Biographies
of the
7th Cavalry

Biographies
of the
7th Cavalry
June 25th 1876

By
Kenneth Hammer

The Old Army Press

The Old Army Press
405 Link Lane
Fort Collins, Colorado 80321

CONTENTS

PREFACE

This book has been prepared as a reference concerning the citizens, enlisted men, officers, Indian scouts and quartermaster employees who were in the Sioux campaign, or were members of the 7th Cavalry in June, 1876, or were in the Little Bighorn River fight.

Names are indexed according to rank by companies and are alphabetically indexed for privates by companies. Indian names are indexed alphabetically by first names. Because names were found recorded differently in various records, it has been impossible to determine with certainty the correct spelling of some names.

The introduction was originally published as The Glory March *by the English Westerners' Society in July, 1966, and is reprinted here through the courtesy of Barry C. Johnson, editor of the English Westerners'* Brand Book.

Ideas and assistance in preparing this book have come from many sources. Grateful appreciation is extended to the many persons cooperating in its preparation. It is needless to say that this is not a final study and additional material from readers is most welcome.

Kenneth Hammer
University of Wisconsin - Whitewater
Whitewater, Wisconsin 53190

THE GLORY MARCH

As a result of the Little Bighorn fight in June, 1876, courageous Lieutenant Colonel George A. Custer came back into the national limelight. Difficulties with President Grant's administration had lately obscured his Indian-fighting exploits. Grant had relieved Custer from his command but at the intercession of Brigadier General Alfred Terry, he was allowed to accompany his regiment on the Sioux expedition.

This expedition was a result of the westward expansion of the nation. The efforts of the Bureau of Indian Affairs to force hostile Indians to live on reservations, instead of marauding the settlement trails, had failed. The subjugation of these hostiles then became the responsibility of the War Department in 1876.

Lieutenant General Philip Sheridan, commanding the Military Division of the Missouri, ordered three columns to strike into hostile territory and punish all Sioux found away from their reservations. On February 7, 1876, General Terry, commanding the Department of Dakota, and Brigadier General George Crook, commanding the Department of the Platte, were instructed to organize large commands for the purpose.

Crook opened the campaign on March 1, riding from Fort Fetterman, Wyoming, with about 800 soldiers. On March 17 his cavalry charged a Cheyenne encampment on the Little Powder River but abandoned the village after a fight. Facing a shortage of supplies, Crook withdrew to Fort Fetterman, with severe cold rendering further campaigning useless.

Crook again left Fetterman on May 29 with 1,100 men, comprising ten companies of the 3rd Cavalry, five companies of the 2nd Cavalry and five companies from the 4th and 9th Infantry. On June 17 he encountered about 1,500 warriors on Rosebud Creek. The fight was, at best, a draw. Crook deemed it wise to withdraw to his wagon train on Goose Creek and await reinforcements. His cavalry was immobilized for over a month.

Terry's column departed from Fort Abraham Lincoln, Dakota, on May 17. It consisted of Terry's staff and the 7th Cavalry - its 12 companies assembled for the first time since its organization in 1866 - with 32 officers and 792 enlisted men; Companies C and G, 17th Infantry and Company B, 6th Infantry, 8 officers and 135 enlisted men; Second Lieutenant William H. Low's platoon of 3 Gatling guns from the 20th Infantry, 2 officers and 32 enlisted men; and Second Lieutenant Charles Varnum's detachment of 40 Indian scouts.

Many of the 7th Cavalry enlisted men were very young, as were the lieutenants. Custer, at 36, was one of the oldest in the regiment. Youth was in the saddle this day.

As part of Terry's force, Colonel John Gibbon left Fort Shaw, Montana, on March 17 with Companies A, B, H, I, and K, 7th Infantry. Company E, 7th Infantry left Camp Baker on March 14 and joined at Crow Agency. Major James S. Brisbin's four companies of the 2nd Cavalry left Fort Ellis on April 1, joined Gibbon and proceeded down the north bank of the Yellowstone River to join Terry and cut off the escape of any hostiles to the north. Gibbon's column now comprised about 27 officers and 426 men.

On June 7 Terry's Column reached Powder River. The steamboat, *Far West*, loaded with supplies, was at the mouth of the Powder and Terry proceeded up the Yellowstone on it to meet Gibbon. He talked with Gibbon on the 9th about plans for the campaign and then returned to Custer's camp. Gibbon countermarched up the Yellowstone and on June 14 took a position nearly opposite the mouth of the Rosebud.

On June 10 dark-eyed Major Marcus A. Reno with Companies B, C, E, F, I, and L, 7th Cavalry, departed on a scout up the Powder, as far south as the Little Powder, thence west to the Mizpah, down that stream to its mouth and down the Tongue to its confluence with the Yellowstone. Exceeding his orders, Reno included the Rosebud in his scout and arrived at its mouth on June 18. His message to Terry indicated that not more than 1,000 warriors were somewhere in the vicinity of the Bighorn River. Not knowing of Crook's fight with the Sioux, Terry concluded that the only hostiles in the region were those mentioned by Reno.

Leaving the walking soldiers and about 134 cavalrymen at Powder River, the remainder of Custer's cavalry joined Reno at 11:30 a.m. on the 21st near the Tongue and then marched to the Rosebud.

Terry planned that Gibbon's and Custer's columns would move so that the hostiles could not escape to the southwest without being intercepted by Crook. The Indians would not go farther west for beyond the Bighorn were the Crows, their deadly enemies. Northward they would be met by Gibbon and to the south lay the Bighorn Mountains where they could not support themselves.

Gibbon was to cross the Yellowstone and march up the Bighorn and Little Bighorn valleys. Terry discussed his plan with Gibbon on the 21st and before noon Gibbon's column was moving up the north bank of the Yellowstone, within an hour after Terry had arrived and before Custer reached camp near the Rosebud.

On the afternoon of the 21st, Terry, Gibbon and others held a conference aboard the *Far West* to advise Custer of his part in the campaign. The two columns would be brought within co-ordinating distance for an attack against the Indians on June 26 — this was understood by Gibbon and Custer that day. Custer said he would march at the rate of 30 miles per day and the campaign was based on this rate of march.

Custer was to follow the trail that Reno had located, and time his march to meet Gibbon for the attack. Custer declined offers of Low's Gatling guns (they would impede his progress) and Brisbin's cavalry, saying that the 7th Cavalry could handle any Indians they met. Custer was given a white scout, George Herendeen, and six Crow scouts who possessed a knowledge of the region.

Low's guns were ferried to the north bank of the Yellowstone to overtake and join Gibbon. Herendeen and the Crows were ferried to the south bank to join Custer. Terry's written instructions were given to Custer and he marched from camp at noon on the 22nd. When Custer said goodbye to Terry and Gibbon, the latter remarked: "Now Custer, don't be greedy but wait for us." Custer made the ambiguous reply: "No, I will not."

During the spring the "Buffalo Indians" under Sitting Bull, the Hunkpapa, had been joined by agency Sioux and hostiles from other tribes. There may have been 15,000 men, women and children, with about 3,500 ablebodied warriors on the Little Bighorn. Probably one-third of the Sioux nation was in camp on June 24. The tribal circles of Northern Cheyenne, Yanktonais, Blackfeet, Sans Arc, Miniconjou, Brule, Oglala and Hunkpapa Sioux probably comprised the most formidable concentration of Indians ever faced by the Army.

They were armed with bows and arrows and a haphazard assortment of vintage flint and percussion trade guns and some Henry, Sharps, Spencer and Winchester repeaters, together with some revolvers of various origins. The hostiles had shown great spirit and cohesiveness in their attack on Crook. Had Terry known this, the plan of attack would undoubtedly have been changed. That the

Indians knew that soldiers were in the field cannot be doubted but not until the morning of the 25th did they realize the regiment was in their vicinity and, even then, there was no preparation for attack or defense.

With about 31 officers, 586 soldiers, 33 Indian scouts and 20 employees and citizens, Custer's column proceeded two miles up the Yellowstone, crossed the Rosebud, marched up that stream for ten miles and went into camp about 4 p.m. At 8 p.m. Custer gave instructions to his officers for the conduct of the march. He believed that 1,000 or 1,500 Indians would be found and he intended to pursue until he caught them.

Each man was armed with the single-shot U. S. Carbine, Model 1873, with 100 rounds of 45-55-405 ammunition, and a .45 calibre revolver with 24 rounds. Sabres were not carried. An improvised pack train included 12 mules each loaded with 2,000 rounds of carbine ammunition, in boxes of 1,000 rounds, and about 160 mules carrying 15 day's rations. Each man carried 12 pounds of oats for his horse.

The march up the Rosebud was resumed at 5 a.m. on the 23rd. Three deserted Indian camps were passed; no hostiles were seen. The column went into bivouac at 5 p.m. after traveling 33 miles.

Camp was broken at 5 a.m. on the 24th. A large Indian camp-site was passed at 7:30 a.m. After halting for lunch, the regiment rested until 5 p.m. The regiment again halted for coffee and hard-tack at 7:45 p.m., marching 28 miles from reveille. Supper over, fires were put out. Scouts came in, reporting that the trail diverged west from the Rosebud towards the Little Bighorn. At 9:25 p.m. Custer called his officers together and said *that beyond a doubt an Indian village was in the Little Bighorn valley* and it would be necessary to cross over from the Rosebud at night to avoid being discovered.

Terry had directed that the upper forks of Tullock's Creek be examined and Herendeen was sent with Custer expressly to communicate the results to Gibbon. Custer was now in the vicinity of the forks but Herendeen was not sent out nor did Varnum's scouts go into that region. Custer may have intended that Herendeen should scout the Tullock the next day. Custer had not abandoned Terry's plan for a combined offensive; no enemy had been seen and there was nothing to indicate the hostiles knew of his location.

March was wearily resumed before 1:00 a.m. on the 25th towards the divide between the Rosebud and the Little Bighorn *where*

Custer intended to halt and rest for the day. The exact position of the hostiles or their numerical strength was not yet known. The scouts told Custer that he could not cross the divide before daylight, so about 2:30 a.m. the column halted and unsaddled after a march of eight miles.

In the meantime Varnum, with some of the scouts, had gone to the Crow's Nest, a high hill on the divide, for observation at dawn. Varnum sent word that an Indian village had been sighted some 15 miles down in the Little Bighorn valley.

Custer hurried forward about 7 a.m. The regiment cautiously moved forward at 8:45 and at 10:07 arrived three miles from the divide and concealed itself in a deep ravine. Custer returned from the Crow's Nest about 11:30, called his officers together and informed them of what the scouts had seen. Mitch Bouyer, at dawn, had sighted large pony herds but Custer, on the Crow's Nest later in the morning, could discern nothing through the morning mist, even with field glasses, and expressed some doubt as to the presence of the village.

During Custer's absence from the column, hostiles were sighted by the scouts, and Indians were seen in the rear of the column. Custer was told of this and, convinced that discovery of the regiment would cause the hostiles to strike their tepees and escape, Custer immediately made the decision to attack. *Probably at this point Custer abandoned the intent of Terry's plan* an attack at mid-day was almost unprecedented in Indian campaigning. The scouts moved out and the regiment marched at 11:45.

Custer led his regiment over the divide and about 12:05 he divided the regiment into four columns. Custer retained Companies C, E, F, I and L - 13 officers, four scouts, two citizens, one interpreter: 215 in all. Grey-haired Captain Frederick Benteen received Companies D, H and K. Companies A, G and M went to Reno. Captain Thomas McDougall's Company B escorted the pack train, augmented by one non-commissioned officer and five privates from each company, accounting for about one-fifth of the regiment.

Benteen, with his 113 men, was ordered to proceed to the left, scout the bluffs about three miles distant, pitch into anything he found and report to Custer. Twice during the first minutes of his march Benteen was further instructed to go to the valley beyond and if he found nothing, to go on to the next valley.

If Custer had an enveloping attack in mind, details were not made known to the others.

Within ten minutes Benteen was lost to view. At 12:12 the rest of the regiment continued down Sundance Creek towards the Little Bighorn, Custer on the right, Reno on the left, with McDougall trailing Reno. After 2:00 p.m. an abandoned tepee was passed. At 2:15 p.m. a heavy dust cloud was seen some distance ahead. From a knoll, Frederick Gerard, a citizen interpreter, saw about 40 Sioux in flight between the regiment and river. He shouted to Custer: "Here are your Indians running like devils." Immediately Custer ordered the scouts in pursuit but they, aware of the immense numbers of hostiles ahead, sullenly refused.

Reno was coming up with his column and First Lieutenant William Cooke, Custer's adjutant, rode over and said: "Custer says to move at as rapid a gait as you think prudent and to charge afterwards, and you will be supported by the whole outfit."

At a fast trot, Reno and his 131 men covered the three miles to the river by 2:30. Cooke and Captain Myles Keogh rode towards the river with Reno's column and then turned back to join Custer. Custer was following behind Reno at a slower gait.

Crossing the river in columns of four, Reno formed his command on the left bank and moved out within ten minutes. Hostiles streamed from the distant village. Gerard, knowing that Custer believed the hostiles were in flight, galloped back and told Cooke about the Sioux in front of Reno. Cooke said he would report this to Custer. We can assume that Cooke told Custer about 2:45.

Custer changed his direction of march, ascended the bluffs on the right bank and moved north paralleling the Little Bighorn.

Sending Private Archibald McIlhargey, and then Private John Mitchell, to Custer with messages that he had the enemy in force at his front, Reno advanced down the valley towards the village, swinging his force into line. He attacked at about 3:15.

The fight was underway. The Indians ahead multiplied until there was a solid front before the village. Reno dismounted his men and withdrew the horses into the timber on his right. Warriors rode through the low hills around Reno's left flank and turned it, part of the scouts there fleeing from the field.

The firing increased to heavy proportions and Reno sustained casualties, although his losses were not critical. About 3:30 he withdrew his dismounted skirmishers into the timber with the horses.

Reno's indecision as to his next move was probably influenced by the realization that his command was being rapidly surrounded. Reno ordered his men to mount, but at that moment, Bloody Knife, an Arikara-Sioux guide, fell at Reno's side with a bullet in his head: his brains were dashed over Reno. Unnerved, Reno ordered his men to dismount and, almost immediately, to mount again. He dashed out of the timber towards the distant bluffs overlooking the valley, followed by the cavalrymen, leaving behind some who were wounded or had lost their horses. The hostiles pursued and killed men in the stampede - there was no organized resistance. Reno reached the bluffs about 4:15, losing one-third of his demoralized column. The hostiles killed three officers, three employees, three Indian scouts and 29 enlisted men in the valley fight and during the flight to the bluffs. Seven enlisted men were wounded and 19 were missing in the timber, but most of them rejoined later.

With his horses wearing out in the rugged terrain, Benteen soon turned to the right towards the trail taken by Reno and Custer. He came on the trail just ahead of the pack train and then watered his horses. Sergeant Daniel Kanipe galloped up with a message from Custer to the pack train urging haste in bringing the reserve ammunition. After Benteen had ridden past the lone teepee, Trumpeter John Martin brought this message: "Benteen. Come on. Big village, Be quick. Bring packs. W. W. Cooke." Indicating the urgency of the reserve ammunition, Cooke further scrawled "P. S. Bring pacs."

Receiving Custer's last message about five miles from the Indian village, Benteen increased his gait. From a hill on the right bank of the Little Bighorn he saw mounted Indians in the valley pursuing Reno's men to the bluffs. Arriving about 4:20 at Reno's position Benteen sent Second Lieutenant Luther Hare to hurry the pack train, which arrived about 4:45. Pending arrival of the packs several officers discussed Custer's situation, which was not then known. That the hostiles had by then withdrawn down the valley in the direction Custer had taken, together with the sound of heavy firing, caused little apprehension in Reno's force. Two distinct volleys from Custer's direction caused an officer to remark that, "Custer was giving it to them for all he was worth." Later opinion was that these volleys were distress signals to bring support to Custer's column.

During Reno's attack and retreat, Custer was, at a fast pace, marching north on the bluffs on the east side of the river *confident that the Indians would try to escape.* Conjecture is a fitting word to describe the events following. Custer's further route is not definitely known. He left Reno's trail about 2:45, advanced down the river about five miles and sent Trumpeter Martin back about 3:15. A diversionary attack on the village by way of a ford may have been attempted by part of Custer's column. If there was such an attack it was repulsed and the remaining cavalry was forced directly north to a hillcrest area. Here the location of the dead of First Lieutenant James Calhoun's Company L indicated that the column was probably struck by Gall's strong attack from the south. Calhoun probably acted as a holding force while Custer tried to meet Crazy Horse's attack from the north. With Calhoun in a death struggle, Keogh's Company I rode towards the left flank and was annihilated en masse.

Captain George Yates held the extreme right (north) flank with Company F. Custer's disposition of a line of dismounted skirmishers due south from his right-flank position was evidenced by the dead from Captain Thomas Custer's Company G and First Lieutenant Algernon Smith's Company E.

As Calhoun's company went down in death, Gall rolled up the left flank; and Crazy Horse enveloped the right flank within a short time. The hostiles rode around to the rear and surrounded Custer's position.

The duration of the action is problematical. The hasty withdrawal of the hostiles against Reno's position after 4:15, and the volleys and heavy firing about 4:30, probably began the main attack. By 4:15 Custer was hemmed in and before 5 o'clock his doom was sealed.

The attack on Custer's column had drawn all but a handful of warriors away from Reno's position, enabling a reorganization after the severe mauling in the valley fight. As the pack train was coming in, Captain Thomas Weir's Company D moved down the river in an attempt to communicate with or join Custer. He proceeded about a mile before halting. The Indians checked Weir about 5 o'clock: Reno started with the wounded to join Weir about 5:30. Retreat up the river to Reno's previous hilltop position began about 6 o'clock and by 6:30 most of the command was back on the hilltop. By 7 o'clock all were back and, as First Lieutenant Edward Godfrey's Company K dashed to safety, the hostiles surrounded the position and poured in a deadly fire. Horses and mules, in a swale near the center of the position, shielded the nearby wounded. Heavy firing continued until dark, about 9 o'clock, when the Indians withdrew, leaving a small force to contain Reno.

That night the valley resounded with the savage life of the great Indian village. Not far away, across the river, lay the silent, white bodies of the dead. Four miles up the river, Reno's men were busy preparing for the morning, when the hostiles would make a mighty effort to kill them.

Reno's intrenchments were not completed when the Indians attacked about 2:30 a.m. on the 26th. Many of the men, especially the wounded, were suffering from thirst. So great was their distress that volunteers were called to get water from the river. Four marksmen were posted on the bluffs to clear the area for the water party. Water was obtained at the price of a few casualties.

Benteen's men were exposed to long-range fire from the surrounding hills and many were wounded. The Indians were growing bolder and, as their fire increased, Benteen prepared a sortie. His men charged from the intrenchments and opened fire. Surprised at this unexpected offensive, the hostiles temporarily withdrew.

In the afternoon the Indians began to withdraw to their camp leaving some hostiles to harass the cavalrymen. With Gibbon approaching, miles to the north, they set fire to the grass in the valley and withdrew up the Little Bighorn about 7 o'clock. By 9:30 all the Indians were gone. Thus ended the Little Bighorn River fight.

Reno's casualties on the hilltop were 18 enlisted men and one citizen killed, and more than 52 wounded. His command still believed that Custer had survived the previous day's fight, had met Gibbon, and was coming to their rescue.

In the meantime Gibbon's column, with Terry accompanying, continued upriver to the mouth of the Bighorn, ferried across the Yellowstone on the *Far West* and moved up the right bank of the Bighorn. The *Far West* followed up the Bighorn to the mouth of the Little Bighorn.

The trail was difficult and the men suffered from the heat, dust and thirst but pushed steadily on. On the night of the 24th they camped on lower Tullock's Creek. On the 25th they marched through the hills towards the mouth of the Little Bighorn and camped that night on the Bighorn, 12 miles below the mouth of the Little Bighorn.

On the morning of the 26th, First Lieutenant James Bradley encountered three Crow scouts who called across the river that Custer's column had been destroyed. Terry doubted this and moved up the Little Bighorn valley. After a hard march he arrived on the morning of the 27th where the Indian village had stood. Here Bradley rode up and reported that 197 bodies had been counted in the foothills to the left. The dead were Custer's command.

About 10 a.m. Terry and his staff reached Reno's position where Terry told the astounded survivors of Custer's fate. That afternoon Benteen rode over to the field and identified Custer's body. In the evening the wounded were brought down from the bluffs.

Early on the 28th, the survivors and Gibbon's forces buried the dead. Over two hundred bodies were interred but not all of the remains were located. The Indians had stripped the dead of their clothing: those nearest the village were so mutilated as to make identification nearly impossible. The graves of those identified were marked.

At sunset the wounded were placed on litters and the march to the mouth of the Little Bighorn began. Here Terry awaited reinforcements. The wounded were placed aboard the *Far West* and taken to Fort Lincoln.

Twenty-five Medals of Honor were awarded for heroic acts in the fight. A total of 262 were killed and over 59 were wounded. Seven of the wounded died later. The only survivor of Custer's fight that was found on the field was Keogh's wounded horse, Comanche, which was taken aboard the *Far West*. Curly, a Crow scout, is credited with surviving the fight, although he took no active part. He remained observing the fight until the Sioux overran the field, and then rode to tell his story to listeners on the *Far West*.

ROSTER OF THE SEVENTH REGIMENT OF CAVALRY
IN JUNE, 1876

Commissioned Officers   Co.

1. Bell, James Montgomery .... D
2. Benteen, Frederick William .... H
3. Braden, Charles L
4. Calhoun, James C
5. Cooke, William Winer .... Staff
6. Craycroft, William Thomas .... B
7. Crittenden, John Jordan .... Att. L
8. Custer, George Armstrong .... Staff
9. Custer, Thomas Ward C
10. DeRudio, Charles Camilus .... E
11. DeWolf, James M. .... Med.
12. Eckerson, Edwin Philip L
13. Edgerly, Winfield Scott .... D
14. French, Thomas Henry .... M
15. Garlington, Ernest Albert .... H
16. Gibson, Francis Marion .... H
17. Godfrey, Edward Settle .... K
18. Hale, Owen .... K
19. Hare, Luther Rector .... K
20. Harrington, Henry Moore C
21. Hodgson, Benjamin Hubert .... B
22. Ilsley, Charles Stilliman .... E
23. Jackson, Henry .... F
24. Keogh, Myles Walter I
25. Larned, Charles William .... F
26. Lord, George Edwin .... Med
27. Mathey, Edward Gustave .... M
28. McDougall, Thomas Mower .... B
29. McIntosh, Donald .... G
30. Merrill, Lewis .... Staff
31. Moylan, Myles .... A
32. Nave, Andrew Humes I
33. Nowlan, Henry James .... Staff
34. Porter, Henry Rinaldo .... Med
35. Porter, James Ezekiel I
36. Reily, William Van Wyck .... E
37. Reno, Marcus Albert .... Staff
38. Sheridan, Michael Vincent L
39. Smith, Algernon Emory .... A
40. Sturgis, James Garland .... M
41. Sturgis, Samuel Davis .... Cmdg
42. Tilford, Joseph Green .... Staff
43. Tourtellotte, John Eaton .... G
44. Varnum, Charles Albert .... A
45. Wallace, George Daniel .... G
46. Weir, Thomas Bell .... D
47. Yates, George Walter .... F

Enlisted Men   Co.

1. Abbots, Harry .... E
2. Abos, James A. .... B
3. Abrams, William G. L
4. Ackerman, Charles .... K
5. Ackison, David .... E
6. Adams, George E. L
7. Adams, Jacob .... H
8. Akers, James .... G
9. Alberts, James H. .... D
10. Alcott, Samuel .... A
11. Allan, Fred E. C
12. Aller, Charles .... A
13. Anderson, Charles L. C
14. Anderson, George .... K
15. Andrews, William L
16. Armstrong, John E. .... A
17. Arndt, Otto .... Band
18. Arnold, Herbert C
19. Ascough, John B. .... D
20. Assadaly, Anthony L
21. Atcheson, Thomas .... F
22. Avery, Charles E. .... H
23. Babcock, Elmer L
24. Bailey, Henry A. I
25. Bailey, John E. .... B
26. Baker, William H. .... E
27. Bancroft, Neil .... A
28. Banks, Charles L
29. Barnett, Charles C. .... G
30. Barry, John I
31. Barry, Peter O. .... B
32. Barsantee, James F. .... B
33. Barth, Robert .... E
34. Bates, Joseph .... M
35. Bauer, Jacob .... K
36. Baumbach, Conrad .... Band
37. Baumgartner, Louis .... A
38. Beck, Benjamin .... Band
39. Bender, Henry L
40. Bennett, James C. C
41. Berwald, Frank .... E
42. Bishley, P. Henry .... H
43. Bischoff, Charles H. C
44. Bishop, Alexander B. .... H
45. Bishop, Charles H. .... H
46. Black, Henry .... H
47. Blair, James C. .... K
48. Blair, Wilbur F. .... A
49. Blake, Thomas .... A
50. Blunt, George .... K
51. Boam, William .... B
52. Bobo, Edwin C
53. Bockerman, August .... A
54. Bohner, Aloys .... D
55. Boissen, Christian .... K
56. Boner, Hugh .... B
57. Boren, Ansgarius .... B
58. Borter, Ludwig .... A
59. Bott, George A. .... A
60. Botzer, Edward .... G
61. Bowers, Frank (F. Volkenstein) M
62. Boyle, James P. .... G

63.	Boyle, Owen	E
64.	Brady, William	F
65.	Brainard, George	B
66.	Brandle, William	C
67.	Brandon, Benjamin	F
68.	Brant, Abraham B.	D
69.	Braun, Frank	M
70.	Braun, Franz C.	I
71.	Brennan, John	C
72.	Bresnahan, Cornelius	K
73.	Brightfield, John	C
74.	Bringes, John	A
75.	Brinkerhoff, Henry M.	G
76.	Briody, John	F
77.	Broadhurst, Joseph F.	I
78.	Brogan, James	E
79.	Bromwell, Latrobe (Latrobe Brommell)	E
80.	Brown, Alexander	G
81.	Brown, Benjamin Franklin	F
82.	Brown, George C.	E
83.	Brown, Hiram E.	F
84.	Brown, James	B
85.	Brown, Joseph	K
86.	Brown, Nathan T.	L
87.	Brown, William	F
88.	Bruce, Patrick	F
89.	Bruns, August	E
90.	Bucknell, Thomas J.	C
91.	Burdick, Benjamin F.	A
92.	Burgdorf, Charles J.	K
93.	Burke, Edmund H.	K
94.	Burke, John	L
95.	Burkhardt, Charles	K
96.	Burkman, John	L
97.	Burli, Edmond	Band
98.	Burnham, Lucien	F
99.	Burns, Charles	B
100.	Bustard, James	I
101.	Butler, James	L
102.	Butler, James W.	F
103.	Caddle, Michael C.	I
104.	Cain, Morris	M
105.	Caldwell, William M.	B
106.	Callahan, John J.	K
107.	Callan, James	B
108.	Callan, Thomas J.	B
109.	Campbell, Charles	G
110.	Campbell, Charles A.	B
111.	Campbell, Jeremiah	K
112.	Cansby, Thomas	Staff
113.	Capes, William	M
114.	Carey, Patrick	M
115.	Cary, John J.	B
116.	Carmody, Thomas	B
117.	Carney, James	F
118.	Carroll, Daniel	B
119.	Carroll, Joseph	Band
120.	Carter, Andrew	Band
121.	Carter, Cassius R.	G
122.	Cashan, William	L
123.	Cather, Armantheus D.	F
124.	Channell, William	H
125.	Chapman, William H.	E
126.	Charley, Vincent	D
127.	Chreer, Ami	L
128.	Clark, Frank	B
129.	Clear, Elihu F.	K
130.	Clyde, Edward	F
131.	Coakley, Patrick	K
132.	Cody, Henry (Henry M. Scollin)	M
133.	Cody, John F.	A
134.	Coleman, Charles	F
135.	Coleman, Thomas W.	B
136.	Collins, John C.	F
137.	Colwell, John R.	L
138.	Conelly, Patrick	H
139.	Conlan, Thomas	D
140.	Conlon, Michael	L
141.	Connell, John	B
142.	Conner, Andrew	A
143.	Connor, Edward	E
144.	Connors, Thomas	I
145.	Considine, Martin	G
146.	Cooney, David	I
147.	Cooper, John	H
148.	Corcoran, John	C
149.	Corcoran, Patrick	K
150.	Cornwall, Michael	G
151.	Cowley, Cornelius	A
152.	Cowley, Stephen	D
153.	Cox, Thomas	D
154.	Crandall, Charles A.	C
155.	Crawford, William L.	K
156.	Creighton, John C. (Charles Chesterwood)	K
157.	Criddle, Christopher	C
158.	Crisfield, William B.	L
159.	Criswell, Benjamin C.	B
160.	Criswell, Harry	B
161.	Crowe, Michael	B
162.	Crowley, Patrick	B
163.	Crump, John	B
164.	Crussy, Melanchton H.	G
165.	Culbertson, Ferdinand A.	A
166.	Cunningham, Albert J.	D
167.	Cunningham, Charles	B
168.	Curtiss, William A.	F
169.	Dalious, James	A
170.	Dann, George	D
171.	Darris, John	E
172.	Davenport, William H.	B
173.	Davern, Edward	F
174.	Davis, Harrison	M
175.	Davis, William	E
176.	Dawsey, David E.	D
177.	Day, John	H
178.	Deetline, Frederick	D
179.	Deihle, Jacob	A
180.	DeLacy, Milton J.	I
181.	Delaney, Michael	K

182.	De Tourriel, Louis	B
183.	Devoto, Augustus L.	B
184.	Dewey, George W.	H
185.	Diamond, Edward	H
186.	Dohman, Anton	F
187.	Dolan, John (Thomas Brown)	M
188.	Doll, Jacob W.	B
189.	Donahue, John	M
190.	Donahue, John F.	K
191.	Donnelly, Timothy	F
192.	Dooley, Patrick	K
193.	Dorn, Richard B.	B
194.	Dose, Henry C.	G
195.	Dougherty, James	B
196.	Downing, Alexander	F
197.	Downing, Thomas P.	I
198.	Drago, Henry	F
199.	Drinan, James	A
200.	Driscoll, Edward C.	I
201.	Duggan, John	L
202.	Durselen, Otto	A
203.	Dwyer, Edmond	G
204.	Dye, William	L
205.	Eades, William	F
206.	Eagan, Thomas P.	E
	(Thomas Hagan)	
207.	Easley, John Thomas	A
208.	Eisenberger, Peter	Band
209.	Eisman, George	C
210.	Engle, Gustave	C
211.	Etzler, William	L
212.	Farber, Conrad	I
213.	Farley, William	H
214.	Farrand, James	C
215.	Farrar, Morris	C
216.	Farrell, Richard	E
217.	Fay, John J.	D
218.	Fehler, Henry	A
219.	Finckle, August	C
220.	Findeisen, Hugo	L
221.	Finley, Jeremiah	C
222.	Finnegan, Thomas J.	F
223.	Fischer, Charles	M
224.	Fisher, Charles	K
225.	Fitzgerald, John	C
226.	Flanagan, James	D
227.	Flood, Phillip	G
228.	Foley, John	C
229.	Foley, John	K
230.	Foster, Samuel James	A
231.	Fowler, Isaac	C
232.	Fox, Frederick	I
233.	Fox, Harvey A.	D
234.	Fox, John	D
235.	Frank, William	B
236.	Franklin, John W.	A
237.	Frederick, Andrew	K
238.	French, Henry Eldon	C
239.	Gaffney, George	I
240.	Gallenne, Jean B. D.	M
241.	Galvan, James J.	L
242.	Gannon, Peter	B
243.	Gardner, William	F
244.	Garlick, Edward	G
245.	Geesbacher, Gabriel	I
246.	Gehrmann, Frederick H.	B
247.	Geiger, George H.	H
248.	Geist, Frank J.	G
249.	George, William H.	H
250.	Gibbs, William	K
251.	Gilbert, John M.	A
252.	Gilbert, Julius	E
253.	Gilbert, William H.	L
254.	Gillette, David C.	I
255.	Glease, George W.	H
256.	Golden, Bernard	M
257.	Golden, Patrick	D
258.	Goldin, Theodore W.	G
	(John Stilwell)	
259.	Gordon, Henry	M
260.	Gordon, Thomas A.	K
261.	Graham, Charles	L
262.	Graham, Thomas	G
263.	Gray, John	B
264.	Gray, William S.	G
265.	Grayson, Edward	G
266.	Green, John	D
267.	Green, Joseph H.	D
268.	Green, Thomas	K
269.	Gregg, William J.	F
270.	Griesner, Julius	Band
271.	Griffin, Patrick	C
272.	Grimes, Andrew	I
273.	Gross, George H.	I
274.	Gunther, Julius	K
275.	Haack, Charles L.	I
276.	Haack, Henry	H
277.	Hackett, John	G
278.	Hagemann, Otto	G
279.	Hager, John	D
280.	Haley, Timothy	H
281.	Hall, Curtis	D
282.	Hall, Edward	D
283.	Hamilton, Andrew	A
284.	Hamilton, Henry	L
285.	Hammon, George W.	F
286.	Hammon, John E.	G
287.	Hanley, Richard P.	C
288.	Hardden, William	D
289.	Hardy, William G.	A
290.	Harlfinger, Gustav	D
291.	Harrington, Weston	L
292.	Harris, David W.	A
293.	Harris, James	D
294.	Harris, Leonard A.	F
295.	Harris, William M.	D
296.	Harrison, Thomas W.	D
297.	Harrison, William H	L
298.	Hathersall, James	C
299.	Hauggi, Louis	L
300.	Hayt, Walter	K
301.	Hayward, George	I

302. Heath, William H.	L	363. Kelly, George	H
303. Hegner, Francis	F	364. Kelly, James	B
304. Heid, George	M	365. Kelly, James	H
305. Heim, John	E	366. Kelly, John P.	F
306. Helmer, Julius	K	367. Kennedy, Francis Johnson	I
307. Henderson, George W.	G	(Francis Johnson)	
308. Henderson, John	E	368. Kenney, Michael	F
309. Henderson, Sykes	E	369. Kerr, Dennis	A
310. Hetesimer, Adam	I	370. Kilfoyle, Martin	G
311. Hetler, Jacob	D	371. Kimm, John G.	E
312. Heyn, William	A	372. King, George H.	A
313. Hiley, John S.	E	373. King, John	C
314. Hill, James	B	374. Kipp, Fremont	D
315. Hoehn, Max	L	375. Klawitter, Ferdinand	B
316. Hohmeyer, Frederick	E	376. Klein, Gustav	F
317. Holahan, Andrew	K	377. Klein, Nikolaus	F
318. Holcomb, Edward P.	I	378. Klotzbucher, Henry	M
319. Holden, Henry	D	379. Knauth, Herman	F
320. Holmstead, Frederick	A	380. Knecht, Andy	E
321. Hood, Charles N.	H	381. Kneubuhler, Joseph	Band
322. Hook, Stanton	A	382. Korn, Gustave	I
323. Horn, George	D	383. Kramer, William	C
324. Horn, Marion E.	I	384. Kretchmer, Joseph	D
325. Horner, Jacob	K	385. Kuehl, Jesse	D
326. Hose, George	K	386. Laden, Joseph	G
327. Houghtaling, Charles	D	387. Lalor, William	M
328. Housen, Edward	D	388. Lambertin, Frank	H
329. Howard, Frank	E	389. Lange, Henry	E
330. Howard, Frank	F	390. Lasley, William W.	K
331. Howell, George	C	391. Lattmann, John	G
332. Huber, William	E	392. Lauper, Frank	G
333. Huff, Jacob (Jacob Emerich)	Band	393. Lawhorn, Thomas	H
334. Hughes, Francis F.	L	394. Lawler, James	G
335. Hughes, Robert H.	K	395. Lee, Mark E.	I
336. Hughes, Thomas	H	396. Lefler, Meig	F
337. Hunt, George	D	397. Lehman, Friederick	I
338. Hunt, John	H	398. Lehmann, Henry	I
339. Hunter, Frank	F	399. Lell, George	H
340. Hurd, James	D	400. Lepper, Frederick	L
341. Hutchinson, Rufus D.	B	401. Lerock, William H.	F
342. Hutter, Anton	E	402. Lewis, David W.	B
343. James, John	E	403. Lewis, John	C
344. James, William B.	E	404. Lewis, Uriah S.	D
345. Jennys, Alonzo	K	405. Liddiard, Herod T.	E
346. Johnson, Benjamin	G	406. Liebermann, Andrew	K
347. Johnson, Samuel	A	407. Liemann, Werner L.	F
348. Jones, Henry P. (John Bush)	I	408. Littlefield, John L.	B
349. Jones, Julien D.	H	409. Lloyd, Edward W.	I
350. Jonson, Emil O.	A	410. Lloyd, Frank	G
351. Jordan, John	C	411. Lobering, Louis	L
352. Jungesbluth, Julius	Band	412. Logue, William J.	L
353. Kanavagh, John	D	413. Lombard, Frank	Band
354. Kane, William	C	414. Lorentz, George	M
355. Kanipe, Daniel Alexander	C	415. Lossee, William A.	F
356. Katzenmaier, Jacob	G	416. Lovett, Meredith	C
357. Kavanagh, Thomas G.	L	417. Loyd, George	G
358. Kavanaugh, Charles	M	418. Lynch, Dennis	F
359. Keefe, John J.	B	419. Lynch, Patrick	I
360. Keegan, Michael	L	420. Lyons, Bernard	F
361. Keller, John J.	D	421. Lyons, Daniel	K
362. Kelley, Patrick	I	422. Madden, Michael P.	K

423. Madson, Christian	F	482. Myers, Frank	F
424. Mahoney, Bartholomew	L	483. Myers, Fred	I
425. Mahoney, Daniel	M	484. Myers, John	D
426. Mahoney, John	C	485. McCabe, John	B
427. Manning, David	D	486. McCall, Joseph	I
428. Manning, James R.	F	487. McCann, Patrick	E
429. Maroney, Matthew	H	488. McCarthy, Charles	L
430. Marshall, Jasper	L	489. McClurg, William	A
431. Marshall, John M.	H	(William Irvine)	
432. Marshall, William A.	D	490. McConnell, Wilson	K
433. Martin, James	G	491. McCormick, James	M
434. Martin, John (Giovanni Martini)	H	492. McCormick, Samuel	G
435. Martin, Michael	D	493. McCreedy, Thomas	C
436. Martin, William	B	494. McCue, Martin	K
437. Mask, George B.	B	495. McCurry, Joseph	H
438. Mason, Henry S.	E	496. McDermott, George M.	A
439. Maxwell, Thomas E.	L	(Michael Burke)	
440. Meador, Thomas E.	H	497. McDermott, Thomas	H
441. Meadwell, John	D	498. McDonald, James	A
(J. R. Meadville)		499. McDonnell, John	G
442. Mecklin, Henry W. B.	H	500. McDonnell, Patrick	D
443. Meier, Frederick	C	501. McEagen, John	G
444. Meier, John H.	M	502. McElroy, Thomas	E
445. Meinicke, Ernest	F	503. McGinnis, John	G
446. Merritt, George A.	Band	504. McGlone, John	M
447. Meyer, Albert H.	E	505. McGonigle, Hugh	G
448. Meyer, August	C	506. McGucker, John	I
449. Meyer, William D.	M	507. McGue, Peter	L
450. Mielke, Max	K	508. McGuiness, John J.	I
451. Miller, Edwin	C	509. McGuire, John	C
452. Miller, Henry	E	510. McGurn, Bernard	B
453. Miller, John	L	511. McHugh, Philip	L
454. Miller, William E.	I	512. McIlhargey, Archibald	I
455. Milton, Francis E.	F	513. McKay, Edward J.	G
456. Milton, Joseph	F	514. McKee, John	G
457. Mitchell, John	I	515. McKenna, John	E
458. Moller, Jan	H	516. McLaughlin, Terrence	B
459. Monroe, Joseph	F	517. McLaughlin, Thomas	H
460. Moodie, William	A	518. McMasters, William	B
461. Moonie, George A.	E	519. McNally, James P.	I
462. Moore, Andrew J.	G	520. McNamara, James	H
463. Moore, Hugh N.	M	521. McPeake, Alexander	L
464. Moore, James E.	B	522. McShane, John	I
465. Moore, Lansing A.	L	523. McVay, John	G
466. Morris, George C.	I	524. McVeigh, David	A
467. Morris, William E.	M	525. McWilliams, David	H
468. Morrison, John	G	526. Nealon, Daniel	H
469. Morrow, William E.	B	527. Neely, Frank	M
470. Morton, Thomas	D	528. Nees, Elder	H
471. Mueller, William	D	529. Newell, Daniel	M
472. Muering, John	A	530. Nicholas, Joshua S.	H
473. Mullen, John (James Hughes)	L	531. Nitsche, Ottocar	C
474. Muller, John	H	532. Nolan, John	K
475. Mullin, Martin	C	533. Northeg, Olans H.	G
476. Murphy, Lawrence	E	534. Noshang, Jacob	I
477. Murphy, Michael	K	535. Nugent, William D.	A
478. Murphy, Robert L.	I	536. Nunan, John	L
479. Murphy, Thomas	K	537. Nursey, Frederick	F
(Thomas Anderson)		538. O'Brien, Thomas	B
480. Murray, Henry	K	539. O'Bryan, John	I
481. Murray, Thomas	B	540. O'Connell, David J.	L

541.	O'Connor, Patrick	E	602.	Rogers, Benjamin F.	G
542.	Ogden, John S.	E	603.	Rogers, Walter B.	L
543.	O'Hara, Miles F.	M	604.	Rollins, Richard	A
544.	O'Mann, William	D	605.	Rood, Edward	E
545.	Omling, Sebastian	F	606.	Rooney, James M.	F
546.	O'Neill, Bernard	Band	607.	Rose, Peter E.	L
547.	O'Neill, James	B	608.	Rossbury, John W.	I
548.	O'Neill, John	B	609.	Roth, Francis	K
549.	O'Neill, Thomas	G	610.	Rott, Louis	K
550.	Orr, Charles M.	C	611.	Rowland, Robert	G
551.	O'Ryan, William	H	612.	Roy, Stanislaus	A
552.	O'Toole, Francis	E	613.	Rudden, Patrick	F
553.	Owens, Eugene	I	614.	Rudolph, George	Band
554.	Pahl, John	H	615.	Russell, James Henry	C
555.	Pandtle, Christopher	E	616.	Russell, Thomas	D
556.	Parker, John	I	617.	Rutten, Roman	M
557.	Patton, John W.	I	618.	Ryan, Daniel	C
558.	Penwell, George B.	K	619.	Ryan, John M.	M
559.	Perkins, Charles	L	620.	Ryan, Stephen L.	B
560.	Petring, Henry	G	621.	Ryder, Hobart	M
561.	Phillips, Edgar	C	622.	Rye, William W.	M
562.	Phillips, John J.	H	623.	Saas, William	I
563.	Pickard, Edwin F.	F	624.	Sadler, William	D
564.	Pigford, Edward A.	M	625.	Sager, Hiram Wallace	B
565.	Pilcher, Albert (Henry Barton)	F	626.	Sanders, Charles	D
566.	Pinkston, John S.	H	627.	Saunders, Richard	F
567.	Pitter, Felix James	I	628.	Schauer, John	K
568.	Pittet, Francis	H	629.	Schele, Henry	E
569.	Porter, John	I	630.	Schlafer, Christian	K
570.	Post, George	I	631.	Schleiffarth, Paul	F
571.	Proctor, George W.	A	632.	Schleiper, Claus	F
572.	Pym, James	B	633.	Schmidt, Charles	L
573.	Quinn, James	I	634.	Schwerer, John	K
574.	Quinn, John	D	635.	Scott, Charles	L
575.	Rafter, John	K	636.	Scott, George D.	D
576.	Ragan, Michael	K	637.	Seafferman, Henry	G
577.	Ragsdale, John S.	A	638.	Seamans, John	M
578.	Raichel, Henry W.	K	639.	Seayers, Thomas	A
579.	Ramell, William	H	640.	Seifert, August	K
580.	Ramsey, Charles	I	641.	Seiler, John	L
581.	Randall, George F.	B	642.	Selby, Crawford	G
582.	Randall, William J.	D	643.	Senn, Robert	M
583.	Rapp, John	G	644.	Severs, James	M
584.	Rauter, John	C	645.	Severs, Samuel	H
585.	Reed, John A.	G	646.	Shade, Samuel S.	C
586.	Reed, William	I	647.	Shanahan, John	G
587.	Rees, William H.	E	648.	Sharrow, William H.	Staff
588.	Reese, William	E	649.	Shea, Daniel	B
589.	Reeves, Francis M.	A	650.	Shea, Jeremiah	C
590.	Reibold, Christian	L	651.	Sherborne, Thomas	Band
591.	Reid, Elwyn S.	D		(Charles Answorth)	
592.	Reiley, Michael	F	652.	Shields, William	E
593.	Reilly, Michael	K	653.	Short, Nathan	C
594.	Rickets, Joseph	M	654.	Shulte, Frederick	F
595.	Riley, James F.	E		(Charles Miller)	
596.	Rivers, John	I	655.	Sicfous, Francis W.	F
597.	Rix, Edward	C	656.	Siebelder, Anton	A
598.	Robb, Eldorado J.	G	657.	Siemon, Charles	L
599.	Robers, Johnathan	K	658.	Siemonson, Bent	L
600.	Roberts, Henry	L	659.	Simons, Patrick	B
601.	Robinson, William	M	660.	Sims, John J.	D

661. Sivertsen, John	M	720. Tolan, Frank	D
662. Slaper, William C.	M	721. Torrey, William A.	E
663. Small, John R.	G	722. Tritten, John G.	Staff
664. Smallwood, William	E	723. Troy, James E.	I
665. Smith, Albert A.	E	724. Trumble, William	B
666. Smith, Frederick	K	725. Tulo, Joseph	G
667. Smith, George E.	M	726. Turley, Henry	M
668. Smith, Henry G.	D	727. Tweed, Thomas S.	L
669. Smith, James (1)	E	728. Vahlert, Jacob	C
670. Smith, James (2)	E	729. Van Allen, Garrett	C
671. Smith, William E.	D	730. Van Bramer, Charles	I
672. Smith, William M.	B	731. Van Pelt, William E.	K
673. Sniffin, Frank	M	732. Van Sant, Cornelius	E
674. Snow, Andrew	L	733. Varden, Frank E.	I
675. Spencer, Able B.	E	734. Varner, Thomas B.	M
676. Spinner, Philipp	B	735. Vetter, Michael	L
677. Sprague, Otto	L	736. Vickory, John	F
678. Stafford, Benjamin F.	E	737. Vinatieri, Felix Villietri)	Band
679. Stanley, Edward	G	738. Voight, Henry C.	M
680. Staples, Samuel S.	I	739. Voit, Otto	H
681. Stark, Frank	C	740. Von Arnim, Julius	C
682. Steintker, John R.	K	741. Voss, Henryy	Staff
683. Stella, Alexander	E	742. Walker, George	E
684. Stephens, George W.	G	743. Walker, Robert	C
685. Sterland, Walter S.	M	744. Wallace, John W.	G
686. Stevenson, Thomas W.	G	745. Wallace, Richard A.	B
687. Stivers, Thomas W.	D	746. Walsh, Frederick	L
688. St. John, Ludwick	C	747. Walsh, Michael J.	H
689. Stoffel, Henry	L	748. Walsh, Thomas	F
690. Stout, Edward	B	749. Walter, Aloyse L.	H
691. Stowers, Thomas J.	B	750. Warner, Oscar T.	C
(James Thomas)		751. Warren, Amos B.	L
692. Stratton, Frank	M	752. Warren, George A.	F
693. Streing, Frederick	M	753. Wasmus, Ernest	K
694. Strode, Elijah T.	A	754. Watson, James	C
695. Stuart, Alpheus	C	755. Way, Thomas N.	F
696. Stungewitz, Ygnatz	C	756. Weaver, George	M
697. Sullivan, Daniel	G	757. Weaver, Henry C.	M
698. Sullivan, John	A	758. Weaver, Howard H.	A
699. Sullivan, Timothy	L	759. Weeks, James	M
700. Summers, David	M	760. Weiss, John	A
701. Sweeney, John W.	F	761. Weiss, Markus	G
702. Sweeney, William	F	762. Welch, Charles H.	D
703. Sweetser, Thomas P.	A	763. Wells, Benjamin J.	G
704. Symms, Darwin L.	I	764. Wells, John S.	E
705. Tanner, James J.	M	765. Wetzel, Adam	B
706. Taply, Daniel	H	766. Whaley, William B.	I
707. Tarbox, Byron L.	L	767. Whitaker, Alfred	C
708. Taube, Emil	K	768. White, Charles	M
709. Taylor, Walter O.	G	769. Whisten, John	M
710. Taylor, William O.	A	770. Whitlow, William	K
711. Teeman, William	F	771. Whytefield, Albert	K
(William A. Adams)		772. Widmayer, Ferdinand	M
712. Tessier, Edmond D.	L	773. Wiedman, Charles T.	M
713. Thadus, John	C	774. Wight, Edwin B.	B
714. Thomas, Herbert P.	I	775. Wilber, James	M
715. Thompson, Peter	C	776. Wild, John	I
716. Thornberry, Levi	M	777. Wilkison, John K.	F
717. Thorp, Michael	F	778. Williams, Charles	M
718. Thorpe, Rollins L.	M	779. Williams, William C.	H
719. Tinkham, Henry L.	B	780. Williamson, Pasavan	G

781. Wilson, George A. .... K
782. Windolph, Charles .... H
   (Charles Wrangel)
783. Winney, DeWitt .... K
784. Witt, Henry .... K
785. Wood, William M. .... M
786. Woodruff, Jerry .... E

787. Woods, Aaron .... B
788. Wright, Willis B. C
789. Wylie, George W. .... D
790. Wyman, Henry C
791. Wynn, James .... D
792. Zametzer, John .... M

Capt. Frederick W. Benteen

Mitch Bouyer, Interpreter

Pvt. John Burkman

1st Lt. James Calhoun

1st Lt. William W. Cooke

Curly, Crow Indian Scout

Boston Custer, Guide

Lt. Col. George A. Custer

Capt. Thomas W. Custer

1st Lt. Charles C. DeRudio   2nd Lt. Winfield S. Edgerly   1st Lt. Francis M. Gibson

1st Lt. Edward S. Godfrey   Hairy Moccasin, Crow Indian Scout   2nd Lt. Henry M. Harrington

2nd Lt. Benjamin H. Hodgson   Sgt. Daniel A. Kanipe   Pvt. Gustave Korn

Capt. Myles W. Keogh

Trumpeter John Martin

Capt. Thomas M. McDougall

1st Lt. Donald McIntosh

Acting Asst. Surgeon
Henry R. Porter

1st Lt. James E. Porter

Harry A. Reed, Attached Civilian

2nd Lt. William V. W. Reily

Major Marcus A. Reno

Charles A. Reynolds, Guide

1st Sgt. John M. Ryan

1st Lt. Algernon E. Smith

2nd Lt. James G. Sturgis

2nd Lt. Charles A. Varnum

Capt. Thomas B. Weir

White-Man-Runs-Him,
Crow Indian Scout

Pvt. Charles Windolph

Capt. George W. Yates

HEADQUARTERS, 7TH CAVALRY, IN 1876

Early in the spring, orders were issued for the regiment to assemble at Fort Abraham Lincoln, Dakota, for duty with the Sioux expedition under Brig. General Alfred Terry. The expedition was against the Sioux Indians who were absent from their reservations and supposed to be located south of the Yellowstone River in Montana Territory. Other commands were to be in the field for the same purpose and it was hoped that their combined efforts would result in subjugation of the hostiles.

Companies E and L arrived from Fort Totten, Dakota, on April 17 and went into quarters. Companies B, G and K arrived from the Department of the Gulf on May 1 and Companies H and M arrived from Fort Rice, Dakota, on May 5. As each company reported, except E and L, they were placed in camp about two miles down river from the post. On May 5 the field staff, band, and Companies A, C, D, E, F, I and L joined the remainder of the regiment in the field camp.

The expedition left Fort Lincoln at 5 AM on May 17 and arrived on the Little Missouri River on May 29 after traveling a distance of 166 miles. They remained in camp on May 30 and on the 31st camp was made 10 miles from that river. Because of a snowstorm the expedition remained in camp on June 1 and 2. On June 7 the expedition arrived on the Powder River and on June 10, Companies B, C, E, F, I and L left under the command of Major Marcus Reno to scout along and between the Powder, Tongue and Rosebud. On June 11 the headquarters, band and six remaining companies and the remainder of the expedition marched to the junction of the Powder and Yellowstone Rivers, arriving there the same day. A supply camp, named *Yellowstone Depot* was established at this place. Headquarters, the band, and Companies A, D, G, H, K and M left on June 15 under the command of Lieutenant Colonel George Custer and marched up the Yellowstone to the mouth of the Tongue River, arriving there on the 18th, and remaining there in camp on the 19th. In the afternoon scouts reported that Major Reno's command was 8 or 10 miles up the Yellowstone. The companies left camp at 8 AM on the 20th and reached Major Reno's camp at 11:30 AM. The supply steamboat *Far West* arrived soon afterwards and at 4 PM, the entire regiment marched toward the mouth of Rosebud Creek, a distance of 16 miles, arriving there at 11 PM. The regiment left the Rosebud camp on June 22 and marched up the Rosebud for 93 miles and then crossed the divide into the valley of the Little Bighorn River on June 25. A large Indian village was located and attacked. The engagement lasted with intervals until the next evening, when the hostiles withdrew.

The regiment was relieved by the arrival of General Terry and forces under Colonel John Gibbon. June 28 was devoted to burying the dead, and the 29th to destroying the Indian camp and making litters for movement of the wounded, and to scouting up the Little Bighorn River. Camp was moved a short distance and the river crossed and the command was mustered. The march was resumed that night with the wounded and camp was made at the mouth of the Little Bighorn at 2:30 AM on July 1. The expedition left the same day and marched 20 miles down the Bighorn River and on July 2 they reached and crossed the Yellowstone at Pease Bottom. On July 3 the steamboat *Far West* with Captain Stephen Baker's company of the 6th Infantry as escort, and having on board the wounded, and Capt. Smith, adc, with dispatches, left at noon and reached

1

Bismarck, Dakota, at 11 PM on July 5. At dawn the next day the families at Fort Lincoln were notified of the disaster.

The expedition left camp on August 8 and marched 35 miles up the Rosebud, where a column under General George Crook joined General Terry's command on August 10. As no column was known to be in the vicinity, the dust raised by Crook's column was supposed to be caused by Indians moving to attack. Chief Trumpeter Hardy was sent down the column on a dead run to warn the command and in a few moments the entire command was in a position to receive whatever was in store for them. The surprise, however, was pleasant when it developed that the opposite forces were friends. The combined forces left the next day and marched to the Powder River, crossing it 40 miles above its mouth, thence to the supply depot at its junction with the Yellowstone, arriving there on the 17th. On August 24 General Crook's command left the depot and marched toward the Black Hills and at the Slim Buttes had a severe fight with hostile Indians.

General Terry's command crossed the Yellowstone on August 27 and marched in a northerly direction, and on August 31 was camped on Fox Creek about 45 miles from Fort Buford. Between September 1 and 9, the regiment was scouting in the vicinity of the Yellowstone. On September 10 the expedition started for the Missouri River and reached it opposite Wolf's Point on September 13. They crossed the Missouri and left Wolf's Point on September 16 and arrived at Fort Buford on September 18, Fort Berthold on September 22, Fort Stevenson on September 23 and Fort Lincoln on September 26 at noon. The band and Companies A, D, C, E, F, I and L occupied quarters and Companies B, G, H, I, K and M went into camp below the post in anticipation of movement down the Missouri River to disarm and dismount the Indians at Standing Rock and Cheyenne Agencies. By the arrival of 503 recruits from St. Louis Barracks the regimental strength was increased to 1244 men. More than 500 new horses were received and assigned to the companies. With further field work soon to be undertaken there was little time in which to reorganize, repair and issue equipment and give the new horses and men enough drill and training to smooth the rough edges. Sixteen officers were absent from the regiment and five inexperienced officers had joined by transfer, making a noticeable shortage in this respect. However, by steady application and long hours of work the regiment was put in shape and by October 17, Headquarters and Companies B, E, F, H, I, K, L and M, 7th Cavalry, with Companies A and H, 17th Infantry, Company D, 20th Infantry, a section of Parrott guns and 28 Indian scouts under the command of Colonel Samuel Sturgis crossed the Missouri River and went into camp. They left on October 20 and marched down the left bank of the Missouri, arriving opposite the Standing Rock Agency on October 22. In the meantime Major Reno with Companies A, C, D and G left Fort Lincoln on October 21 and marched to Fort Rice and thence the next day to Standing Rock Agency on the right bank of the river, the two forces arriving the same day. Their duty having been accomplished at the agency, Major Reno's command arrived back at Fort Lincoln on November 3, having driven 900 ponies from the agency. Colonel Sturgis' command left Standing Rock on October 26 and arrived nearly opposite Cheyenne Agency on October 30. Duty having been performed here, arrangements were made for locating the regiment at winter station. Company F left this camp on November 4, with about 1,000 ponies and arrived at Fort Abercrombie for station on November 14 after traveling a distance of 265 miles. The rest of Colonel Sturgis' column began the return march on

2

November 4. Companies H and M were left at Fort Rice for station on November 10. The column reached Fort Lincoln on November 11 after traveling 185 miles. Companies A and D left Fort Lincoln on November 14 and arrived at Fort Rice for station on the same day after marching a distance of 26 miles. Company C left Fort Lincoln on November 18 and arrived at Fort Totten for station on November 28 after traveling a distance of 182 miles. A number of men were badly frozen on this march. The remaining six companies took winter station at Fort Lincoln.

The following named officers were promoted or assigned to the regiment during the year: 2nd Lieut. Wm. Van Wyck Reily, Lieut. Colonel Elmer Otis, 2nd Lieut. Wm. Robinson, Jr., 2nd Lieut. George Eaton, 1st Lieut. Edwin Eckerson, 2nd Lieut. Daniel Pearson, 2nd Lieut. Hugh Scott, 2nd Lieut. Charles Schofield, 2nd Lieut. Ernest Garlington, 2nd Lieut. John Wilkinson, 2nd Lieut. Albert Russell, 2nd Lieut. George Chase, 2nd Lieut. Edwin Andrus, 2nd Lieut. Loyd McCormick, 2nd Lieut. John Gresham, 2nd Lieut. William Nicholson, 2nd Lieut. Ezra Fuller, 2nd Lieut. Jonathan Biddle, 2nd Lieut. Horatio Sickel, 2nd Lieut. Herbert Slocum, 2nd Lieut. Edwin Brewer.

The following officers were lost to the regiment during the year: Colonel George Custer, 1st Lieut. William Cooke, Regimental Adjutant, 1st Lieut. Algernon Smith, 2nd Lieut. Benjamin Hodgson, Captain Thomas Custer, 1st Lieut. James Calhoun, 2nd Lieut. Henry Harrington, Captain George Yates, 1st Lieut. Donald McIntosh, Captain Myles Keogh, 1st Lieut. James Porter, 2nd Lieut. James Sturgis, 2nd Lieut. Wm. Van Wyck Reily, 2nd Lieut. Edwin Andrus, 1st Lieut. Charles Larned, 2nd Lieut. George Eaton, 2nd Lieut. Charles Schofield, 2nd Lieut. George Chase, 2nd Lieut. Daniel Pearson, Captain Thomas Weir, making a net gain of one officer and leaving 41 officers present and absent.

Field and staff officers were: Colonel Samuel Sturgis, Lieut. Colonel George Custer, Major Joseph Tilford, Major Lewis Merrill, Major Marcus Reno, Lieut. Col. Elmer Otis, 1st Lieut. William Cooke, Regimental Adjutant, 1st Lieut. Henry Nowlan, Regimental Quartermaster, 1st Lieut. Charles Varnum, Regimental Quartermaster, 1st Lieut. George Wallace, Regimental Adjutant, 1st Lieut. Winfield Edgerly, Regimental Quartermaster.

The distance marched by headquarters during the year was 1,731 miles and the distance marched by the Band was 1,361 miles.

The following is a list of members of headquarters and the regimental quartermaster who were casualties in the Little Bighorn River fight. Those killed were: Lieut. Colonel George Custer, 1st Lieut. William Cooke, Regimental Adjutant, Sergeant Major William Sharrow, Chief Trumpeter Henry Voss. Assistant Surgeon George Lord was with the Custer battalion and was killed in the fight. Second Lieutenant John Crittenden, 20th Infantry, was killed in the fight.

In addition, Acting Assistant Surgeon James DeWolf, Boston Custer, Harry Reed, Mark Kellogg, Charles Reynolds and Isaiah Dorman, a Negro interpreter from Fort Rice, were killed.

STAFF AND BAND, QUARTERMASTER AND CITIZENS AT THE LITTLE BIGHORN

	Absent	Present	Wounded	Died OWRT	Killed	Survived
Colonel	1					1
Lieut. Colonel		1			1	
Major	2	1				3
First Lieut.	1	1			1	1
Medical Officer		3			2	1
Veterinarian	1					1
Sgt. Major		1			1	
Chief Trumpeter		1			1	
Saddler Sergt.	1					1
QM Sergeant	1					1
Chief Musician	1					1
Privates-Band	16					16
Guide		3			3	
Scout		1				1
Interpreter		3			2	1
Chief Packer		1	1			1
Packers		9			1	8
Teamster		1				1
Citizens		2			2	
Totals	24	28	1	0	14	38

FIELD STAFF AND BAND ON JUNE 30, 1876

Officers present for duty 3
Officers absent detached service 2
Officers absent leave 1
Enlisted absent detached service 18
Enlisted absent sick 1
Colonel 1
Majors 3
Adjutant 1
Quartermaster 1
Quartermaster Sergeant 1
Chief Musician 1
Saddler Sergeant 1
Privates 16
Total enlisted 19
Aggregate 25
Aggregate in May 28
Officer by appointment 1
Officers killed 2
Enlisted killed 2
Horses serviceable 18
Horses unserviceable 2
Horses lost 4

STURGIS, SAMUEL DAVIS, Colonel

On detached service at St. Louis, Missouri. Born on June 11, 1822, at Shippensburg, Pennsylvania. He entered the Military Academy in 1842 and graduated as the 1303rd graduate on July 1, 1846, ranking 32nd in his class of 59 graduates. Appointed Brevet Second Lieutenant, First Dragoons, commissioned a Second Lieutenant on February 16, 1847. While serving with the 1st Dragoons in the Mexican War he was captured on Feb. 20, 1847, while reconnoitering near Buena Vista and was not released until after the battle. On July 5, 1851, he married Jereusha Wilcox at West Ely, Missouri. Promoted to First Lieutenant on July 15, 1853; served on the western frontier from 1851 to 1854 and was engaged against hostile Apaches in April, 1854. On March 3, 1855, he was promoted to Captain in the First Regiment of Cavalry and during the same year served in the Indian campaign in New Mexico. He rendered gallant service in the Cheyenne expedition in 1857 and was engaged in the Utah expedition in 1858 and fought against the Kiowas and Comanches in 1860. Promoted to Major, 1st Cavalry, on May 3, 1861, when he was in command at Fort Smith, Arkansas. He received the brevet of lieutenant colonel for his gallant and meritorious services in the battle of Wilson's Creek, with rank from August 10, 1861. On the same date he was promoted to Brigadier General, U.S. Volunteers. On March 13, 1865, he was brevetted Brigadier General, U.S.A. for his gallant and meritorious service at South Mountain where he commanded a division. He received the brevet of Major General for his gallant and meritorious services at Fredericksburg. He participated in the campaign in northern Virginia; the Maryland campaign; the Rappahannock campaign and the operations in central Kentucky. He was Chief of Cavalry in the Department of Ohio and in operations in Tennessee, North Carolina and Mississippi. After transfer to the west he was mustered out of volunteer service on August 24, 1865. Appointed Lieutenant Colonel 6th Cavalry, on October 27, 1863, and Colonel, 7th Cavalry, on May 6, 1869; saw service in Indian campaigns but was not in field command of the regiment until after the Little Bighorn River fight. General Sturgis was Governor of the Soldier's Home, Washington, D.C. from 1881 to 1885 and on June 11, 1886, after 40 years service, he retired. Died on September 28, 1889, at St. Paul, Minnesota; interred in Arlington National Cemetery. One of his sons, Lieut. James G. Sturgis was killed in the Little Bighorn River fight. His other son, Samuel D. Sturgis, Jr. entered the Military Academy on July 1, 1880. For additional biographical information see the *Annual Report of the Association of Graduates of the United States Military Academy At West Point, New York, 1890.*

CUSTER, GEORGE ARMSTRONG, Lieutenant Colonel

Killed with the Custer column on June 25. Born December 5, 1839, in New Rumley, Ohio, the son of Emanuel Henry (born December 10, 1806-died November 17, 1892) and Maria Ward Kirkpatrick Custer (born May 31, 1807-died January 13, 1882.) He attended the Military Academy from July 1, 1857 to June 24, 1861, graduating 34 in his class of 34 as the 1966th graduate. Commissioned Second Lieut. Co. G, 2nd Cavalry to rank from his date of graduation. Promoted to First Lieut. 5th Cavalry to rank from July 17, 1862. Promoted to Captain, Staff and AADC to Gen. George McClellan to rank from June 5, 1862. On June 29, 1863, upon the recommendation of Gen. Alfred Pleasonton, he was promoted to Brigadier General, U.S. Volunteers. Brevetted

Major to rank from July 3, 1863 for gallant and meritorious services at the Battle of Gettysburg. On February 9, 1864, while on leave, he married Elizabeth Clift Bacon (born April 3, 1842-died April 1, 1933), daughter of Judge Daniel Stanton and Eleanor Sophia Page Bacon in Monroe, Michigan. Promoted to Captain, 5th Cavalry, May 8, 1864. Brevetted Lieutenant Colonel to rank from May 11, 1864 for his meritorious services in capturing a battery at Yellow Tavern. Brevetted Colonel to rank from September 19, 1864, for gallant and meritorious services at the Battle of Winchester. Brevetted Brigadier General, AUS, to rank from March 13, 1865 for gallant and meritorious services at the Battle of Five Forks. Promoted to Major General, U.S. Volunteers, on April 15, 1865. Appointed Lieutenant Colonel, 7th Cavalry, to rank from July 28, 1866, the date the regiment was organized. Brevetted Major General, AUS, on July 28, 1866, to rank from March 13, 1865. Court-martialed, suspended from pay and rank for one year in 1867. Engaged in the Washita River fight November 28, 1868. In command of the 7th Cavalry on the Yellowstone expedition in 1873 and the Black Hills expedition of 1874. Killed while in command of the 7th Cavalry in the Little Bighorn River fight. Interred on the battlefield on June 28, 1876. Exhumed in July, 1877, and re-interred in the Post Cemetery at the Military Academy on October 10, 1877. Fort Custer, Montana, was named in his honor, as well as many place names throughout the United States.

TILFORD, JOSEPH GREEN, Major

On leave of absence.[1] Born in Kentucky. Entered the Military Academy by appointment from Kentucky on July 1, 1847, and was the 1533rd graduate, ranking 40th in his class of 42 graduates. On July 1, 1851, he was appointed a Brevet Second Lieutenant in the Mounted Rifles. Commissioned Second Lieutenant on January 27, 1853. Promoted to First Lieutenant on June 14, 1858, and Captain on July 31, 1861.[2] He served at the Cavalry School and on frontier duty from 1851 to 1862 and was engaged in actions in New Mexico, Tennessee and was in the campaign against Chattanooga. He received the brevet of Major to rank from February 21, 1862, for his gallant and meritorious services in the battle of Valverde, New Mexico, and the brevet of Lieutenant Colonel to rank from March 13, 1865, for his faithful and meritorious services during the Civil War. Captain Tilford was appointed Major in the Seventh Regiment of Cavalry, on November 27, 1867, and served with the regiment for the next twenty-two years. He did not participate in the Sioux expedition of 1876, being on leave of absence at the time. On September 22, 1883, he received promotion to Lieutenant Colonel and on April 11, 1889, he was promoted to Colonel of the Ninth U.S. Cavalry. He received promotion to Brigadier General and retired on July 1, 1891. Died February 24, 1911 in Washington, D. C.; interred in Arlington National Cemetery, Grave 1205, Section 2. Additional biographical information is in Cullum *Biographical Register of the Officers and Graduates of the U.S. Military Academy at West Point, N.Y. From Its Establishment in 1802, to 1890.*

1. The leave of absence granted Major Tilford (at Fort Rice, Dakota) in Special Order Nr. 71, April 27, 1875, was extended eleven months.
2. The Mounted Rifles was designated the Third Regiment of Cavalry by Act of Congress on August 3, 1861.

MERRILL, LEWIS, Major

On detached service as chief of military staff of the President, at the International Exhibition of 1876 at Philadelphia from March to November, 1876. Born in Pennsylvania. Entered the Military Academy in May, 1851. Graduated in July, 1855, ranking 20th in his class of 34 graduates as the 1696th graduate. Appointed Brevet Second Lieutenant, 1st Dragoons, July 1, 1855. Served in garrison at Jefferson Barracks, Missouri, and on frontier duty at Forts Leavenworth and Riley in 1855. Appointed Second Lieutenant, 2nd Dragoons December 13, 1855. At Carlisle Barracks in 1856 and quelling Kansas disturbances in 1856 to 1858; on the Utah expedition in 1858 and on sick leave in 1859 and in the Kiowa and Comanche campaigns in 1860. Promoted to First Lieutenant April 24, 1861. Promoted to Colonel and Chief of Cavalry Staff of Major Gen. Fremont in August, 1861. He organized and was appointed Colonel of the regiment of Merrill's Horse, Missouri Volunteer Cavalry, August 23, 1861. He was engaged in numerous battles in Missouri and Arkansas, Tennessee and Georgia until 1865. He received promotions through the ranks until March 13, 1865, when he was brevetted Brigadier General, U.S. Volunteers, for his gallant and meritorious services during the war. Mustered out of volunteer service December 14, 1865. Stationed at Fort Leavenworth and other frontier posts from 1866 in staff positions mainly. Commanding troops in northwest South Carolina from March, 1871, to June, 1873, engaged in suppression of Ku Klux Klan activity. He received the thanks of the War Department and of Brig. Gen. Alfred Terry, commanding the Department of the South, for his great work and ability in breaking up the Klan conspiracy. He was on sick leave until August, 1874, and on frontier duty at Fort Rice, Dakota from August to September, 1874. Commanding two battalions of the 7th Cavalry enroute to and in New Orleans to October, 1874; at Shreveport, Louisiana, commanding the District of the Red River to February, 1876, when he became chief of military staff to the President at the Centennial Exhibition. On frontier duty at Fort A. Lincoln, Dakota to May, 1877, when he commanded a battalion of the 7th Cavalry departing for the Nez Perce campaign. Engaged in the Canyon Creek fight on September 14, 1877. At Fort Lincoln to July, 1878, and in the field near Bear Butte, Dakota, to November, 1878. Commanding a battalion at Standing Rock, Dakota, to May, 1880, and then commanding troops guarding construction of the Northern Pacific Railroad to Dec., 1880. Member of the Whittaker court martial in New York City to May, 1881 and then returned to guarding construction of the Northern Pacific until Dec., 1882. Brevetted Brig. Gen. U.S.A., Feb. 27, 1890, for his gallant service at Canyon Creek. Died on Feb. 27, 1896, at age 62.

RENO, MARCUS ALBERT, Major

Commanding Companies A, G and M in the valley fight and Companies A, B, D, G, H, K and M and the pack train in the hilltop fight. Born in Carrollton, Greene County, Illinois in 1832. Entered the Military Academy from Illinois September 1, 1851, and graduated on July 1, 1857 as the 1779th graduate, ranking 20th in his class of 38 graduates. Appointed Brevet Second Lieutenant of Dragoons July 1, 1857, and Second Lieut. 1st Dragoons, June 14, 1858, Served at Fort Dalles, Oregon, and Fort Walla Walla, Washington Terr. until 1861. Promoted to First Lieut. 1st Regiment of Cavalry, April 25, 1861, and Captain, November 12, 1861. Brevetted Major, effective March 17, 1863 for gallant and meritorious services at Kelly's Ford, Virginia, March 17, 1863. Brevetted Lieut. Col. for gallant and meritorious serivces at the Battle of Cedar Creek, October 19, 1864. Appointed Colonel, 12th Penna. Volunteer Cavalry from January 1 to July 20, 1865. Brevet Colonel and Brig. General, U.S. Volunteers, on March 13, 1865, for gallant and meritorious services. Married Mary Hannah Ross. On the western frontier and in the southern states and on staff duty until April, 1873. On frontier duty until 1877. Court-martialed in 1877; suspended from pay and rank for two years. Dismissed from the service April 1, 1880, as a result of a court-martial. Died March 30, 1889, at age 57 at Providence Hospital, Washington, D.C. following an operation. Re-interred at Custer Battlefield National Cemetery. See *The Annual Report Of The Association Of Graduates Of The United States Military Academy*, 1889 and W. A. Graham, *The Reno Court of Inquiry*, pp. 298-300 and Barry Johnson, *Case Of Marcus A. Reno*, The English Westerners' Society Special Publication No. 3, London, 1969.

COOKE, WILLIAM WINER, First Lieutenant
Killed with the Custer battalion on June 25. Born in Mount Pleasant, Brant County, Ontario, Canada, the eldest son of Dr. Alexander Hardy and Sarah Winer Cooke. He entered U.S. military service at Niagara Falls, New York, in 1862. Appointed Second Lieutenant, 24th New York Volunteer Cavalry, on January 26, 1864; promoted to First Lieutenant on December 14, 1865. Honorably mustered out of volunteer service on June 25, 1865. Appointed Second Lieutenant, 7th Cavalry, to rank from July 28, 1866. Promoted to First Lieutenant on July 31, 1867. Regimental Adjutant December 8, 1866, to February 21, 1867, and from January 1, 1871, to June 25, 1876. Lt. Cooke was brevetted Captain on March 2, 1867, for service at the Battle of Petersburg on June 17, 1864; Major on March 2, 1867, for service in the Battle of Dinwiddie Courthouse, Virginia on March 29, 1865; Lieut. Colonel on March 2, 1867 for service in the Battle of Sayler's Creek, Virginia on April 6, 1865. Killed in the fight on the Little Bighorn River. His remains were exhumed in June, 1877 and re-interred at the Custer Battlefield National Monument. Later his remains were again exhumed and re-interred at Hamilton, Ontario, Canada.

NOWLAN, HENRY JAMES, First Lieutenant
Born in Corfu. Entered military service from New York. Appointed First Lieutenant, 14th New York Volunteer Cavalry, on January 17, 1863. Transferred to the 18th New York Volunteer Cavalry June 12, 1865. Promoted to Captain January 15, 1866. Honorably mustered out of volunteer service May 31, 1866. Appointed Second Lieutenant, 7th Cavalry to rank from July 28, 1866, the day the regiment was organized. Promoted to First Lieutenant December 3, 1866. Appointed Regimental Commissary for Subsistence November 1, 1867, to July 15, 1870. Appointed Regimental Quartermaster March 1, 1872, to June 25, 1876. Promoted to Captain effective June 25, 1876, to fill the vacancy created by the death of Captain Myles Keogh. Brevetted Major February 27, 1890 for his gallant service in action against the Nez Perce Indians at Canyon Creek, Montana Territory September 13, 1877. Promoted to Major July 17, 1895. Died November 10, 1898.

LORD, GEORGE EDWIN, Assistant Surgeon

Killed with the Custer battalion on June 25. Born on February 17, 1846, in Boston, Massachusetts. He entered military medical service from Maine on April 27, 1871, when he contracted for duty as an Acting Assistant Surgeon. The contract was made at St. Paul, Minnesota for duty in the Department of Dakota at a monthly compensation of $100. On April 30, 1871, Dr. Lord was on duty at Fort Ripley and on May 31 he was with a detachment of the 20th Infantry at Leech Lake, Minnesota and on the last day of June he was at the Whetstone Agency in Dakota. From the 29th of May, 1872, he was at Fort Randall, Dakota. On October 31 of the same year he took a 30-day leave of absence then returned to Fort Randall on November 21 and was on duty there from November 30 until his contract was cancelled at his own request on November 3, 1873. On May 22, 1874, while residing in Limerick, Maine, he entered a new contract for medical duty in the Department of Dakota for the same pay as in the previous contract. On June 1 he was assigned to duty with the escort for the Northern Boundary Survey Commission (NBSC) and at the end of the month he was at Camp Quaking Aspen serving with Companies E and I of the 6th Infantry who were escort for the NBSC. On July 27 he received a letter inviting him to appear before the Army Medical Board as a candidate for appointment on the medical staff of the army. On the 31st of July he was on duty at Camp Reno in the Sweet Grass Hills, Montana Territory, with the NBSC and on the last day of August, he was on duty in the camp on the North Fork of the Milk River, Montana Territory, with the NBSC. On September 30th he was at Bismarck, Dakota enroute to St. Paul with the NBSC. When he arrived at Department of Dakota Headquarters in St. Paul on October 7, he found that he had been assigned to winter station at Fort Ripley effective the previous day. From October 31 he was a Post Surgeon at Ripley until December 3 when his contract was annulled at his own request in St. Paul. In New York City on January 18, 1875, he signed a new contract for duty as an Acting Assistant Surgeon at the same monthly pay and was ordered to St. Paul for assignment. He was on temporary duty at Fort Snelling from January 25 until February 27 when he departed for New Ulm, Minnesota. He was there on the 28th and enroute to Lac Qui Parle and Yellow Medicine Countries to make an enrollment of the settlers who were suffering because of the grasshopper plague. On March 2 he was at Granite Falls and on the 3rd he was at Minnesota Falls and by the 24th of the month he had returned to Fort Snelling. On May 9 Dr. Lord was relieved from duty at Fort Snelling and proceeded to Fort Abraham Lincoln, Dakota. He left Fort Snelling on May 17 and arrived in Fort Lincoln on May 20 for duty with an expedition to explore in the Black Hills area until July 8 when he received telegraphic orders to return to Fort Snelling. Upon his return he was appointed Assistant Surgeon, U.S. Army, with the rank of First Lieutenant effective from June 26, 1875. On May 17, 1876 Lieut. Lord departed with Brig. General Terry's command from Fort Lincoln to participate in the Sioux expedition. On June 25 at the time that Lieut. Colonel George Custer divided his force prior to the attack on hostile Indians on the Little Bighorn River, Dr. Lord was suffering from an indisposition and Colonel Custer suggested that he remain with the force to the rear, but Lord insisted on going with the regimental staff. His remains were interred on the battlefield on June 28 and exhumed in July, 1877, and re-interred at the Custer Battlefield National Monument. He was survived by his brother, Thomas William Lord, First Lieutenant and RQM, 20th Infantry, Fort Snelling.

DEWOLF, JAMES M., Acting Assistant Surgeon
   Killed on the bluffside in the retreat from the valley fight on June 25.
Born on January 14, 1843, at Mehosparry or Jenningsville, Wyoming County,
Pennsylvania. At the age of 17 he enlisted in the 1st Regiment of Pennsylvania
Volunteer Artillery on August 1, 1861. He was 5'-8" tall with grey eyes, light,
hair and light complexion. He gave his occupation as farmer. He was engaged in
the Battle of Bull Run on Aug. 30, 1862, as a Corporal in Battery A, 1st Penna.
Arty. and was wounded. He was 1/3rd disabled and was discharged as a Corporal
on Oct. 29, 1862, as a result of gunshot wound (necrosis of the ulna). He
resigned his pension and re-enlisted in Battery A, 1st Penna. Arty. in September,
1864. Discharged on June 14, 1865. Enlisted on Oct. 5, 1865, in Co. E, 14th
U.S. Infantry; appointed hospital steward on May 17, 1866, and discharged on
Oct. 5, 1868. He re-enlisted the same day at Camp Lyon, Idaho under the name
of James DeWall as a hospital steward. On Oct. 3, 1871, he was married to
Fannie J. Downing at Camp Warner, Oregon, by Chaplain M. J. Kelly. She was
appointed hospital matron at Camp Warner on Nov. 4, 1871. DeWolf was
discharged on Oct. 5, 1871, and re-enlisted the same day, under the name James
M. DeWolf as a Hospital Steward, U.S.A. He was transferred to Watertown
Arsenal, Watertown, Mass. to enable him to study medicine at Harvard
University which he entered in September, 1873. He graduated from Harvard
School of Medicine on June 26, 1875, with an MD degree. After graduation he
took the Army Medical Examination for Assistant Surgeon but failed to pass. He
was discharged as a Hospital Steward on October 5, 1875, and on October 23
that year he entered into contract as an Acting Assistant Surgeon with the
Surgeon General, U.S.A. at Forkston, Penna. Assigned to Fort Totten, Dakota,
on November 6, 1875, and arrived there on November 14. He participated in the
Sioux expedition of 1876 as an Acting Assistant Surgeon, Headquarters,
Department of Dakota, and was attached to the 7th Cavalry on June 21. Killed
in the Little Bighorn River fight by a gunshot wound through the abdomen and
six wounds in the head and face. His remains were exhumed in July, 1877, and
re-interred in Woodland Cemetery, Norwalk, Ohio, in October, 1877. His widow
married Elijah Dodd June 10, 1879, at Waterville, Ohio and was divorced
November 21, 1912. Fannie DeWolf Dodd died May 19, 1918. As far as is
known there was one son, Verne A. Dodd, who became an eminent physician
and surgeon and until about 1942 was Dean of the Medical School, Ohio State
University. As late as 1955 he was living at Latana, Florida, and Jackson Hole,
Wyoming. Dr. Dodd presented James DeWolf's letters (written April-June, 1876)
and diary to the Custer Battlefield National Monument.

PORTER, HENRY RINALDO, Acting Assistant Surgeon
   In the valley and hilltop fights. Born on February 3, 1848, in New York
Mills, New York, the son of Henry N. and Helen Polson Porter. Graduated from
The Georgetown University School of Medicine in 1872, as Doctor of Medicine.
He signed a contract on June 26, 1872, in Washington for duty as an Acting
Assistant Surgeon and arrived in Arizona on August 25, 1872, and was assigned
to duty at Camp Hualpai, 40 miles north of Prescott. From September 22, 1872,
to April 25, 1873, he was in the field with the 5th Cavalry in the campaign
against the Apache Indians and engaged in several fights including the fight at
Muchos Canyon on September 26, 1872. On Apr. 25, 1873, he became Post
Surgeon at Camp Grant until July 27th when he returned to San Francisco to

have his contract cancelled at his own request. On October 16, 1873, he entered another contract as Acting Assistant Surgeon and was assigned to Camp Hancock, Dakota, where he arrived on the 31st. He remained there until his contract was cancelled at his request on December 1, 1874. He then entered into the partnership of Nicholson & Porter, druggists and stationers, in Bismarck. On September 28, 1875, he again signed a contract for assignment as Acting Assistant Surgeon at Camp Hancock. He was on duty there from November 1, 1875, to May 14, 1876, when he entered a three-month contract for duty with the Sioux expedition. On May 17 he departed with the expedition from Fort Abraham Lincoln enroute to the Powder River. He was engaged in the Little Bighorn River fight on June 25-26 and set up a hospital during the hilltop fight and cared for the wounded. His story of the fight was published in *Compendium of History and Biography of North Dakota*, 160-162, Geo. A. Ogle & Co. 1900. He served throughout the summer campaign until his contract was cancelled on September 30 at Fort Lincoln. On December 2 he entered a contract for duty as Acting Assistant Surgeon at Camp Hancock. This contract was annulled on February 28, 1877. He married Charlotte Viets in September, 1877 in Oberlin, Ohio. In 1879 he testified at the Reno Court of Inquiry. His testimony was not favorable to Major Reno but was laudatory for Captain Frederick Benteen. Engaged in a world tour in 1893 and 1894. Died on the morning of March 3, 1903 in the Hotel Metropole in Agra, India and was interred there. A memorial was erected beside his wife's grave in Oberlin. He was survived by his son, Henry Viets Porter. A Surgical Chest, U.S. Army, No. 2 used by Dr. Porter in the Little Bighorn River fight, is in the Fort Lincoln State Park Museum, North Dakota. See also Wm. Stoddard (ed.) *History of the Great Northwest*, Minneapolis, 1901, The Minneapolis Journal, pp. 145-146.

STEIN, C.A., Veterinarian

Attached for duty with the 7th Cavalry during the Sioux expedition. On duty at Yellowstone Depot, Montana Territory during the Little Bighorn River fight. C. A. Stein was ordered to duty with a detachment of the regiment at Shreveport, Louisiana in 1875.[1] He was relieved from duty in the Department of the Gulf and ordered to report to Fort Abraham Lincoln, Dakota, in December, 1875,[2] but the transfer order was superseded in January, 1876.[3] In a letter from the Adjutant General's Office to the Commanding Officer, 7th Cavalry, January 4, 1876, regarding suspension of transfer until the following spring, Major Merrill stated that Stein had a large family of small children and that they would suffer severely in going to Fort Lincoln at that season and that Stein was too poor to leave them in Louisiana. Stein was ordered, on March 24, 1876, to take charge of a herd of mules, destined for Fort Lincoln.[4] He participated in the Sioux expedition and accompanied the column from Fort Lincoln on May 17, arriving on the Powder River on June 7. He remained at Yellowstone Depot when the 7th Cavalry departed on the campaign to the Little Bighorn River. Grant Marsh, captain of the supply steamboat, the *Far West*, related, just after the Little Bighorn River fight that Stein, "was the most scared man" that he had ever seen.[5] The resignation of Stein, as veterinary surgeon, was accepted to take effect on September 1, 1876.[6]

1. Paragraph 2, Special Order Nr. 129, Headquarters, Department of the Gulf, July 15, 1875.

2. Special Order Nr. 260, War Department, December 20, 1875.
3. Special Order Nr. 1, War Department, January 3, 1876.
4. Special Order Nr. 37, Department of Dakota, March, 1876 and Special Order Nr. 22, Military Division of the Missouri, March, 1876.
5. Joseph Mills Hanson, *Conquest of the Missouri.*
6. Special Order Nr., War Department, August 17, 1876 and the *Army and Navy Journal*, August 26, 1876, p. 36.

SHARROW, WILLIAM H., Sergeant Major

Killed with the Custer battalion on June 25. Born at sea. Second enlistment on September 10, 1874, at age 29 in St. Paul, Minnesota by Lieut. William Cooke. He had blue eyes, light hair, light complexion and was 5'-8" in height. Listed as W. H. Sharrow on the battle monument. A list of personal effects found in Sergeant Sharrow's quarters at Fort Abraham Lincoln, Dakota on October 8, 1876, is in the Descriptive List and Records File, Custer Battlefield National Monument.

VOSS, HENRY, Chief Trumpeter

Killed in battle on June 25. Born in Hanover, Germany. Third enlistment on January 18, 1875, in New York City by Lieut. John Babcock. He had blue eyes, light hair, fair complexion and was 5'-8¾" in height. Listed as Henry Voss on the battle monument.

TRITTEN, JOHN G., Saddler Sergeant

On detached service from June 14, 1876, at Yellowstone Depot, Montana Territory. Born in Canton Rune, Switzerland. Second enlistment on December 22, 1873, at age 27 2/12 in Cincinnati by Lieut. Adam Kramer. Previous occupation was saddler. Transferred from Company L to regimental headquarters. Discharged on December 22, 1878, at Fort Abraham Lincoln, Dakota, upon expiration of service, as a Saddler Sergeant. He had blue eyes, light hair, light complexion and was 5'-7" in height. A manuscript letter copy from Mrs. Anna M. Tritten, September 7, 1875, petitioning for the discharge of John G. Tritten, Saddler Sergeant, 7th Cavalry is in the E. B. Custer Collection, Custer Battlefield National Monument.

CANSBY, THOMAS, Quartermaster Sergeant

On detached service from June 14, 1876, at Yellowstone Depot, Montana Territory. Born in Liverpool, England. Second enlistment on June 1, 1872, at age 25 in Memphis, Tennessee by Captain G. A. Purington. Previous occupation was laborer. Discharged on January 1, 1877, at Fort A. Lincoln upon expiration of service, as a Sergeant of excellent character. He had blue eyes, light hair, fair complexion and was 5'-10¾" in height. He re-enlisted on January 1, 1877. Listed as Thomas Cansby in the Register of Enlistments, U.S. Army, and on his Oath of Enlistment, and elsewhere as Thomas Causby.

SEVENTH CAVALRY BAND

VINATIERI, FELIX VILLIET, Chief Musician

On detached service from June 14, 1876, at Yellowstone Depot, Montana Territory. Born in 1834 in Turin, Italy. Graduated from the music school of the

University of Naples where he taught for a year following graduation. He arrived in the United States before 1859 and was enlisted on August 5, 1861, at Camp Cameron, near Worcester, Massachusetts, for three years as a musician under the name Felix Villiett. Joined for duty and enrolled at Cambridge as Musician, 1st Class, in the 16th Mass. Infantry Band. Appointed band leader in September, 1861. Discharged for disability on July 23, 1862, at Harrison's Landing, Virginia by Samuel Dalton, Adjutant General. He returned to Europe and lived in Lisbon, Portugal, later returning to the states. He was enrolled as Band Leader, 22nd Infantry, at Fort Columbus, New York by Captain Evan Miles on December 26, 1867. Previous occupation was listed as musician. Transferred to Fort Sully, Dakota, and served there three years. Discharged December 26, 1870 at which time he left for Yankton, Dakota, downriver from Fort Sully. He married Anna Frances Fefjar, age 16, in Yankton on October 24, 1871. On May 23, 1873 he was enlisted at age 36 as Chief Musician, 7th Cavalry at St. Paul, Minnesota, by Lieut. William Cooke. In the Yellowstone expedition of 1873 and the Black Hills expedition of 1874. Discharged December 18, 1876, at Fort A. Lincoln, Dakota per Special Order Nr. 251, AGO, Dec. 6, 1876 as a Chief Musician of very good character. he had grey eyes, brown hair, fair complexion and was 5'-2½" in height. Listed as Felice Vinatieri in the Register of Enlistments, U.S. Army and on his Oath of Enlistment and elsewhere as Felix Viniateri and Felix Vineteri. Resided in Yankton at 606 West Second St. Died December 15, 1891, at Yankton and interred in Yankton Protestant Cemetery. Survived by his wife and five sons, Albert, Ehrum, Frank, Felix Samuel and Joseph and three daughters Amelia, Lenora and Matilda.

ARNDT, OTTO, Private
On detached service from June 14, 1876 at Yellowstone Depot, Montana Territory. Born in Bavaria, Germany. Second enlistment on May 19, 1870, at age 26 at Fort Leavenworth by Lieut. Myles Moylan, in Company H, 7th Cavalry. He had been discharged on April 22, 1870 from Company A, 3rd Infantry. Discharged from the 7th Cavalry on December 21, 1877. Re-enlisted on January 12, 1878 at age 31 at Fort Hamilton, New Utrecht, New York, by Lieut. J. D. C. Hoskins in the 3rd Artillery Band. He had grey eyes, dark hair, fair complexion and was 5'-7½" in height.

BAUMBACH, CONRAD, Private
On detached service from June 14, 1876, at Yellowstone Depot, Montana Territory. Born in Berlin, Germany. Enlisted on June 26, 1875, at age 35 at St. Louis Barracks, Missouri by Lieut. James Wheelan in the 2nd Cavalry. Transferred to the 7th Cavalry. He had blue eyes, dark hair, ruddy complexion and was 5'-6" in height and was illiterate.

BECK, BENJAMIN, Private
On detached service from June 14, 1876, at Yellowstone Depot, Montana Territory. Born in Philadelphia, Pennsylvania. Enlisted on January 3, 1876, at age 23 in New York City by Lt. John Babcock. Previous occupation was moulder. Discharged on January 2, 1881, at Fort Meade, Dakota upon expiration of service, as a Private of excellent character. He had brown eyes, light brown hair, fair complexion and was 5'-5¼" in height. The Descriptive List and Records

File, Custer Battlefield National Monument, has a muster and descriptive roll of musicians, General Mounted Service, assigned to the 7th Cavalry by Special Order Nr. 17, Headquarters, St. Louis, February 1, 1876, which includes the name Benjamin Beck.

BURLI, EDMOND, Private
On detached service from June 14, 1876, at Yellowstone Depot, Montana Territory. Born in Klingnow, Switzerland. Enlisted on November 13, 1871 at age 23 in Chicago by Captain Samuel Young. Previous occupation was musician. Deserted on May 14, 1873, at St. Louis; surrendered on November 12, 1873, in St. Louis. Discharged on May 28, 1877, at Fort A. Lincoln, Dakota upon expiration of service, with desertion time made good, as a Private of good character. He had hazel eyes, dark hair, dark complexion and was 5'-6½" in height. Listed as Edward Burlia on the 7th Cavalry Muster Roll, June 30, 1876, and as Edmond Burli in the Register of Enlistments, U.S. Army, and elsewhere as Edmond Burlis.

CARROLL, JOSEPH, Private
On detached service from June 14, 1876, at Yellowstone Depot, Montana Territory. Born in New York City. Third enlistment on July 1, 1875, at age 28 at St. Louis Barracks, Mo. by Captain James Wheelan. Previous occupation was musician. Discharged on June 30, 1880, at Fort Meade, Dakota upon expiration of service, as a Private of good character. He had blue eyes, dark hair, fair complexion and was 5'-4" in height. The Descriptive List and Records File, Custer Battlefield National Monument, has a muster and descriptive roll of musicians, General Mounted Service, assigned to the 7th Cavalry by Special Order Nr. 17, Headquarters, St. Louis, Feb. 1, 1876, which includes the name of Joseph Carroll.

CARTER, ANDREW, Private
On detached service from June 14, 1876, at Yellowstone Depot, Montana Territory. Born in Lincoln, England. Enlisted on September 20, 1875, at age 24 in Cincinnati by Lieut. Patrick Cusack. Previous occupation was laborer. Discharged on January 27, 1877, at Fort A. Lincoln, Dakota, per General Court Martial Order Nr. 59, Department of Dakota, 1876, as a Private with character reference of "None". He had dark eyes, brown hair, ruddy complexion and was 5'-6¼" in height.

EISENBERGER, PETER, Private
On detached service from June 14, 1876, at Yellowstone Depot, Montana Territory. Born in Bavaria, Germany. Enlisted on November 15, 1875, at age 19 in New York City by Lieut. John Babcock. Previous occupation was musician. Discharged on November 14, 1880, at Fort Meade, Dakota upon expiration of his service, as a Private of excellent character. He had dark eyes, dark hair, light complexion and was 5'-5½" in height. Listed as Peter Eisenberger in the Register of Enlistments, U.S. Army and on Special Order Nr. 24, Headquarters, Mounted Recruiting Service, St. Louis Barracks, by which order he was transferred to the 7th Cavalry.

GRIESNER, JULIUS, Private
On detached service from June 14, 1876, at Yellowstone Depot, Montana Territory. Born in Neurode, Germany. Enlisted on March 3, 1875, at age 31 in St. Louis by Lieut. William Volkmar. Previous occupation was musician. Discharged on March 2, 1880, at Fort Meade, Dakota upon expiration of service, as a Private of good character. He had grey eyes, light hair, fair complexion and was 5'-5¾" in height.

HUFF, JACOB (Jacob Emerich), Private
On detached service from June 14, 1876, at Yellowstone Depot, Montana Territory. Born in Bavaria. Enlisted on October 16, 1875, at age 24 in Cincinnati by Lieut. Patrick Cusack. Previous occupation was baker. His enlistment was cancelled and he surrendered on August 5, 1876, as Jacob Huff, deserter from Company F, 22nd Infantry. He had blue eyes, light hair, fair complexion and was 5'-9" in height.

JUNGESBLUTH, JULIUS, Private
On detached service from June 14, 1876, at Yellowstone Depot, Montana Territory. Born in Brunswick, Germany. Second enlistment on February 23, 1876, at age 32 2/3 in St. Louis by Lieut. John Thompson. Previous occupation was soldier. Assigned to the 7th Cavalry on Special Order Nr. 24, Headquarters, Mounted Recruiting Service, St. Louis. Deserted on March 30, 1878. He had hazel eyes, brown hair, dark complexion and was 5'-7" in height.

KNEUBUHLER, JOSEPH, Private
Sick and on detached service from May 4, 1876, at Fort Abraham Lincoln, Dakota. Born in Lucerne, Switzerland. Enlisted on March 14, 1872, at age 21 in Louisville, Kentucky by Lieut. William Cooke. Previous occupation was musician. Served in Companies F and G. Discharged on March 14, 1877, at Fort Lincoln upon expiration of service, as a Private of good character. He had grey eyes, brown hair, fair complexion and was 5'-7" in height.

LOMBARD, FRANK, Private
Sick in the hospital at Fort Abraham Lincoln from May 4, 1876. Born in Naples, Italy. Enlisted on September 22, 1871, at age 22 in Meridian, Mississippi, by Captain George Yates. Previous occupation was musician. Discharged at Fort Lincoln, on September 22, 1876, upon expiration of service, as a Private of very good character. He had dark eyes, black hair, dark complexion and was 5'-3" in height.

MERRITT, GEORGE A., Private
On detached service from May 4, 1876, at Fort Abraham Lincoln, Dakota. Born in Stonington, Connecticut. Enlisted on January 22, 1875 at age 32 in Cincinnati by Lieut. Patrick Cusack. Previous occupation was musician. Discharged on January 21, 1880 at Fort Lincoln, upon expiration of service, as a Private of excellent character. He had grey eyes, sandy hair, fair complexion and was 5'-8¾" in height. Listed as George W. Merritt in the Register of Enlistments, U.S. Army.

O'NEILL, BERNARD, Private

On detached service from June 14, 1876, at Yellowstone Depot, Montana Territory. Born in Kelfurbog, Ireland. Second enlistment on November 28, 1871 at age 30 in Louisville, Kentucky by Lieut. William Cooke. Previous occupation was musician. Discharged on November 28, 1876, at Fort Abraham Lincoln, Dakota, upon expiration of service, as a Private of excellent character. He had brown eyes, black hair, dark complexion and was 5'-7" in height.

RUDOLPH, GEORGE, Private

On detached service from June 14, 1876, at Yellowstone Depot, Montana Territory. Born in Minterheim, Bavaria, Germany. Enlisted on September 21, 1871, at age 18 in Meridian, Mississippi by Captain George Yates. Previous occupation was musician. Discharged on September 21, 1876, at Fort Abraham Lincoln, Dakota upon expiration of service, as a Private of very good character. He had brown eyes, brown hair, fair complexion and was 5'-4½" in height.

SHERBORNE, THOMAS, Private

On detached service from June 14, 1876, at Yellowstone Depot, Montana Territory. Born in Kingston, Hampshire, England. Enlisted under the name Charles Answorth on January 11, 1873, at age 33 in Chicago by Captain Samuel Young. Previous occupation was musician. Assignment to the General Mounted Service Band. His enlistment was cancelled when he surrendered under General Order Nr. 102, AGO, 1873, as Thomas Sherbon, a deserter from the 20th Infantry band. Restored to duty. Discharged from the 7th Cavalry Band in his fourth enlistment on February 14, 1887. Re-enlisted on February 15, that year at Fort Meade, Dakota at age 53 by Lieut. Luther Hare. Assigned to Battery L, 1st Artillery. At this time he was not married. He had dark or grey eyes, dark hair, sallow complexion and was 5'-6½" to 7" in height.

CITIZENS AND QUARTERMASTER EMPLOYEES

KELLOGG, MARCUS HENRY, Civil Correspondent
Killed with the Custer column on June 25. Born in Brighton, Canada on March 31, 1833, the son of Simon and Lorenda Whelpley Kellogg. Employed as a telegrapher and correspondent in LaCrosse, Wisconsin, and later as an assistant editor in Council Bluffs, Iowa. Later he became editorial assistant on *The Bismarck Tribune*. He accompanied the Sioux expedition as correspondent for the Tribune. Three of his articles about the expedition were published in the Tribune. His diary was also preserved. See also J. W. Vaughn, "The Mark H. Kellogg Story," *The Westerners New York Posse Brand Book*, 7:4, 1961.

REED, HARRY ARMSTRONG, Accompanying Citizen
Killed with the Custer column on June 25. Born on April 27, 1858 in Monroe, Michigan, the son of Lydia Reed and the nephew of George and Thomas Custer. His remains were interred on the battlefield and exhumed in January, 1878 and re-interred at Monroe, Michigan. Listed as Arthur Reed on the battle monument.

WAGONER, J. C., Chief Packer
Wounded in the head in the hilltop fight. Employed as Chief Packer in charge of pack train on March 1, 1876, by the 7th Cavalry Quartermaster at a monthly pay of $100. Reported as wounded in *The Bismarck Tribune Extra*, July 6, 1876, and by John Frett in his testimony at the Reno Court of Inquiry. This wound probably occurred while he was among the horses in the hilltop fight. Discharged on September 23, 1876, at the end of the campaign, with payment of $276.66 from July 1–September 23 and of $200.00 from May 1 to June 30, 1876.

ALEXANDER, WILLIAM, Packer
With the pack train on June 25? Employed as a civil packer in April, 1876, for the 7th Cavalry Quartermaster. Hired by Lieut. Eugene Gibbs, 6th Infantry in St. Paul, Minnesota and transferred to Lieut. Henry Nowlan at Fort Abraham Lincoln, Dakota on April 17, 1876. Entitled to draw one ration per day and to transportation back to St. Paul if honorably discharged. Employed until the end of the campaign on September 23, 1876. Payment of $138.33 was made for the period July 1–September 23, and of $100 for the period May 1–June 30, 1876. Not listed in Walter Camp's notes.

BLOODY KNIFE, Guide
Killed in the timber in the valley fight on June 25. Bloody Knife, or Nes-i-ri-pat, was an Arikara-Sioux long employed in government service. His father was a Hunkpapa Sioux and his mother was an Arikara. He was born on the Hunkpapa reservation in what is now North Dakota. As he approached manhood his mother determined to return to her people and he accompanied her. Prior to the building of the Northern Pacific Railroad, the mail for Fort Stevenson and other Missouri River forts was carried overland from Fort Totten, Dakota. The high country east of the Missouri River was at that time a hunting ground of the hostile Sioux who had been driven west from Minnesota after the massacre of 1862, and so often were the mail carriers killed on this route that it became

17

difficult to find anyone to carry the mails. Bloody Knife undertook the task and almost always got the mail through. Enlisted in the Detachment of Indian Scouts at Fort Stevenson, Dakota in 1868. Deserted on Sept. 30, 1868. Soon after the establishment of Fort Abraham Lincoln, Dakota, a number of Arikara scouts were engaged for service at the post and of these Bloody Knife was one of the leaders. He was with Colonel David Stanley's expedition in 1873 escorting the North Pacific Railroad Survey and exploring the valley of the Yellowstone River. He took part in the fight against hostile Sioux on that expedition. He was enlisted on May 30, 1874, for six months at Fort Lincoln by Lieut. Colonel George Custer for duty as a scout. At the time of this enlistment he was 37 years old and was 5'8" tall. He participated in the expedition that explored the Black Hills in July and August, 1874. Discharged on November 30, 1874 upon expiration of his six months' service, as a Private of excellent and reliable character. On March 13, 1876, he was employed by the regimental quartermaster of the 7th Cavalry for duty as a guide with the Sioux expedition then being assembled near Fort Lincoln. He departed with the expedition on May 17. He was with Colonel Custer on the trip to the Crow's Nest in the early morning of June 25. Assigned to the Reno battalion on June 25th; on the skirmish line in the valley fight. Killed in the timber during the valley fight before the retreat to the bluffs by a shot in the head while he was standing near Major Reno. His remains were probably interred in the valley on June 27th, or 28th by Colonel John Gibbon's men. See John Gray, "Bloody Knife, Ree Scout For Custer" *The Westerners Brand Book*, Chicago, 17:12, Feb. 1961.

BOUYER, MITCH, Interpreter

Killed with the Custer column on June 25. Ka-pesh, Minton Bouyer, Ca Pay, Kar-paysh, Michelet Bouer or Boyer, Man-Wearing-Calfskin-Vest. Half-blood Sioux Indian interpreter for the Crow scouts attached to the 7th Cavalry from the 2nd Cavalry on June 22. He accompanied Lieut. Charles Varnum on the trip to the Crow's nest, arriving there about 2:30 on the morning of June 25. Listed as Mitch Boyer on the battle monument. Not listed among the casualties in the *Bismarck Tribune Extra*, July 6, 1876. See Marquis *Memoirs Of A White Crow Indian.* Bouyer may possibly have been a half brother of Baptiste Pourier. At one time he served as a mail carrier between Forts Kearney and C. F. Smith.

CHURCHILL, B. F., Packer

In the hilltop fight. Employed as a teamster from April, 1876, by the 7th Cavalry Quartermaster to drive a team at $30 monthly compensation. His name is listed as B. C. Churchill on the September, 1876, *Report of Persons and Articles Employed and Hired . . .*, 7th Cavalry Quartermaster. Assigned as a packer on June 22 at $50 monthly compensation (the pay of a packer). Employed as a packer from the Yellowstone River to the Little Bighorn River and during the hilltop fight. Discharged at the end of the campaign on September 23, 1876, with payment of $138.33 for the period July 1—September 23. Churchill testified at the Reno Court of Inquiry in Chicago in 1879. At that time he was a rancher at Tongue River, Fort Keogh, Montana Territory.

CUSTER, BOSTON, Guide

Killed with the Custer column on June 25. Born on October 31, 1848, in

New Rumley, Ohio, the brother of George and Thomas Custer. Employed as a forage master from June 5, 1875, at a monthly compensation of $75 issuing and receiving forage. Discharged on March 2, 1876, as forage master and employed on order of the regimental commander by the 7th Cavalry Quartermaster from March 3, 1876, at $100 monthly compensation as a civil guide for the Sioux expedition. He was with the pack train on June 25 but joined the Custer column near the Little Bighorn River and was killed with the column. His remains were interred on the battle field and exhumed in January, 1878, and re-interred at Monroe, Michigan. Listed as Boston Custer on the battle monument.

DORMAN, ISAIAH, Interpreter

Killed in the valley fight on June 25. Civil Negro interpreter from Fort Rice, Dakota, employed from May 15, 1876, by the 7th Cavalry Quartermaster. He was formerly a woodcutter (woodhawk) for Durfee & Peck, and was married to a Santee Sioux woman who spoke the Sioux language. In the winter of 1868 he carried the mail from Fort Rice to Fort Wadsworth (Fort Sisseton), Dakota. He was known to the Indians by the name of "Teat". Not listed among the casualties in the *Bismarck Tribune Extra*, July 6, 1876. Listed only as Isaiah on the battle monument.

"Isaiah Dorman, a negro scout and interpreter, was found with many arrows shot in his body and head, and badly cut and slashed . . ." William Slaper in Brininstool, *Troopers With Custer*, p. 65. See also *Journal of Negro History* Vol. XXXIII, July, 1948, 344-352.

EDWARDS, GEORGE, Teamster-Packer

With the pack train on June 25? Employed on Apr. 1, 1876, as a civil teamster by the 7th Cavalry Quartermaster for service with the Sioux expedition. Paid as a teamster for the period April 1 to June 30. Paid $40 as a packer from July 1 to July 24, and $31 as a teamster for the period July 1-August 1. Discharged on July 24. The dual payment for the period in July may indicate compensation intended as payment for services as a packer from June 22 and in the Little Bighorn River fight.

FLINT, MOSES E., Packer

With the pack train on June 25? Employed as a civil packer by the 7th Cavalry Quartermaster for service with the Sioux expedition. Hired by Lieut. Eugene Gibbs, 6th Infantry in St. Paul, Minnesota and transferred to Lieut. Henry Nowlan at Fort Abraham Lincoln, Dakota on April 17, 1876, with pay of $50.00 commencing April 18. Entitled to draw one ration per day and to transportation back to St. Paul if honorably discharged. Discharged at the end of the campaign on September 23, 1876, and received payment of $138.33 for the period July 1–September 23 and $100 for the period May 1–June 30, 1876. His name is listed in Camp's notes. Listed elsewhere as Moses Flink.

FRETT, JOHN, Packer

With the pack train on June 25. In the hilltop fight. Employed as a civil packer in St. Paul, Minnesota for the 7th Cavalry Quartermaster for the Sioux expedition. Hired by Lieut. Eugene Gibbs at St. Paul; transferred to Lieut. Henry Nowlan at Fort Lincoln, Dakota on April 17, 1876, with pay of $50.00

per month beginning April 18. Entitled to draw one ration per day and to transportation back to St. Paul if honorably discharged. Discharged on July 8, 1876, with payment of $13.33 for the period July 1-8 and payment of $100.00 for the period May 1–June 30, 1876. Listed as John Fretts in the 7th Cavalry AAQM Report, June, 1876. He testified in the Reno Court of Inquiry in Chicago in 1879. See *The Chicago Tribune*, July 28, 1876.

GERARD, FREDERICK F., Interpreter

Missing in the valley fight on June 25. Civil interpreter for the Arikara and Sioux Indian scouts. Employed on May 12, 1876, by the 7th Cavalry Quartermaster at a monthly pay of $75. Assigned to the Reno column on June 25 and was missing in the valley fight, rejoining the command on the hilltop on the night of June 26. Born in 1829 in St. Louis, he went to Fort Pierre in September, 1848 and Fort Clark in 1849. In 1855 he accompanied Basil Clement to the headwaters of the Platte. After returning he went to Fort Berthold as an Indian trader until 1869 when his license was not renewed. Two daughters, Sisters Adelbert and Anastasia, OSB, were born to Gerard and his Arikara wife. Anastasia, born June 25. 1865 was baptized by Father DeSmet on May 21, 1866 at Fort Berthold. Gerard was at Forts Buford and Stevenson and became a government interpreter in 1872. He opened a store in Mandan in 1883; moved to Minneapolis in 1890 where he was employed by Pillsbury Mills as advertising agent. Died on Jan. 13, 1913 at St. Cloud; interred at St. Joseph. Sister Anastasia died Oct. 21, 1959.

HERENDEEN, GEORGE B., Scout

In the valley and hilltop fights. Born on November 28, 1846, at Parkman, Geauga County, Ohio. His parents died when he was 13 years old. After serving in the Civil War he lived with an uncle in Indiana and then went to Denver, Colorado, thence to New Mexico and in 1869 he went to Montana. From February 12 to May 11, 1874 he was with the Yellowstone Wagon Road and Prospecting Expedition. In June, 1875 he went with Fellows Pease and others to a site on the left bank of the Yellowstone and built the Fort Pease Stockade. He was 5'-8" in height and had fair complexion, blue eyes and brown hair. He joined Lieut. Colonel George Custer's column in the Sioux expedition on June 22, 1876. Employed as a scout with a job compensation of $100 for the purpose of carrying messages from Colonel Custer to Colonel John Gibbon. On June 25 he was attached to the Reno battalion and was engaged in the valley fight on the Little Bighorn River. Missing in the retreat to the ford; rejoined the battalion on the hilltop on the same day and fought there during the remainder of the fight. Engaged in the Nez Perce campaign in 1877 as a scout to find the route taken by the Nez Perce under Chief Joseph. On January 27 and 28, 1879 he testified in the Reno Court of Inquiry in Chicago. Following the 1876 Sioux expedition he lived in Bozeman, Montana for about five years and then in Lewistown and Great Falls until 1889 when he moved to Harlem, Montana. Died on June 17, 1918 at Sacred Heart Hospital in Harlem, his death being due to hypostatic pneumonia. Interred in the Harlem Cemetery. Further biographical material is in Barry Johnson "George Herendeen: Montana Scout," *The English Westerner's Brand Book*, 2:3, Apr., 1960 and 2:4, July 1960.

LAINPLOUGH, JOHN, Packer

With the pack train on June 25? Employed as a civil packer by the 7th

Cavalry Quartermaster on May 2, 1876, for service with the Sioux expedition. He received payment of $138.33 for the period July 1 to September 23 when he was discharged. He received payment of $75.00 for the period May 16 to June 30. His name is listed in Walter Camp's notes.

LAWLESS, WILLIAM, Packer
With the pack train on June 25? Employed in St. Paul, Minnesota on April 1, 1876 as a civil packer for the 7th Cavalry Quartermaster. Hired by Lieut. Eugene Gibbs, 6th Infantry at St. Paul and transferred to Lieut. Henry Nowlan at Fort Abraham Lincoln, Dakota on April 17, 1876, for service with the Sioux expedition. Pay was to commence on April 18. Entitled to draw one ration per day and to transportation back to St. Paul if honorably discharged. Discharged on July 24, 1876, and received payment of $40 for the period July 1–July 24, 1876. His name is listed in Walter Camp's notes.

LOESER, CHRIS, Packer
With the pack train on June 25? Employed on March 26, 1876, as a civil packer by the 7th Cavalry Quartermaster. Loeser and J. C. Wagoner were the only packers employed in March and the first that were employed. He was discharged on July 24, 1876, with payment of $40.00 for the period July 1–July 24 and $100 for the May 1–June 30 period. His name is listed in Walter Camp's notes.

MANN, FRANK C., Packer
Killed beside William Nugent in the hilltop fight on June 25. Employed from St. Paul, Minnesota as a civil packer in April, 1876, for the 7th Cavalry Quartermaster. Hired by Lieut. Eugene Gibbs, 6th Infantry in St. Paul and transferred to Lieut. Henry Nowlan on April 17, 1876, at Fort Abraham Lincoln, Dakota for service with the Sioux expedition. Entitled to draw one ration per day and transportation back to St. Paul if honorably discharged. Payment of $91.66 was due for the period May 1-June 25, 1876. Listed as F. G. Mann on the battle monument.

McBRATNEY, HARRY, Packer
With the pack train on June 25? Employed from St. Paul as a civil packer on April 17, 1876, for the 7th Cavalry Quartermaster. Hired by Lieut. Eugene Gibbs, 6th Infantry in St. Paul and transferred to Lieut. Henry Nowlan at Fort Abraham Lincoln, Dakota on April 17, 1876 with pay at $50 monthly to commence from April 18. Entitled to draw one ration per day and to transportation back to St. Paul if honorably discharged. He was discharged on September 23, 1876, at the end of the campaign and payment was made of $138.33 for period July 1-September 23 and of $100 for the period May 1-June 30, 1876. His name is listed in Walter Camp's notes.

MOORE, E. L., Packer
With the pack train on June 25? Employed as a civil packer on May 13, 1876, by the 7th Cavalry Quartermaster. He received payment of $98.33 for the period May 2-June 30, 1876. His name is listed in Walter Camp's notes.

REYNOLDS, CHARLES ALEXANDER, Guide
Killed in the valley fight on June 25. He was shot through the heart when

he stopped near Dr. Henry Porter who was treating a wounded man. Born on March 20, 1842, in Warren County, Illinois, the son of Joseph Boyer and Phebe Bush Reynolds. Attended Abingdon College, Abingdon, Illinois. Moved in 1859, to Pardee, Kansas and the next spring went to the Colorado gold fields. In 1861 he enlisted in the 10th Kansas Volunteers serving in Missouri and Kansas and on escort duty on the Santa Fe Trail. Unsuccessfully engaged in a trading expedition to New Mexico after the Civil War. Became a buffalo hunter on the Republican River for a few years and then moved to the upper Missouri River country and engaged in hunting. In the 1872 Yellowstone Expedition and the 1874 Black Hills Expedition. In 1875 he was on the Yellowstone Survey Expedition. He was a civil guide employed by the 7th Cavalry Quartermaster from April 3, 1876 with $100.00 monthly pay. He accompanied Lieut. Charles Varnum on the trip to the Crow's Nest arriving there about 2:30 on the morning of June 25. Killed in the valley fight that afternoon. His remains were recovered in 1877 by Philetus Norris, Superintendent of Yellowstone Park, and interred, probably, at Norris, Michigan. The Reynold's Diary of the Sioux Expedition is in the Minnesota State Historical Society. See Joseph Henry Taylor *Sketches of Frontier and Indian Life* and John S. Gray, "On the Trail of Lonesome Charley Reynolds," *The Westerner's Brand Book*, Chicago, 14:8, Oct. 1957. The complete text of the Reynolds diary can be found in *Diaries of the Little Big Horn*, by Michael J. Koury.

QUARTERMASTER EMPLOYEES NOT IN THE LITTLE BIGHORN RIVER FIGHT

Abbott, Frederick, S.B. .... General Superintendent
Acty, Herrmann .... Teamster
Aldermann, John .... Teamster
Allen, Charles .... Teamster
Allen, George .... Teamster
Aslen, Isaac .... Teamster
Bartholomew, J.R. .... Teamster
Beal, John .... Teamster
Bennett, James .... Teamster
Blackbird, Eugene .... Teamster
Borowsky, Charles .... Master Mechanic
Bostwick, Louis .... Teamster
Boutiette, Edward .... Teamster
Boykan, William .... Teamster
Briner, J. H. .... Teamster
Brown, Charles .... Master of Transportation
Brown, Charles .... Teamster
Bruer, Samuel .... Teamster
Bunker, Fred .... Teamster
Bushea, I. .... Teamster
Campbell, Gordon .... Teamster, Asst. Wagonmaster
Carter, George .... Teamster
Case, George .... Teamster
Cassidy, C. W. .... Teamster
Childs, Charles .... Teamster
Clark, Thomas .... Teamster
Close, W. A. .... Teamster
Cochran, James .... Teamster
Commonford, J. C. .... Teamster
Connelley, James .... Teamster
Cosgrove, Michael .... Teamster
Crawford, Carlton .... Teamster
Crimble, Charles .... Teamster
Darling, Joseph .... Teamster
Davy, Charles .... Teamster
Dean, George .... Teamster
Demules, Alfred .... Teamster
Demules, Gilbert .... Teamster
Dermott, John J. .... Teamster
Devrant, John .... Teamster
Doris, Andrew .... Teamster
Drew, James .... Teamster
Egan, John .... Teamster
Ferguson, William .... Teamster
Finn, James .... Teamster
Folts, Warren .... Teamster
Ford, William .... Teamster

Fowler, Edward .... Teamster
Franklin, Ed .... Teamster
French, Charles ....Teamster, Asst. Wagonmaster
Glynn, Patrick .... Teamster
Goodrich, William .... Teamster
Granns, Frank .... Teamster
Griffin, John .... Teamster
Grunewald, William .... Teamster
Gutgesell, R. D. .... Teamster
Hadley, Orange .... Asst. Wagonmaster
Hart, Charles .... Teamster
Hartsgrove, Charles .... Teamster
Hegarty, William .... Teamster
Hempton, Edward .... Teamster
Henderson, Frank .... Teamster
Hickey, Patrick .... Blacksmith
Hill, Philip .... Teamster
Hoffmann, John .... Teamster
Howard, Frank .... Teamster
Hutchins, H. C. .... Wheelwright
Jones, John .... Teamster
Karney, James .... Teamster
Keefe, Thomas .... Teamster
Kelley, Martin (1) .... Teamster
Kelley, Martin (2) .... Teamster
Kennedy, L. .... Teamster
Kincaid, B. F. .... Teamster
Kincaid, George .... Teamster
Lafarge, M. .... Teamster
Lander, Ben .... Teamster
Lanning, Thomas .... Teamster
Leahy, Con .... Teamster
Lee, Edward .... Teamster
Levere, Joseph .... Teamster
Logan, Austin .... Teamster
Louis, Augustus .... Teamster
Lowe, C. H. .... Teamster
Macy, George .... Blacksmith
Marlow, Samuel .... Teamster
Martel, Anderson .... Teamster
Mason, Frank .... Teamster
Maxwell, Harry .... Teamster
Meuson, John .... Teamster
Meyer, T. F. .... Teamster
Miller, John .... Teamster
Mooney, Thomas .... Teamster
Muzzy, Frank .... Teamster
Myers, George .... Teamster
McCullom, John .... Teamster
McGee, James .... Asst. Wagonmaster

McGovern, A. . . . . Teamster
McKusick, Charles . . . . Teamster
McPherson, David . . . . Teamster
Niering, Robert . . . . Teamster
Noyes, Wilber , ... Teamster
Page, Runn . . . . Teamster
Parens, Fred . . . . Teamster
Pearson, Isaac . . . . Teamster
Phups, I. . . . . Teamster
Reese, William . . . . Teamster
Richardson, D. . . . . Teamster
Riley, James . . . . Teamster
Riley, John (1) . . . . Teamster
Riley, John (2) . . . . Teamster
Roberts, Robert . . . . Teamster
Rosengreen, Olez . . . . Teamster
Rounnsavelle, Frank . . . . Teamster
Ryan, Thomas . . . . Teamster
Ryland, Henry . . . . Teamster
Sevins, Oliver . . . . Teamster
Shields, William . . . . Teamster
Sinks, Oscar . . . . Teamster
Slack, J. H. . . . . Asst. Wagonmaster
Slew, W. C. . . . . Teamster
Smith, Charles . . . . Teamster
Smith, David . . . . Teamster
Smith, D. L. . . . . Teamster
Smullins, Pat . . . . Teamster
Stone, James . . . . Teamster
Stoning, E. C. . . . . Teamster
Sullivan . . . . Teamster
Thomas, Joseph . . . . Teamster
Thomas, Thomas . . . . Saddler
Tomarto, H. R. . . . . Teamster
Treshman, George . . . . Wheelwright
Victory, James . . . . Teamster
Walker, William . . . . Teamster
Warren, Henry . . . . Teamster
Warren, William . . . . Teamster
Welsch, Oscar . . . . Asst. Wagonmaster
Whipple, William . . . . Teamster
Willis, Gilbert . . . . Teamster
York, Peter . . . . Teamster
Young, Francis . . . . Teamster
Yuba, Charles . . . . Teamster

DETACHMENT OF INDIAN SCOUTS
7TH CAVALRY, AT THE LITTLE BIGHORN

	Absent	Present	Wounded	Killed	Survived
Leaders		2		1	1
Privates	18	25	1	1	42
Totals	18	27	1	2	43

INDIAN SCOUTS

BAKER, WILLIAM, Private
Present for duty on June 30. Half blood Ree Indian scout and interpreter born at Fort Berthold. Presumably his father was George Baker, a woodhawk from Baden, Germany who lived on the Missouri River above Fort Rice, Dakota. Enlisted at age 24 in the 7th Cavalry on May 4, 1876, for six months by Lieut. Charles Varnum at Fort A. Lincoln. In the expedition exploring the Black Hills in 1874. Present for duty at the mouth of the Little Bighorn River on June 30, 1876. Re-enlisted on the Yellowstone River, Montana Terr. on November 4, 1876. Baker had two sons, Lewis and James; see *The Arikara Narrative,* p. 165.

BARKING WOLF, Private
Sick at Yellowstone Depot. On detached service carrying messages in the field from June 22. Si-to-wa-ra, Si-ti-wa-nar, Scabby Wolf. Arikara Indian scout enlisted on May 9, 1876 at age 21 in the 7th Cavalry for six months by Lieut. Charles Varnum at Fort A. Lincoln, Dakota. He was in the party with Bear-Come-Out to rescue Red Bear in the march of the expedition to Powder River. He carried the mail from Camp Nr. 13 on May 31 to Fort Lincoln with Left Hand and returned to the expedition. On detached service carrying messages in the field from June 22. Sick at Yellowstone Depot at the time of the Little Bighorn River fight. The name Scabby Wolf is not listed on the Muster Roll of Lieut. Charles Varnum, 7th Cavalry.

BEAR, Private
In the valley and hilltop fights. *Coonough,* Red Foolish Bear, Red Angry Bear, Angry Bear. Arikara Indian scout. Third enlistment at age 29 in the 7th Cavalry on May 9, 1876, by Lieut. Charles Varnum at Fort A. Lincoln. On scouting duty on the night of June 24 with Forked Horn. Accompanied Lieut. Varnum on the trip to the Crow's Nest arriving there about 2:30 on the morning of June 25. With the Reno battalion on the skirmish line in the valley fight. One of ten Indians who engaged in the valley fight. In the retreat to the bluffs. In the hilltop fight. In the party which tried to carry a message from the hilltop but were forced back. In the first party to Custer Hill on June 27. Present for duty on June 30 at camp at the mouth of the Little Bighorn River. In the scouting party on the Yellowstone from July 2 with Forked Horn.

BEAR COME OUT, Private
Did not cross the river into the valley fight. *Ma-tour-e-namn-pa-pa,* Bear-Comes-Out, Bear Waiting, Ma-tok-sha, Mato-e-napa. Dakota Sioux Indian scout. Tenth enlistment at age 49 in the 7th Cavalry on February 3, 1876, for six months by Lieut. William Cooke at Fort A. Lincoln. On the scouting trip from Camp Nr. 19 at Powder River with Young Hawk. With the Reno battalion on June 25 but did not cross the river into the valley fight. He joined the six scouts on the ridgetop who captured Sioux ponies. On duty as a pony herder. Returned to Yellowstone Depot. Listed as missing in action since June 26 on the Muster Roll of Lieut. Charles Varnum, 7th Cavalry. See John Gray "Ree Scouts With Custer" *The Westerners' Brand Book,* XX:12, Feb, 1964, Chicago.

BEAR RUNNING IN THE TIMBER, Private
Not in the valley fight. *Ma-ta-chun-way-a-gamun*, *Ma-ta-chiss-way-a-ga-will*, Bear-Going-In-The-Woods. Caroo. Dakota Sioux scout. First enlistment at age 40 on November 11, 1875, for six months by Lieut. James Calhoun at Fort A. Lincoln. Discharged May 11, 1876, upon expiration of service and re-enlisted on the same day by Lieut. Charles Varnum at Fort Lincoln. Joined the detachment on May 1. On the scouting party on the Powder River with Young Hawk from Camp Nr. 19 on June 10. With the Reno battalion on June 25 but did not cross the river into the valley fight. Became rear guard for the captured Sioux ponies. Returned to Yellowstone Depot. Listed as missing in action since June 26 on the Muster Roll of Lieut. Charles Varnum, 7th Cavalry.

BEAR'S EYES, Private
At Fort A. Lincoln on May 17. *Coonough-che-rak*, Coonough-chee-reek, Bear's Eye, Wolf Stands In The Cold, Wolf-Standing-In-The-Cold, Walking In The Cold. Arikara Indian scout. Seventh enlistment at age 31 on April 1, 1876, in the 7th Cavalry for six months by Lieut. William Cooke at Fort A. Lincoln. On detached service at Fort Lincoln on May 17. Returned from the 17th Infantry to the 7th Cavalry on June 21. Brother in law of Good Elk (Red Bear) and Boy Chief. Re-enlisted on October 1, 1876.

BLACK CALF, Private
At Yellowstone Depot. *Hanue-ca-tis*, Wolf, Cha-ra-ta. Arikara Indian scout. First enlistment at age 19 in the 7th Cavalry on April 26, 1876 for six months by Lieut. William Cooke at Fort A. Lincoln. He was riding a colt in the expedition. Sick at Yellowstone Depot in the care of Long Bear at the time of the Little Bighorn River fight. Listed as missing in action since June 26 on the Muster Roll of Lieut. Charles Varnum, 7th Cavalry.

BLACK FOX, Private
Chil-ira-two-ca-tis Chewa-koo-katit. Arikara Indian scout. Fourth enlistment at age 19 in the 7th Cavalry on May 9, 1876, for six months by Lieut. Charles Varnum at Fort A. Lincoln. On scouting duty on the night of June 24 with Forked Horn and with the expedition on June 24. He accompanied Lieut. Varnum on the trip to the Crow's Nest arriving there about 2:30 on the morning of June 25. He left with Curly, the Crow scout, met the pack train, backtracked to near the present site of Busby, separated from Curly and went down Rosebud Creek. Listed as missing in action since June 26 on the Muster Roll of Lieut. Charles Varnum, 7th Cavalry.

BLACK PORCUPINE, Private
At Fort A. Lincoln on May 17. *La-uir-ce-tis*, Sawi-catit. Arikara Indian scout. First enlistment at age 21 in the 7th Cavalry on May 9, 1876, for six months by Lieut. Charles Varnum at Fort A. Lincoln. On detached service at Fort Lincoln on May 17. At Yellowstone Depot at the time of the Little Bighorn River fight. Re-enlisted on November 11, 1876.

BOB TAILED BULL, Private
Killed in the valley fight on June 25. *Hocus-ta-ris*, Hucus-ta-nix, Bob-tail-Bull. Hocus-ter-ricks. Arikara Indian scout. First enlistment at age 45

for six months in the 7th Cavalry on April 26, 1876, by Lieut. William Cooke at Fort A. Lincoln. He was the first leader of the Ree scouts. Leader of the rescue party for Good Elk in the march of the expedition to Powder River. Leader of the first scouting party on June 22. On a scouting party from noon to June 24. With Col. George Custer on the trip to the Crow's Nest. With the Reno battalion in the afternoon of June 25. One of ten Indians who engaged in the valley fight. Killed on the left of the skirmish line in the valley fight. There is a reference to Bob Tailed Bull in *Collections* of the State Historical Society of North Dakota, VI, p. 53. See also Dale Schoenberger "Custer's Scouts" *Montana* XVI:2 Spring, 1966, Helena.

BULL, Private
Did not cross the river into the valley fight. *Hocus.* Arikara Indian scout. Second enlistment at age 19 in the 7th Cavalry on May 9, 1876, for six months by Lieut. Charles Varnum at Fort A. Lincoln. On the scouting party on the night of June 24 with Forked Horn and with the expedition on June 24. Accompanied Lieut. Varnum on the trip to the Crow's Nest arriving there about 2:30 on the morning of June 25. Assigned to the Reno battalion in the afternoon of June 25. His horse was exhausted and Bull could not keep up with the battalion. Joined the six scouts on the ridgetop who had captured Sioux ponies. Performed rear guard duty for the pony herd. Returned to Yellowstone Depot. Listed as missing in action since June 26 on the Muster Roll of Lieut. Varnum. 7th Cavalry. Bull and Strike Bear were companions on the expedition.

BULL-IN-THE-WATER, Private
Did not cross the river into the valley fight. *Hocus-ty-arit*, Hocus-tyarit, Bull-Stands—In-The-Water. Arikara Indian scout. Third enlistment at age 29 in the 7th Cavalry for six months on May 9, 1876, by Lieut. Charles Varnum at Fort A. Lincoln. On the scouting trip from Camp Nr. 4 and with the expedition on June 24. Assigned to the Reno battalion on June 25 but did not cross the Little Bighorn River into the valley fight. Joined the six scouts on the ridgetop who had captured Sioux ponies, and became a pony herder. Returned to Yellowstone Depot. Listed as missing in action since June 26 on the Muster Roll of Lieut. Charles Varnum, 7th Cavalry.

BUSH, Private
Na-pa-run-ough, Napa-ran-nogh, Red Wolf, Red Brush. Arikara Indian scout. Sixth enlistment at age 28 on April 26, 1876, in the 7th Cavalry for six months by Lieut. William Cooke at Fort A. Lincoln. Did not cross the river into the valley fight, returned to Yellowstone Depot. Listed as missing in action since June 26 on the Muster Roll of Lieut. Charles Varnum, 7th Cavalry. He was a brother of Sioux, one of the Arikara scouts. Re-enlisted on October 26, 1876.

CLIMBS THE BLUFF, Private
Not in the Little Bighorn River fight. *To-an-chitt-two-nochs*, *Te-nu-chitt-ho-nochs*, Teru-chitkoo-nocho, Charging-Up-The-Hill. Arikara Indian scout. Seventh enlistment on November 1, 1875 at Fort A. Lincoln by Lieut. James Calhoun. Eighth enlistment at age 31 on May 1, 1876, in the 7th Cavalry for six months by Lieut. William Cooke at Fort A. Lincoln. On detached service carrying messages in the field from June 1. At Yellowstone Depot about June 24. In the party with Wolf Runs carrying messages from Yellowstone Depot to

George Custer on June 25. In the scouting party on the Yellowstone River from July 2 with Forked Horn.

CROSS, WILLIAM, Private

Billy Cross, E-esk. Half-blood Dakota Sioux Indian scout. Third enlistment at age 22 on April 17, 1876, in the 7th Cavalry for six months by Lieut. William Cooke. He may have participated in herding the captured Sioux ponies on June 25. Listed as missing in action since June 26 on the Muster Roll of Lieut. Charles Varnum, 7th Cavalry. His story, as told to a news correspondent on July 4, 1876, is in the *Chicago Tribune* July 15, 1876.

CURLY, Private

With the Custer column on June 25. Curley, Shes-his, Shesh-sheash, Shuh-shee-ahsh. Crow Indian born about 1856-58 on the Little Rosebud, Montana Territory, the son of Strong Bear (Inside The Mouth) and Strikes By The Side Of The Water. Enlisted as a scout in the 7th Infantry on April 10, 1876, for six months by Lieut. James Bradley at Crow Agency, M.T. At Fort Pease, M.T. on scouting duty on April 30, 1876. On detached service with the 7th Cavalry from June 21. He accompanied Lieut. Charles Varnum on the trip to the Crow's Nest arriving there about 2:30 on the morning of June 25. With the Custer column on the afternoon of June 25, and witnessed the fight of the Custer column. Carried the news of the fight to the steamboat *Far West* .Listed as absent without leave from June 26 on the Muster Roll of Lieut. Bradley, 7th Infantry. Discharged on Sept. 30, 1876, at Fort Abraham Lincoln by reason of muster out of detachment. On Aug. 31, 1876, he was on detached service (from Aug. 20) at Fort Shaw. Divorced Bird Woman in 1886 and married Takes A Shield, Crow Indian. Pensioned from Dec. 31, 1920. Died on May 21, 1923, of pneumonia at his log ranch near Crow Agency, Montana. Interred at the Custer Battlefield National Cemetery. Grave 1447 (1063)A on May 23, 1923. Takes A Shield was pensioned from May 23, 1923 until she remarried on Dec. 1, 1925.

CURLEY HEAD, Private

Carrying dispatches in the field from June 22. *Bich-ga-ri-su*, Hair, Curly Head. Arikara Indian scout. First enlistment at age 19 on April 27, 1876, in the 7th Cavalry for six months by Lieut. William Cooke at Fort A. Lincoln. On detached service carrying mail from Rosebud Creek to Yellowstone Depot on June 22. In the party with Wolf Runs carrying mail from Yellowstone Depot to Lieut. Col. George Custer on June 25. He was not in the Little Bighorn River fight. Re-enlisted on October 27, 1876.

FOOLISH BEAR, Private

Carrying dispatches in the field from June 22. *Coonough-sen-gauch*, Crooked Foot. Arikara Indian scout. Discharged from enlistment on January 13, 1876. Sixth enlistment at age 28 in the 7th Cavalry for six months on May 9, 1876, by Lieut. Charles Varnum at Fort A. Lincoln. He carried mail from the Turkey Buzzard Camp (Camp Nr. 8) to Fort Lincoln with One Horn and then returned to the expedition. He carried mail from Rosebud Creek to Yellowstone Depot on June 22. Sick at Yellowstone Depot on June 25.

32

FORKED HORN, Private

In the valley and hilltop fights. *Arri-chitt*, Aree-chit, Crooked Horn. Arikara Indian scout born about 1815. Ninth enlistment at a listed age of 37 on April 27, 1876, in the 7th Cavalry for six months by Lieut. William Cooke at Fort A. Lincoln. On the scouting party from Powder River with Young Hawk from Camp Nr. 19 on June 10. With the expedition on June 24. Accompanied Lieut. Varnum on the trip to the Crow's Nest arriving there about 2:30 on the morning of June 25. One of ten scouts who engaged in the valley fight. On the right side of the skirmish line with the Reno battalion. In the retreat to the bluffs and in the hilltop fight. In the party that tried to carry a message from the hilltop but was forced back by the hostiles. Together with Young Hawk he made the first contact, after the hilltop fight, with Colonel John Gibbon's men on June 27, and then returned to the Reno battalion on the hilltop. In the first party to Custer Hill from the hilltop on June 27. Present for duty on June 30 at the camp at the mouth of the Little Bighorn River. Leading a scouting party on the Yellowstone River for ten days from July 2. Re-enlisted October 27, 1876. He was the father of Young Hawk. Died in 1894.

GOES AHEAD, Private

With the Custer column on June 25. Bah-suk-ush, Basuk-ose, Ma-suck-cosh, The First One, Goes First, The One Ahead, Comes Leading, Man-With-Fur-Belt, Child of the Stars. Crow Indian scout born about 1852 on the Platte River. Enlisted in the 7th Infantry on April 10, 1876, for six months by Lieut. James Bradley at Crow Agency, Montana Territory. On detached service from June 21 with Major Marcus Reno, 7th Cavalry. Assigned to the Custer column on the afternoon of June 25. Withdrew from the Custer column about 3:15 p.m. and joined Strike Bear on the ridgetop; in the hilltop fight for a short time. Withdrew and made contact with Colonel John Gibbon's Montana column and then returned to Crow Agency with White-Man-Runs-Him and Hairy Moccasin. Died on May 31, 1919; interred on June 5, 1919 in the Custer Battlefield National Cemetery, Grave 1443 (1060)A. His wife, Pretty Shield, died on April 30, 1944 at the age of 92 and was interred on May 3, 1944 in the Custer Battlefield National Cemetery, Grave 1443A.

GOOD ELK, Private

In the valley fight. *Wan-nee*, Red Bear, Handsome Elk. Arikara Indian scout discharged from second enlistment on April 1, 1873. In the Black Hills expedition in July and August, 1874, Third enlistment at age 27 on May 13, 1876, in the 7th Cavalry for six months by Lieut. Charles Varnum at Fort A. Lincoln. He did not accompany the expedition on May 17 but remained at Fort Lincoln. Good Elk took the place of One Horn on the return trip to the expedition from Fort Lincoln after One Horn had brought the mail from the Turkey Buzzard Camp. Good Elk was with Soldier on the scouting trip on June 22. He was one of ten Indian scouts in the valley fight; he was on the skirmish line. Joined the six scouts who had captured Sioux ponies and became a pony herder. Returned to Yellowstone Depot. Listed as missing in action since June 26 on the Muster Roll of Lieut. Charles Varnum, 7th Cavalry. Brother of Boy Chief; brother-in-law of Bear's Eyes and uncle of Young Hawk.

GOOD FACE, Private

With the pack train. Joined scouts on the ridgetop. Sea-ri, Pretty Face.

Arikara Indian scout. First enlistment at age 21 on May 9, 1876, in the 7th Cavalry for six months by Lieut. Charles Varnum at Fort A. Lincoln. Detailed to duty with the pack train on June 25. Joined the six scouts on the ridgetop who had captured Sioux ponies and became a pony herder. Returned to Yellowstone Depot. Listed as missing in action since June 26 on the Muster Roll of Lieut. Varnum, 7th Cavalry. Re-enlisted on November 11, 1876.

GOOSE, Private
Severely wounded in the retreat from the valley fight. In the hilltop fight. *Co-sk, Co-et*, Arikara Indian scout discharged from his fourth enlistment on April 17, 1876. In the expedition exploring the Black Hills in July and August, 1874. Fifth enlistment at age 20 on April 26, 1876, in the 7th Cavalry for six months by Lieut. William Cooke at Fort A. Lincoln Crossed the Little Bighorn River with the Reno battalion on June 25. One of ten Indian scouts who engaged in the valley fight. On the skirmish line with the Reno battalion. Severely wounded by a shot in his right hand in the retreat after crossing the ford. In the hilltop fight and in the party that tried to carry a message from the hilltop but was forced back by the hostiles. In the first party to Custer Hill from the hilltop on June 27. Present for duty on June 30 at camp at the mouth of the Little Bighorn River. Transported to Fort Berthold, Dakota, on the steamer *Far West*. Nephew of Soldier.

HAIRY MOCCASIN, Private
With the Custer column on June 25. Sah-pee-wish-ush- Isapi-Wishish, Hairy Moccasins, Esh-sup-pee-me-shish, Esup-ewyshes. Crow Indian scout enlisted in the 7th Infantry on April 10, 1876 for six months by Lieut. James Bradley at Crow Agency, Montana Territory. On detached service with Major **Marcus** Reno from June 21. Assigned to the Custer column on the afternoon of June 25. Withdrew from the Custer column about 3:15 pm and joined Strike Bear on the ridgetop; in the hilltop fight for a short time. Withdrew and made contact with Colonel John Gibbon's Montana column and then returned to Crow Agency with White-Man-Runs-Him and Goes Ahead.

HALF-YELLOW-FACE, Private
In the valley and hilltop fights. Iss-too-sah-shee-dah, Esh-too-sah-shee-dah, Paints-His-Face-Half Yellow, Big Belly. Esh-chew-sar-she-lesh Crow Indian scout enlisted in the 7th Infantry on April 10 1876, for six months by Lieut. James Bradley at Crow Agency, Montana Territory. He was the leader of the Crow scouts. On detached service from June 21 with the 7th Cavalry. Assigned to Major Reno's column. Accompanied Lieut. Charles Varnum on the trip to the Crow's Nest arriving there about 2:30 on the morning of June 25. One of the ten Indian scouts who participated in the valley fight; on the skirmish line with the Reno column. In the hilltop fight.

HORN IN FRONT, Private
Carrying messages from Yellowstone Depot on June 25. *Arinn-quis-coo,* Awin-quis-coo, Horns-In-Front. Arikara Indian scout discharged from fifth enlistment on January 13, 1876. Sixth enlistment at age 42 on May 9, 1876, in the 7th Cavalry for six months by Lieut. Charles Varnum at Fort A. Lincoln. Sick at Camp Nr. 19 or 20 at the mouth of the Powder River in the care of Long

Bear. On detached service at Yellowstone Depot from June 15. In the party with Wolf Runs carrying mail from Yellowstone Depot to the 7th Cavalry on June 25. Returned from the 17th Infantry to the 7th Cavalry on June 21. He was not in the Little Bighorn River fight. In the scouting party on the Yellowstone River from July 2 with Forked Horn.

HOWLING WOLF, Private
On detached service at Yellowstone Depot from June 15. *Schi-ri-ti-wa-no,* Iche-reti-wana, Arikara Indian scout discharged from his second enlistment on April 17, 1876. Third enlistment at age 21 on April 26, 1876, in the 7th Cavalry for six months by Lieut. William Cooke at Fort A. Lincoln. Sent on June 22 with mail from Rosebud Creek to Yellowstone Depot. In the party with Wolf Runs carrying mail from Yellowstone Depot to the 7th Cavalry on June 25. He was not in the Little Bighorn River fight.

JACKSON, ROBERT, Private
At Fort Abraham Lincoln. Quarter blood Pikuni Blackfoot Indian scout. Discharged from third enlistment on December 24, 1875. Fourth enlistment at age 22 on December 25, 1875 in the 7th Cavalry for six months by Lieut. William Cooke at Fort A. Lincoln. In the expedition exploring the Yellowstone River Valley in 1873 and the Black Hills expedition in the summer of 1874. He may have formerly been enlisted as a scout in the 6th Infantry. Discharged on June 25, 1876, at Fort Lincoln, upon expiration of service. Not recorded as having re-enlisted on the Muster Roll of Lieut. Varnum, 7th Cavalry. In the winter campaign with General Nelson Miles in 1876-77.

JACKSON, WILLIAM, Private
In the valley and hilltop fights. Billy Jackson. Quarter blood Pikuni Blackfoot Indian scout born on August 27, 1856 at Fort Benton, Montana Terr, the son of Thomas Jackson. He was the younger brother of Robert Jackson. Discharged from his second enlistment on December 24, 1875. Third enlistment at age 20 on December 25, 1875 in the 7th Cavalry for six months by Lieut. William Cooke at Fort A. Lincoln. He was disciplined at Camp Nr. 12 for firing his revolver at a snake. With the Reno battalion on the afternoon of June 25. One of ten Indian scouts who engaged in the valley fight. Missing in the valley fight. Rejoined the battalion on the night of June 26 after the hilltop fight. Discharged at camp on the Little Bighorn River effective June 25, 1876, by Lieut. Charles Varnum. Re-enlisted the same day. Present for duty on June 30 at camp at the mouth of the Little Bighorn River. Participated in the expedition exploring the Yellowstone River valley in 1873 and the Black Hills expedition in 1874. He may have been formerly enlisted as a scout in the 6th Infantry. In the winter campaign with General Nelson Miles in 1876-77. Died in 1901 at Cutbank Creek, Blackfoot Indian Reservation, Montana.

LAYING DOWN, Private
Not in the valley or hilltop fights. *Si-ta-roa-ra,* Boy Chief, Ti-sha. Arikara Indian scout. First enlistment at age 18 on May 9, 1876, in the 7th Cavalry for six months by Lieut. Charles Varnum at Fort A. Lincoln. After crossing the Little Bighorn River he turned to the right to capture a herd of Sioux ponies and drive them across the river to the ridgetop. He then left to join the scouts on the skirmish line to find his brother, Good Elk (Red Bear), but was driven back near the ford. Became a rear guard for the pony herd. Returned to Yellowstone

Depot. Brother-in-law of Bear's Eyes. Laying Down is not mentioned in *The Arikara Narrative*, Vol. 6, *Collections* of the State Historical Society of North Dakota, 1920.

LEFT HAND, Private
Not in the Little Bighorn River fight. *Quigh*, Cuch-ha, Left Handed. Arikara Indian scout discharged from his eighth enlistment on December 1, 1875. Ninth enlistment on December 9, 1875 at age 46 in the 7th Cavalry for six months by Lieut. William Cooke. Discharged effective June 9, 1876, upon expiration of service at Fort Lincoln. Re-enlisted June 10, 1876. He carried the mail with Scabby Wolf from Camp Nr. 13 to Fort Lincoln (and returned?). Returned to the 7th Cavalry on June 21 from the 17th Infantry. See the Muster Roll of Lieut. J. M. Burns, 17th Infantry, Detachment of Indian Scouts.

LITTLE BRAVE, Private
Killed in the valley fight. *Naha-cus-chu*, Na-hocus-chisee-pustch, Stub, Little Soldier. Arikara Indian scout discharged from fourth enlistment on October 18, 1874. Fifth enlistment at age 26 on May 9, 1876 in the 7th Cavalry for six months by Lieut. Charles Varnum at Fort A. Lincoln. He was in the scouting party with Bobtail Bull on June 22 and with Lieut. Col. George Custer on the trip to the Crow's Nest. He was with the Reno battalion on the afternoon of June 25 and was one of ten Indian scouts who were in the valley fight. With the battalion on the skirmish line. According to Dustin he died near the ford (p. 131) from a wound in the right shoulder; see also *The Arikara Narrative*, p. 126. According to Forrest he was killed on the skirmish line in the first attack, p. 355. Listed as Soldier on the battle monument. Not listed among the casualties in the *Bismarck Tribune Extra*, July 6, 1876.

LONG BEAR, Private
Carrying messages from Yellowstone Depot, on June 25. *Coonough-ti-Ku-chris*, Coonough-tapeta, Tall Bear, High Bear. Arikara Indian scout discharged from his sixth enlistment on July 12, 1874. Seventh enlistment at age 45 on May 9, 1876 in the 7th Cavalry for six months by Lieut. Charles Varnum at Fort A. Lincoln. On detached service at Yellowstone Depot from June 15. Stayed behind the expedition at Camp Nr. 20. At Yellowstone Depot on June 22. In the party with Wolf Runs carrying mail from Yellowstone Depot to the 7th Cavalry on June 25. Not in the Little Bighorn River fight. In the scouting party on the Yellowstone River from July 2 with Forked Horn.

ONE FEATHER, Private
Crossed the river with the Reno column. *Ha-cui-tis*, Arikara Indian scout. First enlistment at age 45 on May 9, 1876 in the 7th Cavalry for six months by Lieut. Charles Varnum at Fort A. Lincoln. He went on the Powder River scouting trip with Young Hawk from Camp Nr. 19 on June 10. With the Reno column on the afternoon of June 25. After crossing the Little Bighorn he turned to the right to capture a herd of Sioux ponies and drive them across the river to the ridgetop. Returned to Yellowstone Depot. Listed as missing in action since June 26 on the Muster Roll of Lieut. Varnum, 7th Cavalry. He was a brother of Good Elk.

ONE HORN, Private
Probably enroute from Fort A. Lincoln to Yellowstone Depot on June 25.

Ach-no-arri-cas, Ach-ko-are-co. Arikara Indian scout discharged from his seventh enlistment on July 11, 1875. Eighth enlistment at age 25 on April 26, 1876, in the 7th Cavalry for six months by Lieut. William Cooke at Fort A. Lincoln. On detached service at Fort Lincoln on May 17. Carried mail from Turkey Buzzard Camp (Camp Nr. 8) to Fort Lincoln with Red Foolish Bear. He was replaced as mail carrier by Good Elk (Red Bear) and One Horn stayed in Fort Lincoln. Returned from the 17th Infantry to the 7th Cavalry on June 21. He was not in the Little Bighorn River fight.

OWL, Private
On detached service at Fort A. Lincoln from June 17. *Horn,* Ho-ne. Arikara Indian scout. First enlistment at age 19 on May 13, 1876, in the 7th Cavalry for six months by Lieut. Charles Varnum at Fort A. Lincoln. He enlisted with Good Elk and Wagon. On detached service from June 17 at Fort Lincoln. Re-enlisted on November 13, 1876.

ROUND WOODEN CLOUD, Private
Crossed the river with the Reno column. *Much-pa-ga-chunn-ga,* Machpeya-chunga-lashka, Round Woodey Cloud, Round Wooley Cloud, Buffalo Ancestor, Buffalo Body, Whole Buffalo, Pta-a-te. Dakota Sioux Indian scout born in Dakota Territory. Discharged from his first enlistment on October 6, 1875. Second enlistment at age 41 on March 31, 1876, in the 7th Cavalry for six months by Lieut. William Cooke at Fort A. Lincoln. On the scouting trip from Camp Nr. 19 at Powder River with Young Hawk. With the Reno battalion on June 25. After crossing the river with the battalion he turned to the right to capture a herd of Sioux ponies and drive them across the river to the ridgetop. On duty as a pony herder. Returned to Yellowstone Depot. Listed as missing in action since June 26 on the Muster Roll of Lieut. Varnum, 7th Cavalry. Enlisted as a scout on May 5, 1877, at Fort Lincoln for six months. Discharged on November 5, 1877, at Fort Lincoln upon expiration of service by Major Joseph Tilford, with good character reference. At this time his listed age was 41 years and he was 5'-11" in height. Enlisted in Lieut. George Young's Detachment of Indian Scouts on April 14, 1881 for six months. Discharged October 13, 1881, by Lieut. Col. H. L. Chipman, 7th Infantry, at Fort Buford, Dakota, upon expiration of service. His listed age was then 38 and he was 5'-9" in height. Enlisted in Lieut. Francis Woodbridge's Detachment of Indian Scouts on October 14, 1881 for six months. Discharged on April 13, 1882, by Lieut. Col. H. L. Chipman at Fort Buford upon expiration of service with good character reference. His listed age was then 37 and he was 5'-9" in height.

RUSHING BULL, Private
Did not cross the river into the valley fight. *Hocus-ne-ginn,* Hocus-pa-cut-rer, Hocus-naquin, Running Bull, Charging Bull. Arikara Indian scout enlisted at age 45 on May 9, 1876, in the 7th Cavalry for six months by Lieut. Charles Varnum at Fort A. Lincoln. He was with the expedition on June 25 but did not cross the Little Bighorn River into the valley fight. Joined the six scouts on the ridgetop who had captured Sioux ponies and performed duty as pony herder. Returned to Yellowstone Depot. Listed as missing in action since June 26 on the Muster Roll of Lieut. Varnum, 7th Cavalry. Discharged by Col. Samuel Sturgis at Fort Lincoln in November, 1876, upon expiration of service

with good character reference. His age was then 45 and he was 5'-9" in height. Re-enlisted November 11, 1876.

SIOUX, Private
Crossed the river with the Reno column. *Sen-nen-urt*, Sen-nen-net, Little Sioux, One Wolf. Arikara Indian scout born at Fort Clark, Dakota. Discharged from his fourth enlistment on November 18, 1875. Fifth enlistment at age 21 on February 3, 1876, in the 7th Cavalry for six months by Lieut. William Cooke at Fort A. Lincoln. He was returned from the 17th Infantry to the 7th Cavalry on June 21. With the Reno column on the afternoon of June 25. After crossing the Little Bighorn River he turned to the right to capture a herd of Sioux ponies and drive them across the river to the ridgetop. On rear guard duty for the pony herd. Returned to Yellowstone Depot. Listed as missing in action since June 26 on the Muster Roll of Lieut. Varnum, 7th Cavalry. He was a nephew of Bloody Knife and brother of Bear Come Out (Red Wolf). Re-enlisted on July 3, 1876, on the Yellowstone River.

SOLDIER, Private
Did not cross the Little Bighorn into the valley fight. *Kananch*, Hoo-nanch, Hkoo-no-neh. Arikara Indian scout born in 1831. Discharged from twelfth enlistment on May 3, 1874. Thirteenth enlistment at age 43 on April 26, 1876, in the 7th Cavalry by Lieut. William Cooke at Fort A. Lincoln. Second leader of the Arikara scouts. Leader of the second scouting party on June 22. With the Reno column on the afternoon of June 25, but he was left behind on the march down Reno Creek because his pony was in poor condition. He did not cross the river into the valley fight. Joined the six scouts on the ridgetop who had captured Sioux ponies. Performed rear guard duty. Returned to Yellowstone Depot. Listed as missing in action since June 26 on the Muster Roll of Lieut. Varnum, 7th Cavalry. He served about six years as a scout at Fort Stevenson, Dakota. He was an uncle of Goose and of Strike Bear. A sketch of Soldier is in *Collections* of the State Historical Society of North Dakota, VI, p. 79.

STAB, Private
Did not cross the river into the valley fight. *Ca-wars,* Stabbed. Arikara Indian scout. First enlistment at age 45 on May 9, 1876, in the 7th Cavalry for six months by Lieut. Charles Varnum at Fort A. Lincoln. With the expedition on June 24. On June 25 he was detailed to follow a trail with Benteen to the left of the Reno column. He rejoined Soldier below the abandoned Indian tipi and then rejoined Rushing Bull and White Eagle and followed the trail of the Custer column. He did not cross the river into the valley fight. Joined the six scouts on the ridgetop who had captured Sioux ponies and became a rear guard for the pony herd. Returned to Yellowstone Depot. Listed as missing in action since June 26 on the Muster Roll of Lieut. Varnum, 7th Cavalry. His name is erroneously mentioned in Major Marcus Reno's report of July 5, 1876, as having been killed. He was killed in 1882 by Dakota Sioux in the Little Missouri River bad lands in Dakota. He was an uncle of Sioux, an Arikara scout.

STRIKE BEAR, Private
Crossed the river with the Reno column. *Coonough-ta-cha,* Red Star, Strikes the Bear. Arikara Indian scout born in 1858, at Fort Clark, Dakota. First

enlistment at age 21 on May 9, 1876, in the 7th Cavalry for six months by Lieut. Charles Varnum at Fort A. Lincoln. He was on scouting duty from Camp Nr. 4 and on scouting duty with Soldier on June 22 and with the expedition on June 24. Strike Bear and Bull were companions on the expedition. On scouting duty with Forked Horn on the night of June 24. Accompanied Lieut. Varnum on the trip to the Crow's Nest arriving there about 2:30 on the morning of June 25. With Bull he carried a message from Lieut. Varnum to Lieut. Col. George Custer. He was with Col. Custer on the trip to the Crow's Nest. After crossing the river with the Reno column he turned to the right to capture a herd of Sioux ponies and drive them across the river to the ridgetop. On duty as a pony herder. Returned to Yellowstone Depot. Listed as missing in action since June 26 on the Muster Roll of Lieut. Varnum, 7th Cavalry. His name was changed to Red Star after the Sioux expedition.

STRIKE THE LODGE, Private

Did not cross the river into the valley first. *Tay-kee-che,* Tay-kee-chee, Tay Ku Chi, Strikes-The Lodge. Arikara Indian born in Dakota Territory. Second enlistment on July 13, 1875 for six months in the Fort Lincoln Detachment of Indian Scouts. Discharged at Fort Lincoln January 13, 1876 by Major Marcus Reno upon expiration of enlistment at a listed age of 28, with a character reference of good. He was 5'-9" in height and had black eyes, black hair and dark complexion. Third enlistment at age 29 on May 9, 1876 in the 7th Cavalry for six months by Lieut. Charles Varnum at Fort Lincoln. He accompanied Lieut. Varnum on the trip to the Crow's Nest, arriving there about 2:30 on the morning of June 25. With the Reno column on June 25 but he did not cross the river into the valley fight. Joined the six scouts on the ridgetop who had captured ponies. Became a rear guard for the pony herd. Returned to Yellowstone Depot. Listed as missing in action since June 26 on the Muster Roll of Lieut. Varnum, 7th Cavalry. Discharged November 9, 1876 at Fort Lincoln at age 29 upon expiration of enlistment by Col. Samuel Sturgis with a character reference of good. Re-enlisted November 11, 1876.

STRIKE TWO, Private

Crossed the river with the Reno column. *Ti-ta-wa-ri-cho,* Sita-ka-wisha, Strikes Two. Arikara Indian born at Fort Clark, Dakota. Fourth enlistment at age 29 in the 7th Cavalry for six months by Lieut. Charles Varnum on May 9, 1876, at Fort A. Lincoln. He was the first to reach the abandoned Indian tipi on the march down Reno Creek from the divide between Rosebud Creek and the Little Bighorn. After crossing the Little Bighorn he turned to the right to capture a herd of Sioux ponies and drive them across the river to the ridgetop. Rear guard for the pony herd. Returned to Yellowstone Depot. Listed as missing in action since June 26 on the Muster Roll of Lieut. Varnum, 7th Cavalry.

WAGON, Private

At Yellowstone Depot on June 24. *Saparam,* Sappa-rannee-was. Arikara Indian enlisted with Good Elk at age 20 in the 7th Cavalry for six months by Lieut. Charles Varnum at Fort A. Lincoln. On detached service at Fort Lincoln on May 17. At Yellowstone Depot about June 24. In the scouting party on the Yellowstone River from July 2 with Forked Horn.

WHITE CLOUD, Private
　　　Did not cross river into the valley fight. *Much-pa-a-ska,* Much-pa-a-cha, Mach-pe-as-ka, Machpe-eska. Dakota Sioux scout enlisted in the 7th Cavalry on November 13, 1875 for six months by Lieut. James Calhoun at Fort A. Lincoln. Third enlistment at age 21 on May 14, 1876 in the 7th Cavalry for six months by Lieut. Charles Varnum at Fort A. Lincoln. He was on the scouting party from Camp Nr. 19 at Powder River with Young Hawk. Assigned to the Reno column on the afternoon of June 25 but did not cross the Little Bighorn into the valley fight. Joined the six scouts on the ridgetop who had captured Sioux ponies. Became rear guard for pony herd. Returned to Yellowstone Depot. Carried messages from Yellowstone Depot to the steamer *Far West* at the mouth of the Little Bighorn. Listed as missing in action since June 26 on the Muster Roll of Lieut. Varnum, 7th Cavalry.

WHITE EAGLE, Private
　　　Did not cross river into the valley fight. *Na-ta-sta-ca*, Nota-staka. Arikara Indian scout enlisted at age 24 on May 9, 1876 in the 7th Cavalry for six months by Lieut. Charles Varnum at Fort A. Lincoln. Assigned to the Reno column on June 25. His small pony was exhausted and White Eagle could not keep up with the column. He did not cross the Little Bighorn into the valley fight. Joined the six scouts on the ridgetop who had captured Sioux ponies and became a pony herder. Returned to Yellowstone Depot. Listed as missing in action since June 26 on the Muster Roll of Lieut. Varnum, 7th Cavalry.

WHITE-MAN-RUNS-HIM, Private
　　　With the Custer battalion on June 25. Ma-esta-she-it-coo-roosh, Mahr-stah-shee-dah-ku-roosh, Mias-tas-hede-Karoos, Mahr-itah-thee-dah-ka-roosh, Crow-Who-Talks-Gros Ventre. Crow Indian scout enlisted in the 7th Infantry on April 10, 1876 for six months by Lieut. James Bradley at Crow Agency, Montana Territory. On detached service with Major Marcus Reno, 7th Cavalry from June 21. Accompanied Lieut. Charles Varnum on the trip to the Crow's Nest arriving there about 2:30 on the morning of June 25. Assigned to the Custer column in the afternoon of June 25. He withdrew from the column about 3:15 pm and joined Strike Bear on the ridgetop; in the hilltop fight for a short time. Withdrew and made contact with Colonel John Gibbon's Montana column and then returned to Crow Agency. His earlier name was White Buffalo That Turns Around, Be-shay-es-chay-e-coo-sis. He died on June 2, 1929 at Crow Agency and was interred in the Custer Battlefield National Cemetery, Grave 1467 (1007)A.

WHITE SWAN, Private
　　　Wounded in the valley fight. Mee-nah-tsee-us, Me-lar-cheash, Strikes Enemy. Crow Indian scout enlisted in the 7th Infantry on April 10, 1876 for six months by Lieut. James Bradley at Crow Agency, Montana. On detached service with the 7th Cavalry from June 21. Accompanied Lieut. Charles Varnum on the trip to the Crow's Nest arriving there about 2:30 on the morning of June 25. One of ten Indians in the valley fight where he was severely wounded in the right hand and leg (possibly by Whirlwind, a Cheyenne Indian) after the retreat, after crossing the ford. Died on August 12, 1904 at Crow Agency, Montana. Interred in the Custer Battlefield National Cemetery, Grave 460A.

WOLF RUNS, Private

Carrying mail to the 7th Cavalry on June 25. *Schri-ri-to-nuch,* Sci-ri-tu-nuch, Running Wolf. Arikara Indian scout born in 1856 at Fort Clark, Dakota. First enlistment at age 21 on May 9, 1876 in the 7th Cavalry for six months by Lieut. Charles Varnum at Fort A. Lincoln. He carried the mail from Rosebud Creek to Yellowstone Depot on June 22. Leader of a party carrying mail from Yellowstone Depot to the 7th Cavalry on June 25. Not in the Little Bighorn River fight. In the scouting party on the Yellowstone River from July 2 with Forked Horn. Discharged in November, 1876.

YOUNG HAWK, Private

In the valley and hilltop fights. *Ach-ta-wi-si-henune,* Striped Horn, Crazy Head, Achta-wisi-hum. Arikara Indian scout born in 1859. Fourth enlistment at age 21 on May 9, 1876 in the 7th Cavalry for six months by Lieut. Charles Varnum at Fort A. Lincoln. On the march to the Powder River he cooked meat for George Custer. On the Powder River scouting trip from Camp Nr. 19 on June 10. One of the ten Indian scouts engaged in the valley fight. He was on the right side of the skirmish line, between Goose and Half Yellow Face. In the retreat to the bluffs and the hilltop fight. In the party that tried to carry a message from the hilltop but was forced back by hostiles. In the first party to Custer Hill from the hilltop on June 27. Together with Forked Horn he made the first contact, after the hilltop fight, with Colonel John Gibbon's Montana column, through Lieut. Jacobs on June 27, and then returned to the Reno battalion on the hilltop. Present for duty on June 30 at camp at the mouth of the Little Bighorn. He accompanied Goose, the wounded scout on the trip to the steamer *Far West.* In the scouting party on the Yellowstone River from July 2 with Forked Horn. He was the son of Forked Horn. Young Hawk was in the Black Hills expedition in 1874.

41

COMPANY A IN 1876

The company remained a part of the garrison at Fort A. Lincoln, Dakota, until May 5th and then joined the regiment in camp below the post to take part in the Sioux expedition under the command of Brigadier General Alfred Terry. The company left Fort Lincoln on May 17th and returned on September 26 and went into quarters. Company A was one of the four companies under the command of Major Marcus Reno to go to Standing Rock Agency via the west bank of the Missouri River to assist in disarming and dismounting the Indians at that agency. The company left on October 21st and returned on November 3rd. On November 12th the company left Fort Lincoln and arrived at Fort Rice for winter station on the same day. Total distance marched by the company in the year was 1542 miles.

The following members were casualties in the Little Bighorn River fight on June 25-26. Killed: Lieut. Algernon Smith; Corporal James Dalious, Privates James Drinan, James McDonald, John Armstrong, William Moodie, Richard Rollins, Thomas Sweetser, and John Sullivan. Those wounded were First Sergeant William Heyn, Corporal George King; Privates Jacob Deihl, Frederick Holmstead, Elijah Strode, Samuel Foster and Francis Reeves. Corporal King died on July 2nd of his wounds.

Officers serving with Company A in the year were Captain Myles Moylan, First Lieutenants Algernon Smith and Andrew Nave; Second Lieutenants Charles Varnum and Ezra Fuller*. Lieut. Nave was transferred from Co. I and promoted to First Lieut. to occupy the vacancy created by the death of Lieut. Smith. Lieut. Fuller was transferred from the 8th Cavalry to occupy the vacancy created by the promotion of Lieut. Varnum.

* *Ezra Bond Fuller was born in Rockford, Ill. October 4, 1848 and entered military service from Illinois. Enlisted as a Private Co. E, 141 Ill. Inf. May 17, 1864, and was discharged October 10, 1864. Enlisted as a Private Co. M, 8th Ill. Cav. Feb. 2, 1865 and was discharged July 17, 1865. Appointed a cadet at the Military Academy July 1, 1869. Graduated 12th in his class in 1873. Appointed 2nd Lieut. 8th U.S. Cavalry, June 13, 1873. Transferred to 7th Cavalry June 26, 1876. Promoted to 1st Lieut. September 30, 1877. Reg. QM, November 2, 1887, to November 6, 1891. Brevet Captain February 27, 1890 for gallant service in action against Indians at Canyon Creek, Mont. Sept. 13, 1877. Promoted to Captain March 22, 1892; Major 10th Cavalry May 31, 1901. Transferred to 7th Cavalry, Oct. 2, 1902.*

COMPANY A AT THE LITTLE BIGHORN

	Absent	Present	Wounded	Died OWRT	Killed	Survived
Captain		1				1
1st Lieut		1			1	
2nd Lieut		1	1			1
1st Sgt.		1	1			1
Sergt.	1	5				6
Corporal		2	1	1	1	
Trumpeter		2				2
Saddler		1				1
Farrier		1				1
Wagoner						
Blacksmith		1				1
Private	5	34	5		7	32
Totals	6	50	8	1	9	46

COMPANY A ON JUNE 30, 1876

Officer present for duty 1
Officer present special duty 1
Enlisted present for duty 28
Enlisted present extra duty 4
Enlisted absent detached service 6
Enlisted absent sick 7
Captain 1
2nd Lieutenant 1
1st Sergeant 1
Sergeants 6
Trumpeters 2
Farrier and blacksmith 2
Saddler 1
Privates 32
Total enlisted 44
Aggregate 46
Aggregate last month 57
Officer killed 1
Enlisted expiration of service 1
Enlisted killed 8
Wounded 7
Horses serviceable 38
Horses lost in action or died 14

MOYLAN, MYLES, Captain

Born on December 17, 1838 in Amesbury, Massachusetts, the son of Thomas and Margaret Riley Moylan. He resided in Massachusetts until he enlisted from Essex as a Private. Co. C, 2nd Dragoons on June 8, 1857. He was engaged in Colonel Albert Johnston's expedition to Utah that year. From 1859 to 1860 Moylan was in Nebraska and was engaged against hostile Indians at Blackwater Springs, Kansas with the 2nd Dragoons, on July 11, 1860. Promoted to Corporal, Co. C on Oct. 1, 1858; to Sergeant on Oct. 1, 1860 and to First Sergeant on May 17, 1861. Discharged on April 1, 1862 and re-enlisted, holding the rank of First Sergeant until March 28, 1863 when he was appointed Second Lieutenant, 5th Cavalry. Participated in Gen. Lyon's campaign in southwestern Missouri and was engaged in the battle of Wilson's Creek and the action at Fort Henry and Fort Donelson. In 1862 he was in the engagement at Shiloh and the siege of Corinth and the affair at Pocahontas Farm on Sept. 26 and the battle of Corinth on Oct. 3-4. Engaged in the action at Beverly Ford and the skirmish at Aldie and the actions at Middleburg and Snicker's Gap and Ashby's Gap. In the battle of Gettysburg and the Gettysburg campaign. Dismissed from the service on Oct. 25, 1863, for being in the city of Washington without permission. Under the name of Charles Thomas he enlisted in Co. A, 4th Mass. Vol. Cav. on Dec. 2, 1863 and was promoted to Sergeant on Dec. 26, 1863. Promoted to First Lieutenant on Jan. 25, 1864 and to Captain on Dec. 1, 1864. Brevetted Major, USV for his gallant and distinguished services in Virginia. Honorably mustered out of service on Nov. 26, 1865. Enlisted on Jan. 25, 1866; assigned to Carlisle Barracks, Pa. Transferred to the 7th Cavalry on Aug. 20. 1866; promoted to Sergeant Major on Sept. 1, 1866. Promoted to First Lieutenant on Dec. 16, 1866 and to Captain on March 1, 1872. He served with the regiment for 26 years in Kansas, Kentucky, Dakota and Montana Territories, having been stationed at Fort Leavenworth, Elizabethtown, Forts Rice, Abraham Lincoln, Randall and Meade. Engaged in the Washita River fight on Nov. 27, 1868, and in the Yellowstone expedition in 1873 and the Black Hills expedition in 1874 and the Sioux expedition in 1876. In the Snake Creek fight on Sept. 30, 1877 Moylan was severely wounded. On Nov. 5, 1887 he was in action against Crow Indians in Montana and on Dec. 29, 1890 he participated in the fight on Wounded Knee Creek in South Dakota. Promoted to Major, 10th Cavalry on April 9, 1892. Retired on his own application after 35 years of service. On Nov. 27, 1894 he was awarded the Medal of Honor for his action in the Nez Perce campaign in 1877. Died on Dec. 11, 1909; interred in San Diego.

SMITH, ALGERNON EMORY, First Lieutenant

Born on September 17, 1842 in Newport, New York. He enlisted in Company K, 7th U.S. Infantry in June 1862; discharged upon appointment as a Second Lieutenant 117th New York Volunteers on August 20, 1862. Promoted to First Lieutenant in the same regiment on September 20, 1862. Commanded Co. G, 117th NYV from February, 1863 to October, 1863 when he was detailed as aide-de-camp. Lieut. Smith participated in the siege of Charleston and the assault on Fort Wagner in July, 1863 and was at John's Island, Cold Harbor and Petersburg and Drewry's Bluff and the operations in front of Bermuda Hundred in May, 1864. Promoted to Captain on Oct. 12, 1864. In the Army of the James he was engaged in the siege and charges on Petersburg and in the engagement at Fort Gilmer and the battles on Darbytown Road and the assault on Fort Fisher on January 13-15, 1865, where he was severely wounded. He was hospitalized for two months before returning to duty. Brevetted Major, USV, effective March 13, 1865 for his service in leading a charge at Fort Fisher. Honorably mustered out of volunteer service on May 15, 1865. On August 9, 1867 he was appointed a Second Lieutenant, 7th Cavalry. Brevetted First Lieutenant, USA, effective Aug. 9, 1867 for his service in the battle of Drewry's Bluff and Captain on the same date for his service in the capture of Fort Fisher. Engaged in the Washita fight on Nov. 27, 1868. Promoted to First Lieutenant on Dec. 5, 1868. He was stationed in Kentucky in the early 1870s and then participated in Col. David Stanley's expedition escorting the Northern Pacific Railroad Survey and exploring the valley of the Yellowstone River. He was AAQM and ACS for Lieut. Col. George Custer's expedition exploring the Black Hills in the summer of 1874. On May 17, 1876, he departed with the 7th Cavalry to participate in the Sioux expedition under the command of Brig. Gen. Alfred Terry. While acting regimental quartermaster and commanding Company E of the 7th Cavalry, Lieut. Smith was killed at the Little Bighorn River on June 25. In July, 1877 his remains were exhumed from the battlefield and re-interred on August 3, 1877 in the Fort Leavenworth National Cemetery, Grave 1486A. He was survived by his wife, Henrietta and several children.

VARNUM, CHARLES ALBERT, Second Lieutenant

In the valley and hilltop fights. Commanding the detachment of Indian scouts in the valley fight. Wounded in the leg. Born on June 21, 1849, in Troy, New York, the son of John and Nancy Elizabeth Green Varnum. Resided in Dracut, Massachusetts until 1866 when the family moved to Florida. On August 18, 1866, Varnum sailed for Tampico, Mexico as a paymaster clerk on the USS *Tallapoosa* and returned the following spring. He entered the Military Academy on September 1, 1868 and was the 2427th graduate, ranking 17 in the class of 57 graduates. Commissioned Second Lieutenant, Seventh Regiment of Cavalry, on June 14, 1872, and reported for duty with Company A in Elizabethtown, Kentucky. In the spring of 1873 the regiment was ordered to Dakota and ten companies detrained at Yankton, Dakota, and in May, marched up the Missouri River and joined the expedition of Colonel David Stanley, escorting the Northern Pacific Railroad Survey and exploring the valley of the Yellowstone River. Varnum was engaged on August 4 in a fight with hostile Sioux on the Yellowstone River near the mouth of the Tongue River. He was engaged again on August 11 near the mouth of the Bighorn River. Participated in the Black Hills expedition in July and August, 1874. In 1875 he was scouting from Fort Randall, Dakota. Engaged in the Sioux expedition and the Little Bighorn River fight in 1876. Promoted to First Lieutenant to rank from June 25, 1876 and transferred to Company C. From November 14, 1876, he was regimental quartermaster until October 31, 1879. He participated in the 1877 campaign against the Nez Perce Indians. Varnum was promoted to Captain on July 22, 1890, while commanding Troop B at Fort Riley, Kansas. Engaged in the fight on Wounded Knee Creek, South Dakota, on December 29, 1890, against Big Foot's band of hostile Sioux, and awarded the Medal of Honor on September 22, 1897, for his conduct in this fight. In 1895 Captain Varnum was detached and detailed as Professor of Military Science at the University of Wyoming in Laramie where he remained until the opening of the Spanish-American War. He purchased horses for the Rough Riders, mustered in an Oklahoma regiment and rejoined

46

the 7th Cavalry at Fort Sill. He left for Cuba in January, 1899. He returned in May and was stricken with typhoid fever. Returned to duty the following summer as Adjutant General, Department of Colorado with station at Denver. Promoted to Major on Feb. 2, 1901 and Lieutenant Colonel on April 10, 1905. He retired for disability on Oct. 31, 1907. On April 6, 1919 he was relieved from further duty, the last surviving officer of the Little Bighorn River fight. He died on Feb. 26, 1936 in San Francisco at the age of 86 and was interred in the National Cemetery.

HEYN, WILLIAM, First Sergeant
In the valley and hilltop fights. Wounded in the left knee in the valley fight on June 25. Transported to Fort Abraham Lincoln, Dakota on the steamer *Far West*. Born in Bremen, Germany. Second enlistment on April 6, 1872, at age 26 in New York City by Captain Edwin Sumner. Promoted to First Sergeant December 8, 1873, on Company Order Nr. 20, December 8, 1873. Transferred to GSAGO. Discharged April 6, 1877, at Washington, D.C. upon expiration of service, as a Private of very good character. He had blue eyes, brown hair, fair complexion and was 5'-7¾" in height. Listed elsewhere as Hynes.

ALCOTT, SAMUEL, Sergeant
On detached service from June 15, 1876, at Yellowstone Depot, Montana Territory. Born in Allegany, Pennsylvania. Enlisted on January 10, 1872, at age 21 in Troy, New York by Lieut. Oscar Elting. Previous occupation was file cutter. Discharged on January 10, 1877, at Fort Rice, Dakota upon expiration of service, as a Sergeant of excellent character. He had brown eyes, black hair, dark complexion and was 5'-6" in height.

CULBERTSON, FERDINAND A., Sergeant
In the valley and hilltop fights. Born in Pittsburgh, Pennsylvania. Second enlistment on February 1, 1873, at age 27 in St. Louis by Lieut. James Peale. Previous occupation was clerk. Reduced from Sergeant to Private by Captain Myles Moylan September 14, 1876, at camp on the Missouri River for carelessness in failing to extinguish a camp fire. Discharged on February 1, 1878, at Fort Abraham Lincoln, Dakota upon expiration of service, as a Sergeant of excellent character. Re-enlisted. Testified at the Reno Court of Inquiry in Chicago on January 30, 1879. He had grey eyes, brown hair, fair complexion and was 5'-9¾" in height.

EASLEY, JOHN THOMAS, Sergeant
Born in Montgomery County, Illinois. Enlisted on December 21, 1874, at age 21 in St. Louis by Lieut. William Volkmar. Previous occupation was laborer. Deserted on October 17, 1876. He had brown eyes, light hair, fair complexion and was 5'-8¼" in height.

FEHLER, HENRY, Sergeant
Born in Hanover, Germany. Enlisted on August 14, 1872, at age 35 in St. Louis by Lieut Oscar Elting. Previous occupation was laborer. Discharged on June 24, 1877, at camp near the Tongue River, Montana Territory per Special Order Nr. 70, Department of Dakota, 1877, as a Private of fair character. He had blue eyes, light hair, fair complexion and was 5'-8½" in height. The Descriptive

47

List and Records File, Custer Battlefield National Monument, includes a letter from the Adjutant General's Office, October 31, 1870, to the commanding officer, 7th Cavalry, in which the recommendation of Colonel Samuel Sturgis for the assignments of Privates Henry Fehler, James Forsyth and Harry Bryden to the 7th Cavalry were not approved. Paragraph 2 of the letter refers to the return of an enclosed discharge of Private Fehler.

McDERMOTT, GEORGE M. (Michael Burke), Sergeant

Born in Galway, County Clare, Ireland. Enlisted on January 21, 1870, at age 22 at 100 Walker Street, New York City. Assigned to Battery I, 5th Artillery. Deserted on July 21, 1871 and was enlisted in Company A, 7th Cavalry on January 15, 1872 in New York City, at the age of 24 under the name of Michael Burke, by Lieut. John Mahnken. Previous occupation was laborer. He surrendered on November 16, 1873 under General Order Nr. 102, AGO, 1873, as George McDermott, deserter from Battery I, 5th Artillery. Discharged on May 16, 1877, as First Sergeant of Company A with excellent character. He was re-enlisted on the same day, twelve miles east of Fort Buford, Dakota at age 27 2/12 by Lieut. George Wallace. Killed on September 30, 1877, in the Snake Creek fight near the Bear Paw Mountains in Montana Territory in an engagement with Chief Joseph's band of Nez Perce Indians. He was then First Sergeant of Company A. Re-interred at the Custer Battlefield National Cemetery, Grave 1413 (3) B. He had blue eyes, light hair, fair complexion and was 5'-8¼" to 8½" in height. Mention of Sergeant McDermott is made in Ami Mulford *Fighting Indians In The Seventh Cavalry*, p. 126.

ROY, STANISLAUS, Sergeant

In the hilltop fight. Born in France. Second enlistment on January 19, 1875, at age 28 in Cincinnati, Ohio by Lieut. Patrick Cusack. Awarded the Medal of Honor on October 5, 1878 with the citation, "Brought water to the wounded under most galling fire of the enemy and at great danger to life," in the Little Bighorn River fight. Discharged January 18, 1880 at Fort Meade, Dakota upon expiration of service, as a Sergeant of excellent character. Re-enlisted. In October, 1887 he was still a Sergeant in Company A. He had brown eyes, brown hair, light complexion and was 5'-5¼" in height. Listed as Stanislus Roy in the Register of Enlistments, U.S. Army. In the Sioux Indian Museum, Rapid City, South Dakota, there is a painting of a horse and cavalry trooper. The horse, it is claimed, belonged to Sergeant Stanislaus Roy. It was ridden from Fort Meade, Dakota to Fort Riley when the Seventh Cavalry changed posts in 1888 and remained at this post until he died in 1892 or 1893. The horse was mounted by Prof. Dyche of the University of Kansas and was exhibited at the World Fairs in Chicago and St. Louis. The painting is about 5' x 7'. This is somewhat reminscent of Keogh's horse Comanche.

CODY, JOHN F., Corporal

Born in Philadelphia, Pennsylvania. Enlisted June 22, 1871, at age 37 in Elizabethtown, Kentucky by Capt. Robbins. Previous occupation was soldier. Discharged on June 22, 1876 at Fort A. Lincoln, Dakota upon expiration of service, as a Corporal of excellent character. He had grey eyes, fair hair, fair complexion and was 5'-10½" in height.

DALIOUS, JAMES, Corporal
    Killed in battle on June 25. Born in Sunburg, Pennsylvania. Enlisted on November 5, 1872, at age 21 in Toledo, Ohio by Captain Samuel Young. Previous occupation was railroader. Deserted on March 26, 1875; apprehended on March 27, 1875. He had brown eyes, dark hair, ruddy complexion and was 5'-10½" in height. Listed as James Dalious on the battle monument. Listed elsewhere as Henry Dalton, James Dallions, and Henry Dallans.

KING, GEORGE H., Corporal
    Died on July 2, 1876 on the steamer *Far West*, at Pease Bottom, Montana Territory, of wounds received in the hilltop fight on June 26. Born in Philadelphia, Pennsylvania. Second enlistment on October 2, 1875, at age 27 in Pittsburgh by Lieut. Thomas Gregg. His remains were re-interred at the Custer Battlefield National Cemetery, Grave 1418 (2) B. Not listed on the battle monument. Listed elsewhere as G. K. King. He had hazel eyes, brown hair, fair complexion and was 5'-10½" in height.

HARDY, WILLIAM G., Trumpeter
    Born in Staten Island, New York. Enlisted on December 15, 1874, at age 24 in Boston by Lieut. William Harper, Jr. Previous occupation was trumpeter. Discharged on December 14, 1879 at Fort Meade, Dakota upon expiration of Service, as a Trumpeter of "good character when sober." He had grey eyes, light hair, fair complexion and was 5'-6 3/8" in height.

McVEIGH, DAVID, Trumpeter
    Born in Philadelphia, Pennsylvania. Enlisted on October 29, 1872, at age 21 in Philadelphia by Captain Samuel Whitside. Previous occupation was musician. Discharged on June 24, 1877 at camp on the Tongue River, Montana Territory per Special Order Nr. 70, Department of Dakota, 1877, as a Trumpeter of excellent character. He had blue eyes, light brown hair, fair complexion and was 5'-7" in height.

MUERING, JOHN, Saddler
    Born in St. Louis, Missouri. Enlisted on December 5, 1875, at age 27 in St. Louis by Lieut. William Volkmar. Previous occupation was soldier. Assigned to Company A. Discharged on December 4, 1879 at Fort Meade, Dakota upon expiration of service, as a Saddler of excellent character. He had grey eyes, sandy hair, fair complexion and was 5'-10" in height.

BRINGES, JOHN, Farrier
    Born in Hanover, Germany. Second enlistment on September 22, 1871, at age 26 in Elizabethtown, Kentucky by Lieut. Algernon Smith. Discharged on September 22, 1876 at Fort Berthold, Dakota upon expiration of service, as a Farrier of excellent character. He had blue eyes, brown hair, ruddy complexion and was 5'-9" in height.

HAMILTON, ANDREW, Blacksmith
    Born in Port Glasgow, Scotland. Enlisted on April 17, 1872, at age 23 in New York City by Lieut. John Mahnken. Previous occupation was blacksmith. Assigned to Company A. Discharged on April 17, 1877 at Fort Rice, Dakota

upon expiration of service, as a Private of excellent character. He had grey eyes, light hair, fair complexion and was 5'-6" in height.

ALLER, CHARLES, Private
Born in Germany. Enlisted December 9, 1874, at age 27 in New York City by Lieut. Thomas Gregg. Previous occupation was cooper. Deserted April 24, 1877; surrendered September 15, 1877. Escaped on October 23, 1877. He had blue eyes, brown hair, fair complexion and was 5'-7¾" in height.

ARMSTRONG, JOHN E., Private
Killed in battle on June 25. Born in Philadelphia. Third enlistment on April 2, 1875, at age 33 in New York City by Lieut. John Babcock. Previous occupation was saddler. Listed as J. E. Armstrong on the battle monument and elsewhere as J. C. Armstrong. He had blue eyes, light brown hair, fair complexion and was 5'-8¾" in height.

BANCROFT, NEIL, Private
In the valley and hilltop fights. Born in Oswego, New York. Enlisted on September 20, 1873, at age 27 10/12 in Chicago by Captain Henry Carroll. Previous occupation was lumberman. Discharged on September 20, 1878, at Camp James G. Sturgis, Dakota upon expiration of service, as a Private of good character. Awarded the Medal of Honor on October 5, 1878, for bringing water for the wounded under a most galling fire from the enemy during the Little Bighorn River fight. He had grey eyes, fair hair, fair complexion and was 5'-6¾" in height.

BAUMGARTNER, LOUIS, Private
Born in Baden, Germany. Enlisted on February 3, 1872, at age 22 in Cincinnati by Lieut. Myles Moylan. Previous occupation was laborer. Discharged on February 3, 1877, at Fort Rice, Dakota upon expiration of service, as a Private of very good character. He had brown eyes, brown hair, fair complexion and was 5'-6½" in height. The Returns of Alterations and Casualties, Company A, Dec. 1887, lists Louis Baumgartner as First Sergeant of Company A, on furlough at Bristol, Pennsylvania. He re-enlisted on December 22, 1887, at Fort Keogh, Montana, with a character reference of excellent.

BLAIR, WILBUR F., Private
Born in Lewisburg, Pennsylvania. Enlisted on September 18, 1872, at age 31 in Harrisburg, Pennsylvania by Lieut. John Mahnken. Previous occupation was printer. Discharged on June 24, 1877, near the Tongue River, Montana Territory, per Special Order Nr. 70, Department of Dakota, 1877, as a Private of good character. He had hazel eyes, dark hair, ruddy complexion and was 5'-6" in height.

BLAKE, THOMAS, Private
Born in New York City. Enlisted on January 15, 1872, at age 21 in New York City by Lieut. John Mahnken. Previous occupation was clerk. Discharged on January 15, 1877, at Fort Rice, Dakota upon expiration of service, as a Private of very good character. He had grey eyes, dark hair, dark complexion and was 5'-8½" in height.

BOCKERMAN, AUGUST, Private
On detached service with the band from June 15, 1876, at Yellowstone Depot, Montana Territory. Born in Elberfield, Prussia. Enlisted on February 12, 1872, at age 21 in Chicago by Captain Samuel Young. Pervious occupation was bookkeeper. Discharged from Company A on February 12, 1877, at Fort Abraham Lincoln, Dakota upon expiration of service, as a Private of excellent character. He had blue eyes, light hair, light complexion and was 5'-11" in height.

BORTER, LUDWIG, Private
Born in De Walle, Switzerland. Enlisted on October 4, 1873, at age 23 in New York City by Lieut. Edward Hunter. Previous occupation was farmer. Deserted on March 26, 1875; apprehended on June 13, 1876, and again deserted on August 6, 1876. He had grey eyes, brown hair, dark complexion and was 5'-5" in height. Not listed on the 7th Cavalry Returns, June 30, 1876.

BOTT, GEORGE A., Private
Born in Fort Wayne, Indiana. Enlisted on September 16, 1875, at age 22 in Cincinnati by Lieut. Patrick Cusack. Previous occupation was clerk. Discharged on September 15, 1880 at Fort Meade, Dakota upon expiration of service, as a Private of good character. He had grey eyes, brown hair, fair complexion and was 5'-7" in height.

BURDICK, BENJAMIN F., Private
On detached service from June 15, 1876 at Yellowstone Depot, Montana Territory. Born in Grafton, New York. Enlisted on January 13, 1872, at age 21 in Troy, New York by Lieut. Oscar Elting. Previous occupation was cooper. Discharged on January 13, 1877 at Fort Rice, Dakota upon expiration of service, as a Private of very good character. He had blue eyes, brown hair, fair complexion and was 5'-8¾" in height.

COWLEY, CORNELIUS, Private
Born in Ireland. Enlisted on December 9, 1874, at age 28 in Boston by Lieut. William Harper, Jr. Previous occupation was stonemason. Discharged on November 1, 1876 at Fort Abraham Lincoln, Dakota for disability, as a Private of good character. He had blue eyes, brown hair, fair complexion and was 5'-8" in height.

CONNER, ANDREW, Private
Born in Limerick, Ireland. Enlisted on November 8, 1872, at age 30 in Lowell, Mass. by Captain Moses Harris. Previous occupation was moulder. Discharged on November 8, 1877 at Fort Rice, Dakota upon expiration of service, as a Private of excellent character. He had blue eyes, grey hair, florid complexion and was 5'-4¾" in height.

DEIHLE, JACOB, Private
Wounded in the face in the hilltop fight on June 26. Transported to Fort Abraham Lincoln, Dakota on the steamer *Far West*. Born in Wurtemburg, Germany. Enlisted on October 1, 1875, at age 22 in New York City by Lieut. John Babcock. His previous occupation was bartender. Discharged on September 3, 1880, at Fort Meade, Dakota upon expiration of his service, as a Private of

excellent character. Second enlistment on November 30, 1880, at age 27 in Louisville, Kentucky by Captain H. W. Wessells, Jr. At this time he was not married. Assigned to Company D, 8th Cavalry. Discharged on September 11, 1884, at the Post of San Antonio, Texas, for chronic rheumatism in the right knee and ankle, contracted while on duty at the Post of San Antonio in February, 1884, and for impairment of motion of his right wrist due to fracture at Fort Clark, Texas in May, 1882. Listed as Jacob Deihle in the Register of Enlistments, U.S. Army and on his Oath of Enlistment. He had grey eyes, brown hair, ruddy complextion and was 5'-6½" in height.

DRINAN, JAMES, Private

Killed in battle on June 25. Born in Cork, Ireland. Enlisted on December 2, 1874, at age 21 in Boston by Lieut. William Harper, Jr. Previous occupation was laborer. He had grey eyes, light brown hair, dark complexion and was 5'-7 3/8" in height. Listed as James Drinan on the battle monument and elsewhere as Drinaw and Drinans.

DURSELEN, OTTO, Private

Born in Frankfort, Germany. Enlisted on December 5, 1874, at age 24 in New York City by Lieut. Thomas Gregg. Previous occupation was clerk. Promoted to Sergeant. Killed on September 30, 1877, in an engagement with Nez Perce Indians under Chief Joseph near the Bear Paw Mountains, Montana Territory. His remains were re-interred in the Custer Battlefield National Cemetery, Grave 1413 (3) B. He had blue eyes, brown hair, fair complexion and was 5'-9½" in height. Listed as Otto Durselen in the Register of Enlistments, U.S. Army and on his Oath of Enlistment. Listed elsewhere as Derslow and Durselow.

FOSTER, SAMUEL JAMES, Private

Wounded in the right arm on June 25. Transported to Fort Abraham Lincoln, Dakota on the steamer *Far West*. Born in Clay County, Kentucky. Enlisted on May 9, 1872, at age 22 in Manchester, Kentucky by Lieut. Algernon Smith. Discharged on May 9, 1877 at Fort Rice, Dakota upon expiration of service, as a Private of excellent character. He had black eyes, brown hair, dark complexion and was 5'-6½" in height.

FRANKLIN, JOHN W., Private

Born in Providence, Rhode Island. Enlisted on January 11, 1875, at age 24 in St. Louis by Lieut. William Volkmar. Previous occupation was hostler. Deserted on February 2, 1877; apprehended on February 11, 1880. Dishonorably discharged on March 15, 1880 at David's Island, New York per General Court Martial Order Nr. 18, AGO, 1880. He had grey eyes, brown hair, dark complexion and was 5'-9" in height.

GILBERT, JOHN M., Private

Born in Cork, Ireland. Enlisted on October 6, 1875, at age 21 in St. Louis by Lieut. John Thompson. Previous occupation was laborer. Deserted on April 28, 1877. He had hazel eyes, brown hair, fair complexion and was 5'-7" in height.

HARRIS, DAVID W., Private
In the hilltop fight. Born in Indianapolis, Indiana. Enlisted on September 29, 1873, at age 21 in Cincinnati by Lieut. Adam Kramer. Previous occupation was laborer. Awarded the Medal of Honor on October 5, 1878, for bringing water to the wounded at great danger to his life and under a most galling fire from the enemy, in the Little Bighorn River fight. Discharged on September 29, 1878, at Camp James G. Sturgis, Dakota upon expiration of service, as a Private of good character. He had blue eyes, brown hair, florid complexion and was 5'-6¼" in height.

HOLMSTEAD, FREDERICK, Private
Wounded in the left wrist on June 25. Transported to Fort Abraham Lincoln, Dakota on the steamer *Far West*. Born in Copenhagen, Denmark. Enlisted on November 6, 1872, at age 23 in New York City by Captain Edwin Sumner. Previous occupation was clerk. Discharged on November 6, 1877 at Fort Abraham Lincoln, Dakota upon expiration of service, as a Private of excellent character. He had brown eyes, brown hair, fair complexion and was 5'-8¼" in height. Listed elsewhere as Homstead, Homestead, and Homsted.

HOOK, STANTON, Private
Born in Coshocton, Ohio. Enlisted on October 12, 1875, at age 30 in Cincinnati by Lieut. Patrick Cusack. Previous occupation was saddler. Discharged on October 11, 1880 at Fort Meade, Dakota upon expiration of service, as a Saddler of excellent character. He had blue eyes, brown hair, fair complexion and was 5'-7¼" in height.

JOHNSON, SAMUEL, Private
Born in Troy, New York. Enlisted on October 25, 1872, at age 21 in Troy by Captain Theodore Wint. Previous occupation was engineer. Discharged on June 24, 1877 at camp near the Tongue River, Montana Territory per Special Order Nr. 70, Department of Dakota, 1877, as a Private of good character. He had brown eyes, brown hair, sallow complexion and was 5'-5¾" in height.

JONSON, EMIL O., Private
Born in Kilmar, Sweden. Enlisted on June 22, 1874, at age 21 in St. Paul, Minnesota by Lieut. William Cooke. Deserted on January 21, 1875; surrendered on April 12, 1875 and again deserted on January 24, 1878. He had dark eyes, light hair, light complexion and was 5'-6½" in height. Listed as E. O. Jonsan in the Register of Enlistments, U.S. Army.

KERR, DENNIS, Private
On detached service from May 5, 1876 at Fort Abraham Lincoln, Dakota. Born in Antrim, Ireland. Fourth enlistment on March 13, 1872, at age 35 in Elizabethtown, Kentucky, by Lieut. True. Previous occupation was soldier. Discharged on March 13, 1877 at Fort Rice, Dakota upon expiration of service, as a Private of excellent character. He had blue eyes, light hair, fair complexion and was 5'-7¼" in height.

MOODIE, WILLIAM, Private
Killed in battle on June 25 in the Reno-Benteen fight. Born in Edinburgh, Scotland. Enlisted on December 15, 1874, at age 33 in New York City by Lieut.

Thomas Gregg. Previous occupation was coachman. He had grey eyes, brown hair, florid complexion and was 5'-8" in height. Listed as Wm. Moodie on the battle monument and elsewhere as Moody.

McCLURG, WILLIAM (William Irvine), Private
Born in Belfast, Ireland. Enlisted on September 23, 1875, at age 21 in Cincinnati by Lieut. Patrick Cusack. Previous occupation was laborer. Deserted on March 22, 1878; surrendered on March 9, 1882. He enlisted in violation of the 50th Article of War in Company F, 22nd Infantry as William Irvine. Discharged on May 24, 1882 at Fort Duncan, Texas per General Court Martial Order Nr. 13, Department of Texas, 1882, as a Private. He had blue eyes, brown hair, ruddy complexion and was 5'-8" in height.

McDONALD, JAMES, Private
Killed in battle on June 25. Born in Boston. Enlisted on September 29, 1875, at age 22 in Boston by Lieut. Henry Lawton. His previous occupation was laborer. He had grey eyes, brown hair, fair complexion and was 5'-6" in height. Listed as James McDonald on the battle monument.

NUGENT, WILLIAM D., Private
In the valley and hilltop fights. Born in Grayson County, Kentucky. Enlisted on August 5, 1872, at age 21 in Elizabethtown, Kentucky by Lieut. Algernon Smith. Previous occupation was farmer. Discharged on August 5, 1877 at Fort Rice, Dakota upon expiration of service, as a Private with character not known. He had grey eyes, brown hair, dark complexion and was 5'-8½" in height. In 1927 he resided on Rural Route 1, Jefferson, Kansas.

PROCTOR, GEORGE W., Private
Born in Manchester, New Hampshire. Enlisted on July 15, 1872, at age 22 in New York City by Captain Edwin Sumner. Previous occupation was teamster. Discharged on June 24, 1877 at camp on the Tongue River, Montana Territory, per Special Order Nr. 70, Department of Dakota, 1877, as a Private of excellent character. He had grey eyes, brown hair, dark complexion and was 5'-10¼" in height. Listed as George W. Procttor in the Register of Enlistments, U.S. Army.

RAGSDALE, JOHN S., Private
On detached service from June 15, 1876 at Yellowstone Depot, Montana Territory. Born in Hardin County, Kentucky. Enlisted on July 23, 1872, at age 22 in Elizabethtown, Kentucky by Lieut. Algernon Smith. Previous occupation was farmer. Acquitted of a charge of desertion on General Court Martial Order Nr. 8, Department of Dakota, January 20, 1876. Discharged on June 24, 1877 at camp on the Tongue River, Montana Territory per Special Order Nr. 70, Department of Dakota, 1877, as a Private of good character. He had blue eyes, light hair, fair complexion and was 5'-7" in height. In 1927 he resided at the National Military Home, Dayton, Ohio.

REEVES, FRANCIS M., Private
Wounded in the left side and body on June 25. Transported to Fort Abraham Lincoln, Dakota on the steamer *Far West*. Born in Bluffton, Indiana. Enlisted on October 7. 1875. at age 28 in St. Louis by Lieut. John Thompson.

Previous occupation was teamster. Discharged on December 20, 1878 at Fort Lincoln for disability, as a Private of excellent character. He had grey eyes, light hair, florid complexion and was 5'-5¾" in height.

ROLLINS, RICHARD, Private
Killed in battle on June 25. Born in Breckenridge County, Kentucky. Enlisted on November 26, 1872, at age 23 in Elizabethtown, Kentucky by Lieut. Algernon Smith. Previous occupation was farmer. He had blue eyes, brown hair, fair complexion and was 5'-10¾" in height. Listed as Rich'd Rollins on the battle monument, and in the Register of Enlistments, U.S. Army. Listed elsewhere as R. Rowlins and Richard Rawlins.

SEAYERS, THOMAS, Private
Born in Pikesville, Canada. Enlisted on September 10, 1875, at age 21 in Cincinnati by Lieut. Patrick Cusack. Previous occupation was baker. Deserted on June 4, 1878; surrendered on September 28, 1878. Dishonorably discharged on February 5, 1879 at Fort Abraham Lincoln, Dakota per General Court Martial Order Nr. 4, Department of Dakota, 1879. He had brown eyes, brown hair, dark complexion and was 5'-5¾" in height.

SIEBELDER, ANTON, Private
Born in Lichlewold, Germany. Second enlistment on April 2, 1872, at age 36 4/12 in Elizabethtown, Kentucky by Lieut. Francis Gibson. Previous occupation was carpenter. Discharged on April 2, 1877 at Fort Rice, Dakota upon expiration of service, as a Private of excellent character. Re-enlisted on December 27, 1877 at Fort Abraham Lincoln, Dakota by Lieut. Ernest Garlington and discharged on December 26, 1882 at Fort Meade, Dakota upon expiration of service, as a Private of excellent character. He had blue eyes, brown hair, fair complexion and was 5'-10" in height. Listed as Anton Seibelder in the Register of Enlistments, U.S. Army.

STRODE, ELIJAH T., Private
Orderly for Lieut. Charles Varnum. Wounded in the right ankle in the valley fight on June 25. Transported to Fort Abraham Lincoln, Dakota, on the steamer *Far West*. Born in Monroe County, Kentucky. Enlisted on October 15, 1872, at age 21 7/12 in Elizabethtown, Kentucky by Lieut. Algernon Smith. Previous occupation was farmer. Assigned to Company A; transferred to Company H. Discharged on June 24, 1877, at camp on the Tongue River, Montana Territory per Special Order Nr. 70, Department of Dakota, 1877, as a Private of good character. He re-enlisted and was promoted to Sergeant, Company D, in 1877. Wounded on September 30, 1877, in the Snake Creek fight, Montana Territory in an engagement with Chief Joseph's band of Nez Perce, near the Bear Paw Mountains. Murdered on February 14, 1881, at Fort Yates, Dakota. Interred in the Fort Meade (Dakota) Post Cemetery, Grave 1-11. He had brown eyes, brown hair, fair complexion and was 5'-9¾" in height. Listed as Elija T. Strode in the Register of Enlistments, U.S. Army and elsewhere as Strond, Elijah Stroude, and Elijah T. Stroud.

SULLIVAN, JOHN, Private
Killed in battle on June 25. Born in Dublin, Ireland. Enlisted on December 7, 1874, at age 23 in Boston by Lieut. William Harper, Jr. Previous occupation

was laborer. He had grey eyes, brown hair, medium complexion and was 5'-6 1/8" in height. (Died in hospital at Fort Abercrombie, Dakota?) Listed in Company F by John Ryan in the *Billings* (Mon.) *Gazette* June 25, 1923. Listed as Jno. Sullivan on the battle monument.

SWEETSER, THOMAS P., Private
     Killed in battle on June 25. Born in Redding, Massachusetts. Enlisted on September 8, 1875, at age 25 in Boston by Lieut. William Harper, Jr. Previous occupation was carpenter. Listed as T. P. Sweetser on the battle monument, and elsewhere as Switzer. He had blue eyes, brown hair, dark complexion and was 5'-7¾" in height.

TAYLOR, WILLIAM O., Private
     In the valley and hilltop fights. Born in Canadaigua, New York. Enlisted on January 17, 1872, at age 21 in Troy, New York by Lieut. Oscar Elting. Previous occupation was cutler. He joined Company M on February 14, 1872 per AGO Order Nr. 2, February 10, 1872. Transferred to Company A on February 17, 1876 to take effect on March 1, 1876. Discharged January 17, 1877, at Fort Rice, Dakota upon expiration of service, with a character reference as a poor soldier. He had hazel eyes, brown hair, fair complexion and was 5'-5¾" in height. He resided in Orange, Massachusetts in 1910.

WEAVER, HOWARD H., Private
     Born in Willamantic, Connecticut. Enlisted on November 4, 1872, at age 21 10/12 in Springfield, Massachusetts by Captain Theodore Wint. Previous occupation was machinist. Wounded on September 30, 1877, in the Snake Creek fight near the Bear Paw Mountains, Montana Territory in an engagement with Chief Joseph's band of Nez Perce Indians. Discharged on November 4, 1877, at Fort Rice, Dakota upon expiration of service, as a Private of excellent character. He had grey eyes, auburn hair, ruddy complexion and was 5'-5¾" in height. Mentioned in *"Thrilling Experiences of Comrade William D. Nugent"*, in *Winners of the West*, February, June, 1926, June, 1932.

WEISS, JOHN, Private
     On detached service from May 5, 1876 at Fort Abraham Lincoln, Dakota. Born in Cincinnati, Ohio. Enlisted on June 17, <u>1870</u>, at age 21 in Cincinnati by Lieut. J. C. White. Previous occupation was farmer. Assigned to Company A, 7th Cavalry. Discharged on August 20, 1876. Second enlistment on November 30, 1876, at the age of 27 at Fort Lincoln by Lieut. George Wallace. Discharged on November 9, 1881 from Company L, 7th Cavalry. Third enlistment on February 27, 1882, in Cincinnati by Lieut. William Davis, Jr. He had blue eyes, brown hair, light complexion and was 5'-8½" to 9" in height. In 1927 he resided at 310 3rd Ave. Durango, Colorado

COMPANY B IN 1876

The company remained a part of the garrison at Shreveport, Louisiana until April 19 and then departed by rail with Co. G. The transfer from Shreveport, in the Department of the Gulf, to Fort Abraham Lincoln, in the Department of Dakota, covered a distance of 2,583 miles. Company B arrived in St. Paul on April 23, having joined Company K enroute. The companies left St. Paul on April 28 and arrived at Fort Lincoln on May 1 and went into camp below the post awaiting the departure of the Sioux expedition. The regiment left Fort Lincoln on May 17 and returned on September 26. Company B again went into camp below the post. The company was one of eight companies, under the command of Colonel Samuel Sturgis, that went to Cheyenne Agency, via the left bank of the Missouri, to disarm and dismount the Indians there. The company departed October 17 and returned on November 11 for winter station. The distance marched by the company in the year was 2,006 miles.

The following members were casualties in the Little Bighorn River fight. Killed: Second Lieut. Benjamin Hodgson and Privates Richard Dorn and George Mask. Those wounded were Sergeant Thomas Murray, Corporal William Smith and Private Charles Cunningham. Private Richard Wallace was drowned in camp near Yellowstone River while crossing a small stream to go on picket guard. Private Thomas O'Brien died in the hospital at Fort Buford, Dakota on September 15 of typhoid fever.

Officers serving with the company in the year were Captain Thomas McDougall, First Lieutenant William Craycroft and Second Lieutenants Benjamin Hodgson, William Robinson and William Nicholson.* Lieut. Robinson was replacement for Lieut. Hodgson.** Lieut. Nicholson was replacement for Lieut. Robinson who was transferred to Company F.

* William John Nicholson was born in the District of Columbia and entered military service from there. He was appointed Second Lieut. 7th Cavalry on August 15, 1876. Promoted to First Lieut. Jan. 16, 1884, and to Captain on August 27, 1896. Appointed Major and Chief Ordnance Officer, U.S. Volunteers on July 18, 1898. Honorably discharged from volunteer service on March 13, 1899. Transferred to 12th Cavalry April 13, 1901.

**William Wallace Robinson, Jr. was born in Ohio and appointed to military service from Wisconsin. He enlisted as Private, Co. E, 7th Wisconsin Volunteer Infantry March 17, 1865 and was discharged July 3, 1865 effective from June 30, 1865. Appointed Cadet, USMA, July 1, 1865. Graduated 32nd in his class. Appointed Second Lieut. 3rd Cavalry June 15, 1869. Transferred to the 7th Cavalry effective June 26, 1876 and assigned to Company B. Transferred to Company F. Promoted to First Lieut. Aug. 14, 1876. Regimental QM Nov. 7, 1883 to Nov. 7, 1887. Captain and Assist QM on June 1, 1891. Major, QM, U.S. Volunteers, Aug. 14, 1900 and Major, QM, U.S. Army, Nov. 14, 1900.

COMPANY B AT THE LITTLE BIGHORN

	Absent	Present	Wounded	Died OWRT	Killed	Survived
Captain		1				1
1st Lieut.	1					1
2nd Lieut.		1			1	
1st Sgt.		1				1
Sergt.	1	4	2			5
Corporal		3	1			3
Trumpeter		2				2
Saddler		1				1
Farrier		1				1
Wagoner						
Blacksmith		1				1
Private	4	53	1		2	55
Totals	6	68	4	0	3	71

COMPANY B ON JUNE 30, 1876

Officers present for duty 1
Enlisted present for duty 60
Enlisted present extra duty 4
Officers absent detached service 1
Enlisted absent detached service 2
Enlisted absent sick 1
Enlisted absent arrest 2
Captain 1
First Lieutenant 1
First Sergeant 1
Sergeants 5
Corporals 4
Trumpeters 2
Farrier and blacksmith 2
Saddler 1
Privates 54
Total enlisted 69
Aggregate 71
Aggregate in May 74
Enlisted lost by **transfer** 1
Officers killed 1
Enlisted gained by transfer 1
Enlisted killed 2
Wounded 4
Horses serviceable 40
Horses unservicable 3
Horses lost 9

THOMAS MOWER McDOUGALL, Captain, Company B

In the hilltop fight. Born May 21, 1845, in Prairie du Chien, Wisconsin, the son of Brevet Brig. General Charles McDougall, Medical Corps. Entered military service from Kansas and served in the Civil War. At the age of 18 he was appointed Second Lieutenant in the 10th Louisiana Volunteers of African Descent (on February 18, 1864 to rank from January 22, 1864). The 10th Louisiana Volunteers were re-designated to 48th U.S. Colored Infantry. At the battle of Lakeville, Mississippi he was severely wounded. He served with General Grant at the siege of Vicksburg in 1863 and was honorably mustered out of volunteer service on June 1, 1865 at Benton Barracks, Missouri. On June 2, 1865 he was commissioned a Captain, Company G, 5th U.S. Volunteer Infantry and was mustered out of volunteer service on August 10, 1865 at Fort Leavenworth. From civil life he was offered a commission as a Second Lieutenant, 14th Infantry on May 10, 1866; he accepted the commission on July 21, 1866 at Fort Laramie. On September 21, 1866, he was transferred to the 32nd Infantry and received promotion to First Lieutenant to rank from January 14, 1867. During the reorganization of the army he was transferred to the 21st Infantry on April 19, 1869 and was unassigned on October 21, 1869. Assigned to the 7th Cavalry on December 30, 1870, and was stationed in South Carolina during the Ku Klux Klan troubles in that state. For eighteen years he was stationed in the Dakotas and was engaged in some notable Indian campaigns. Promoted to Captain on December 15, 1875. On May 17, 1876, he departed from Fort Abraham Lincoln, Dakota with the 7th Cavalry to participate in the expedition against hostile Indians. On the march on June 25 to the Little Bighorn River he was in command of Company B, the pack train escort, and he was engaged with Major Reno's battalion in the hilltop fight. Captain McDougall remained in the 7th Cavalry until he was retired for disability in line of duty on July 22, 1890. For his Civil War service, he was promoted to Major of Cavalry (Ret) on May 24, 1904 to rank from April 23, 1904. Major McDougall died July 3, 1909, at Brandon, Vermont. Funeral services were held in the Dahlgren Chapel of the Sacred Heart, Georgetown University on July 7 and he was interned in the National Cemetery, Arlington, Virginia. He was survived by his two sisters, Mrs. Josephine McDougall Buel and Mrs. Edwin B. Babbitt.

CRAYCROFT, WILLIAM THOMAS, First Lieutenant

Born January 28, 1847 in Springfield, Kentucky. He entered the U.S. Military Academy on July 1, 1865 by appointment from Kentucky. He was the 2290th graduate ranking 18 of 39 graduates in the class of 1869. He was commissioned a Second Lieutenant in the 7th Cavalry on June 15, 1869 and accepted the appointment on July 7th at Springfield, Kentucky. Lieuts. James Porter and Charles Braden were academy classmates also assigned to the 7th Cavalry. After graduation leave, Craycroft joined the regiment at Fort Wallace, Kansas on October 17, 1869. He served on various posts on the frontier and took part in Colonel David Stanley's Yellowstone expedition, escorting the Northern Pacific Railroad Survey and exploring the valley of the Yellowstone River in Montana Territory from May 7 to September 21, 1873. On December 2, 1875, he was transferred to Company B, 7th Cavalry, at Shreveport, Louisiana and promoted to First Lieutenant to occupy the vacancy created by the transfer and promotion of Lieut. Thomas Custer, who was transferred to command of Company C. Lieut. Craycroft did not participate in the Sioux expedition of 1876, being on detached service at the time. From October 17, 1876, he was on sick leave until his retirement on June 28, 1878, for disability in line of duty. After retirement he resided in Samar, Missouri and at Bridgeport, Connecticut, where he worked in an industrial school. He passed away on October 31, 1906, at the age of 60 in Dallas, Texas, his death being due to apoplexy. He was survived by his brother, Hunter A. Craycroft of Dallas.

HODGSON, BENJAMIN HUBERT, Second Lieutenant
Killed in the valley fight, at the ford, on June 25. Born in Philadelphia about June, 1848. Entered the Military Academy July 1, 1865, by appointment from Pennsylvania. He was the 2356th graduate, ranking 45th in his class of 58 graduates on June 15, 1870. Commissioned Second Lieutenant, 7th Cavalry, June 15, 1870; accepted the commission on August 9, 1870. After graduation leave he joined the regiment and went on scouting duty in Colorado until November when he went to winter station at Fort Leavenworth. From March, 1871 until October, 1871 he was at Unionville, S. C., Columbia, S. C. and thence to Spartanburg, S. C. where he remained until March, 1873. At Memphis, Tennessee and enroute to Yankton, Dakota, in April. On May 7th, ten companies of the regiment departed from Yankton to join Colonel David Stanley's expedition on the Yellowstone River until September, 1873. In winter station at Fort Abraham Lincoln, Dakota until July, 1874, when he departed with the regiment on the Black Hills expedition. Returned to Fort Lincoln in September; assigned to station at Shreveport, Louisiana, where he remained until April, 1876, except while attending a court martial and a Congressional Committee December, 1874, to February 23, 1875, and a leave of absence from April 1 to October 1, 1875. He returned with his company to Fort Lincoln and on May 17, 1876, he departed with Company B, 7th Cavalry to participate in the Sioux expedition. He was Acting Adjutant of Companies A, G and M at the time of his death. The vacancy in the regiment created by his death was filled by Lieut. William Robinson, Jr. Hodgson's remains were interred on the Reno-Benteen field on the morning of June 27 and exhumed in July, 1877; re-interred in Laurel Hill Cemetery, Philadelphia, in October, 1877.

HILL, JAMES, First Sergeant
Born in Edinburgh, Scotland. Enlisted March 22, 1875, at age 36 in New Orleans, Louisiana by Captain Frederick Benteen. Appointed Ordnance Sergeant, 7th Cavalry, on January 20, 1877. Discharged in March 3, 1880, at Fort Sanders, Wyoming, per Special Order Nr.43,AGO,1880, as an Ordnance Sergeant of good character. He had blue eyes, light hair, fair complexion and was 5'10" in height. Died in 1906 in Wooster, Ohio.

CARROLL, DANIEL, Sergeant
On detached service with the band from May 17, 1876 at Fort Abraham Lincoln, Dakota. Born in Chicago. Second enlistment on December 19, 1871 at the age 21 in New York City by Captain Edwin Sumner. Discharged December 19, 1876, at Fort Lincoln upon expiration of service, as a Sergeant of very good character. He had brown eyes, black hair, fair complexion and was 5'-7½" in height.

CRISWELL, BENJAMIN, Sergeant
In the valley and hilltop fights. Wounded in the neck in the hilltop fight on June 25. Born in Marshall County, West Virginia. Second enlistment on

February 23, 1876, in Shreveport, Louisiana by Lieut. Ben Hodgson. Discharged April 3, 1878, at Standing Rock, Dakota per Special Order Nr.63,AGO,1878, as a Sergeant of excellent character. Awarded the Medal of Honor October 5, 1878, for recovering the body of Lieut. Hodgson, bringing up ammunition and encouraging the men in the most exposed conditions under heavy fire in the Little Bighorn River fight. He had hazel eyes, black hair, dark complexion and was 5'-6¼" in height.

GANNON, PETER, Sergeant
Born in Manchester, England. Second enlistment on July 16, 1872 at age 28 in New York City by Captain Edwin Sumner. Deserted on May 5, 1873; apprehended on August 23, 1873. Discharged in July 16, 1877, at camp near Sentinel Buttes, Montana Territory, upon expiration of service, as a Sergeant of good character. He had blue eyes, brown hair, light complexion and was 5'-6¾" in height.

HUTCHINSON, RUFUS D., Sergeant
In the hilltop fight. Born in Butlersville, Ohio. Enlisted on September 25, 1873, at age 23 in Cincinnati by Lieut. Adam Kramer. Previous occupation was farmer. Discharged on September 25, 1878, at Standing Rock Agency, (Fort Yates) Dakota, upon expiration of service, as First Sergeant, with excellent character. Awarded the Medal of Honor October 5, 1878, as a member of the water party bringing water to the wounded, guarding and carrying the wounded, and posting and directing the men in his charge, under a galling fire from the enemy, in the Little Bighorn River fight. He had blue eyes, light hair, fair complexion and was 5'-10" in height.

MURRAY, THOMAS, Sergeant
Wounded in the hilltop fight on June 26. Born in Managhan, Ireland. Second enlistment on August 17, 1871, at age 35 in Unionville, South Carolina by Captain William Thompson. Discharged August 17, 1876, at the Powder River, Montana Territory upon expiration of service, as a Sergeant of excellent character. Awarded the Medal of Honor October 5, 1878, for bringing in the pack train on June 25 and bringing rations to the firing line on June 26 and bringing water to the wounded during the Little Bighorn River fight. He had blue eyes, brown hair, ruddy complexion and was 5'-8½" in height.

DOUGHERTY, JAMES, Corporal
Escort for the pack mules. In the hilltop fight. Born in Oxford, New Jersey. Enlisted December 5, 1872, at age 21 in Wilkes Barre, Pennsylvania by Captain Eugene Beaumont. Previous occupation was brakeman on the Delaware, Lackawanna & Western Railway. Appointed Corporal on December 18, 1875. Discharged December 5, 1877, at Standing Rock Agency, Dakota upon expiration of service, as a Sergeant of good character. Recommended for a medal by Captain Thomas McDougall for "gallantry in action at the Little Big Horn June 25 and 26, 1876." Re-enlisted in May, 1878. Discharged in 1883 and returned to Pennsylvania where he worked as a brakeman. Died of tuberculosis. He had grey eyes, dark hair, ruddy complexion and was 5'-7¾" in height.

SMITH, WILLIAM M., Corporal
Wounded in the hilltop fight on June 26. Returned to duty. Born in

Trenton, New Jersey. Enlisted on July 11, 1872, at age 21 in Philadelphia by Captain Samuel Whitside. Previous occupation was blacksmith. Discharged February 9, 1877, at Fort Abraham Lincoln, Dakota for disability, as a Corporal. He had light blue eyes, dark hair, ruddy complexion and was 5'-5½" in height. Listed elsewhere as W. F. Smith.

WETZEL, ADAM, Corporal

Born in St. Louis, Missouri. Second enlistment on July 5, 1872, at age 26 in Spartanburg, South Carolina by Captain William Thompson. Discharged July 5, 1877, at camp on the Little Missouri River, Montana Territory upon expiration of service, as a Private of good character. He had blue eyes, sandy hair, fair complexion and was 5'-7" in height.

CONNELL, JOHN, Trumpeter

Born in Ogdensburg, New York, Enlisted on February 6, 1872, at age 21 in Erie, Pennsylvania by Lieut. James Peale. Previous occupation was porter. Discharged February 6, 1877, at Fort Abraham Lincoln, Dakota upon expiration of service, as a Trumpeter of very good character. He had blue eyes, brown hair, light complexion and was 5'-7" in height.

KELLY, JAMES, Trumpeter

Born in Bangor, Maine. Enlisted on January 4, 1876 at age 23 in St. Louis by Lieut. John Thompson. Previous occupation was plumber. Sentenced to three months confinement at his post and $10.99 fine per General Court Martial Order Nr.10, Department of the Gulf, March, 1876. Dishonorably discharged January 5, 1877, at Fort Abraham Lincoln, Dakota per Special Order Nr.264,AGO,1877. He had blue eyes, brown hair, fair complexion and was 5'-4" in height. Listed as James Kelly in the Register of Enlistments, U.S. Army, and elsewhere as Kelley.

BAILEY, JOHN E., Saddler

Born in Joe Davis County, Illinois. Second enlistment on December 10, 1875, at age 30 in Shreveport, Louisiana by Lieut. James M. Bell. Discharged December 9, 1880, at Fort Yates, Dakota upon expiration of service, as a Saddler of very good character. Listed as John A. Bailey in the Register of Enlistments, U.S. Army. He had blue eyes, dark hair, dark complexion and was 5'-11½" in height. Interred in Fort Meade (Dakota) Post Cemetery?

MOORE, JAMES E., Farrier

In the hilltop fight. Accompanied Captain Thomas McDougall on the night of June 26 to recover the body of Lieut. Benj. Hodgson. Born in Hebron, Ohio. Second enlistment on August 28, 1871, at age 24 in Unionville, South Carolina by Lieut. William Thompson. Discharged August 6, 1876, at Rosebud Creek, Montana Territory upon expiration of service, as a Farrier of excellent character. He had blue eyes, brown hair, fair complexion and was 5'-10" in height.

CRUMP, JOHN, Blacksmith

Born in Germany. Enlisted on April 14, 1876 at age 22 in St. Louis, by Lieut. John Thompson. Previous occupation was blacksmith. Assigned to Company B. Deserted on March 29, 1877. He had grey eyes, light hair, fair complexion and was 5'-7" in height.

ABOS, JAMES A., Private
In confinement from May 1, 1876, at Fort Richardson, Texas. Born in Albany, New York. Enlisted on December 10, 1874, at age 17 5/12 in New York City by Lieut. Thomas Gregg. Previous occupation was hostler. Deserted on March 29, 1876; surrendered on April 6, 1876. He was sentenced to one year imprisonment at hard labor and to forfeit all pay, per General Court Martial Order Nr.89, Headquarters, U.S. Army, July, 1876. Deserted on February 2, 1877. He had grey eyes, brown hair, fair complexion and was 5'-8¼" in height.

BARRY, PETER O., Private
On detached duty in Commissary Department per Regimental Order. Born in Washington, D.C. Second enlistment July 16, 1872, at age 27 in Spartanburg, South Carolina by Captain William Thompson. Discharged July 16, 1877, at camp near Cedar Creek, Montana Territory upon expiration of service, as a Private of good character. He had brown eyes, brown hair, dark complexion and was 5'-9½" in height.

BARSANTEE, JAMES F., Private
Born in Boston, Massachusetts. Enlisted on March 8, 1876 at age 23 in Boston by Lieut. Henry Lawton. Previous occupation was sailor. Assigned to Company B. Deserted on March 29, 1877. He had hazel eyes, brown hair, fair complexion and was 5'-5½" in height.

BOAM, WILLIAM, Private
Born in Manchester, England. Enlisted on December 22, 1874, at age 21 9/12 in Boston by Lieut. William Harper, Jr. Previous occupation was sailor. Discharged on April 12, 1877, at Fort Abraham Lincoln, Dakota for disability, as a Private of good character. He had grey eyes, brown hair, medium complexion and was 5'-9" in height.

BONER, HUGH, Private
Born in Boston, Mass. Enlisted on March 18, 1876, at age 21¼ in Boston by Lieut. Henry Lawton. Previous occupation was laborer. Deserted July 7, 1876; apprehended on July 13, 1876; again deserted on Sept. 6, 1876. He had grey eyes, dark hair and dark complexion and was 5'-7½" in height. Listed as Hugh Boner in the Register of Enlistments, U.S. Army and on his Oath of Enlistment and elsewhere as Bohner.

BOREN, ANSGARIUS, Private
Born in Linkoben, Sweden. Enlisted on Feb. 12, 1872, at age 22 in Chicago, Illinois by Capt. Samuel Young. Previous occupation was student. Deserted on April 6, 1874; apprehended on April 14, 1874. Discharged February 12, 1877 at Fort A. Lincoln, Dakota upon expiration of service, as Private of good character. He had blue eyes, light hair, light complexion and was 5'-5¼" in height.

BRAINARD, GEORGE, Private
Orderly at Headquarters, Department of Dakota. Born in Brooklyn, Ohio. Enlisted on January 22, 1872, at age 25 in Cleveland, Ohio by Lieut. James Peale. Previous occupation was teamster. Discharged January 22, 1877, at Fort Abraham Lincoln, Dakota upon expiration of service, as Private of very good

character. He has blue eyes, light hair, light complexion and was 5'-9½" in height.

BROWN, JAMES, Private
Born in County Queens, Ireland. Enlisted on March 23, 1876, at age 22 in Baltimore by Lieut. William Wallace. Previous occupation was moulder. Assigned to Company B. Discharged March 22, 1881, at Fort Yates, Dakota upon expiration of service, as a Private of good character. He had blue eyes, black hair, dark complexion and was 5'-6½" in height.

BURNS, CHARLES, Private
Born in Howard County, Indiana. Enlisted on March 8, 1876, at age 28 in Baltimore by Lieut. William Wallace. Previous occupation was soldier. Assigned to Company B. Discharged March 7, 1881 at Fort Yates, Dakota upon expiration of service, as a Private of good character. He had blue eyes, brown hair, florid complexion and was 5'-9" in height. Not listed on the Company B Muster Roll for June 30, 1876.

CALDWELL, WILLIAM M., Private
Born in Pennsylvania. Enlisted on March 23, 1876, at the age 21 in Baltimore by Lieut. William Wallace. Previous occupation was laborer. Assigned to Company B. Deserted on April 22, 1877. He had blue eyes, black hair, fair complexion and was 5'-7" in height.

CALLAN, JAMES, Private
Born in Scotland. Enlisted on March 11, 1876 at age 27 in Baltimore, Maryland by Lieut. Thomas Gregg. Previous occupation was shoemaker. Deserted on February 2, 1877; apprehended on January 10, 1880. Discharged on April 13, 1880 at Fort Wayne, Michigan, per General Court Martial Order Nr.29, Department of the East, 1880 as a Private with a character reference of "None". He had grey eyes, dark hair, fair complexion and was 5'-7" in height.

CALLAN, THOMAS J., Private
Born in Louth, Ireland. Enlisted on March 10, 1876, at age 22 in Boston by Lieut. Henry Lawton. Previous occupation was morocco dresser. Discharged March 9, 1881, at Fort Yates, Dakota upon expiration of service, as a Private of good character. He had blue eyes, dark hair, fair complexion and was 5'-9½" in height. Awarded the Medal of Honor on October 24, 1896, for conspicuous gallantry and intrepidity as a member of the water party in the Little Bighorn River fight. He volunteered and succeeded in obtaining water for the wounded and he displayed conspicuous good conduct in assisting to drive away the Indians. Died March 6, 1906, in Yonkers, New York.

CAMPBELL, CHARLES A., Private
Born in Boon County, Illinois. Enlisted on January 22, 1872, at age 27 in Cincinnati, Ohio by Lieut. Myles Moylan. Previous occupation was painter. Discharged January 22, 1877, at Fort A. Lincoln, Dakota upon expiration of service, as a Private. He had hazel eyes, light brown hair, ruddy complexion and was 5'-8½" in height.

CARY, JOHN J., Private
Born in Troy, New York. Enlisted on October 25, 1872 at age 21 in Troy by Captain Theodore Wint. Previous occupation was hostler. Discharged July 23, 1877 at Cedar Creek, Montana Territory per General Order Nr.47,AGO,1877, as a Private of good character. He had blue eyes, brown hair, sallow complexion and was 5'-5½" in height. Listed as John J. Cary in the Register of Enlistments, U.S. Army and elsewhere as John J. Carey and John J. Casey.

CARMODY, THOMAS, Private
Born in New York City. Second enlistment on August 1, 1874, at age 30 at Fort Abraham Lincoln, Dakota, by Lieut, William Thompson. Discharged July 31, 1879 at Fort Yates, Dakota upon expiration of service, as a Private of good character. He had blue eyes, brown hair, fair complexion and was 5'-4½" in height.

CLARK, FRANK, Private
Born in Sheldon, Vermont. Enlisted on March 16, 1876, at age 21 4/12 in Boston by Lieut. Henry Lawton. Previous occupation was teamster. Assigned to Company B. Deserted on March 29, 1877. He had brown eyes, black hair, dark complexion and was 5'-6¼" in height.

COLEMAN, THOMAS W., Private
Born in Troy, New York. Enlisted on January 4, 1872, at age 22 in Troy by Lieut. Oscar Elting. Previous occupation was carpenter. Discharged January 4, 1877, at Fort Abraham Lincoln, Dakota upon expiration of service, as a Private of very good character. He had grey eyes, brown hair, fair complexion and was 5'-5 1/8" in height.

CRISWELL, HARRY, Private
Born in Marshall, West Virginia. Enlisted on April 11, 1876, at age 21 in Pittsburgh by Lieut. Thomas Gregg. Previous occupation was farmer. Assigned to Company B. Deserted on March 25, 1879. He had dark brown eyes, dark brown hair, fair complexion and was 5'-7" in height. Brother of Sergeant Ben. Criswell(?).

CROWE, MICHAEL, Private
Born in County Cork, Ireland. First enlistment on July 8, 1867, in New York City by Capt. Samuel Ferris. Assigned to the 34th Infantry. Transferred to Co. A, 16th Infantry. Discharged July 8, 1870. Re-enlisted July 9, 1870, at age 21 in Cincinnati, Ohio by Capt. Thomas Brent. Assigned to Co. E, 7th Cavalry. Discharged July 9, 1875. Third enlistment on July 9, 1875, at age 26 at White River, Dakota by Lieut. Thomas McDougall. Transferred from Co. E on June 1, 1876, to Co. B per Special Order Nr.49, Headquarters, 7th Cavalry. Discharged July 8, 1880, at Camp Houston, Dakota, 138 miles west of Fort A. Lincoln, upon expiration of service, as a Private of good character. Fourth enlistment on July 9, 1880 at age 31 at Camp Houston. At this time he was unmarried. He had grey eyes, brown hair, fair complexion and was 5'-4½" in height. Listed as Michael Crow in the Register of Enlistments, U.S. Army. He died at 1:30 pm June 8, 1883, of heart disease, as a Private in Troop B, 7th Cavalry. Interred at 4 pm June 9 at Fort Yates, Dakota.

CROWLEY, PATRICK, Private
Born in Bangor, Maine. Enlisted on December 14, 1875, at age 21 11/12 in Boston by Lieut. William Harper, Jr. Previous occupation was butcher. Deserted on September 27, 1877. He had grey eyes, brown hair, fair complexion and was 5'-6¼" in height.

CUNNINGHAM, CHARLES, Private
Wounded in the neck in the hilltop fight on June 25. Returned to duty. Born in Hudson, New York. Enlisted on December 8, 1874, at age 29 in New York City by Lieut. Thomas Gregg. Previous occupation was cooper. Awarded the Medal of Honor on October 5, 1878 for remaining on the firing line in the hilltop fight. He declined to leave the line when wounded, although drawing heavy fire, and fought bravely the next day. Discharged December 9, 1879, at Fort Yates, Dakota upon expiration of service, as a Private of good character. He had grey eyes, light hair, fair complexion and was 5'-7¼" in height.

DAVENPORT, WILLIAM H., Private
Born in Williamsburg, New York. Enlisted on March 15, 1876 at age 22 in Boston by Lieut. Henry Lawton. Previous occupation was policeman. Assigned to Company B. Discharged on December 19, 1877 at Fort Abraham Lincoln, Dakota for disability, as a Private of good character. He had blue eyes, light brown hair, fair complexion and was 5'-9¼" in height.

DE TOURREIL, LOUIS, Private
Born in Tours, France. Enlisted on April 3, 1876 at age 21 in New York City by Lieut. John Babcock. Previous occupation was farmer. Assigned to Company B. Deserted on September 30, 1876. He had blue eyes, brown hair, dark complexion and was 5'-5" in height. Listed as Louis De Tourreil in the Register of Enlistments, U.S. Army and elsewhere as Louis De Tourriel.

DEVOTO, AUGUSTUS L., Private
Born in Genoa, Italy. Enlisted on October 1, 1873, at age 21½ at St. Louis Barracks, Missouri by Captain Charles Bendire. Previous occupation was bookbinder. Discharged October 4, 1878, at Standing Rock Agency (Fort Yates), Dakota upon expiration of service, as a Private of good character. He had hazel eyes, black hair, dark complexion and was 5'-9" in height.

DOLL, JACOB W., Private
Born in Russel, England. Enlisted on March 21, 1876 at age 26 in Baltimore by Lieut. William Wallace. Previous occupation was baker. Assigned to Company B. Deserted on November 19, 1877. He had brown eyes, black hair, fair complexion and was 5'-7" in height.

DORN, RICHARD B., Private
Killed in battle on June 25. Born in Bronson, Branch County, Michigan on February 12, 1853, the son of John and Bridget Dorn, both from Ireland. Enlisted on January 30, 1872, at a stated age of 21 in Chicago by Captain Samuel Young. He had grey eyes, dark hair, dark complexion and was 5'-9" in height. Listed as Rich'd Dorn on the battle monument and elsewhere as Doran.

FRANK, WILLIAM, Private
Born in Magdeburg, Prussia. Fifth enlistment on October 12, 1875 at age 39 in St. Louis by Lieut, John Thompson. Previous occupation was tailor. Discharged April 28, 1879 at Fort Yates, Dakota for disability, as a Private of excellent character. He had hazel eyes, brown hair, light complexion and was 5'-8¼" in height.

GEHRMANN, FREDERICK H., Private
Born in Baltimore, Maryland. Enlisted on March 13, 1876, at age 21 in Baltimore by Lieut. William Wallace. Previous occupation was laborer. Assigned to Company B. Discharged March 12, 1881, at Fort Yates, Dakota upon expiration of service, as a Private of excellent character. He had blue eyes, brown hair, ruddy complexion and was 5'-9¼" in height.

GRAY, JOHN, Private
Born in Troy, New York. Enlisted on March 23, 1876, at age 21 11/12 in Boston by Lieut. Henry Lawton. Previous occupation was laborer. Assigned to Company B. Discharged March 22, 1881, at Fort Yates, Dakota upon expiration of service, as a Private of very good character. He had grey eyes, brown hair, fair complexion and was 5'-9¾" in height.

KEEFE, JOHN J., Private
Born in Kerry, Ireland. Enlisted on April 11, 1876, in Boston by Lieut. Henry Lawton. Previous occupation was shoemaker. Assigned to Company B. Discharged on February 9, 1877, at Fort Abraham Lincoln, Dakota for disability, as a Private. He had blue eyes, brown hair, fair complexion and was 5'-5¾" in height.

KLAWITTER, FERDINAND, Private
On detached service from May 17, 1876 at Fort Abraham Lincoln, Dakota. Born in Prussia. Enlisted on January 20, 1875, at age 28 in Shreveport, Louisiana by Lieut. James M. Bell. Previous occupation was soldier. Discharged February 3, 1878, at Fort Rice, Dakota for disability as a Private of Excellent character. He had blue eyes, light hair, fair complexion and was 5'-7¼" in height. The Descriptive List and Records File, Custer Battlefield National Monument, has a letter, Headquarters, Company A, 7th Cavalry, February 7, 1873, Elizabethtown, Kentucky to Lieut. William Cooke, Adjutant 7th Cavalry requesting that Private Ferdinand Klawitter, then on detached service at Yorkville, S. C. be ordered to rejoin his company at Elizabethtown and notes that he has been on detached service since March 1, 1871.

LEWIS, DAVID W., Private
In confinement from April 26, 1876 at Fort Barrancas, Florida. Born in St. Louis, Missouri. Enlisted on July 13, 1875 at age 21½ at Shreveport, Louisiana by Lieut. James M. Bell. Previous occupation was laborer. Deserted March 29, 1876; surrendered on April 26, 1876. Discharged on July 12, 1880 at Camp Houston, Dakota upon expiration of service, as a Sergeant of excellent character. He had grey eyes, black hair, florid complexion and was 5'-10" in height.

LITTLEFIELD, JOHN L., Private
Born in Portland, Maine. Enlisted on March 28, 1876 at age 24 in Boston, Massachusetts by Lieut. Henry Lawton. Previous occupation was drummer. Deserted on July 7, 1876; apprehended on July 13, 1876; again deserted on January 22, 1877. He had blue eyes, brown hair, fair complexion and was 5'-10" in height.

MARTIN, WILLIAM, Private
Born in London, England. Enlisted on September 4, 1873, at age 23 in St. Louis by Captain Charles Bendire. Previous occupation was laborer. Discharged September 4, 1878, at Standing Rock Agency (Fort Yates), Dakota upon expiration of service, as a Private of good character. He had blue eyes, brown hair, fair complexion and was 5'-5¼" in height.

MASK, GEORGE B., Private
Killed in the hilltop fight on June 25. Born in Pittsburgh, Pennsylvania. Enlisted on November 15, 1872, at age 22 11/12 in Pittsburgh by Lieut. Calbraith Rodgers. Previous occupation was moulder. He had grey eyes, brown hair, fair complexion and was 5'-4" in height. Listed as G. B. Mask on the battle monument and elsewhere as C. B. Mask.

MORROW, WILLIAM E., Private
Born in Boston, Massachusetts. Enlisted on March 24, 1876 at age 21 5/12 in Boston by Lieut. Henry Lawton. Previous occupation was barber. Assigned to Company B. Deserted on April 12, 1877. He had hazel eyes, dark hair, fair complexion and was 5'-6¼" in height.

McCABE, JOHN, Private
Born in Cavan, Ireland. Second enlistment on April 11, 1876, at age 24 in New York City by Lieut. John Babcock. Assigned to Company B. Discharged October 19, 1880 at Fort Yates, Dakota for disability. He had brown eyes, brown hair, fair complexion and was 5'-8¼" in height.

McGURN, BERNARD, Private
Born in Newton, Massachusetts. Enlisted on March 23, 1876, at age 24 in Boston by Lieut. Henry Lawton. Previous occupation was plumber. Assigned to Company B. Discharged March 22, 1881, at Fort Yates, Dakota upon expiration of service, as a Private of very good character. He had blue eyes, brown hair, ruddy complexion and was 5'-7 7/8" in height.

McLAUGHLIN, TERENCE, Private
Born in Harrisburg, Pennsylvania. Enlisted on March 13, 1876, at age 24 in New York City by Lieut. John Babcock. Previous occupation was polisher. Assigned to Company B. Discharged March 21, 1881, at Fort Yates, Dakota upon expiration of service, as a Sergeant of excellent character. He had hazel eyes, brown hair, fair complexion and was 5'-6¾" in height. Listed as Terence McLaughlin in the Register of Enlistments, U.S. Army and elsewhere as Terrence McLaughlin.

McMASTERS, WILLIAM, Private
Born in Glasgow, Scotland. Enlisted on December 14, 1874, at age 29 in

Boston by Lieut. William Harper, Jr. Previous occupation was brickmason. Discharged December 13, 1879, at Fort Yates, Dakota, upon expiration of service, as a Private of good character. He had grey eyes, brown hair, ruddy complexion and was 5'-6½" in height.

O'BRIEN, THOMAS, Private
Born in Limerick, Ireland. Enlisted on March 31, 1876, at age 22 in Boston by Lieut. Henry Lawton. Previous occupation was currier. Assigned to Company B. Died September 15, 1876, at Fort Buford, Dakota of typhoid fever. His remains were re-interred in the Custer Battlefield National Cemetery, Grave 226A. He had blue eyes, light hair, fair complexion and was 5'-5½" in height.

O'NEILL, JAMES, Private
Sick in the hospital from May 17, 1876 at Fort Abraham Lincoln, Dakota. Born in Liverpool, England. Enlisted on November 8, 1872, at age 21 in Cincinnati by Lieut. James Wheelan. Previous occupation was laborer. Discharged on September 18, 1876, at Fort Lincoln for disability, as a Private. He had blue eyes, brown hair, florid complexion and was 5'-4¼" in height.

O'NEILL, JOHN, Private
Born in Tipperary, Ireland. Enlisted on January 8, 1872, at age 23 in New York City by Captain Edwin Sumner. Previous occupation was cooper. Discharged January 8, 1877, at Fort Abraham Lincoln, Dakota upon expiration of service, as a Private of excellent character. Re-enlisted January 10, 1877, at Fort Lincoln, by Lieut. George Wallace. Discharged January 9, 1882, at Fort Yates, Dakota upon expiration of service, as a Private of good character. He had brown eyes, black hair, dark complexion and was 5'-6" in height.

PYM, JAMES, Private
In the hilltop fight. Born in Oxfordshire, England. Enlisted December 11, 1874, at age 22 in Boston by Lieut. William Harper, Jr. Previous occupation was laborer. Awarded the Medal of Honor October 5, 1878, for volunteering and securing water under heavy fire in the Little Bighorn River fight. He had blue eyes, light hair, fair complexion and was 5'-7" in height. ". . .Jim Pym seemed to us in Miles City very unassertive, quiet and ordinary. To show you the kind he was, I once saw another man pull a gun on him in front of my shop. He took the gun out of the fellow's hand, tossed it away, knocked his assailant down, kicked him, and told him to leave town and not show his face in it again. The fellow left. Jim and Mrs. Jim, as we knew her, lived in a little log shack near Bill Reece's dance hall. Jim was mighty good to her. One day, a younger man was visiting with her at Jim's house, or at the dance hall. Unexpectedly Jim came on the scene. What was the younger man to expect, caught like that, from a man like Jim Pym? Certainly he looked for no mercy; doubtless he felt he would be killed like a rat. So he pulled his own gun without a word, and shot Jim dead. . ." Neil Clark, "He Captured the Vanishing West Before It Vanished" a story about Laton Huffman in *The American Magazine*, Feb. 1927, p. 74.

RANDALL, GEORGE F., Private
Born in Northfield, Vermont. Enlisted on December 15, 1874, at age 21 2/12 in Boston by Lieut. William Harper, Jr. Previous occupation was farmer.

Discharged December 14, 1879 at Fort Yates, Dakota, upon expiration of service, as a Farrier of good character. He had blue eyes, light hair, fair complexion and was 5'-7 1/8" in height.

RYAN, STEPHEN L., Private
During the hilltop fight he aided Captain Thomas McDougall in recovering and burying Lieut. Ben Hodgson's body. Born in Ireland. Fourth enlistment on December 1, 1874, at age 35 in Shreveport, Louisiana by Lieut. James M. Bell. Discharged November 30, 1879 at Fort Yates, Dakota, upon expiration of service, as a Private of good character. He had blue eyes, brown hair, fair complexion and was 5'-6" in height.

SAGER, HIRAM WALLACE, Private
In the hilltop fight. Born in Westport (or Whitehall), New York, Nov. 27, 1850, the youngest of the 12 children of David and Laura Wallace Sager. David was the son of Michael Sager of Pigeon Hill, Sutton, Quebec Prov. Canada. Laura was the daughter of Joshua Wallace, a Scotsman of Sutton, who died there at age 90. Laura Sager was buried at Siota Cemetery, Low Hampton, New York. Her marble headstone lists the names of two sons killed in the Civil war. Hiram Sager lived near Westport until Oct. 26, 1872, when he was enlisted at a stated age of 21 10/12 in Troy, New York, by Capt. Theodore Wint. Previous occupation was farmer. Assigned to Co. B, 7th Cav. while at Jefferson Barracks, Mo. Stationed at Shreveport, La. and Spartanburg, S. C. Deserted Apr. 6, 1874, apprehended Apr. 14, 1874. He was a member of the expedition to the Black Hills in 1874. He took part in the Little Bighorn River fight and was in other Indian fights. Discharged July 23, 1877, at Cedar Creek, Mont. Terr. per Gen Order Nr.47,AGO,1877, as a Private of good character. He had blue eyes, brown hair, ruddy complexion and was 5'-10" in height. Re-enlisted Apr. 9, 1878; served with troops that guarded construction crews of the Northern Pacific railway in Montana. On Dec. 8, 1880, at Bismarck, Dak. he married Margaret Ann Easton, formerly of Osakis, Minn., who was employed at Fort Yates, where Sager was stationed. Margaret was born Oct. 8, 1856 at New London, Minn., the daughter of Matthew and Margaret Easton. Hiram Sager was promoted to Sergeant, Troop B, effective Jan. 1, 1882. Discharged Apr. 8, 1883, upon expiration of service at Ft. Yates, as a Sergeant of excellent character. He departed that day for Campbell County, Dak. Before the end of the year Hiram, with his two brothers, Charles W. and Carlton W. had settled on claims fronting the Missouri River just west of LaGrace, Dak. Sometime before 1890 Charles and Hiram moved to new claims near Mound City, Dak. Margaret, wife of Hiram, taught school and their children were among her pupils. Their children were Edgar Roy; Laura Wallace; Bessie Ethel; Bertha Agnes; Paul Easton and Hollis Walter. Hiram Sager attended the first state convention in 1889. Appointed sheriff of Campbell County Nov. 4, 1890, and served that office 7 years. Appointed aide-de-camp and Colonel on Nov. 29, 1893, on the staff of Arthur Mellette, first governor of South Dakota. In April, 1899, the family moved to Spokane, Wash., after living in South Dakota for 16 years. Hiram worked on a farm, then as a street railway conductor. In 1906, after an illness, he was in charge of a Washington Water Power Co. electric substation until his death on Dec. 21, 1907. He was interred in Greenwood Cemetery, Spokane. Margaret, his wife, died Sept. 13, 1932 and was also interred in Greenwood Cemetery.

SHEA, DANIEL, Private
 Born in County Cork, Ireland. Enlisted on December 11, 1874, at age 22 in New York City by Lieut. Thomas Gregg. Previous occupation was laborer. Discharged December 10, 1879, at Fort Yates, Dakota upon expiration of service, as a Private of good character. He had blue eyes, brown hair, fair complexion and was 5'-7¼" in height.

SIMONS, PATRICK, Private
 Born in Sligo, Ireland. Enlisted on March 14, 1876, at age 21 in Baltimore by Lieut. William Wallace. Previous occupation was laborer. Assigned to Company B. Deserted on June 29, 1879. Released from service in February 1892 under an Act of Congress approved April 11, 1890. He had grey eyes, brown hair, ruddy complexion and was 5'-7¼" in height.

SPINNER, PHILIPP, Private
 In the valley and hilltop fights. Born in Baden, Germany. Enlisted on December 12, 1870, at age 24 4/12 at Fort Leavenworth by Lieut. Myles Moylan. Assigned to Company B, 7th Cavalry. Discharged December 12, 1875. Second enlistment on December 12, 1875 at the age of 29 in Shreveport, Louisiana by Lieut. James M. Bell. Discharged December 11, 1880, at Fort Yates, Dakota upon expiration of service, as a Private of good character. Third enlistment, in Company B, on January 4, 1881 in St. Louis by Lieut. Peter Bomus. Discharged January 3, 1886. Fourth enlistment on January 25, 1886 in Fort Leavenworth by Lieut. J. E. Macklin. At this time he was unmarried. He was transfered from Troop B, 3rd Cavalry to Troop B, 7th Cavalry and discharged on January 24, 1891. His fifth enlistment was on January 25, 1891, at age 45½ in Stanton, Nebraska by Lieut. Loyd McCormick. He had grey eyes, light brown hair, fair to ruddy complexion and was 5'-4½" to 6½" in height. Listed as Philipp Spinner in the Registers of Enlistments, U.S. Army, and his Oaths of Enlistments are so signed. Spinner was shot to death in Wisconsin in 1895.

STOUT, EDWARD, Private
 Born in Calhoun, Missouri. Second enlistment on January 25, 1875, at age 33 in Shreveport, Louisiana by Lieut. James M. Bell. Discharged January 24, 1880 at Fort Yates, Dakota upon expiration of service, as a Private of good character. He had brown eyes, brown hair, light complexion and was 5'-11" in height.

STOWERS, THOMAS J. (James Thomas), Private
 Born in Bucks County, Pennsylvania, December 3, 1848. Enlisted on September 3, 1864 at Norristown, Pennsylvania as a Private, Co. D, 119th Pennsylvania Infantry and served in campaigns in the winter of 1864-1865. Discharged June 28, 1865. Re-enlisted December 1, 1874 at age 26 in Chicago by Lieut. John Babcock. Previous occupation was farmer. Joined Co. B, 7th Cavalry at St. Louis Barracks, Missouri. Appointed Corporal March 7, 1879. Discharged November 30, 1879, at Fort Yates, Dakota, upon expiration of service, as a Corporal of excellent character. Listed as James Thomas in the Register of Enlistments U.S. Army. He had blue or hazel eyes, light or sandy hair, fair complexion and was 5'-5" to 7" in height. His pension, under the Act

of June 27, 1890, was $12.00 per month. A disability pension of $24.00 per month, for total deafness and general debility, was allowed under Special Act (Private Nr. 27i) dated March 28, 1902. The pension was increased to $30.00 on November 20, 1918, and to $32.00 on December 3, 1920. Admitted to the National Military Home, Dayton, Ohio on December 5, 1918, under the name of Thomas J. Stowers. He also resided at 108 Claiborne St. Nashville, Tennessee and at Michigan Ave. and 11th St. Nashville. He never married. Died on July 26, 1933, at Baxter, Tennessee and was interred the same day at Baxter.

TINKHAM, HENRY L. , Private
Born in Montpelier, Vermont. Enlisted on March 30, 1876, at age 21 4/12 in Boston by Lieut. Henry Lawton. Previous occupation was farmer. Assigned to Company B. Deserted April 22, 1877. He had blue eyes, brown hair, fair complexion and was 5'-8¾" in height.

TRUMBLE, WILLIAM, Private
Born in Iowa. Enlisted on September 9, 1873, at age 21 in Cincinnati by Lieut. Adam Kramer. Previous occupation was laborer. Discharged September 9, 1878 at Standing Rock, Dakota, upon expiration of service, as a Private of good character. Re-enlisted September 21, 1878, in St. Louis by Lieut. W. C. Forbush, and was assigned to Troop M. Discharged September 20, 1883. Third enlistment on September 22, 1883, at Fort Meade, Dakota by Lieut. Loyd McCormick; assigned to Troop E. At this time he was not married. Discharged January 19, 1889. Fourth enlistment on January 26, 1889 at the age of 39½ at Fort Sill, Indian Territory by Lieut. G. O. Cress. Assigned to Troop C, 8th Cavalry. He had grey eyes, brown hair, florid complexion and was 5'-8" in height and was illiterate. His name is listed as William Trimble in the Register of Enlistments, U. S. Army and as William Trumble on his Oath of Enlistment.

WALLACE, RICHARD A., Private
Born in Boston. Enlisted on December 7, 1874 at age 22 in Boston by Lieut. William Harper, Jr. Previous occupation was teamster. Drowned on July 25, 1876 near the mouth of the Bighorn River, Montana Territory while crossing stream to go on picket guard. He had grey eyes, dark hair, sallow complexion and was 5'-7½" in height.

WIGHT, EDWIN B., Private
Born in Cass County, Maine. Enlisted on March 29, 1876, at age 24 in Boston by Lieut. Henry Lawton. Previous occupation was stonemason. Assigned to Company B. Discharged March 28, 1881 at Fort Yates, Dakota upon expiration of service, as a Private of very good character. He had blue eyes, brown hair, ruddy complexion and was 5'-8½" in height.

WOODS, AARON, Private
Born in Philadelphia. Enlisted on September 2, 1873, at age 21 in Philadelphia by Lieut. William Volkmar. Previous occupation was laborer. Discharged September 2, 1878, at Standing Rock Agency, Dakota, as a Private of good character. He had brown eyes, dark hair, ruddy complexion and was 5'-7½" in height.

COMPANY C IN 1876

The company remained a part of the garrison at Fort A. Lincoln, Dak. until May 5 when they joined the regiment in camp below the post in preparation for the departure of the Sioux expedition. The regiment left Fort Lincoln on May 17.

Company C participated in a scouting expedition for 22 miles up the Little Missouri River and returned on May 30. The regiment was engaged in the Little Bighorn River fight until relieved on June 27 by forces under Brig. Gen. Terry. The regiment returned to Fort Lincoln on Sept. 26 where the company occupied quarters. The company moved into camp on October 16 and on October 21, Companies A, C, D and G, under the command of Maj. Marcus Reno left for Standing Rock Agency to disarm and dismount the Indians there. They arrived at the agency on October 22 and returned to Fort Lincoln on November 3 and moved into camp on November 12. On Nov. 18 the company left for Fort Totten, Dak. for winter station and arrived at Fort Seward on November 23 and left there on Nov. 25 and arrived at Fort Totten on Nov. 28. The company marched 1992 miles in the year.

The following were casualties in the Little Bighorn River fight. Killed: Capt. Thomas Custer, First Lieut. James Calhoun, Second Lieut. Henry Harrington. First Sergt. Edwin Bobo, Sergeants Jeremiah Finley and August Finckle, Corporals Henry French, John Foley and Daniel Ryan, Trumpeters Thomas Bucknell and William Kramer, Saddler George Howell, Blacksmith John King, Privates Fred Allan, John Brightfield, Christopher Criddle, George Eiseman, Gustave Engle, James Farrand, Patrick Griffin, James Hathersall, John Lewis, August Meyer, Frederick Meier, Edgar Phillips, John Rauter, Edward Rix, James Russell, Samuel Shade, Jeremiah, Shea, Nathan Short, Ludwick St John, Alpheus Stuart, Ygnatz Stungewitz, John Thadus, Garret Van Allen, Oscar Warner, Willis Wright and Henry Wyman. Those wounded were: Privates James Bennett, John McGuire, Peter Thompson, and Alfred Whitaker. Private James Bennett died at Fort Lincoln on July 6 of wounds received in the fight.

Officers serving with the company in the year were Capt. Thomas Custer, Captain Henry Jackson (replacement for Capt. Custer), First Lieut. James Calhoun, Lieut. Charles Varnum (replacement for Lieut. Calhoun), Second Lieuts. Henry Harrington, George Oscar Eaton (transferred from 5th Cavalry to occupy vacancy created by death of Lieut. Harrington) and Horatio Sickel, Jr.* (transferred to 7th Cavalry to occupy the vacancy created by the transfer of Lieut. Eaton).

* *Lieut. Horatio Gates Sickel, Jr. was born in Pennsylvania and was appointed to the USMA from that state on Sept. 1, 1872. He graduated on June 14, 1876 and was appointed 2nd Lieut. 14th Inf. on June 15. He was transferred to the 5th Cavalry on July 28, 1876. The appointment by transfer, to be 2nd Lieut. 5th Cav. was revoked by GO 103,AGO,76. He was transferred to the 7th Cav. same order, to date from July 28, 1876. Promoted 1st Lieut. Dec. 17, 1882.*

73

COMPANY C AT THE LITTLE BIGHORN

	Absent	Present	Wounded	Died OWRT	Killed	Survived
Captain		1			1	
1st Lieut.		1			1	
2nd Lieut.		1			1	
1st Sgt.		1			1	
Sergt.	1	4			2	3
Corporal		4			3	1
Trumpeter		2			2	
Saddler		1			1	
Farrier		1				1
Wagoner		1				1
Blacksmith		1			1	
Private	6	44	4	1	26	23
Totals	7	62	4	1	39	29

COMPANY C ON JUNE 30, 1876

Enlisted present for duty 15
Enlisted present extra duty 5
Enlisted absent detached service 3
Enlisted absent sick 5
Enlisted absent in arrest 2
Sergeants 3
Corporals 1
Farrier 1
Wagoner 1
Privates 24
Total enlisted 30
Aggregate 30
Aggregate in May 69
Officers killed 3
Enlisted killed 36
Attached civil correspondent killed 1
Wounded 4
Horses serviceable 10
Horses unservicable 2
Horses lost 46

CUSTER, THOMAS WARD, Captain

Killed with the Custer battalion on June 25. Born on March 15, 1845, in New Rumley, Ohio. He enlisted on September 2, 1861 as a Private, Company H, 21st Ohio Volunteer Infantry and engaged in the battle of Stone's River, December 31, 1862-January 3, 1863. In the escort of Maj. Gen. James Negley from April 2 to December, 1863, and participated in the battle of Chickamauga September 19-20, the battle of Jonesboro and the skirmish at Missionary Ridge on November 24, where he was in the escort for General Grant. He re-enlisted as a veteran volunteer on January 1, 1864, and engaged in the battle of Kenesaw Mountain in 1864. From June 23 to August, 1864, he was detailed in the escort of General Palmer and he was later in the escort of General Thomas. In the engagements under General Sherman in the campaign from Chattanooga to Atlanta, and on to Galesville, Alabama. Mustered out as a Corporal on October 23, 1864, to accept a commission as Second Lieutenant, Company B, 6th Michigan Cavalry with rank from July 11, 1864. From November 8, 1864, he served as aide-de-camp to his brother, Maj. Gen. George Custer until he was mustered out of volunteer service. Participated in the battle of Waynesboro March 2, 1865, and the battle of Dinwiddie Courthouse on March 31 and at Five Forks and Namozine Church and Sayler's Creek. Received the Medal of Honor for his distinguished conduct at Namozine Church and a second Medal of Honor for his gallant conduct at Sayler's Creek. After the Civil War he served in Texas until mustered out on April 24, 1866. He received appointment as Second Lieutenant, 1st Cavalry, effective from February 23, 1866, and resigned on July 27, 1866, to accept a First Lieutenancy in the 7th Cavalry to rank from July 28, 1866. He was Acting Quartermaster on December 8, 1866, and served as regimental quartermaster from December 3, 1866, until March 10, 1867. He received the brevets of First Lieutenant, Captain and Major for his services at Waynesboro, Sayler's Creek and Namozine Church. Participated in the arrest of Rain-In-The-Face at Standing Rock Agency, Dakota in January, 1875. Promoted to Captain December 2, 1875. Departing from Fort Abraham Lincoln, Dakota on May 17, 1876, Captain Custer participated in the Sioux expedition in command of Company C. His remains were interred on the battlefield and exhumed in July, 1877 and re-interred in Grave 1488A, Fort Leavenworth National Cemetery, August 3, 1877.

CALHOUN, JAMES, First Lieutenant

Killed with the Custer battalion on June 25 while in command of Company L. Born on August 24, 1845, in Cincinnati, Ohio. Entered military service from Ohio as a Private on January 14, 1864 in Company D, 14th Infantry. Promoted to First Sergeant on February 1, 1865; served with the 14th Infantry until October 24, 1867. On July 31, 1867, he was commissioned a Second Lieutenant, 32nd Infantry, at Camp Warner, Oregon. He served in the field in Arizona and at Camp Grant until July, 1869. On April 19, 1869, he was transferred to the 21st Infantry (when the 32nd Regiment was consolidated with the 21st). Lieut. Calhoun requested transfer to the 7th Cavalry. On October 29, 1870, during the reorganization of the army, he was placed on the list of supernumeraries and was unassigned and awaiting orders until January 1, 1871, when he was assigned to the 7th Cavalry. Promoted to First Lieutenant effective January 9, 1871, while at Bagdad, Kentucky. He was enroute, with a detachment of recruits, to join the 7th Cavalry in February, 1871, and was on duty with the regiment until July, 1871, when he attended a court of inquiry in Arizona until November, 1871. Rejoined his regiment in Kentucky and served there until July, 1872. In 1872 he married Margaret Emma Custer, sister of George and Thomas Custer. From Kentucky, Lieut. Calhoun was transferred to North Carolina where he served until March, 1873. He was in Colonel David Stanley's expedition, escorting the Northern Pacific Railroad Survey and exploring the valley of the Yellowstone River in Montana from May 7 to September 21, 1873, and then in winter station at Fort Lincoln, Dakota. In the expedition exploring the Black Hills in July and August, 1874, and at Fort Seward, Dakota from March 23 to April 17, 1876. On May 17, 1876, he departed from Fort Abraham Lincoln with the 7th Cavalry to participate in the Sioux expedition. Killed while on duty with Company L in the Little Bighorn River fight on June 25. His remains were exhumed from the battlefield in July, 1877 and re-interred in Grave 1489A, Fort Leavenworth National Cemetery on August 3, 1877. He was survived by his wife, Margaret.

HARRINGTON, HENRY MOORE, Second Lieutenant

Missing with the Custer battalion and presumed killed on June 25. Born on April 30, 1849, in Albion, Orleans County, New York. Entered the U.S. Military Academy on July 1, 1868 by appointment from Coldwater, Michigan. He was the 2429th graduate of the Academy, ranking 19th in his class of 57 graduates, graduating June 14, 1872. On that date he was appointed a Second Lieutenant in the Seventh Regiment of Cavalry. He accepted the commission on August 5. From October 31, 1872, to March 31, 1873, he was on garrison duty at Charlotte, North Carolina and in April of that year he departed from Yankton, Dakota for frontier duty. On Colonel David Stanley's expedition, escorting the Northern Pacific Railroad Survey and exploring the valley of the Yellowstone River from May 7 to September 21, 1873. His company then went into winter station at Fort Rice, Dakota until June, 1874. On leave of absence from October 19 to November 10, 1873. Engaged in Lieut. Colonel George Custer's expedition exploring the Black Hills in July and August, 1874, when he returned with his company to Fort Rice. From October 10, 1875 to March 9, 1876, he was on leave of absence and was at Fort Seward, Dakota, from March 9 to April 17 when his company proceeded to Fort Abraham Lincoln, Dakota. On May 17, 1876, he departed from Fort Lincoln with Company C, 7th Cavalry to participate in the Sioux expedition. He was 27 years old at the time of his death and was survived by his wife, Grace Harrington, and daughter Grace Aileen (born at Fort A. Lincoln). The story is related that Mrs. Harrington, while living in the east after her husband's death, disappeared and was missing two years. She was found in a small town in Texas suffering from amnesia and pneumonia. Her daughter, Grace Aileen, was postmistress at the Military Academy for many years. *The Fargo* (N.D.) *Forum*, May 16, 1947, p. 27.

BOBO, EDWIN, First Sergeant

Killed with the Custer battalion on June 25. Born in Franklin County, Ohio. Second enlistment on December 23, 1872, at age 27 in Charlotte, North Carolina by Lieut. Wolfe. Previous occupation was clerk. He had hazel eyes, brown hair, fair complexion and was 5'-6½" in height. Listed as Edwin Bobo on the battle monument.

AUGUST FINCKLE, Sergeant

Killed in battle on June 25. Born in Berlin, Germany. Enlisted on January

27, 1872, at age 27 in Chicago by Captain Samuel Young. Previous occupation was clerk. He had grey eyes, dark hair, dark complexion and was 6'-0½" in height. Listed as August Finckle on the battle monument.

FINLEY, JEREMIAH, Sergeant
Killed in battle on June 25. Born in Tipperary, Ireland. Arrived in the United States in 1860 and served in the Civil War. Second enlistment on Sept. 18, 1873, at age 32 at camp on the Heart River, Dakota, by Lieut. James Calhoun. Previous occupation was laborer. Finley was a tailor in the regiment and made the buckskin jacket that George Custer wore on the Sioux expedition. Listed as Jere. Finley on the battle monument. He had grey eyes, brown hair, light complexion and was 5'-7" in height. He was survived by his widow and son, Jeremiah M. Finley (born five months after his father's death). His widow married Private John Donahue of Company K and later resided at Oberon, North Dakota.

HANLEY, RICHARD P., Sergeant
With the pack train in the hilltop fight. Born in Boston. Fifth enlistment on September 18, 1873, at age 30 in Cincinnati by Lieut. Adam Kramer. Discharged on September 18, 1878, at Camp James G. Sturgis, Dakota upon expiration of service, as a Sergeant of excellent character. He had blue eyes, dark hair, fair complexion and was 5'-11½" in height. Awarded the Medal of Honor on October 5, 1878 for re-capturing a stampeded mule loaded with ammunition. He caught the pack mule single-handed and without orders within the enemy lines and under a galling fire lasting some twenty minutes in the Little Bighorn River fight.

KANIPE, DANIEL ALEXANDER, Sergeant
Carried messages from Lieut. Col. George Custer to Captain McDougall, Company B, in command of guard for pack train. Born on April 15, 1853 near Marion, McDowell County, North Carolina, the son of Jacob Knipe and Isabella Mosteller Knipe. Enlisted on August 7, 1872, at a represented age of 21 in Lincolnton, North Carolina by Captain Verling Hart. Previous occupation was farmer. Participated in Colonel David Stanley's Yellowstone expedition, escorting the Northern Pacific Railroad Survey and exploring the valley of the Yellowstone River, May-September, 1873 and the expedition exploring the Black Hills in July and August, 1874. He married Missouri Ann Wyskoff Bobo, widow of First Sergeant Edwin Bobo, on April 12, 1877. Discharged on August 7, 1877, at Fort Totten, Dakota upon expiration of service, as a Sergeant of excellent character. He was a Captain in the 19th North Carolina Militia in World War I. Died on July 18, 1926, at Marion, North Carolina. He had hazel eyes, light hair, fair complexion and was 5'-11" in height. Listed as Daniel Knipe in the Register of Enlistments, U.S. Army.

MILLER, EDWIN, Sergeant
On detached service from May 5, 1876, at Fort Abraham Lincoln, Dakota. Born in Hanover, Germany. Second enlistment on November 30, 1872, at age 23 in Charlotte, North Carolina by Lieut. James Calhoun. Previous occupation was clerk. Discharged on November 30, 1877, at Fort Lincoln upon expiration of service, as a Sergeant of good character. He had hazel eyes, dark hair, dark

complexion and was 5'-10" in height. The Descriptive List and Records File, Custer Battlefield National Monument, has a letter to the Commanding Officer, 7th Cavalry, December 15, 1868, listing Private Edwin Miller, Company E, 7th Cavalry, as having surrendered or having been apprehended from desertion on July 12, 1868.

CRANDALL, CHARLES A., Corporal
Born in New Milford, Connecticut. Enlisted on December 9, 1872 at age 24 in Scranton, Pennsylvania by Captain Eugene Beaumont. Previous occupation was lawyer. Discharged December 9, 1877 at Fort A. Lincoln, Dakota upon expiration of service, as a Private, with character reference of "a good soldier." He had grey eyes, brown hair, dark complexion and was 5'-10½" in height.

FOLEY, JOHN, Corporal
Killed in battle on June 25. Born in Salem, Massachusetts. Enlisted on September 18, 1873, at age 23 in Boston by Lieut. James Ropes. Previous occupation was shoecutter. He had blue eyes, grey hair, ruddy complexion and was 5'-8½" in height. Listed as Jno. Foley on the battle monument.

FRENCH, HENRY ELDON, Corporal
Killed in battle on June 25. Born in Portsmouth, New Hampshire. Enlisted on January 22, 1872 at age 22 in Brooklyn, New York by Lieut. John Mahnken. Previous occupation was painter. He had hazel eyes, brown hair, fair complexion and was 5'-6" in height. Listed as H. E. French on the battle monument.

RYAN, DANIEL, Corporal
Killed in battle on June 25. Born in Syracuse, New York, Enlisted on December 18, 1872 at age 21 in New York City by Captain Edwin Sumner. Previous occupation was laborer. He had grey eyes, dark hair, fair complexion and was 5'-7¼" in height. Listed as Dan'l Ryan on the battle monument.

BUCKNELL, THOMAS J., Trumpeter
Killed in battle on June 25. Born in Cincinnati. Second enlistment on September 23, 1875, at age 26 in Cincinnati by Lieut. Patrick Cusack. He had grey eyes, light hair, light complexion and was 5'-8¼" in height. Listed as T. J. Bucknell on the battle monument.

KRAMER, WILLIAM, Trumpeter
Killed in battle on June 25. Born in Reading, Pennsylvania. Enlisted on October 7, 1875 at age 27 in Cincinnati by Lieutenant Patrick Cusack. Previous occupation was painter. He had grey eyes, brown hair, ruddy complexion and was 5'-5¾" in height. Listed as Wm. Kramer on the battle monument. Not listed in *The Bismarck Tribune* Extra, July 6, 1876.

HOWELL, GEORGE, Saddler
Killed in battle on June 25. Born in Cold Springs, New York. Second enlistment on December 4, 1872 at age 26 in New York City by Captain Edwin Sumner. Previous occupation was harness maker. He had grey eyes, dark hair, fair complexion and was 5'-5¾" in height. Listed as Geo. Howell on the battle monument and elsewhere as Hamel and Hammel.

FITZGERALD, JOHN, Farrier

Born in Staffordshire, England. Fourth enlistment on January 19, 1872, at age 30 in New York City by Lieut. John Mahnken. Discharged on January 19, 1877 at Fort Totten, Dakota upon expiration of service, as a Farrier. He had blue eyes, brown hair, fair complexion and was 5'-4" in height. Peter Thompson, in his account of the fight, related that Brennan and Fitzgerald turned their horses to the rear when they had gone two miles beyond the lone tepee, just before the Little Bighorn River fight.

STARK, FRANK, Wagoner

On detached service at Yellowstone Depot, Montana Territory? Born in Bavaria, Germany. Second enlistment on September 7, 1875, at age 26 in St. Louis by Lieut. William Harper, Jr. Discharged on September 6, 1880, at Belle Fourche, Dakota, upon expiration of service, as a Private of good character. He had hazel eyes, brown hair, fair complexion and was 5'-7½" in height. Listed as Frank Stark in the Register of Enlistments, U.S. Army and elsewhere as Starck.

KING, JOHN, Blacksmith

Killed in battle on June 25. Born in Basel, Switzerland. Enlisted on September 22, 1875, at age 26 in Cincinnati by Lieut. Patrick Cusack. Previous occupation was horseshoer. He had grey eyes, brown hair, dark complexion and was 5'-5¼" in height. Listed as Jno. King on the battle monument.

ALLAN, FRED E., Private

Killed in battle on June 25. Born in Milton, England. Enlisted on October 3, 1873, at age 25 in Boston, Mass. by Lieut. James Ropes. Previous occupation was watchmaker. He had brown eyes, black hair, dark complexion and was 5'-8 1/8" in height. Listed on the battle monument as F.E. Allan and as Fred E. Allan in the Register of Enlistments, U.S. Army.

ANDERSON, CHARLES L., Private

Deserted at camp on the Powder River, Montana Territory on June 20, 1876. Born in Albion, New York. Enlisted on August 15, 1875, at age 29 in Boston by Lieut. Henry Lawton. Previous occupation was sailor. He had grey eyes, dark hair, dark complexion and was 5'-8¼" in height. At the time of desertion, there was due the U.S. for Ordnance stores, $67.39.

ARNOLD, HERBERT, Private

On detached service from May 5, 1876 at Fort Abraham Lincoln, Dakota. Born in Rocky Hill, Connecticut. Enlisted on October 30, 1872, at age 21 in Springfield, Massachusetts by Captain Theodore Wint. Previous occupation was burnisher. Discharged on June 16, 1877, at Fort Totten, Dakota per Special Order NR.72, Department of Dakota, 1877 as a Corporal of very good character,. He had grey eyes, brown hair, ruddy complexion and was 5'-7½" in height.

BENNETT, JAMES C., Private

Wounded in the body in the hilltop fight on June 26. Died at 3 o'clock, July 5, on the steamer *Far West*. Born in Shelby, Ohio. Second enlistment on September 11, 1875 at age 27 in New York City by Lieut. John Babcock.

Previous occupation was clerk. He had grey eyes, dark hair, dark complexion and was 5'-6¼" in height. Listed elsewhere as Charles Bennett and James E. Bennett. Recorded in the Returns of the 7th Cavalry as having died on July 6. Recorded in the Register of Enlistments, U.S. Army, as having died on July 5.

BISCHOFF, CHARLES H., Private
Born in Bremen, Germany. Enlisted on November 23, 1872 at age 21 in Philadelphia by Captain Samuel Whitside. Previous occupation was barber. Discharged on November 23, 1877 at Fort Abraham Lincoln, Dakota upon expiration of service, as a Sergeant of excellent character. He had blue eyes, light hair, fair complexion and was 5'-4½" in height.

BRANDLE, WILLIAM, Private
Born in Wurtemburg, Germany. Enlisted on Oct. 8, 1873 at age 21 in St. Louis by Capt. Charles Bendire. Previous occupation was laborer. Discharged on Oct. 8, 1878 at Camp James G. Sturgis, Dakota upon expiration of service, as a Sergeant of excellent character. He had hazel eyes, brown hair, fair complexion and was 5'-9¼" in height. Listed as William Brandle in the Register of Enlistments, U.S. Army, and elsewhere as Brandal.

BRENNAN, JOHN, Private
Born in County Waterford, Ireland. Enlisted on September 24, 1875 at age 26 in St. Louis by Lieut. John Thompson. Previous occupation was laborer. Dishonorably discharged on December 4, 1879 at Fort Meade, Dakota per Special Order Nr.265,AGO,1879, as a Private. He had grey eyes, brown hair, light complexion and was 5'-5¾" in height. Peter Thompson related that Brennan and John Fitzgerald turned their horses to the rear after they had gone two miles beyond the lone tepee just before the Little Bighorn River fight.

BRIGHTFIELD, JOHN, Private
Killed in battle on June 25. Born in Dearborn County, Indiana. Enlisted on October 7, 1875 at age 22 in Cincinnati by Lieut. Patrick Cusack. Previous occupation was cabinetmaker. He had brown eyes, brown hair, dark complexion and was 5'-9¼" in height. Listed as Jno. Brightfield on the battle monument.

CORCORAN, JOHN, Private
In confinement from May 5, 1876 at Fort A. Lincoln, Dakota. Born in Staffordshire, England. Enlisted in October 8, 1873, at age 21 in Philadelphia, Pa. by Lieut William Volkmar. Previous occupation was boltmaker. Discharged on October 8, 1878, at Camp James G. Sturgis, Dakota, upon expiration of service, as a Private. He had blue eyes, dark hair, ruddy complexion and was 5'-8" in height.

CRIDDLE, CHRISTOPHER, Private
Killed in battle on June 25. Born in New Canton, Virginia. Enlisted on September 22, 1875 at age 24 in Cincinnati by Lieut. Patrick Cusack. Previous occupation was laborer. He had grey eyes, brown hair, dark complexion and was 5'-8" in height. Listed as Christopher Criddle on the battle monument.

EISEMAN, GEORGE, Private
Killed in battle on June 25. Born in Philadelphia. Enlisted on January 15,

1872 at age 21 in Philadelphia by Captain Samuel Whitside. Previous occupation was brushmaker. He had blue eyes, dark hair, fair complexion and was 5'-5¼" in height. Listed as Geo. Eiseman on the Company C Muster Roll, June 30, 1876 and on the battle monument, and as Geo. Eisemann in the Register of Enlistments, U.S. Army.

ENGLE, GUSTAVE, Private
Killed in battle on June 25. Born in Wurtemburg, Germany. Second enlistment on September 27, 1875 at age 26 in Cincinnati by Lieut. Patrick Cusack. He had brown eyes, brown hair, fair complexion and was 5'-8" in height. Listed as Gustave Engle on the battle monument and as Gustave Engel in the Register of Enlistments, U.S. Army.

FARRAND, JAMES, Private
Killed with the Custer battalion on June 25. Born in Washington County, Illinois. Second enlistment on November 16, (10?), 1875 at age 36 at Fort Abraham Lincoln, Dakota by Lieut. James Calhoun. Previous occupation was carpenter. He had dark eyes, black hair, dark complexion and was 5'-8" in height. Listed as James Farrand on the battle monument.

FARRAR, MORRIS, Private
Born in Amesbury, Massachusetts. He was enlisted on January 23, 1872, at age 26 in New York City by Lieut. John Mahnken. Previous occupation was grinder. Discharged on January 23, 1877, at Fort Totten, Dakota upon expiration of his service, as a Sergeant of excellent character. Re-enlisted on September 1, 1881 in Company C, 7th Cavalry, in Boston by Captain Sam Ferris, at the age of 35. Listed as Morris Farrar in the Register of Enlistments, U.S. Army and on his Oath of Enlistment. He had blue or brown eyes, black hair, dark complexion and was 5'-8¾ to 9" in height.

FOWLER, ISAAC, Private
Born in Dark County, Ohio. Enlisted on September 29, 1873 at age 29 in Cincinnati by Lieut. Adam Kramer. Previous occupation was farmer. Discharged on September 29, 1878 at Camp James G. Sturgis upon expiration of service, as a Private of good character. He had brown eyes, dark hair, fair complexion and was 5'-7¼" in height.

GRIFFIN, PATRICK, Private
Killed in battle on June 25. Born in Dingle Kerry, Ireland, the son of Edward and Rebecca Lowe Griffin. Enlisted on October 16, 1872 at age 24 in Toledo, Ohio by Captain Samuel Young. He had black eyes, dark hair, ruddy complexion and was 5'-9" in height. Listed as Pat'k Griffin on the battle monument.

HATHERSALL, JAMES, Private
Killed in battle on June 25. Born in Liverpool, England. Second enlistment on September 13, 1875 at age 26 in New York City by Lieut. John Babcock. He had blue eyes, light hair, fair complexion and was 5'-6" in height. Listed as James Hathersall on the battle monument and as Hattisoll in the *Bismarck Tribune* Extra, July 6, 1876.

JORDAN, JOHN, Private

Born in New York City. Second enlistment on November 28, 1875 at age 33 at Fort Abraham Lincoln, Dakota by Lieut. James Calhoun. Discharged on November 27, 1880 at Fort Meade, Dakota upon expiration of service, as a Farrier of excellent character. He had hazel eyes, black hair, dark complexion and was 5'-5¼" in height.

KANE, WILLIAM, Private

In the hilltop fight. Born in Kerry, Ireland. Second enlistment on November 21, 1872 at age 38 in St. Louis by Lieut. Oscar Elting. Discharged on November 27, 1877 at Fort Totten, Dakota upon expiration of service, as a Private of excellent character. He had grey eyes, brown hair, fair complexion and was 5'-7½" in height.

LEWIS, JOHN, Private

Killed in battle on June 25. Born in Povey County, Pennsylvania. Second enlistment on December 11, 1872 at age 26 in Charlotte, North Carolina by Lieut. Wolfe. He had grey eyes, brown hair, fair complexion and was 5'-8" in height. His name is listed as Jno. Lewis on the battle monument and elsewhere as Johnathan Lewis.

LOVETT, MEREDITH, Private

In confinement from May 5, 1876, at Fort Abraham Lincoln, Dakota. Born in Delaware County, Penn. Enlisted on August 16, 1873, at age 21 in Philadelphia by Lieut. William Volkmar. Previous occupation was laborer. Deserted April 14, 1875; apprehended May 7, 1875. Dishonorably discharged March 26, 1877, at Fort Totten, Dakota per General Court Martial Order Nr.45, Department of Dakota, 1877, as a Private. He had blue eyes, dark hair, ruddy complexion and was 5'-7¾" in height. Listed elsewhere as Meredith Lovelt.

McCREEDY, THOMAS, Private

On detached service from May 5, 1876 at Fort Abraham Lincoln, Dakota. Born in Dublin, Ireland. Enlisted on October 22, 1872 at age 21 in Philadelphia by Captain Samuel Whitside. Previous occupation was morocco finisher. Discharged on October 22, 1877, at Sulphur Creek, Dakota, upon expiration of service, as a Corporal of excellent character. He had grey eyes, brown hair, ruddy complexion and was 5'-7¾" in height.

MAHONEY, JOHN, Private

With the pack train detail on June 25? Born in Cork, Ireland. Enlisted on September 24, 1875 at age 27 in St. Louis by Lieut. John Thompson. Previous occupation was laborer. Discharged on September 30, 1880 at Fort Meade, Dakota upon expiration of service, as a Private of excellent character. He had blue eyes, dark hair, dark complexion and was 5'-7" in height.

MEYER, AUGUST, Private

Killed in battle on June 25. Born in Hanover, Germany. Enlisted on October 11, 1875 at age 28 in Cincinnati by Lieut. Patrick Cusack. Previous occupation was teamster. He had blue eyes, brown hair, dark complexion and was 5'-6" in height. Listed as Mayer (1) in the *Bismarck Tribune* Extra July 6, 1876. Listed as August Meyer on the battle monument.

MEIER, FREDERICK, Private
Killed in battle on June 25. Born in Delmenhort, Germany. Enlisted on December 24, 1875 at age 21 in St. Louis Barracks, Missouri by Lieut. John Thompson. Previous occupation was tailor. Assigned to Company C. He had hazel eyes, brown hair, fair complexion and was 5'-6½" in height. Listed as Fred'k Meier on the battle monument and as Frederick Meier in the Register of Enlistments, U.S. Army. Listed as Mayer (2) in the *Bismarck Tribune* Extra, July 6, 1876. Listed as Fred Meier on the Company C Muster Roll June 30, 1876.

McGUIRE, JOHN, Private
Wounded in the right arm in the hilltop fight on June 26. Transported to Fort Abraham Lincoln, Dakota on the supply steamer *Far West*. Born in Indiana County, Pennsylvania. Enlisted on October 4, 1875 at age 21 in Pittsburgh by Lieut. Thomas Gregg. Previous occupation was farmer. Discharged on October 3, 1880 at Fort Meade, Dakota upon expiration of service, as a Private of very good character. He had brown eyes, brown hair, florid complexion and was 5'-8" in height. Listed elsewhere as Maguire.

MULLIN, MARTIN, Private
With the pack train detail on June 25? Born in Cork, Ireland. Enlisted on January 3, 1873 at age 25 2/12 in Pittsburgh by Lieut. Calbraith Rodgers. Previous occupation was laborer. Deserted on January 23, 1873; apprehended on January 27, 1873 at St. Louis, Missouri. Sentenced to 30 days confinement and a $10 fine on May 2, 1876. Discharged on January 3, 1878 at Fort Totten, Dakota upon expiration of service, as a Private. He had blue eyes, brown hair, fair complexion and was 5'-5" in height.

NITSCHE, OTTOCAR, Private
Born in Germany. Enlisted on December 6, 1872 at age 22 in New York City by Captain Edwin Sumner. Previous occupation was merchant. Discharged on December 6, 1877 at Fort Totten, Dakota upon expiration of service, as a Corporal of excellent character. He had blue eyes, light hair, fair complexion and was 5'-5¼" in height.

ORR, CHARLES M., Private
With the pack train detail on June 25? Born in Parris, Canada. Enlisted on September 24, 1875 at age 28 in St. Louis by Lieut. John Thompson. Previous occupation was painter. Discharged on September 23, 1880, at Fort Meade, Dakota upon expiration of service, as a Private of very good character. He had blue eyes, brown hair, complexion and was 5'-9¾" in height.

PHILLIPS, EDGAR, Private
Killed in battle on June 25. Born in Lynn, Massachusetts. Enlisted on September 24, 1875 at age 22 in Chicago by Lieut. Edmund Luff. Previous occupation was farmer. He had blue eyes, light hair, fair complexion and was 5'-5¾" in height. Listed as Edgar Phillips on the battle monument and as Edgar Philips on the Company C Muster Roll June 30, 1876.

RAUTER, JOHN, Private
Killed in battle on June 25. Born in Tyrol, Switzerland. Enlisted on October 4, 1873 at age 27 in Philadelphia by Lieut. William Volkmar. Previous

occupation was butcher. He had blue eyes, dark hair, dark complexion and was 5'-9¾" in height. Listed as Jno. Rauter on the battle monument and on his Oath of Enlistment and elsewhere as Ranter.

RIX, EDWARD, Private
Killed in battle on June 25. Born in Lowell, Massachusetts. Enlisted on October 1, 1873 at age 23 2/12 in Chicago by Captain Henry Carroll. Previous occupation was railroader. He had grey eyes, light brown hair, fair complexion and was 5'-5¾" in height. Listed as Edw'd Rix on the battle monument and elsewhere as Edward Rice.

RUSSELL, JAMES HENRY, Private
Killed in battle on June 25. Born in Corpus Christi, Texas. His father was a member of the first legislature of Florida and a Major in the Confederate States Army. James was enlisted on September 11, 1873, at age 21 8/12 in Boston by Lieut. James Ropes. Previous occupation was schoolteacher. He had grey eyes, brown hair, fair complexion and was 5'5" in height. Listed as J. H. Russell on the battle monument.

SHADE, SAMUEL S., Private
Killed in battle on June 25. Born in Jamestown, Pennsylvania. Enlisted on August 3, 1875 at age 28 in Baltimore by Lieut. Charles Cresson. Previous occupation was schoolteacher. He had blue eyes, light hair, fair complexion and was 5'-8¾" in height. Listed as S. S. Shade on the battle monument.

SHEA, JEREMIAH, Private
Killed in battle on June 25. Born in London, England. Enlisted on September 6, 1875 at age 21½ in Boston by Lieut. William Harper, Jr. Previous occupation was hostler. He had grey eyes, brown hair, ruddy complexion and was 5'-6¼" in height. Listed as Jere Shea on the battle monument.

SHORT, NATHAN, Private
Killed in battle on June 25. Born in Lehigh County, Pennsylvania. Enlisted on October 9, 1875 at age 21 in St. Louis by Lieut. John Thompson. Previous occupation was laborer. He had grey eyes, brown hair, fair complexion and was 5'-7" in height. Listed as Nathan Short on the battle monument.

ST. JOHN, LUDWICK, Private
Killed in battle on June 25. Born in Columbia, Missouri. Second enlistment on December 15, 1874, at age 30 at Fort Rice, Dakota by Lieut Edward Mathey. Deserted on May 8, 1875, at Fort Rice; surrendered on June 25, 1875, at Rock Island Arsenal, Illinois. A General Court Martial, with Major Joseph Tilford presiding, was convened on September 23, 1875, at Fort Rice for the trial of St. John. Sentenced to eight months confinement with loss of pay and allowance for the same period, per General Court Martial Order Nr. 73, Headquarters, Department of Dakota, November 20, 1875. The unexpired portion of the sentence was remitted and he was released from confinement on April 28, 1876, per Special Order Nr. 56, Department of Dakota. He had grey eyes, brown hair, fair complexion and was 5'-9" in height. Listed as Ludwig St. John on the battle monument.

STUART, ALPHEUS, Private
    Killed in battle on June 25. Born in New York City. Second enlistment on September 20, 1875 at age 33, in Cincinnati by Lieut. Patrick Cusack. He had grey eyes, dark hair, fair complexion and was 5'-10½" in height. Listed as Alpheus Stuart on the battle monument.

STUNGEWITZ, YGNATZ, Private
    Killed in battle on June 25. Born in Kuuno, Russia. Enlisted on September 15, 1873 at age 26 in New York City by Lieut. Edward Hunter. Previous occupation was clerk. He had blue eyes, light hair, fair complexion and he was 5'-8½" in height. Listed as Ignatz Stungwitz on the battle monument and as Ygnatz Stungewitz in the Register of Enlistments, U.S. Army and the Company C Muster Roll, June 30, 1876.

THADUS, JOHN, Private
    Killed in battle on June 25. Born in Guilford County, North Carolina. Enlisted on August 17, 1875 at age 21 in Baltimore by Lieut. Charles Cresson. Previous occupation was farmer. He had black eyes, dark hair, dark complexion and was 5'-6¾" in height. Listed as John Thadus on the battle monument and elsewhere as Thadius.

THOMPSON, PETER, Private
    Assigned to the battalion under Lt. Col. George Custer; his horse became exhausted and he joined Major Reno's command on the hilltop. Wounded in the right hand while with the water party on June 26. Transported to Fort Abraham Lincoln, Dakota on the steamer *Far West*. Born in Fifeshire, Scotland on Dec. 28, 1853. Birthdate has also been listed as Dec. 28, 1854 and Dec. 28, 1856. He arrived in the United States in 1865 and settled with his parents in Banksville (Pittsburgh), Penna. Thence he moved to Indiana County, Penna. He was enlisted on September 21, 1875, at a represented age of 21. Enlisted in Pittsburgh by Lieut. Thomas Gregg. Previous occupation was miner. Transferred to Jefferson Barracks, Mo. and assigned to Company C, 7th Cavalry at Fort Lincoln. Issued the Medal of Honor on October 5, 1878, as a member of the water party in the Little Bighorn River fight with the citation. ". . . after having voluntarily brought water to the wounded in which effort he was shot through the head, he made two more successful trips for the same purpose notwithstanding the remonstrances of his sergeant." Discharged Sept. 20, 1880, at Fort Meade, Dakota upon expiration of service, as a Private of excellent character. He had brown eyes, brown hair, ruddy complexion and was 5'-8¾" in height. He managed a ranch northeast of Alzada, Montana, until his death. Died at the Soldier's Home, Hot Springs, S.D. on Dec. 3, 1928, at age 75 and was interred in the Masonic Section of West Lead Cemetery, Lead, S.D. on Dec. 4. He was survived by his son, Peter, who continued operation of his father's ranch. A typescript by Peter Thompson is in the possession of the North Dakota State Historical Society. A typescript copy titled, *The Experience of a Private Soldier In The Custer Massacre* is in the Vickers Collection, Custer Battlefield National Monument, and similar material is in Jesse Brown *Black Hills Trails*.

VAHLERT, JACOB, Private
    Sick in the hospital from May 5, 1876 at Fort Abraham Lincoln, Dakota.

Born in Nassau, Germany. Enlisted on September 29, 1875 at age 21 in New York City by Lieut. John Babcock. Previous occupation was butcher. Discharged on August 25, 1876 at Fort Lincoln, for disability, as a Private of good character. He had hazel eyes, light hair, fair complexion and was 5'-11¾" in height.

VAN ALLEN, GARRETT, Private
Killed in battle on June 25. Born in New Brunswick, New Jersey. Enlisted on October 2, 1873 at age 27 in New York City by Lieut. Edward Hunter. Previous occupation was farmer. He had blue eyes, brown hair, black complexion and was 5'-7" in height. Listed as Garrett Van Allen on the battle monument, and in the Register of Enlistments, U.S. Army.

VON ARNIM, JULIUS, Private
Born in Germany. Second enlistment on August 16, 1871, at age 33 in Louisville, Kentucky by Lieut. William Cooke. Discharged August 16, 1876 at Fort A. Lincoln, Dakota upon expiration of service, as a Private of excellent character. Listed as Julius Von Arnim in the Register of Enlistments, U.S. Army and elsewhere as Julius Van Arnim. He had brown eyes, dark hair, dark complexion and was 5'-3¼" in height.

WALKER, ROBERT, Private
Born in Boston. Enlisted on August 20, 1875 at age 22 in Boston by Lieut. William Harper, Jr. Previous occupation was safemaker. Deserted on February 2, 1877; apprehended on May 21, 1878. Discharged on June 15, 1878, at Fort Independence, Massachusetts, per General Court Martial Order Nr.45, Department of the East, 1878. He had brown eyes, black hair, dark complexion and was 5'-7¼" in height.

WARNER, OSCAR T., Private
Killed in battle on June 25. Born in Berne, New York. Enlisted on October 8, 1875 at age 35 in St. Louis by Lieut. John Thompson. Previous occupation was carpenter. He had blue eyes, brown hair, fair complexion and was 5'-5¾" in height. Listed as O. T. Warner on the battle monument and elsewhere as Warren.

WATSON, JAMES, Private
In the hilltop fight. Born in Hudson, New York. Enlisted on September 10, 1875 at age 25 in Cincinnati by Lieut. Patrick Cusack. Previous occupation was laborer. In the march to the Little Bighorn River, Watson's horse became exhausted at about the same time as Peter Thompson's horse gave out. Watson undoubtedly joined Major Reno's command on the hilltop. Discharged on September 9, 1880, at Fort Meade, Dakota upon expiration of service, as a Private of very good character. He had blue eyes, brown hair, fair complexion and was 5'-6½" in height.

WHITAKER, ALFRED, Private
Wounded in the right elbow in the hilltop fight on June 26. Transported to Fort Abraham Lincoln, Dakota on the steamer *Far West*. Born in New Orleans, Louisiana. Enlisted on September 26, 1873 at age 26 in Philadelphia by Lieut. William Volkmar. Previous occupation was blacksmith. Discharged on September 26, 1878 at Camp James G. Sturgis, Dakota upon expiration of service, as a

Private of very good character. He had blue eyes, dark hair, fair complexion and was 5'-6" in height. Listed elsewhere as Whittaker.

WRIGHT, WILLIS B., Private
Killed in battle on June 25. Born in Oskaloosa, Iowa on June 7, 1859. He was enlisted on August 25, 1875 at a represented age of 21 in Cincinnati, Ohio by Lieut. Patrick Cusack. Previous occupation was laborer. He had blue eyes, brown hair, ruddy complexion and was 5'-6½" in height. Listed as W. B. Right on the battle monument. His brother, Allen C. Wright, later resided in Hot Springs, S. D.

WYMAN, HENRY, Private
Killed in battle on June 25. Born in Woburn, Massachusetts. Enlisted on August 22, 1873 at age 33 in Boston by Lieut. James Ropes. Previous occupation was machinist. He had brown eyes, dark hair, dark complexion and was 5'-6¼" in height. Listed as Henry Wyman on the battle monument.

88

COMPANY D IN 1876

The company remained a part of the garrison at Fort A. Lincoln, Dakota until May 5 when they joined the regiment in camp below the post to take part in the Sioux expedition. The regiment left Fort Lincoln on May 17 and returned on September 26.

Company D was one of the four companies under the command of Major Marcus Reno who left Fort Lincoln on October 21 to go to Standing Rock Agency, Dakota via the right bank of the Missouri River to disarm and dismount the Indians at the agency. The company returned to Fort Lincoln on Nov. 3, and left on Nov. 12 and arrived the same day at Fort Rice, Dakota for winter station. Distance marched in the year was 1,542 miles.

The following members were casualties in the fight on the Little Bighorn River, Montana Territory. Killed: Farrier Vincent Charley, Privates Edward Housen and Patrick Golden. Wounded: Privates Patrick McDonnell and Jacob Hetler. Private James Carey died at Fort Lincoln on February 4 of pneumonia.

Officers serving with the company in the year were Captain Thomas Weir, First Lieutenants James M. Bell and Edwin Eckerson and Second Lieutenants Winfield Edgerly and Edwin Brewer. Captain Weir died on December 9 while on recruiting duty in New York City. Lieut. Daniel Crosby Pearson was transferred from the 2nd Cavalry to fill the vacancy created by the promotion of Lieut. Edgerly but he declined the transfer. Lieut. Brewer was assigned to fill the vacancy.*

* *Edwin Parker Brewer was born in, and appointed to military service, from Ohio. He was a Cadet at the Military Academy July 1 to November 14, 1871. Appointed 2nd Lieut. 7th Cavalry, Aug. 31, 1876 and accepted Sept. 4, 1876. Promoted to 1st Lieut. September 23, 1885 and to Captain, December 8, 1896.*

COMPANY D AT THE LITTLE BIGHORN

	Absent	Present	Wounded	Died OWRT	Killed	Survived
Captain		1				1
1st Lieut.	1					1
2nd Lieut.		1				1
1st Sgt.		1				1
Sergt.	1	3				4
Corporal	1	1				2
Trumpeter		1				1
Saddler		1				1
Farrier		1			1	
Wagoner						
Blacksmith		1				1
Private	12	41	2		2	51
Total	15	52	2	0	3	64

COMPANY D ON JUNE 30, 1876

Officers present for duty 2
Enlisted present for duty 45
Officers absent with leave 1
Enlisted absent detached service 14
Enlisted absent sick 2
Captain 1
First Lieutenant 1
Second Lieutenant 1
First Sergeant 1
Sergeants 4
Corporals 2
Trumpeter 1
Blacksmith 1
Saddler 1
Privates 51
Total enlisted 61
Aggregate 64
Aggregate last month 67
Enlisted killed 3
Wounded 2
Horses serviceable 47
Horses unserviceable 2
Horses lost 6

WEIR, THOMAS BELL, Captain

In the hilltop fight commanding Company D. Born in Nashville, Ohio on September 28, 1838. He graduated from the University of Michigan in June, 1861 and entered military service on August 27, 1861 in Company B, 3rd Michigan Cavalry and served through all the grades until he was appointed Second Lieutenant, Company B, effective October 13, 1861. In the expedition against New Madrid, the battle of Farmington, the siege of Corinth, the battle of Iuka, the second battle of Corinth and the battle of Coffeeville. Effective June 19, 1862 he was promoted to First Lieutenant and was taken prisoner by the Confederates on June 26, 1862, and remained with the enemy until January 8, 1863. Rejoined the regiment and served with it until May, 1865. Promoted to Captain effective from November 1, 1862. After the reduction of Mobile his regiment went to San Antonio where Captain Weir was on Brevet Major General George Custer's staff as Acting Assistant Inspector General until he was mustered out with the regiment on February 12, 1866. Promoted to Major effective from January 18, 1865 and to Lieutenant Colonel to rank from November 6, 1865. Appointed First Lieutenant, 7th Cavalry, with rank from July 28, 1866, the date that the regiment was organized. On July 31, 1867 he received the brevet of Major, USA, for service in the battle of Farmington and on the same date he received the brevet of Lieutenant Colonel for his services in the engagement with General Forrest near Ripley, Mississippi on December 1, 1863. Captain Weir participated in the Sioux expedition of 1876 in command of Company D and on June 25 his company, a part of Captain Benteen's battalion, was engaged in scouting and in a severe fight on a hilltop near the Little Bighorn River. The fatigue and exposure of the campaign impaired his health and he was detailed to take charge of the cavalry recruiting office in New York City. Here his constitution broke down completely. He died suddenly on December 9, 1876 at the age of 38. On December 14, his remains were interred on Governor's Island, New York Harbor with full military honors. He was survived by his sister, Mrs. Samuel Brown, of Greenville, Mississippi. Listed elsewhere as Thomas Benton Weir.

BELL, JAMES MONTGOMERY, First Lieutenant

On leave of absence. Born in Pennsylvania. Entered military service as a Private, 86th Ohio Volunteer Infantry, May to June, 1862. Appointed a First Lieutenant in the same regiment on June 10, 1862 and was mustered out on September 25, 1862. On June 30, 1863, he was commissioned Captain of an Independent Company, Pennsylvania Cavalry engaged in protecting the state against Lee's invasion and in the action at North Mountain. Mustered out on August 9, 1863. On October 8, 1863, he was appointed Captain, 13th Pennsylvania Volunteer Cavalry and was engaged in the operations at Mine Run, the battles of the Wilderness, Spottsylvania, North Anna, the actions at Ream's Station and Coggin's Point where he was wounded. He was in the actions at White Oak Road and the battle of Hatcher's Run and the battle of Bentonville, the action at Raleigh. Honorably mustered out on July 14, 1865. Commissioned Second Lieutenant, 7th Cavalry, on July 28, 1866, the date that the regiment was organized. Brevetted First Lieutenant, Captain and Major, USA. Promoted to First Lieutenant on April 2, 1867. In the summer of 1873 he was engaged as an escort for the survey of the international boundary between the United States and Canada. Promoted to Captain of Cavalry effective June 25, 1876, to occupy the vacancy created by the death of Captain George Yates, killed in the Little Bighorn River fight. Captain Bell was engaged in the 1877 Nez Perce campaign and the action at Canyon Creek on September 13, 1877, for which action he received the brevet of Lieutenant Colonel. On January 2, 1881, Bell took part in the surrender of Gall's band of Sioux at Poplar Creek. During the summers of 1880-82 he was engaged as escort to construction parties of the Northern Pacific Railroad. Promoted to Major, 1st Cavalry on May 23, 1896, and on July 5, 1899, he was promoted to Colonel of the 27th U.S. Volunteer Infantry. On January 10, 1900, he was promoted to Lieutenant Colonel, U.S.A., 8th Cavalry and Brigadier General, U.S.V. on January 20, 1900. Honorably discharged from volunteer service on June 20, 1901. Promoted to Colonel, 8th Cavalry on March 24, 1901, and Brigadier General, U.S.A. on September 17, 1901 and retired on October 1, 1901.

EDGERLY, WINFIELD SCOTT, Second Lieutenant

On scouting duty and in the hilltop fight with Company D. Born in Farmington, New Hampshire on May 29, 1846. Entered military service at the Military Academy on July 1, 1866. Graduated on June 15, 1870, ranking 50th in his class of 58 graduates; the 2361st graduate of the Academy. Appointed Second Lieutenant, Company D, 7th Cavalry on June 15, 1870 and joined the regiment near Fort Riley, Kansas. During the reconstruction period he served at various posts in the southern states until 1873 when he proceeded to Fort Snelling for escort duty with the International Boundary Survey Commission. In 1876 the regiment assembled at Fort Abraham Lincoln, Dakota, and departed on the Sioux expedition. Lieut. Edgerly fought in the Little Bighorn River fight and rendered conspicuously gallant service. Promoted to First Lieutenant to rank from June 25, 1876, to occupy the vacancy created by the promotion of Lieut. James M. Bell. He served on frontier duty until 1883 when he went to Cincinnati for duty with the General Recruiting Service. Promoted to Captain of Cavalry on September 22, 1883; joined his troop at Fort Leavenworth in 1884. On duty at Fort Keogh in 1885-86 and then transferred to Fort Riley. He participated in the fight on Wounded Knee Creek, South Dakota on December 29, 1890 where he rendered conspicuously valuable service. He served in Texas from 1892 to 1895 and then for a year at the State College, Orino, Maine as an instructor and the following two years as National Guard instructor at Concord, New Hampshire. On June 8, 1898, he was promoted to Lieut. Colonel U.S. Volunteers and Major, 6th Cavalry on July 9, 1898. Transferred to the 7th Cavalry on January 5, 1899, which he joined in Cuba. Promoted to Lieut. Colonel. 10th Cavalry on February 19, 1901 and transferred back to the 7th Cavalry on March 20, 1901. On February 17, 1902, he was promoted to Colonel, 2nd Cavalry and joined the regiment at Fort Myer, Virginia. The following year he took the regiment to the Philippine Islands. There he received promotion to Brigadier General on June 28, 1905. In 1907 he was in Germany as an observer of army maneuvers. Retired on December 29, 1909, after 43 years service. Recalled for a short period in World War I and commanded the mobilization camp at Concord, New Hampshire. Died September 10, 1927 at Farmington; interred in the National Cemetery, Arlington, Virginia.

MARTIN, MICHAEL, First Sergeant

Born in Dublin, Ireland. Second enlistment on December 7, 1872, at age 37 in Opelika, Alabama by Lieut. Winfield Edgerly. Killed by a shot in the chest in the Snake Creek fight near the Bear Paw Mountains, Montana Territory, on September 30, 1877, the morning of Chief Joseph's surrender to Colonel Nelson Miles. He had grey eyes, fair hair, fair complexion and was 5'-6½" in height. Re-interred in the Custer Battlefield National Cemetery, Grave 1412 (2) B. Surviving were his wife, Mary, and children.

FLANAGAN, JAMES, Sergeant

Born in Innis, County Clare, Ireland in 1847. He served in the 11th Ohio Volunteer Cavalry in the Civil War and then enlisted in the 2nd U.S. Cavalry. Enlisted in the 7th Cavalry on November 15, 1871, at a represented age of 35 in Louisville, Kentucky by Lieut. William Cooke. Discharged on November 15, 1876, at Fort Rice, Dakota upon expiration of service, as a Sergeant of excellent character. Re-enlisted. Wounded on September 30, 1877, in the Snake Creek fight near the Bear Paw Mountains, Montana Territory, in an engagement with Chief Joseph's band of Nez Perce Indians. He had blue eyes, brown hair, light complexion and was 5'-10½" in height. Died in 1921; interred in a Mandan, North Dakota cemetery. Material by Sergeant Flanagan, titled *Last Custer Scout*, is in the files of the Order of Indian Wars.

HARRISON, THOMAS W., Sergeant

Born in Sligo, Ireland. Second enlistment on August 10, 1871, at age 22 in Mount Vernon, Kentucky by Captain Thomas Weir. Previous occupation was soldier. Discharged on August 5, 1876, at camp at the mouth of Rosebud Creek, Montana Territory per General Order Nr.24,AGO,1859, as a Sergeant. He had blue eyes, brown hair, fair complexion and was 5'-9½" in height.

RUSSELL, THOMAS, Sergeant

Born in Oxford, Indiana. Enlisted on August 5, 1872, at age 24 in Chicago by Captain Samuel Young. Previous occupation was laborer. Discharged on June 23, 1877, at camp on the Tongue River, Montana Territory per Special Order Nr.70, Department of Dakota, 1877, as a Sergeant of excellent character. He had brown eyes, dark hair, dark complexion and was 5'-4" in height.

MORTON, THOMAS, Sergeant

Sick in the hospital from May 5, 1876 at Fort Abraham Lincoln, Dakota. Born in Darke County, Ohio. Second enlistment on November 18, 1871 at age 30 in Chester, South Carolina by Captain Thomas Weir. Discharged on November 18, 1876 at Fort Lincoln upon expiration of service, as a Sergeant of good character. Re-enlisted on November 18, 1876. Letter from AGO, October 17, 1876, to Commanding General, Department of Dakota, authorized Sergeant Morton to go on a four-month furlough with permission to go beyond the sea, effective upon his re-enlistment on November 18, 1876. Letter copy in the *Descriptive List and Records File*, Custer Battlefield National Monument. He had dark eyes, brown hair, fair complexion and was 5'-9½" in height.

WYLIE, GEORGE W., Corporal

Born in New Orleans, Louisiana. Enlisted on March 17, 1873, at age 25 in Memphis, Tennessee by Lieut. Winfield Edgerly. Previous occupation was laborer. Wounded on September 30, 1877, in the Snake Creek fight near the Bear Paw Mountains, Montana Territory, in a fight with Chief Joseph's band of

Nez Perce Indians. Discharged March 17, 1878, at Fort Rice, Dakota, upon expiration of service, as a Corporal of good character. He had blue eyes, light hair, fair complexion and was 5'-8¼" in height. He married about 1906. Interred at Fort Leavenworth, Kansas. His wife was interred there several years after his death.

CUNNINGHAM, ALBERT J., Corporal

On detached service from June 15, 1876 at Yellowstone Depot, Montana Territory. Born in Leeds, England. Second enlistment on January 20, 1872, at age 34 in Chester, South Carolina by Capt. Thomas Weir. Previous occupation was soldier. Discharged on January 20, 1877, at Fort Rice, Dakota upon expiration of service, as a Corporal with character reference of, "capable and faithful". He had blue eyes, dark hair, fair complexion and was 5'-5" in height.

BOHNER, ALOYS, Trumpeter

Born in Baden, Germany. Third enlistment on January 12, 1874 at age 44 in St. Paul, Minnesota by Lieut. Henry Nowlan. Previous occupation was musician. Discharged on January 12, 1879, at Fort Abraham Lincoln, Dakota upon expiration of service, as the Chief Trumpeter, with excellent character. He had hazel eyes, brown hair, dark complexion and was 5'-7¾" in height. The Descriptive List and Records File, Custer Battlefield National Monument, includes Special Order Nr.18, Headquarters, District of the Upper Arkansas, October 28, 1867 which indicates that Bohner was a member of the 7th Cavalry in 1867.

MYERS, JOHN, Saddler

Born in Wurtemburg, Germany. Second enlistment on January 1, 1872, at age 35 in Chester, South Carolina by Captain Thomas Weir. Previous occupation was soldier. Discharged on January 1, 1877 at Fort Rice, Dakota upon expiration of service, as a Saddler of good character. He had hazel eyes, black hair, ruddy complexion and was 5'-7½" in height.

DEETLINE, FREDERICK, Blacksmith

In the hilltop fight. Born in Wittenberg (or Offenheim), Germany. First enlistment on July 21, 1870, at age 24 in the 17th Infantry at Baltimore, Maryland, by Captain J. F. Randleto. Previous occupation was laborer. Discharged from Company C, 22nd Infantry on July 21, 1875 upon expiration of service. He had slate blue or grey eyes, brown hair, fair complexion and was 5'-9½" to 11" in height and was illiterate. His second enlistment was on August 5, 1875, at age 29 in Baltimore by Lieut. Charles Cresson. Wounded on September 30, 1877, in the Snake Creek fight near the Bear Paw Mountains, Montana Territory in an engagement with Chief Joseph's Nez Perce Indians. He sustained a bullet wound below the right shoulder coming out of the back of the right shoulder. Awarded the Medal of Honor on October 5, 1878, for voluntarily bringing water to the wounded under fire in the Little Bighorn River fight. Discharged from Company D, 7th Cavalry, on August 4, 1880 at Fort Yates, Dakota upon expiration of service, as a Sergeant of excellent character. Third enlistment was on June 21, 1881 at St. Louis by Lieut. Peter Bomus. Discharged from Troop G, 5th Cavalry, on June 20, 1886. Fourth enlistment on September 8, 1886, at Fort Walla Walla, Washington Territory by Lieut. Charles Schofield.

Discharged from Troop B, 2nd Cavalry on September 7, 1891. Fifth enlistment on September 29, 1891 at Fort Reno, Oklahoma. Assigned to Troop G, 5th Cavalry. Listed as Frederick Deetline in the Register of Enlistments, U.S. Army, and elsewhere as Frederick Dettlein.

CHARLEY, VINCENT, Farrier

Killed in battle at the Little Bighorn River. Born in Lucerne (Lutzern) Switzerland. Enlisted on March 4, 1871, at age 22 in Chicago by Captain Samuel Young. Previous occupation was farmer. Discharged on March 4, 1876, at Fort Abraham Lincoln, Dakota upon expiration of service, as a Farrier. Re-enlisted on March 5, 1876, at age 27 at Fort Lincoln by Captain Thomas Weir. He had hazel eyes, red hair, sandy complexion and was 5'-10¼" in height. Listed as Chas. Vincent on the battle monument.

ALBERTS, JAMES H., Private

Born in Woodstock, Illinois. Enlisted on September 24, 1875, at age 28 in St. Louis by Captain Owen Hale. Previous occupation was farmer. Promoted to Sergeant. Killed on September 30, 1877 in the Snake Creek fight near the Bear Paw Mountains, Montana Territory by Nez Perce Indians. Re-interred at the Custer Battlefield National Cemetery, Grave 1412 (B). He was 5'5¾" in height and had blue eyes, brown hair and fair complexion. Listed elsewhere as James M. Albert.

ASCOUGH, JOHN B., Private

Born in Philadelphia, Pennsylvania. Enlisted on September 3, 1872, at age 28 in Philadelphia by Captain Samuel Whitside. Previous occupation was shoemaker. Discharged on June 23, 1877 at camp near the Tongue River, Montana Territory per Special Order Nr.70, Department of Dakota, 1877 as a Corporal of very good character. He had brown eyes, dark hair, ruddy complexion and was 5'-9¼" in height.

BRANT, ABRAHAM B., Private

In the hilltop fight. Born in New York City. Enlisted on September 27, 1875 at age 26 in St. Louis by Lieut. William Thompson. Previous occupation was civil engineer. Awarded the Medal of Honor for bringing water to the wounded under a most galling fire in the Little Bighorn River fight. Died on October 4, 1878 in camp near Camp Ruhlen, Dakota of accidental gunshot wounds in the abdomen, by his own hand. He was shot while handing his revolver to the First Sergeant. He had hazel eyes, light hair, fair complexion and was 5'5 7/8" in height. Listed elsewhere as Abram B. Brant.

CONLAN, THOMAS, Private

On detached service from June 15, 1876 at Yellowstone Depot, Montana Territory. Born in Ayrshire, Scotland. Enlisted on September 18, 1875 at age 21 11/12 in Boston, Mass. by Lieut. Henry Lawton. Previous occupation was marble cutter. Deserted on December 21, 1876; apprehended on December 21, 1876. Dishonorably discharged on March 12, 1877, at Fort Rice, Dakota per General Court Martial Order Nr.8, Department of Dakota, 1877. This soldier had blue eyes, brown hair, dark complexion and was 5'-6¾" in height.

COWLEY, STEPHEN, Private
On detached service from June 15, 1876 at Yellowstone Depot, Montana Territory. Born in Sligo, Ireland. Enlisted on November 14, 1872 at age 24 in Chicago by Captain Samuel Young. Previous occupation was butcher. Discharged on November 14, 1877 at Fort A. Lincoln, Dakota upon expiration of service, as a Private of excellent character. He had brown eyes, brown hair, florid complexion and was 5'-6½" in height.

COX, THOMAS, Private
Born in Cincinnati, Ohio. Enlisted on September 22, 1873 at age 29 in Philadelphia by Lieut. William Volkmar. Previous occupation was brickmaker. Discharged on September 22, 1878 at Camp James G. Sturgis, Dakota, upon expiration of service, as a Corporal of excellent character. He had blue eyes, dark hair, ruddy complexion and was 5'-8" in height.

DANN, GEORGE, Private
Born in Elmira, New York. Enlisted on June 3, 1873 at age 21 at Fort Snelling, Minnesota by Captain Thomas Weir. Previous occupation was laborer. Deserted on March 19, 1878; surrendered on March 13, 1881. Discharged on July 29, 1881 at Fort Leavenworth, Kansas per Special Order Nr.162, AGO 1881, as a Private of no character. He had blue eyes, light hair, fair complexion and was 5'-8¾" in height.

DAWSEY, DAVID E., Private
Born in Belleville, Ohio. Enlisted on December 17, 1872, at age 21 in Toledo, Ohio by Captain Samuel Young. Previous occupation was farmer. Killed on September 30, 1877, in the Snake Creek fight near the Bear Paw Mountains, Montana Territory, in a fight with Chief Joseph's band of Nez Perce Indians. Re-interred in the Custer Battlefield National Cemetery, Grave 1412 (2) B. He had grey eyes, sandy hair, sandy complexion and was 5'-4½" in height.

FAY, JOHN J., Private
Born in Chicago, Illinois. Enlisted on September 8, 1873, at age 21 in Detroit, Michigan by Lieut. Johnathan Stevenson. Previous occupation was plasterer. Discharged on September 15, 1877, at Fort Rice, Dakota, for disability, as a Private of very good character. He had grey eyes, brown hair, fair complexion and was 5'-5" in height.

FOX, HARVEY A., Private
On detached service from June 15, 1876, at Yellowstone Depot, Montana Territory. Born in Alexander County, North Carolina. Enlisted on July 27, 1871 at age 23 in Mount Vernon, Kentucky by Captain Thomas Weir. Previous occupation was farmer. Discharged on July 27, 1876 at camp at the mouth of Rosebud Creek, Montana Territory, upon expiration of his service, as a Private. He had grey eyes, fair hair, fair complexion and was 5'-6" in height. Listed elsewhere as Harry Fox.

FOX, JOHN, Private
Born in Buffalo, New York. Enlisted on September 24, 1875 at age 28 in St. Louis by Lieut. John Thompson. Previous occupation was cooper. Discharged on September 23, 1880 at Fort Yates, Dakota upon expiration of service, as a Sergeant of good character. He had blue eyes, dark hair, dark

complexion and was 5'-8½" in height. In 1927 he was residing at the U.S. Soldier's Home, Washington, D. C.

GOLDEN, PATRICK M., Private
Killed in the hilltop fight, by a shot in the head, on June 26. Born in Sligo, Ireland. Enlisted on Jan. 22, 1872, at age 22 in Boston by Lieut. Moses Harris. Previous occupation was slater. He had blue eyes, brown hair, fair complexion and was 5'-9¼" in height. His name is listed as Pat'k Golden on the battle monument and as Patrick Goldan in the Register of Enlistments U.S. Army. Lieut. Winfield Edgerly wrote his wife on July 4th following the Little Bighorn River fight and his letter had the note: ". . . as soon as the charge was completed we were ordered to get in the pits again. Private Stivers who had been in the pit with me saw Golden in a pit and asked him whose it was. He said he didn't know and as there was room enough for three men there Stivers and I got into it. We hadn't been there a minute before a shot came throwing dirt all over us and striking Golden in the head. He never knew what hit him but died instantly." "Echoes From Custer's Last Fight," *Military Affairs,* XVII:4, Winter, 1953, p. 173. Edward Pigford, however, told Earle Forrest ("Fighting With Custer" in *The Morning Observer,* Washington, Pennsylvania, Oct. 3-19, 1932) a somewhat different story, "A soldier named Golden was in the trench beside me. We had been talking at intervals during the battle that afternoon, and when the fighting stopped shortly after dark I started to talk to him again. He didn't answer as I rattled on, and at last when I reached out my hand and touched his head it was covered with blood."

GREEN, JOHN, Private
On detached service from June 15, 1876, at Yellowstone Deport, Montana Territory. Born in Racine, Wisconsin. Enlisted on February 5, 1872, at age 21 in Chicago by Captain Samuel Young. Previous occupation was laborer. Discharged on February 5, 1877, at Fort Rice, Dakota upon expiration of his service, as a Private of excellent character. He had grey eyes, light hair, light complexion and was 5'-7" in height.

GREEN, JOSEPH H., Private
Born in Lectrim, Ireland. Enlisted on January 22, 1872, at age 22 in Boston by Lieut. Moses Harris. Previous occupation was milkhand. Discharged on January 22, 1877, at Fort Rice, Dakota upon expiration of service, as a Private of good character. He had blue eyes brown hair, fair complexion and was 5'-5¾" in height.

HAGER, JOHN, Private
Born in Buffalo, New York. Enlisted on January 10, 1872, at age 23 in Buffalo by Lieut. Albert Forse. Previous occupation was laborer. Discharged on January 10, 1877, at Fort Rice, Dakota upon expiration of service, as a Private of excellent character. Re-enlisted on Nov. 6, 1878, at age 29, at Fort Union, New Mexico by Lieut. Geo. Kinzie. Discharged from Co. C, 15th Infantry on Nov. 5, 1883. Third enlistment on Nov. 17, 1883 at Fort Leavenworth, Kansas by Lieut. Douglas Scott in Co. C, 15th Inf. He had hazel eyes, brown hair, fair to ruddy complexion and was 5'-8½" in height. Listed as John Hager in the Register of Enlistments, U.S. Army.

HALL, CURTIS, Private
    Born in Lycoming County, Pennsylvania. Enlisted on December 9, 1872, at age 21 in Louisville, Kentucky by Lieut. Peter Vroom. Previous occupation was harness maker. Discharged on December 9, 1877, at Fort Rice, Dakota upon expiration of service, as a Saddler of excellent character. He had hazel eyes, brown hair, ruddy complexion and was 5'-11" in height.

HALL, EDWARD, Private
    On detached service from May 5, 1876, with the band at Fort Abraham Lincoln, Dakota. Born in Winfield, New York. Enlisted on January 4, 1872 at age 21 in Troy, New York by Lieut. Oscar Elting. Previous occupation was teamster. Discharged on January 4, 1877 at Fort Rice, Dakota upon expiration of service, as a Private of excellent character. He had blue eyes, light brown hair, fair complexion and was 5'-5½" in height.

HARDDEN, WILLIAM, Private
    Born in New York City. Enlisted on January 27, 1872 at age 21 in Syracuse, New York by Lieut. Albert Forse. Previous occupation was laborer. Discharged on January 22, 1877 at Fort Abercrombie, Dakota upon expiration of service, as a Private of excellent character. He had grey eyes, sandy hair, dark complexion and was 5'-8" in height.

HARLFINGER, GUSTAV, Private
    On detached service from June 15, 1876 at Yellowstone Depot, Montana Territory. Born in Baden, Germany. First enlistment on August 8, 1866 in Philadelphia by Captain Mix. Assigned to Company D, 7th Cavalry. Second enlistment on September 7, 1871 at age 24 in Mount Vernon, Kentucky by Captain Thomas Weir. Assigned to Company D, 7th Cavalry. Discharged on August 5, 1876 in camp at the mouth of Rosebud Creek, Montana Territory per General Order Nr.24, AGO, 1859, as a Private. He had hazel eyes, light hair, fair complexion and was 5'-6¾" in height. His name is listed as Gustav Harlfinger on his Oath of Enlistment, U.S. Army and elsewhere as Gustave Hartfinger.

HARRIS, JAMES, Private
    Born in Yarmouth, Nova Scotia. Enlisted on September 21, 1875 at age 21 1/12 in Boston by Lieut. Henry Lawton. Previous occupation was painter. Discharged on September 20, 1880 at Fort Yates, Dakota upon expiration of service as a Private of excellent character. He had grey eyes, dark hair, fair complexion and was 5'-6½" in height.

HARRIS, WILLIAM M., Private
    In the hilltop fight. Born in Madison County, Kentucky. Enlisted on August 25, 1871, at age 21 in Mount Vernon, Kentucky. Previous occupation was farmer. Discharged on August 5, 1876, at camp at the mouth of the Rosebud Creek, Montana Territory, per General Order Nr. 24, AGO, 1859, as a Private. Awarded the Medal of Honor on October 5, 1878 for voluntarily bringing water to the wounded under fire of the enemy in the Little Bighorn River fight. He had grey eyes, light hair, fair complexion and was 5'-10½" in height.

HETLER, JACOB, Private

Wounded in the left leg on June 25, and in the back on June 26. Born in Mansfield, Ohio. Enlisted on February 3, 1872, at age 21 in Chicago by Capt. Samuel Young. Previous occupation was carpenter. After enlistment he was sent to Jefferson Barracks, Missouri, and then transferred to Co. D, 7th Cavalry at Opelika, Alabama, until September, 1872, thence to Montgomery, Alabama for six weeks and returned to Opelika; thence to Memphis, Tennessee. He went to Cairo, Illinois by riverboat and by rail to Fort Snelling, Minnesota. In June, 1874, he went to the end of the St. Paul & Pacific Railroad at Breckenridge, Minnesota, and then walked to Fargo, Dakota. A week later he walked to Fort Pembina, Dakota, on the Canadian border, where he arrived on June 25 to provide escort for the Northern Boundary Survey Commission. He remained in winter station at Fort Totten, Dakota, for two winters, thence to Fort Abraham Lincoln, Dakota, in 1875. In the Sioux expedition in 1876; discharged on Feb. 3, 1877, at Fort Rice, Dakota, upon expiration of service, as a Private of good character. He had blue eyes, light hair, light complexion and was 5'-6" in height. In 1927 he resided on Rural Route 3, Greenwich, Ohio.

HOLDEN, HENRY, Private

Born in London, England. Third enlistment on January 9, 1872 at a represented age of 33 in Chicago by Captain Samuel Young. Discharged on January 9, 1877 at Fort Rice, Dakota upon expiration of service, as a Corporal of good character. Awarded the Medal of Honor on October 5, 1878 for bringing up ammunition under a galling fire from the enemy, in the Little Bighorn River fight. He had grey eyes, light hair, light complexion and was 5'-5" in height.

HORN, GEORGE, Private

Born in Andalusia, Spain. Enlisted on January 12, 1872, at age 28 in Buffalo, New York by Lieut. Albert Forse. Discharged on January 12, 1877 at Fort Rice, Dakota upon expiration of service, as a Private of good character. He had dark eyes, dark hair, fair complexion and was 5'-6" in height.

HOUSEN, EDWARD, Private

Killed in battle. Born in Pittsburgh, Pennsylvania. Enlisted on July 5, 1870, at age 22 in Cincinnati by Capt. Thomas Brent. Previous occupation was farmer. Listed as Edward Housen on the battle monument and elsewhere as Hansen.

HOUGHTALING, CHARLES H., Private

On detached service from the regiment from June 29, 1876 on duty at the Yellowstone River. Born in Hudson City, New York. Second enlistment on September 8, 1871, at age 27 in New York City by Captain Edwin Sumner. Previous occupation was druggist. Discharged on September 8, 1876, at Fort Buford, Dakota upon expiration of service, as a Sergeant. Third enlistment on September 8, 1876, at Fort Buford by Captain Thomas Weir. Discharged on March 30, 1877, to date from February 28, 1877, at Fort Rice, Dakota per Special Orders Nr. 59, AGO, 1877, as a Private. He had hazel eyes, black hair, dark complexion and was 5'-3" to 4½" in height. Listed as Charles H. Houghtaling and Charles H. Houghtalin in Registers of Enlistments, U.S. Army.

HUNT, GEORGE, Private
    Born in Boston. Enlisted on June 2, 1873, at age 22 at Fort Snelling, Minnesota by Lieut. Winfield Edgerly. Previous occupation was laborer. Discharged on June 1, 1878 at Fort Rice, Dakota upon expiration of service, as a Private of fair character. He had blue eyes, light brown hair, ruddy complexion and was 5'-7" in height.

HURD, JAMES, Private
    Born in Jessamine County, Kentucky. Enlisted on August 30, 1871, at age 22 in Mount Vernon, Kentucky. Previous occupation was farmer. Discharged on August 5, 1876, at camp at the mouth of Rosebud Creek, Montana Territory per General Order Nr. 24, AGO, 1859, as a Private. Second enlistment on September 4, 1876, at Fort Abraham Lincoln, Dakota at the age of 27, by Captain Thomas Weir. Discharged on September 3, 1881 at Fort Yates, Dakota upon expiration of service, as a Private of very good character. He had blue eyes, black hair, dark complexion and was 5'-6" in height.

KANAVAGH, JOHN, Private
    Born in Rascommon, Ireland. Enlisted on January 3, 1872 at age 21 in Jersey City, New Jersey by Captain Edwin Sumner. Previous occupation was teamster. Discharged on January 3, 1877 at Fort Rice, Dakota upon expiration of service, as a Private of excellent character. He had grey eyes, brown hair, ruddy complexion and was 5'-6" in height.

KELLER, JOHN J., Private
    Born in Lancaster, Tennessee. Second enlistment on October 19, 1873, at age 27 at Fort Snelling, Minnesota by Lieut. Henry Nowlan. Discharged on October 19, 1878, at Helena, Montana Territory upon expiration of service, as a Private. He had blue eyes, dark hair, ruddy complexion and was 5'-6¾" in height. In 1908 he resided at 36 E. Cutler, St. Helena, Montana.

KIPP, FREMONT, Private
    Born in Noble Hill, Ohio. Enlisted on December 2, 1872, at age 21 in Columbus, Ohio by Lieut. James Wheelan. Previous occupation was laborer. Discharged on December 2, 1877, at camp near Fort Buford, Dakota, upon expiration of service, as a Sergeant of excellent character. He had brown eyes, brown hair, dark complexion and was 5'-8¾" in height. In 1927 he was residing at the U.S. Soldier's Home, Washington, D. C.

KRETCHMER, JOSEPH, Private
    Born in Silesia, Germany. Second enlistment on September 20, 1872, at age 34 in Cincinnati by Lieut. James Wheelan. Discharged on September 20, 1877, at Fort Abercrombie, Dakota upon expiration of service, as a Private of good character. He had blue eyes, brown hair, florid complexion and was 5'-4" in height.

KUEHL, JESSE, Private
    On detached service from June 16, 1876, at Yellowstone Depot, Montana Territory. Born in Los Angeles, California. Enlisted on October 9, 1875 at age 21 in St. Louis by Lieut. John Thompson. Previous occupation was barber. Deserted on March 27, 1877; apprehended on February 18, 1878. Dishonorably

discharged June 29, 1878 at Fort Rice, Dakota per General Court Martial Order Nr. 47, Department of Dakota, 1878, as a Private. Sentenced to two years confinement in September, 1878. He had brown eyes, brown hair, dark complexion and was 5'-7 1/8" in height. Listed elsewhere as Jesse Kuchl.

LEWIS, URIAH S., Private

On detached service with the band from June 15, 1876 at Yellowstone Depot, Montana Territory. Born in Montgomery County, Pennsylvania. Enlisted on August 18, 1873, at age 21 in Philadelphia by Lieut. William Volkmar. Previous occupation was painter. Released from confinement per General Court Martial Order Nr. 8, Department of Dakota, January 20, 1876. Wounded on September 30, 1877, in the Snake Creek fight near the Bear Paw Mountains, Montana Territory in an engagement with Chief Joseph's band of Nez Perce Indians. Discharged on August 18, 1878, at Camp James G. Sturgis, Dakota upon expiration of service, as a Private of excellent character. He had blue eyes, brown hair, fair complexion and was 5'-10" in height. Listed elsewhere as Uriah L. Lewis.

MANNING, DAVID, Private

Born in Dublin, Ireland. Enlisted on October 1, 1873 at age 26 in Boston by Lieut. James Ropes. Previous occupation was shoemaker. Discharged on October 1, 1878 at Camp James G. Sturgis, Dakota upon expiration of service, as a Private of excellent character. He had grey eyes, sandy hair, florid complexion and was 5'-8¼" in height.

MARSHALL, WILLIAM A., Private

Born in Germany. Enlisted on September 25, 1875, at age 24 in Chicago by Lieut. Edmund Luff. Previous occupation was teamster. Wounded on September 30, 1877, in the Snake Creek fight near the Bear Paw Mountains, Montana Territory in an engagement with Chief Joseph's band of Nez Perce Indians. Discharged September 24, 1880, at Fort Yates, Dakota, upon expiration of service, as a Sergeant of excellent character. He had grey eyes, light brown hair, fair complexion and was 5'-7" in height.

MEADWELL, JOHN (J. R. Meadville), Private

Born in Butler County, Pennsylvania. Enlisted on September 13, 1875, at age 21 in Pittsburgh by Lieut. Thomas Gregg. Discharged on July 25, 1876, at camp near the mouth of Rosebud Creek, Montana Territory, per Special Order Nr. 24, AGO, June 24, 1876, as a Private. Re-enlisted. Wounded on September 30, 1877, in the Snake Creek fight near the Bear Paw Mountains, Montana Territory in an engagement with Chief Joseph's band of Nez Perce Indians. He had brown eyes, brown hair, fair complexion and was 5'7½" in height.

McDONNELL, PATRICK, Private

Wounded in the left leg in the hilltop fight on June 25. Transported to Fort Abraham Lincoln, Dakota on the steamer *Far West*. Born in Ireland. Enlisted on November 16, 1872, at age 21 9/12 in Pittsburgh by Lieut. Calbraith Rodgers. Previous occupation was laborer. Discharged on March 1, 1877 at Fort Rice, Dakota for disability, as a Private of excellent character. He had grey eyes, dark hair, fair complexion and was 5'-6" in height.

MUELLER, WILLIAM, Private
On detached service with the band from May 5, 1876, at Fort Abraham Lincoln, Dakota. Born in Altenburg, Germany. Enlisted on October 6, 1875, at age 34 in St. Louis by Lieut. John Thompson. Previous occupation was laborer. Discharged on October 5, 1880 at Fort Yates, Dakota upon expiration of service, as a Private of excellent character. He had blue eyes, brown hair, dark complexion and was 5'-7 1/8" in height.

O'MANN, WILLIAM, Private
Born in Hamilton County, Indiana. Enlisted on October 12, 1875 at age 26 in Cincinnati by Lieut. Patrick Cusack. Previous occupation was hostler. Discharged on October 11, 1880, at Fort Yates, Dakota upon expiration of service, as a Private of good character. He had brown eyes, brown hair, dark complexion and was 5'-8" in height. His name is listed as William Omann in the Register of Enlistments, U.S. Army.

QUINN, JOHN, Private
On detached service from June 15, 1876 at Yellowstone Depot, Montana Territory. Born in Hartford, Connecticut. Enlisted on June 19, 1875 at age 23 in Boston by Lieut. William Harper, Jr. Previous occupation was blacksmith. Wounded on September 30, 1877 in the Snake Creek fight near the Bear Paw Mountains, Montana Territory in an engagement with Chief Joseph's band of Nez Perce Indians. He was then a Corporal. Discharged on June 18, 1880, at Fort Yates, Dakota upon expiration of service, as a Sergeant of good character. He had blue eyes, brown hair, fair complexion and was 5'-7¾" in height.

RANDALL, WILLIAM J., Private
Born in Pittsburgh, Pennsylvania. Enlisted on September 15, 1875, at age 25 in Cincinnati by Lieut. Patrick Cusack. Previous occupation was carpenter. Killed on September 30, 1877 in the Snake Creek fight, near the Bear Paw Mountains, Montana Territory in an engagement with Chief Joseph's band of Nez Perce Indians. Re-interred in the Custer Battlefield National Monument, Grave 1412 (2) B. He had brown eyes, brown hair, dark complexion and was 5'-7¼" in height. Listed elsewhere as Rander.

REID, ELWYN S., Private
Born in Green, New York. Enlisted on October 26, 1872, at age 27 5/12 in Albany, New York by Captain Theodore Wint. Previous occupation was carpenter. Discharged on June 23, 1877, at camp on the Tongue River, Montana Territory per Special Order Nr. 70, Department of Dakota, 1877, as a Private of excellent character. He had hazel eyes, brown hair, dark complexion and was 5'-10" in height.

SADLER, WILLIAM, Private
On detached service from June 15, 1876 at Yellowstone Depot, Montana Territory. Born in Frankfort, Germany. Enlisted on August 9, 1875, at age 21 in New York City by Lieut. John Babcock. Previous occupation was saddler. Discharged on August 8, 1880, at Fort Yates, Dakota upon expiration of service, as a Private of excellent character. He had grey eyes, light hair, fair complexion and was 5'-7" in height.

SANDERS, CHARLES, Private
   Orderly for Lieut. W. S. Edgerly on June 25, in the valley and hilltop fights.
Born in Saxony, Germany. Third enlistment on January 26, 1872, at age 28 in
Chicago by Captain Samuel Young. His enlistment was cancelled because of
desertion on December 11, 1867 from the General Service, U.S. Army under the
same name. Lieut. Edgerly wrote after the Little Bighorn River fight that,
"When I handed my carbine to Pvt. Saunders [sic], I noticed a broad grin on his
face altho' he was sitting in a perfect shower of bullets. I didn't have time to
question him then, but the next day after the firing had ceased I asked him what
he was laughing at at such a time. He replied, 'I was laughing to see what poor
shots those Indians were; they were shooting too low and their bullets were
spattering dust like drops of rain.' I never saw a cooler man under fire than
Saunders." He was discharged on January 26, 1877, at Fort Abraham Lincoln,
Dakota upon expiration of service, as a Private of good character. He had hazel
eyes, dark hair, dark complexion and was 5'-10½" in height.

SCOTT, GEORGE D., Private
   In the hilltop fight. Born in Lancaster County, Kentucky. Enlisted on
September 7, 1871 at age 21 in Mount Vernon, Kentucky by Captain Thomas
Weir. Previous occupation was farmer. Discharged on August 5, 1876 at camp at
the mouth of Rosebud Creek, Montana Territory, per General Order Nr. 24,
AGO, 59 Awarded the Medal of Honor on October 5, 1878 for voluntarily
bringing water to the wounded under fire in the Little Bighorn River fight. He
had blue eyes, brown hair, fair complexion and was 5'-8" in height.

SIMS, JOHN J., Private
   On detached service from June 15, 1876, at Yellowstone Depot, Montana
Territory. Born in Johnson County, Ill. Enlisted on October 1, 1875, at age 23
in St. Louis by Captain Owen Hale. Previous occupation was painter. Deserted
on February 20, 1877; surrendered on February 25, 1877. Discharged on May
10, 1877, at Fort Rice, Dakota, per General Court Martial Order Nr. 21,
Department of Dakota, as a Private. He had blue eyes, brown hair, dark
complexion and was 5'-7¾" in height. Listed as John J. Sims in the Register of
Enlistments, U.S. Army and elsewhere as John J. Sems.

SMITH, HENRY G., Private
   Born in Lake County, Indiana. Enlisted on September 8, 1875 at age 26 in
Chicago by Lieut. Edmund Luff. Previous occupation was butcher. Deserted on
February 19, 1877. He had grey eyes, brown hair, dark complexion and was
5'-9" in height.

SMITH, WILLIAM E., Private
   Born in Rouses Point, New York. Enlisted on September 13, 1875, at age
22, in Boston by Lieut. Henry Lawton. Previous occupation was farmer.
Deserted on March 28, 1877; apprehended on March 28, 1877. Discharged on
September 12, 1880, at Camp Houston, Dakota, upon expiration of service, as a
Private of excellent character. He had grey eyes, dark hair, dark complexion and
was 5'-5½" in height.

STIVERS, THOMAS W., Private
   In the hilltop fight. Born in Madison County, Kentucky. Enlisted on.

September 16, 1871 at age 21 2/12 in Mount Vernon, Kentucky by Captain Thomas Weir. Previous occupation was clerk. Discharged on August 5, 1876, at camp at the mouth of Rosebud Creek, Montana Territory. Awarded the Medal of Honor on October 5, 1878 with the citation, "voluntarily brought water to the wounded under fire," in the Little Bighorn River fight. Listed as Thomas W. Stivers in the Register of Enlistments, U.S. Army, and elsewhere as Thomas W. Stevens. He had blue eyes, dark brown hair, and fair complexion and was 5'-5" in height.

TOLAN, FRANK, Private
    In the hilltop fight. Born in Malone, New York. Enlisted on August 31, 1875, at age 21¼ in Boston by Lieut. William Harper, Jr. Previous occupation was farmer. Awarded the Medal of Honor on October 5, 1878 for voluntarily bringing water to the wounded under fire in the Little Bighorn River fight. Discharged on August 30, 1880, at Fort Yates, Dakota upon expiration of service, as a Private of fair character. He had grey eyes, brown hair, fair complexion and was 5'-8" in height.

WELCH, CHARLES H., Private
    In the hilltop fight. Born in New York City. Enlisted on June 3, 1873, at age 23 at Fort Snelling, Minnesota by Captain Thomas Weir. Previous occupation was laborer. Wounded on September 30, 1877, in the Snake Creek fight, near the Bear Paw Mountains, Montana Territory in an engagement with Chief Joseph's band of Nez Perce Indians (he was then in the grade of Sergeant). Discharged on June 2, 1878, at Fort Rice, Dakota for disability, as a Sergeant. Awarded the Medal of Honor on October 5, 1878, for voluntarily bringing water to the wounded under fire in the Little Bighorn River fight. He had grey eyes, brown hair, fair complexion and was 5'-7¾" in height.

WYNN, JAMES, Private
    In the hilltop fight. Born in Dublin, Ireland. Second enlistment on March 12, 1873, at age 37 in Livingston, Alabama by Lieut. Winfield Edgerly. Lieut. Edgerly, after the Little Bighorn River fight, wrote of Wynn in the movement from the hilltop to join Custer, "We had in our troop a corpulent old tailor, known throughout the regiment as "Jimmy" Wynn, who was riding an old horse, blind in one eye, and oridnarily very quiet. The instant he mounted, his horse started for the rear at full speed and one of the most laughable sights I ever saw was "Jimmy" pulling at the reins with both hands, his carbine dangling at his side, a veritable fat John Gilpin. He wasn't able to stop until he reached the horses of the rest of the command." Wynn was discharged March 12, 1878, at Fort Rice, Dakota upon expiration of service, as a Private of excellent character. He had grey eyes, grey hair, ruddy complexion and was 5'-5" in height.

COMPANY E IN 1876

The company was stationed at Fort Totten, Dakota. On January 6 Lieut. McDougall, with a detachment of the company, removed trespassing Indians who had located themselves on the reservation. The company left Fort Totten on March 10 with Co. L and arrived at Jamestown, Dakota, on March 13, having marched 83 miles. Lieut. McDougall, having been promoted, was transferred to Company B on March 22, after Lieut. Algernon Smith had arrived from Fort Abraham Lincoln and assumed command.

On April 17 the company arrived at Fort Lincoln to join the Sioux expedition. The regiment left Fort Lincoln on May 17 and returned on September 26 and the company went into quarters.

Company E was one of eight companies under the command of Colonel Samuel Sturgis that went to the Cheyenne Agency via the left bank of the Missouri River to disarm and dismount the Indians there. The company left Fort Lincoln on October 17 and returned on November 11 for winter station. The company marched 2,191 miles in the year.

The following members were casualties in the Little Bighorn River fight. Killed: Lieut. Wm. Reily, First Sergeant Frederick Hohmeyer, Sergeants John Ogden, William James, Corporals Albert Meyer, George Brown, Thomas Eagan (Thomas Hagan) and Henry Mason, Trumpeters Thomas McElroy and George Moonie, Privates William Baker, Robert Barth, Owen Boyle, James Brogan, Edward Connor, John Darris, William Davis, Richard Farrell, John Heim, John Henderson, Sykes Henderson, John Hiley, William Huber, Andy Knecht, Herod Liddiard, Patrick O'Connor, Wm. Rees, Edward Rood, Henry Schele, William Smallwood, Albert Smith, James Smith (1), James Smith (2), Benjamin Stafford, Alexander Stella, William Torrey, Cornelius Van Sant and George Walker. Sergeant James Riley was wounded while with the command under Major Marcus Reno.

Officers serving with the company in the year were Captain Charles Ilsley, First Lieutenants Thomas McDougall and Charles DeRudio and Second Lieutenants William Reily and Hugh Lenox Scott. Lieut. Scott was transferred to the 7th Cavalry to fill the vacancy created by the death of Lieut. Reily.

COMPANY E AT THE LITTLE BIGHORN

	Absent	Present	Wounded	Died OWRT	Killed	Survived
Captain	1					1
1st Lieut.		1				1
2nd Lieut.		1			1	
1st Sergt.		1			1	
Sergeant	1	4	1		2	3
Corporal		4			4	
Trumpeter		2			2	
Saddler		1				1
Farrier		1				1
Blacksmith		1				1
Private	6	39			27	18
Totals	8	55	1	0	37	26

COMPANY E ON JUNE 30, 1876

Officers present for duty 1
Enlisted present for duty 13
Enlisted present extra duty 2
Officers absent detached service 1
Enlisted absent detached service 4
Enlisted absent with leave 1
Enlisted absent sick 3
Enlisted absent in arrest 1
Captain 1
First Lieutenant 1
Sergeants 3
Farrier and blacksmith 2
Saddler 1
Privates 18
Total enlisted 24
Aggregate 26
Aggregate in May 63
Enlisted by transfer 1
Enlisted transferred 1
Enlisted killed 37
Wounded 1
Horses serviceable 11
Horses lost 44

ILSLEY, CHARLES STILLIMAN, Captain

On detached service as aide-de-camp to General John Pope. Born in Maine. He entered military service from Maine by enlisting in Company C, 71st New York State Militia from April 20 to July 30, 1861, during which period he was engaged in the first battle of Bull Run. Appointed Captain, 15th Maine Volunteer Infantry on December 23, 1861 and was engaged at Ship Island and Fort Pickens. Participated in the battle of New Orleans and the actions at Thibodeaux, Louisiana, Mustang Island and Fort Esperanza. He was on General Ransom's staff until April, 1864, and was in the Red River campaign, the battles of Sabine Crossroads, Pleasant Hill and Cane River. In Sheridan's Shenandoah Valley campaign and the battle of Winchester. On the staff of General Seward from November, 1864, to May, 1865. Mustered out of volunteer service on Mar. 25, 1865, and appointed Captain, 5th New York Volunteer Artillery, on April 3, 1865. On the staff of General Fessenden to June, 1865, and aide-de-camp to General Emory to July, 1865. On July 19, 1865, he was mustered out of volunteer service. Appointed Second Lieutenant, 16th Infantry with rank from February 23, 1866; promoted to First Lieutenant to rank from the same date. Received the brevet of Captain on March 2, 1867, for his gallant and meritorious services during the war. From January, 1868 to 1879 he was aide-de-camp to General John Pope who was then commanding the Department of the Lakes. On Apr. 17, 1869, he was unassigned and on December 15, 1870, he was assigned to the 1st Cavalry and transferred to the 7th Cavalry on December 23, 1870. Promoted to Captain of Company E on July 11, 1871. Captain Ilsley did not participate in the Sioux expedition of 1876 because of his continued assignment as aide-de-camp to General Pope who, during that period, commanded the Department of the Missouri at Fort Leavenworth. He was relieved from duty as aide-de-camp to General Pope in August, 1879, at his own request and joined his company at Fort Meade, Dakota, in September, 1879. On June 30, 1892, he was promoted to Major, 9th Cavalry and to Lieutenant Colonel, 6th Cavalry on March 29, 1899. He retired on April 8, 1899 and died on April 17, 1899.

DeRUDIO, CHARLES CAMILUS, First Lieutenant

In command of Company A in the valley and hilltop fights. Born Carlo Camillo di Rudio in Belluno, Italy on August 26, 1832. He was educated at the Austrian Military Academy and served on the staff of General Garabaldi in Italy. Departed from London for New York on February 8, 1864, and entered military service as a Private, 79th Highlanders, New York Volunteers in which regiment he served from August 25 to October 17, 1864. Commissioned a Second Lieutenant in Company D, 2nd U.S. Colored Infantry on October 17 to date from November 11 and was honorably mustered out with the regiment on January 5, 1866. He was appointed a Second Lieutenant, 2nd Infantry on August 31, 1867 but his appointment was cancelled. It was renewed on October 25, 1867. During the reorganization of the army in 1869 he was unassigned. Assigned to the 7th Cavalry on July 14 of that year and promoted to First Lieutenant on December 15, 1875, to occupy the vacancy created by the promotion of First Lieutenant Thomas McDougall. On May 17, 1876, he departed from Fort Abraham Lincoln, Dakota with Company E to participate in the Sioux expedition. During the Little Bighorn River fight he was on duty with Company A and was engaged in the valley fight. In the ensuing retreat to the hilltop, he was missing but rejoined the command on the bluffs on the night of

June 25. DeRudio was promoted to Captain of Cavalry on December 17, 1882, and accepted the promotion on January 31, 1883, while stationed at Fort Meade, Dakota. From June 30, 1894, to October 5, 1895, he was stationed at Fort Sam Houston and from the latter date to May 2, 1896, he was at Fort Bayard, New Mexico. From May 2 to August 26, 1896, he was in San Diego waiting retirement and on that day he was retired by law at the age of 64. He received promotion to Major, retired and accepted the promotion on June 3, 1909 while residing in Los Angeles. Died November 1, 1910 in Los Angeles.

REILY, WILLIAM VAN WYCK, Second Lieutenant

Killed with Company F in the Custer battalion on June 25. Born December 12, 1853 in Washington, D.C. Attended Georgetown College with two years in school in Germany. Appointed to the Naval Academy on September 22, 1870; resigned on October 17, 1872. After leaving the Academy he was on a surveying expedition in Nicaragua for eight months and for two years, prior to commissioning in the army, he superintended the breaking up of old monitors. He was appointed a Second Lieutenant, 10th Cavalry on October 15, 1875, and was transferred to Company E, 7th Cavalry, effective January 26, 1876 to occupy the vacancy created by the promotion of Lieutenant William Craycroft. On May 17, 1876, he departed with the 7th Cavalry from Fort Abraham Lincoln, Dakota to participate in the Sioux expedition. His remains were interred on the battlefield on June 28 and exhumed in July, 1877 and re-interred at Washington, D. C.

HOHMEYER, FREDERICK, First Sergeant

Killed with the Custer battalion (in the ravine) on June 25. Born in Darmstadt, Germany. Third enlistment on May 10, 1875 at age 26 in Opelika, Alabama by Lieut. Thomas McDougall. He had grey eyes, light hair, dark complexion and was 5'-7½" in height. Listed as Fred'k Hohmeyer on the battle monument. Captain Thomas M. McDougall, in a letter dated May 18, 1909, to Brig. Gen. E. S. Godfrey described the manner in which the bodies of the men of Company E were covered over. He said, ". . . Only a few of the men could be recognized. I knew Sergeant Hohmyer [Hohmeyer] at once; he had one sock left on his foot with his name on it."

JAMES, WILLIAM B., Sergeant

Killed in battle on June 25. Born in Pembrokeshire, Wales. Enlisted on February 5, 1872 at age 23 in Chicago by Captain Samuel Young. Previous occupation was coachman. Listed as W. B. James on the battle monument. He had hazel eyes, light hair, light complexion and was 5'-9" in height.

MURPHY, LAWRENCE, Sergeant

Born in Kerry, Ireland. Enlisted on December 30, 1871, at age 22 in Boston by Lieut. Moses Harris. Previous occupation was laborer. Discharged on December 30, 1876, at Fort Abraham Lincoln, Dakota upon expiration of service, as a Sergeant. He had blue eyes, brown hair, fair complexion and was 5'-5¾" in height.

OGDEN, JOHN S., Sergeant

Killed in battle on June 25. Born in Newberry, Massachusetts. Second enlistment on November 15, 1872, at age 27 in Unionville, South Carolina by Lieut. Thomas McDougall. He had grey eyes, light hair, light complexion and was 5'-8" in height. Listed as J. S. Ogden on the battle monument and elsewhere as Egnen and Egden.

RILEY, JAMES F., Sergeant
Wounded in the back and the left leg in the hilltop fight on June 26 while on duty with the pack train. Transported to Fort Abraham Lincoln, Dakota on the steamboat *Far West*. Born in Baltimore, Maryland. Enlisted on August 10, 1866, in Baltimore. Honorably discharged on August 10, 1871 at Spartanburg, South Carolina as a Wagoner in Company E, 7th Cavalry. Second enlistment on August 11, 1871, at age 26 at Spartanburg by Major Marcus Reno. Discharged on August 11, 1876, at Fort Lincoln upon expiration of service, as a Sergeant of excellent character. He had blue eyes, brown hair, fair complexion and was 5'-11" in height. Listed as James F. Riley in the Register of Enlistments, U.S. Army and elsewhere as James T. Reilly.

WELLS, JOHN S., Sergeant
On furlough from May 17, 1876, from Fort Abraham Lincoln, Dakota. Born in Rose, Ohio. Second enlistment on January 11, 1872, at age 39 in Unionville, South Carolina by Lieut. Thomas McDougall. Previous occupation was soldier. Discharged on January 11, 1877 at Fort Lincoln upon expiration of his service, as a Sergeant of very good character. He had blue eyes, light hair, light complexion and was 5'-9¾" in height.

BROWN, GEORGE C., Corporal
Killed in battle on June 25. Born in Baltimore, Maryland. Enlisted on October 19, 1872, at age 21 in Philadelphia by Captain Samuel Whitside. Previous occupation was candymaker. He had brown eyes, brown hair, ruddy complexion and was 5'-5½" in height. Listed as G. C. Brown on the battle monument and elsewhere as C. S. Brown and Bloom.

EAGAN, THOMAS P. (Thomas Hagan), Corporal
Killed in battle on June 25. Born in Ireland, the son of Thomas Luke Eagan. Eagan was enlisted under the name of Thomas Hagan on September 12, 1873 at age 25 at St. Louis Barracks by Captain Charles Bendire. Previous occupation was laborer. He had grey eyes, sandy hair, light complexion and was 5'-5½" in height. Listed as Thos. Hagan on the battle monument. Thomas Eagan wrote this last letter to his half-sister, Ella Adele Eagan Barbour:

Fort Totten, D.T.
March 5th, 1876

Dear Sister,
i take the preasent oppertunity of letting you no that i will soon be on the move again. We ar to start the 10th of this month for the Big horn country. The Indians are getting bad again. i think that we will have some hard times this summer. The old Chief Sitting Bull says that he will not make peace with the whites as long as he has a man to fight. The weather very cold hear at preasent and very likely to stay so for two months yet. Ella, you need not rite to me again until you hear frome me again. Give my love to Sister Mary & Brother Jonny. Remember me to your husband. As soon as i get back of the campaign i

will rite you. That is if i do not get my hair lifted by some Indian. Well i will close, so no more at preasent.

From your loving brother,

T. P. Eagan

P.S. If you hear from Hubert tell him not to rite until he hears from me.

TPE

MASON, HENRY S., Corporal
Killed in battle on June 25. Born in Brownville, Indiana. Second enlistment on August 4, 1875 at age 28 in Louisville, Kentucky by Lieut. William Beck. He had grey eyes, sandy hair, fair complexion and was 5'-11¼" in height. Listed as H. S. Mason on the battle monument. The Descriptive List and Records File, Custer Battlefield National Monument, has Company Order Nr. 11, July 10, 1874, Company F, Black Hills Expedition Camp, Grand River, Dakota in which Sergeant Henry S. Mason was reduced to Private for gross neglect of duty.

MEYER, ALBERT H., Corporal
Killed in battle on June 25. Born in Germany. Enlisted on September 27, 1873 at age 21 in New York City by Captain Edward Hunter. Previous occupation was bartender. He had blue eyes, light hair, fair complexion and was 5'-8" in height. Listed as A. H. Meyer on the battle monument.

McELROY, THOMAS, Trumpeter
Killed in battle on June 25. Born in Neagh, Ireland. He came to the United States in 1863 and enlisted during the Civil War and was wounded. He was enlisted as a Trumpeter in Company G, 1st U.S. Infantry and was discharged at Fort Totten, Dakota. Enlisted in the 7th Cavalry on July 3, 1875 at age 30 at Fort Randall, Dakota by Lieut. William Craycroft. Previous occupation was musician. He had blue eyes, dark hair, ruddy complexion and was 5'-5½" in height. Listed as Thos. McElroy on the battle monument. His widow married John Furey, Company E, 7th Cavalry. His son born March 28, 1874, took his stepfather's name and was known as Thomas Francis Furey.

MOONIE, GEORGE A., Trumpeter
Killed in battle on June 25. Born in Boston. Enlisted on March 18, 1875 at age 20 in Boston by Lieut. William Harper, Jr. Previous occupation was clerk. He had hazel eyes, dark hair, fair complexion and was 5'-6 3/8" in height. Listed as G. A. Moonie on the battle monument and elsewhere as Mooney.

SHIELDS, WILLIAM, Saddler
Born in Vincennes, Indiana. Third enlistment on September 29, 1874, at age 33 at Fort Abraham Lincoln, Dakota, by Lieut. Thomas McDougall. Discharged on September 28, 1879, at Fort Meade, Dakota upon expiration of service, as a Saddler of excellent character. He had grey eyes, brown hair, fair complexion and was 5'-8" in height.

SPENCER, ABLE B., Farrier
Born in Rock County, Wisconsin. Enlisted on January 13, 1872, at age 27 in Chicago by Captain Samuel Young. Previous occupation was farmer.

110

Discharged on January 8, 1877, at Fort Abraham Lincoln, Dakota upon expiration of service, as a Private of good character. He had hazel eyes, dark hair, dark complexion and was 5'-7¾" in height. Listed as Able Spencer in the Register of Enlistments, U.S. Army and elsewhere as Abel K. Spencer.

MILLER, HENRY, Blacksmith
In the pack train detail on June 25? Born in Baltimore, Maryland. Enlisted on November 13, 1871, at age 27 11/12 in Memphis, Tennessee by Captain George Purington. Previous occupation was blacksmith. Discharged on November 13, 1876 at Fort Abraham Lincoln, Dakota upon expiration of service, as a Blacksmith. He had blue eyes, brown hair, light complexion and was 5'-9" in height.

ABBOTS, HARRY, Private
On Extra Duty as hospital attendant from May 17, 1876. Born in New York City. Enlisted on October 8, 1875, at age 22 in Louisville, Kentucky, by Lieut. William Beck. Previous occupation was bricklayer. Discharged on December 3, 1877, at Fort Abraham Lincoln, Dakota for disability, as a Private. He had hazel eyes, dark hair, dark complexion and was 5'-9¼" in height.

ACKISON, DAVID, Private
Sick with consumption. Transported to Fort Buford, Dakota on the steamboat *Far West*, where he was landed on July 4. Born in Troy, New York. Enlisted on October 1, 1873, at age 21¼ in Pittsburgh by Lieut. Randolph Norwood. Previous occupation was railroader. Discharged on October 1, 1878 at Camp Ruhlen, Dakota upon expiration of service, as a Private of good character. He had grey eyes, brown hair, fair complexion and was 5'-5" in height. Listed as David Ackison in the Register of Enlistments, U.S. Army and the 7th Cavalry, Company E, Muster Roll June 30, 1876. Listed elsewhere as Ackinson.

BAKER, WILLIAM H., Private
Killed in battle on June 25. Born in Pope County, Illinois. Second enlistment on November 1, 1875, at age 26 in New York City by Lieut. John Babcock. He had blue eyes, brown hair, fair complexion and was 5'-9" in height. Listed as W. H. Baker on the battle monument.

BARTH, ROBERT, Private
Killed in battle on June 25. Born in Uforzheim, Germany. Enlisted on December 6, 1872, at age 22 in Albany, New York by Captain Theodore Wint. Previous occupation was jeweler. He had grey eyes, brown hair, fair complexion and was 5'-10½" in height. Listed as Rob't Barth on the battle monument, and elsewhere as Bauth.

BERWALD, FRANK, Private
Born in Poland. Enlisted on January 25, 1873, at age 22 in Pittsburgh, Pennsylvania by Lieut. Randolph Norwood. Previous occupation was blacksmith. Discharged on January 25, 1878 at Fort Abraham Lincoln, Dakota upon expiration of service, as a Sergeant of good character. He had grey eyes, brown hair, florid complexion and was 5'-5¾" in height.

BOYLE, OWEN, Private

Killed in battle on June 25. Born in Waterford, Ireland. Enlisted on December 19, 1874, at age 31 in Boston by Lieut. William Harper, Jr. Previous occupation was soldier. He had grey eyes, dark hair, fair complexion and was 5'-6" in height. Listed as Owen Boyle on the battle monument.

BROGAN, JAMES, Private

Killed in battle on June 25. Born in Pittsburgh, Pennsylvania. Second enlistment on April 1, 1876, at age 26 at Fort Seward, Dakota by Lieut. Algernon Smith. He had hazel eyes, brown hair, ruddy complexion and was 5'-8¼" in height. Listed as James Brogan on the battle monument and elsewhere as Bragew and Brogen.

BROMWELL, LATROBE, Private

Born in Frederick County, Maryland. Enlisted on July 12, 1870, at a stated age of 25 in Baltimore in Company G, 2nd Cavalry by Lieut. Lynde. Previous occupation was clerk. Discharged on July 12, 1875, as a Private. Re-enlisted on August 9, 1875, at a stated age of 28 in Baltimore by Lieut. Charles Cresson in Company E, 7th Cavalry. Discharged on August 8, 1880 at Fort Meade, Dakota upon expiration of service, as a Sergeant of excellent character. Re-enlisted on August 9, 1880, at the age of 33 at Fort Meade, Dakota by Lieut. Loyd McCormick and assigned to Company E. Transferred to non-commissioned staff for duty as regimental quartermaster sergeant. Discharged on August 8, 1885 at Fort Meade, Dakota, as regimental quartermaster sergeant. Re-enlisted on August 9, 1885 in the 7th Cavalry at Fort Meade. At this time he was married and had three children. From January 1, 1884 to July 25, 1887 he was stationed at Fort Meade. From July 25, 1887 to September 1, 1887 he was enroute to and at Guide Rock, Nebraska. From September 1, 1887 to November 11, 1889 he was at Fort Riley, Kansas. Discharged on November 11, 1889 by order and at his own request, as regimental quartermaster sergeant. In December, 1889 the new cavalry consolidated mess at Fort Riley was opened with Lieut. Luther Hare in charge. "Tobe" Brommell became the chief cook after his discharge. He re-enlisted on Januray 25, 1892 in the 7th Cavalry at Fort Riley and was stationed there until December 31, 1893. Discharged on January 24, 1897 as regimental quartermaster sergeant. Re-enlisted on January 25, 1897 in the 7th Cavalry and retired on January 14, 1900 as regimental quartermaster sergeant. All service prior to January 25, 1892 was under the name of Latrobe Brommell. Listed as Latrobe Brommell in the Register of Enlistments, U.S. Army and as Latrobe Bromwell on his Oath of Enlistment. He had grey eyes, light hair, light complexion and was 5'-6" in height. A Training School for Cooks and Bakers, Mounted Service School, Fort Riley was established on February 15, 1905 with Tobe Brommell in charge of cooking. Captain M. S. Murray, Commissary, USA was the school commander. Patrick Dunne, formerly a color Sergeant in the 5th Cavalry was appointed Commissary Sergeant in 1908 and appointed Chief Cook to relieve Tobe Brommell upon his retirement about 1909. See W. F. Pride, *The History of Fort Riley*, 1926.

BRUNS, AUGUST, Private

On detached service from May 17, 1876, at Fort Abraham Lincoln,

Dakota. Born in Brunswick, Germany. Participated in the Black Hills expedition in 1874. Re-enlisted in October 20, 1875, at age 37 in New York City by Lieut. John Babcock. Previous occupation was musician. Discharged on November 19, 1880, at Fort Meade, Dakota, upon expiration of service, as a Private of excellent character. He had hazel eyes, dark hair, sallow complexion and was 5'-8½" in height. Listed as August Bruns in the Register of Enlistments, U.S. Army and elsewhere as Brumms. After his discharge he opened a small boot and shoe repair shop in Mandan, Dakota. A bass viol that belonged to Bruns is in the Fort A. Lincoln State Park Museum.

CHAPMAN, WILLIAM H., Private
Born in Glastonbury, Connecticut. Enlisted on March 13, 1876, at age 24 in Boston, by Lieut. Henry Lawton. Previous occupation was farmer. Transferred from Company B on June 1, 1876 in the field, per Special Order Nr. 49, Headquarters, 7th Cavalry. Deserted on October 15, 1876; surrendered on July 7, 1886. Discharged on July 30, 1886 at Fort Meade, Dakota, to date from Oct. 15, 1876 per Special Order Nr. 175, AGO, 1886, as a Private with a character reference of "None". This soldier had grey eyes, dark hair, ruddy complexion and was 5'-9¼" in height.

CONNOR, EDWARD, Private
Killed in battle on June 25. Born in Clare, Ireland. Second enlistment on December 5, 1872, at age 26 at Unionville, S. C. by Lieut. Isaiah McDonald. He had hazel eyes, brown hair, ruddy complexion and was 5'-8½" in height. Listed as Edward Connor on his Oath of Enlistment and the Register of Enlistments, U.S. Army. Listed in Co. I in the *Bismarck Tribune* Extra, July 6, 1876.

DARRIS, JOHN, Private
Killed in battle with Company E on June 25. Born in Goshen, New York. Enlisted on September 9, 1875, at age 29 in Cincinnati by Lieut. Patrick Cusack. Previous occupation was fireman. He had blue eyes, brown hair, dark complexion and was 5'-6½" in height. Listed as Jno. Darris on the battle monument and elsewhere as Darrah and Doring and Daring.

DAVIS, WILLIAM, Private
Killed in battle on June 25. Born in Vandalia, Illinois. Enlisted on December 19, 1874, at age 23 in St. Louis by Lieut. William Volkmar. Previous occupation was laborer. Deserted on February 25, 1875; apprehended on February 28, 1875. He had grey eyes, brown hair, fair complexion and was 5'-6" in height. Listed as Wm. Davis on the battle monument.

FARRELL, RICHARD, Private
Killed in battle on June 25. Born in Dublin, Ireland. Enlisted on September 29, 1875, at age 24 in St. Louis by Captain Owen Hale. Previous occupation was laborer. He had grey eyes, brown hair, fair complexion and was 5'-8¾" in height. Listed as Rich'd Farrell on the battle monument.

GILBERT, JULIUS, Private
On detached service from May 17, 1876 at Fort Abraham Lincoln, Dakota. Born in Belfort, France. Enlisted on December 11, 1874, at age 21 in

New York City by Lieut. Thomas Gregg. Previous occupation was farmer. Discharged on December 10, 1879 at Fort Meade, Dakota upon expiration of service, as a Private of good character. He had hazel eyes, brown hair, fair complexion and was 5'-7¾" in height.

HEIM, JOHN, Private
Killed in battle on June 25. Born in St. Louis, Missouri. Enlisted on January 19, 1875, at age 23 in St. Louis by Lieut. William Volkmar. Previous occupation was clerk. He had brown eyes, light hair, fair complexion and was 5'-1" in height. Listed as Jno. Heim on the battle monument and elsewhere as Hime.

HENDERSON, JOHN, Private
Killed in battle on June 25. Born in Cork, Ireland. Second enlistment on September 22, 1875, at age 26 in New York City by Lieut. John Babcock. He had grey eyes, light hair, fair complexion and was 5'-7¾" in height. Listed as Jno. Henderson on the battle monument.

HENDERSON, SYKES, Private
Killed in battle on June 25. Born in Armstrong County, Pennsylvania. Second enlistment on December 3, 1872, at age 27 in Unionville, South Carolina by Lieut. Thomas McDougall. He had brown eyes, brown hair, fair complexion and was 5'-8" in height. Listed as Sykes Henderson on the battle monument.

HILEY, JOHN S., Private
Killed in battle on June 25. Born in Rugby, England. Enlisted on January 20, 1872, at age 23 in New York City by Lieut. John Mahnken. Previous occupation was clerk. He had hazel eyes, light brown hair, fair complexion and was 6'-0" in height. His name is listed as J. S. Hiley on the battle monument and elsewhere as John G. Hiley.

HOWARD, FRANK, Private
On detached service from May 17, 1876, at Fort Abraham Lincoln, Dakota. Born in Waukegan, Illinois. Enlisted on February 8, 1872, at age 22 in Chicago by Captain Samuel Young. Previous occupation was farmer. Discharged on February 8, 1877 at Fort Lincoln upon expiration of service, as a Private of good character. He had brown eyes, black hair, dark complexion and was 5'-8" in height.

HUBER, WILLIAM, Private
Killed in battle on June 25. Born in Wurtemburg, Germany. Enlisted on December 21, 1874, at age 21 in Cincinnati, Ohio by Lieut. Patrick Cusack. Previous occupation was gunsmith. He had grey eyes, light brown hair, fair complexion and was 5'-7" in height. Listed as Wm. Huber on the battle monument and elsewhere as Hieber.

HUTTER, ANTON, Private
In an insane asylum in Washington, D. C. from June 19, 1872. Born in Bavaria, Germany. Enlisted on February 9, 1872, at age 21 in Rochester, New York by Lieut. Albert Forse. Previous occupation was laborer. He was dropped

from the rolls on February 8, 1877, upon expiration of his period of service, while he was an inmate of the insane asylum. Discharged on October 18, 1878, with character good so far as known. He had hazel eyes, dark hair, fair complexion and was 5'-10½" in height.

JAMES, JOHN, Private
Born in Rome, Italy. Enlisted on May 13, 1872, at age 24 in Louisville, Kentucky by Lieut. William Cooke. Previous occupation was soldier. Discharged on May 13, 1877, at Fort Abraham Lincoln, Dakota, upon expiration of service, as a Corporal of good character. He had grey eyes, brown hair, dark complexion and was 5'-7½" in height.

KIMM, JOHN G., Private
With the pack train detail on June 25? Born in New York City. Third enlistment on January 18, 1872, at age 24 in Cincinnati, Ohio by Lieut. Myles Moylan. Discharged on January 18, 1877, at Fort Abraham Lincoln, Dakota upon expiration of service, as a Private of good character. He had grey eyes, black hair, florid complexion and was 5'-10½" in height.

KNECHT, ANDY, Private
Killed in battle on June 25. Born in Cincinnati, Ohio. Enlisted on September 22, 1873, at age 21½ at St. Louis Barracks, Missouri by Captain Charles Bendire. Previous occupation was butcher. He had hazel eyes, light brown hair, light complexion and was 5'-6½" in height. Listed as Andy Knecht on the battle monument and elsewhere as Andrew Knight.

LANGE, HENRY, Private
With the pack train detail on June 25? Born in Hanover, Germany. Enlisted on January 6, 1872, at age 21 in Chicago by Captain Samuel Young. Previous occupation was laborer. Discharged on January 6, 1877, at Fort Abraham Lincoln, Dakota upon expiration of service, as a Private of good character. He had grey eyes, light hair, light complexion and was 5'-8" in height. Listed as Henry Lange in the Register of Enlistments, U.S. Army and elsewhere as Lang.

LIDDIARD, HEROD T., Private
Killed in battle on June 25. Born in London, England. Enlisted on December 4, 1872, at age 21 in Troy, New York by Captain Theodore Wint. Previous occupation was boatman. He had blue eyes, light hair, fair complexion and was 5'-5¼" in height. Listed on the battle monument as H. T. Liddiard and elsewhere as Leddison.

McCANN, PATRICK, Private
In confinement from May 17, 1876 at Fort Abraham Lincoln, Dakota. Born in Monahan, Ireland. Enlisted on December 19, 1874, at age 21 5/12 in Boston by Lieut. William Harper, Jr. Previous occupation was laborer. Sentenced to one year confinement without pay on May 2, 1876. He had grey eyes, brown hair, fair complexion and was 5'-6 1/8" in height.

McKENNA, JOHN, Private
Born in Limerick, Ireland. Enlisted on December 19, 1874, at age 31 in

Boston by Lieut. William Harper, Jr. Previous occupation was hostler. Assigned to Company E, 7th Cavalry. Transferred to Company I. Discharged on December 18, 1879, at Fort Abraham Lincoln, Dakota upon expiration of service, as a Sergeant of excellent character. He had hazel eyes, dark hair, medium complexion and was 5'-8¾" in height. He was not in the Little Bighorn River fight and is not listed on the 7th Cavalry Muster Rolls June 30, 1876.

O'CONNOR, PATRICK, Private
Killed in battle on June 25. Born in Langford, Ireland. Enlisted on September 18, 1873, at age 21 in New York City by Lieut. William Winter. Previous occupation was shoemaker. He had blue eyes, light hair, fair complexion and was 5'-5½" in height. Listed as Pat'k O'Connor on the battle monument and elsewhere as Conner.

O'TOOLE, FRANCIS, Private
In the pack train detail on June 25? Born in County Mayo, Ireland. Enlisted on December 5, 1872, at age 33 in New York City by Captain Edwin Sumner. Previous occupation was soldier. Discharged on December 5, 1877 at Fort Abraham Lincoln, Dakota upon expiration of service, as a Sergeant of good character. He had blue eyes, brown hair fair complexion and was 5'-9½" in height.

PANDTLE, CHRISTOPHER, Private
On extra duty as hospital attendant from May 1, 1876. Born in Germany. Enlisted on October 28, 1872, at age 23 in Pittsburgh, Pennsylvania by Lieut. Calbraith Rodgers. Previous occupation was sawyer. Discharged June 10, 1877, at Fort A. Lincoln, Dakota per Special Order Nr. 47, Department of Dakota, 1877, as a Private of good character. He had brown eyes, light hair, fair complexion and was 5'-4½" in height.

REES, WILLIAM H., Private
Killed in battle on June 25. Born in Washington, Pennsylvania. Enlisted on December 5, 1872, at age 34 in St. Louis by Lieut. Oscar Elting. Previous occupation was laborer. He had grey eyes, sandy hair, fair complexion and was 6'-1" in height. Listed as W. H. Rees on the battle monument.

REESE, WILLIAM, Private
Born in Philadelphia. Enlisted on September 27, 1873, at age 27 in Philadelphia by Lieut. William Volkmar. Previous occupation was brushmaker. Discharged on September 27, 1878 at Fort Abraham Lincoln, Dakota upon expiration of service, as a Farrier of good character. He had blue eyes, light brown hair, fair complexion and was 5'-10" in height. Listed elsewhere as Ruse.

ROOD, EDWARD, Private
Killed in battle on June 25. Born in Tiago County, New York. Enlisted on September 19, 1873, at age 25 in New York City by Lieut. Edward Hunter. Previous occupation was fireman. He had hazel eyes, black hair, dark complexion and was 5'-7" in height. Listed as Edw'd Rood on the battle monument.

SCHELE, HENRY, Private
Killed in battle on June 25. Born in Hanover, Germany. Second enlistment on December 19, 1872, at age 29 in Unionville, South Carolina by Lieut. Thomas McDougall. He had blue eyes, light hair, fair complexion and was 5'-6" in height. Listed as Henry Schele on the battle monument and elsewhere as Schoole and Charles Schele.

SMALLWOOD, WILLIAM, Private
Killed in battle on June 25. Born in Jonesville, Indiana. Enlisted on December 18, 1874, at age 22 in Cincinnati, Ohio by Lieut. Patrick Cusack. Previous occupation was farmer. He had brown eyes, brown hair, dark complexion and was 5'-8½" in height. Listed as Wm. Smallwood on the battle monument.

SMITH, ALBERT A., Private
Killed in battle on June 25. Born in Queen County, New York. Enlisted on January 1, 1873, at age 34 at Unionville, South Carolina by Lieut. Thomas McDougall. Previous occupation was soldier. He had grey eyes, brown hair, fair complexion and was 5'-5¾" in height. Listed as Albert A. Smith on the battle monument.

SMITH, JAMES (1), Private
Killed in battle on June 25. Born in Tipperary, Ireland. Third enlistment on May 20, 1874, at age 32 at Fort Abraham Lincoln, Dakota by Lieut. George Wallace. He had hazel eyes, brown hair, ruddy complexion and was 5'-6" in height. Listed as James Smith. 1st, on the battle monument.

SMITH, JAMES (2), Private
Killed in battle on June 25. Born in Lynn, Massachusetts. Enlisted on December 1, 1874, at age 27 in St. Louis by Lieut. William Volkmar. Previous occupation was shoemaker. He had hazel eyes, black hair, dark complexion and was 5'-4½" in height. Listed as James Smith, 2d on the battle monument.

STAFFORD, BENJAMIN F., Private
Killed in battle on June 25. Born in Boston. Enlisted on October 8, 1873, at age 27 in Boston by Lieut. James Ropes. Previous occupation was currier. He had brown eyes, black hair, fair complexion and was 5'-5¼" in height. Listed as Benj. Stafford on the battle monument.

STELLA, ALEXANDER, Private
Killed in battle on June 25. Born in Athens, Greece. Enlisted on December 1, 1874, at age 21 in St. Louis by Lieut. William Volkmar. Previous occupation was cook. He had brown eyes, black hair, dark complexion and was 5'-6" in height. Listed as Alex. Stella on the battle monument.

TORREY, WILLIAM A., Private
Killed in battle on June 25. Born in Weymouth, Massachusetts. Enlisted on November 12, 1872, at age 22 4/12 in Boston, by Captain Moses Harris. Previous occupation was bootmaker. He had grey eyes, light hair, fair complexion and was 5'-4½" in height. Listed as W. A. Torrey on the battle monument and elsewhere as Tarr.

VAN SANT, CORNELIUS, Private

Killed in battle on June 25. Born in Cincinnati, Ohio. Enlisted on September 5, 1872, at age 22 4/12 in Cincinnati by Lieut. James Wheelan. Previous occupation was clerk. He had blue eyes, brown hair, fair complexion and was 5'-7¼" in height. Listed as Cornelius Van Sant on the battle monument and as Cornelius Vansant in the Register of Enlistments, U.S. Army and elsewhere as Vaugant.

WALKER, GEORGE, Private

Killed in battle on June 25. Born in Providence, Rhode Island. Enlisted on December 12, 1874, at age 22 in New York City by Lieut. Thomas Gregg. Previous occupation was hostler. He had grey eyes, brown hair, florid complexion and was 5'-6½" in height. Listed as Geo. Walker on the battle monument.

WOODRUFF, JERRY, Private

On detached service from May 17, 1876 at Fort Abraham Lincoln, Dakota. Born in Montjoy, Pennsylvania. Second enlistment on November 8, 1875, at age 27 at Fort Lincoln by Lieut. James Calhoun. Previous occupation was soldier. Discharged on November 7, 1880 at Fort Meade, Dakota upon expiration of service, as a Private of excellent character. He had grey eyes, brown hair, florid complexion and was 5'-6½" in height.

COMPANY F IN 1876

The company was stationed at Fort Abraham Lincoln, Dakota, until May 5 when it joined the regiment in camp below the post in preparation for the Sioux expedition. The regiment left Fort Lincoln on May 17. On May 30 the company was on a scouting trip up the Little Missouri River for 22 miles and return. The expedition returned to Ft. Lincoln on September 26 where the company occupied quarters. Company F was one of eight companies under the command of Colonel Samuel Sturgis which went to the Cheyenne Agency via the left bank of the Missouri to disarm and dismount the Indians there. The company left camp opposite the agency on November 4 in charge of 1,000 ponies and arrived at Ft. Abercrombie, Dakota, for winter station on November 14 after traveling 265 miles. Distance traveled in the year was 2,136 miles.

The following members were casualties in the Little Bighorn River fight. Those killed were Captain George Yates, Second Lieut. William Reily, First Sergeant Michael Kenney, Sergeants Frederick Nursey, John Vickory, John Wilkison, Corporals Charles Coleman, William Teeman and John Briody, Trumpeter Thomas Way, Farrier Benjamin Brandon, Blacksmith James Manning, Privates Thomas Atcheson, William Brady, Benjamin Brown, William Brown, Patrick Bruce, Lucien Burnham, James Carney, Armantheus Cather, Anton Dohman, Timothy Donnelly, William Gardner, George Hammon, John P. Kelly, Gustav Klein, Herman Knauth, William Lerock, Werner Liemann, William Lossee, Christian Madson, Francis Milton, Joseph Monroe, Sebastian Omling, Patrick Rudden, Richard Saunders, Francis Sicfous and George Warren. Private John Sullivan died in the hospital at Fort Abercrombie, Dakota, on December 7 with a disease of the lungs.

Officers serving with the company in the year were Captain George Yates, Captain James M. Bell, First Lieutenants Henry Jackson and William Robinson and Second Lieutenants Charles Larned, William Reily, Charles Schofield and Herbert Slocum.*

---

* *Charles Brewster Schofield was a replacement for Lieut. Chas. Larned who was promoted to First Lieutenant. The transfer, of Lieut. Schofield from the Second Cavalry, was not completed and he was replaced by Lieut. H. J. Slocum.*
Herbert Jermain Slocum was born in Ohio and appointed to the Military Academy from Illinois, which he entered on July 1, 1872. He graduated June 22, 1876, and was commissioned in the 25th Infantry effective June 21. He accepted the commission on July 26. Transferred to the Second Cavalry on August 18 and to the Seventh Cavalry on September 20 to be effective from July 28. Promoted to First Lieut. on Sept. 22, 1883, and Capt. on Aug. 26, 1896. Appointed Major, Inspector General, Volunteers, May 12, 1899. Assigned to Quartermaster Department July 25, 1902. Bvt. 1st Lieut. Feb. 27, 1890, for his gallant services against Chief Joseph's band of Nez Perce Indians at Canyon Creek, Montana Terr. on Sept. 13, 1877.

COMPANY F AT THE LITTLE BIGHORN

	Absent	Present	Wounded	Died OWRT	Killed	Survived
Captain		1			1	
1st Lieut.	1					1
2nd Lieut.	1					1
1st Sergt.		1			1	
Sergt.	1	4			3	2
Corporal		4			3	1
Trumpeter		1			1	
Saddler		1				1
Farrier		1			1	
Blacksmith		1			1	
Private	7	48			26	29
Totals	10	62	0	0	37	35

COMPANY F ON JUNE 30, 1876

Enlisted present for duty 11
Enlisted present extra duty 13
Enlisted present sick 1
Officers absent detached service 2
Enlisted absent detached service 6
Enlisted absent in arrest 2
First Lieutenant 1
Second Lieutenant 1
Sergeants 2
Corporal 1
Saddler 1
Privates 29
Total enlisted 33
Aggregate 35
Aggregate in May 72
Officers killed 1
Enlisted killed 36
Horses serviceable 12
Horses unserviceable 3
Horses lost 42

YATES, GEORGE WALTER, Captain

Killed on June 25 with the Custer battalion while commanding Company F. Born on February 26, 1843, in Albany, New York. At the age of 18 he enlisted in Company A, 4th Michigan Volunteer Infantry at Geneva, New York and served with the regiment in the first battle of Bull Run and the Seven Days Battle. Commissioned First Lieutenant and regimental adjutant on September 26, 1862, and was engaged with the regiment at Beverly Ford, Sharpsburg, Antietam and was wounded at Fredericksburg. He served with the regiment until the summer of 1863 when he was appointed to the staff of General Alfred Pleasonton and participated in the actions of the Army of the Potomac in 1863 including the engagement at Chancellorsville and the battle at Gettysburg. Honorably mustered out of volunteer service July 3, 1864, to date from June 28, 1864. On August 24, 1864 he enrolled from civil life as First Lieutenant and Adjutant of the 45th Missouri Volunteer Infantry. Promoted to Captain of Company G, 13th Missouri Volunteer Cavalry to rank from September 22, 1864. Brevetted Major, U.S.V. for his gallant and meritorious services during the war and Lieutenant Colonel, U.S.V. for his conspicuous gallantry at Beverly Ford, Fredericksburg, and Gettysburg. Honorably mustered out of volunteer service on January 11, 1866. Appointed Second Lieutenant, 2nd Cavalry to date from March 26, 1866; joined the regiment in May, 1866. On August 19, 1867, he accepted appointment as a Captain, 7th Cavalry and joined the regiment at Fort Leavenworth on November 20, 1867. Engaged in the expedition exploring the Black Hills in July and August, 1874, and in 1875 he commanded a detachment of the 7th Cavalry in the arrest of Rain-In-The-Face at Standing Rock Agency, Dakota. On May 17, 1876, he departed from Fort Abraham Lincoln, Dakota to engage in the Sioux expedition. Survived by his wife, Annie, and three children, George, Charles, and Annie. The vacancy in the regiment created by his death was occupied by Captain James M. Bell. Captain Yates was interred on the battlefield on June 28. His remains were exhumed in July, 1877, and re-interred on August 3, 1877, in the Fort Leavenworth National Cemetery. The post at Standing Rock Agency was established on December 30, 1878, and named Fort Yates in his honor.

JACKSON, HENRY, First Lieutenant

On detached service in the Office of the Chief Signal Officer, Washington, D.C. Born in England. Entered military service from Illinois as a Private and Corporal, Company A, 14th Illinois Volunteer Cavalry. He was Sergeant Major of the 5th U.S. Colored Cavalry from December 28, 1863 to May 13, 1865. On May 14, 1865 he was appointed a Second Lieutenant in the same regiment; promoted to First Lieutenant on December 28, 1865. Honorably mustered out of service on March 16, 1866. Appointed Second Lieutenant, 7th Cavalry to rank from July 28, 1866, the date that the regiment was organized. He accepted the commission on November 12, 1866 and received promotion to First Lieutenant on July 31, 1867 and accepted the promotion on October 22, 1867. Lieut. Jackson did not participate in the Sioux expedition as he was on detached service in the Office of the Chief Signal Officer, U.S. Army, Washington, D.C. He was ordered on June 12, 1876 to join his regiment at once. He received promotion to Captain of Cavalry effective June 25, 1876 and was transferred to Company C from Company F, 7th Cavalry to occupy the vacancy created by the death of Captain Thomas Custer, who was killed in the Little Bighorn River fight. On August 27, 1896 he was promoted to Major of the Third Cavalry and on January 23, 1900 he was promoted to Lieutenant Colonel of the Fifth Cavalry. He received promotion to Colonel, Third Cavalry, on April 29, 1901 and retired on May 31, 1901.

LARNED, CHARLES WILLIAM, Second Lieutenant

On detached service at the U.S. Military Academy. Born in New York, the son of William Larned, Additional Paymaster, U.S. Army. Entered the Military Academy on July 1, 1866, by appointment at large from Illinois. He was the 2339th graduate, ranking 28th in his class of 58 graduates. He was commissioned a Second Lieutenant in the 3rd Regiment of Cavalry on June 15, 1870. His Academy classmates who joined the 7th Cavalry were Lieuts. Hodgson and Edgerly. He applied for transfer to the 7th Regiment of Cavalry and received the assignment on October 10, 1870. He was on frontier duty in camp near Detroit, Kansas until the following month when the regiment went into winter station at Fort Leavenworth until March of the following year. From then until April, 1873, he was in garrison at Louisville, Ky. except for leave from June 27, 1871, to February 17, 1872, when he rejoined. In April, 1873, the regiment was assembled at Yankton, Dakota. A great snowstorm delayed the regiment but on May 7th they departed from Yankton, following the Missouri River to Fort Rice, Dakota, from where the regiment departed on the Yellowstone expedition under the command of Colonel David Stanley. Lt. Larned, during the expedition was engaged in the fight on the Bighorn River, Montana against Sioux Indians on August 11, 1873. He reached Fort Abraham Lincoln, Dakota, on September 29, 1873, and went on leave of absence until December 24 of that year. From that time until July 18, 1874, he was on detached service with the War Department. On August 30, 1874, he was assigned to duty at the Military Academy as Assistant Professor of Drawing where he remained. Promoted to First Lieutenant, 7th Cavalry, effective June 25, 1876, to occupy the vacancy created by the promotion and transfer of Lieutenant Henry Jackson. Lieut. Larned was appointed Professor of Drawing at the Academy on July 25, 1876, upon the retirement of Professor Robert Walter Weir, who had served 42 years in the drawing department. Lieut. Larned received the rank of Colonel, Acting, on June 28, 1902.

KENNEY, MICHAEL, First Sergeant

Killed in battle on June 25. Born in Galway, Ireland. Re-enlisted on March 7, 1871, at age 21 at Fort Leavenworth by Lieut. William Cooke. Discharged on March 7, 1876 at Fort Abraham Lincoln, Dakota upon expiration of service, as a Sergeant of excellent character. Third enlistment on March 7, 1876, at age 26 at Fort Lincoln by Captain George Yates. He had grey eyes, brown hair, fair complexion and was 5'-7¼" in height. Listed as Mich'l Kenney on the battle monument and elsewhere as Keeney.

CURTISS, WILLIAM A., Sergeant

Born in Albany, New York. Second enlistment on August 28, 1872, at age 26 in New York City by Captain Edwin Sumner. Acquitted of a charge of prejudicial conduct, per General Court Martial Order No. 8, Department of Dakota, January 20, 1876. Appointed First Sergeant from Sergeant on Special

Order Nr. 78, Headquarters, 7th Cavalry, September 25, 1876, to date from September 1, 1876. Discharged August 28, 1877, at camp at New Law Agency, Montana Territory, upon expiration of service, as a First Sergeant. He had brown eyes, brown hair, dark complexion and was 5'-8¼" in height. Listed as William Curtiss in the Register of Enlistments, U.S. Army and elsewhere as William Curtis.

DRAGO, HENRY, Sergeant

On detached service from May 13, 1876, at Fort Abraham Lincoln, Dakota in charge of company property. Born in Lucas County, Ohio. Second enlistment on August 15, 1871, at age 28 in Louisville, Kentucky by Lieut. William Cooke. Discharged on August 15, 1876 at Fort Lincoln upon expiration of his service, as a Sergeant of excellent character. He had hazel eyes, dark hair, dark complexion and was 5'-7" in height. Appointed Sergeant on Special Order No. 7, Headquarters, 7th Cavalry, September 25, 1876, to date from September 1, 1876.

NURSEY, FREDERICK, Sergeant

Killed in battle on June 25. Born in Suffolk, England. Enlisted on March 23, 1871, at age 22¼ in Pittsburgh, Pennsylvania by Lieut. James M. Bell. Previous occupation was clerk. Assigned to Company F. Discharged on March 23, 1876, at Fort Abraham Lincoln, Dakota upon expiration of service, as a Sergeant of excellent character. Re-enlisted on March 23, 1876, at the age of 27 at Fort Lincoln by Captain George Yates. He had blue eyes, light hair, fair complexion and was 5'-5½" in height. Listed as Fred'k Nursey on the battle monument.

VICKORY, JOHN, Sergeant

Killed in battle on June 25. Born in Toronto, Canada. Second enlistment on September 9, 1874, at age 27 at Fort Abraham Lincoln, Dakota by Captain George Yates. He had blue eyes, brown hair, dark complexion and was 5'-10" in height. Listed as Jno. Vickory on the battle monument and elsewhere as Vickery, Vickroy and Victor. John Burkman in G. D. Wagner *Old Neutriment* related somewhat vaguely that Private Jack Victor [sic] the regimental color bearer, was killed with the Custer column and that his right arm was cut off at the shoulder.

WILKISON, JOHN K., Sergeant

Killed with the Custer column on June 25. Born in Salem, New York. Enlisted on January 5, 1872, at age 24 5/12 in Troy, New York by Lieut. Oscar Elting. Previous occupation was farmer. He had gray eyes, dark brown hair, florid complexion and was 5'-7¾" in height. Listed as J. K. Wilkinson on the battle monument and as John K. Wilkison in the Register of Enlistments, U.S. Army and on his Oath of Enlistment.

CLYDE, EDWARD, Corporal

Born in Waukesha, Wisconsin. Deserted on April 1, 1871; and was a surrendered deserter under General Order Nr. 102, AGO, 1873. Appointed a Sergeant on Special Order Nr. 78, Headquarters 7th Cavalry on September 25, 1876. to be effective September 27, 1876. His fourth enlistment was on July 20,

1878, in Company F, 7th Cavalry at Fort Totten, Dakota by Captain James M. Bell. He was enlisted for the fifth time on July 20, 1883, at the age of 37 at Fort Buford, Dakota, in Company F, 7th Cavalry by Lieut. James Wheelan. He had blue eyes, red hair, ruddy complexion and was 5'-10" in height.

COLEMAN, CHARLES, Corporal
Killed in battle on June 25. Born in Terre Haute, Indiana. Enlisted on September 9, 1873, at age 22 in Cincinnati, Ohio by Lieut. Adam Kramer. Previous occupation was laborer. He had blue eyes, dark hair, ruddy complexion and was 5'-5¼" in height. Listed as Chas. Coleman on the battle monument.

TEEMAN, WILLIAM, Corporal
Killed in battle on June 25. Born in Denmark. Enlisted on September 30, 1867, at age 21 in Pittsburgh, Pennsylvania by Captain Henry Raymond. Assigned to the 4th Artillery. Previous occupation was laborer. Discharged on September 30, 1870, upon expiration of service and re-enlisted on the same day at the age of 24 at Fort Riley, Kansas by Lieut. Arthur Morris; assigned to Battery B, 4th Artillery. He deserted and was enlisted on August 27, 1872, at a represented age of 23 in Cincinnati, Ohio by Lieut. James Wheelan. He represented his birthplace, on this enlistment, as Buffalo, New York. Assigned to Company F, 7th Cavalry under his enlistment name of William A. Adams. His enlistment was cancelled when he voluntarily surrendered on November 19, 1873, under General Order Nr. 102, AGO, 1873 as William Teeman, a deserter from Battery B, 4th Artillery. He had grey eyes, light brown hair, fair to dark complexion and was 5'-9" in height. Listed as Wm. Teeman on the battle monument and elsewhere as Feeman and Freeman.

BRIODY, JOHN, Corporal
Killed in battle on June 25. Born in New York City. Second enlistment on August 13, 1872, at age 25 in New York City by Captain Edwin Sumner. He had blue eyes, brown hair, dark complexion and was 5'-5" in height. Listed as John Briody on the battle monument.

WAY, THOMAS N., Trumpeter
Killed in battle on June 25. Born in Chester County, Pennsylvania. Second enlistment on July 11, 1875, at age 28 in Chicago by Captain Samuel Young. He had hazel eyes, dark hair, dark complexion and was 5'-7" in height. Listed as T.N.Way on the battle monument.

SCHLEIPER, CLAUS, Saddler
Born in Germany. Second enlistment on December 17, 1871, at age 34 in Louisville, Kentucky by Lieut. William H. Clapp. Previous occupation was saddler. Discharged on December 17, 1876, at Fort Abercrombie, Dakota upon expiration of service, as a Saddler of excellent character. He had brown eyes, dark hair, light complexion and was 5'-9¾" in height. Listed as Claus Schlieper in the Register of Enlistments, U.S. Army.

BRANDON, BENJAMIN, Farrier
Killed in battle on June 25. Born in Hopkinsville, Kentucky. Second enlistment on November 1, 1875, at age 44 at Fort Abraham Lincoln, Dakota by

Captain George Yates. He had hazel eyes, black hair, ruddy complexion and was 5'-6½" in height. Listed as Benj. Brandon on the battle monument.

MANNING, JAMES R., Blacksmith
Killed in battle on June 25. Born in Houston County, Georgia. Enlisted in Company I on January 25, 1873, at age 29 in Louisville, Kentucky by Lieut. Peter Vroom. Previous occupation was blacksmith. Transferred to Company F. He had hazel eyes, black hair, dark complexion and was 5'-8½" in height. Listed as J. R. Manning on the battle monument.

ATCHESON, THOMAS, Private
Killed in battle on June 25. Born in County Antrim, Ireland. Second enlistment on August 21, 1871, at age 36 in Meridian, Mississippi, by Captain George Yates. He had hazel eyes, dark hair and was 5'-5¼" in height. Listed as Thos. Atcheson on the battle monument and in the Registers of Enlistments, U.S. Army and elsewhere as Thomas Atchison.

BRADY, WILLIAM, Private
Killed in battle on June 25. Born in Pittsburgh, Pennsylvania. Enlisted on September 15, 1875, at age 27 in Cincinnati, Ohio by Lieut. Patrick Cusack. Previous occupation was plumber. He had blue eyes, brown hair, ruddy complexion and was 5'-6½" in height. Listed as Wm. Brady on the battle monument.

BROWN, BENJAMIN FRANKLIN, Private
Killed in battle on June 25. Born in Taylor County, Kentucky. Enlisted on March 12, 1872, at age 22 in Louisville, Kentucky by Lieut. Charles Larned. Previous occupation was farmer. This soldier had hazel eyes, light hair, fair complexion and was 5'-9" in height. Listed as B. F. Brown on the battle monument.

BROWN, HIRAM E. Private
On detached duty in Quartermaster Department as teamster. Born in Mount Vernon, Ohio. Second enlistment on March 8, 1876, at age 29 at Fort Abraham Lincoln, Dakota by Captain George Yates. Discharged on March 7, 1881, at Fort Buford, Dakota upon expiration of service, as a Corporal of very good character. He had brown eyes, brown hair, fair complexion and was 5'-8¼" in height.

BROWN, WILLIAM, Private
Killed in battle on June 25. Born in Hamburg, Germany. Second enlistment on December 10, 1872, at age 39 in Louisville, Kentucky by Lieut. William Cooke. He had blue eyes, brown hair, fair complexion and was 5'-5" in height. Listed as Wm. Brown on the battle monument.

BRUCE, PATRICK, Private
Killed in battle on June 25. Born in Cork, Ireland. Third enlistment on May 1, 1876, at age 31 at Fort Abraham Lincoln, Dakota by Captain George Yates. He had blue eyes, brown hair, ruddy complexion and was 5'-7" in height. Listed as Pat'k Bruce on the battle monument.

BURNHAM, LUCIEN, Private
    Killed in battle on June 25. Born in Conkling, New York. Enlisted on December 9, 1872, at age 21 in Scranton, Pennsylvania by Captain Eugene Beaumont. Previous occupation was sawyer. He had grey eyes, red hair, ruddy complexion and was 5'-8 5/8" in height. Listed as Lucien Burnham on the battle monument and elsewhere as Burham.

BUTLER, JAMES W., Private
    Born in Riverton, New Jersey. Second enlistment on September 18, 1874, at age 33 at Fort Abraham Lincoln, Dakota, by Captain George Yates. Discharged on September 19, 1879, at Fort Totten, Dakota upon expiration of service, as a Private of good character. He had blue eyes, auburn hair, ruddy complexion and was 5'-6" in height.

CARNEY, JAMES, Private
    Killed in battle on June 25. Born in West Meath, Ireland. Second enlistment on December 9, 1872, at age 29 in St. Louis by Lieut. Oscar Elting. He had grey eyes, black hair, dark complexion and was 5'-4¼" in height. Listed as James Carney on the battle monument and elsewhere as James Carey.

CATHER, ARMANTHEUS D., Private
    Killed in battle on June 25. Born in Shippensville, Pennsylvania. Enlisted on November 8, 1872, at age 22 in Pittsburgh by Lieut. Calbraith Rodgers. Previous occupation was pumper. He had grey eyes, brown hair, fair complexion and was 5'-8½" in height. Listed as A. D. Cather on the battle monument.

COLLINS, JOHN C., Private
    Born in Syracuse, New York. Second enlistment on June 22, 1875, at age 34 in St. Louis by Captain James Wheelan. Previous occupation was soldier. Sick at St. Louis Barracks per Company F Muster Roll, October 31, 1876. Assigned to Co. F; transferred to Co. K. Discharged June 21, 1880, at Fort Meade, Dakota upon expiration of service, as a Private. He had grey eyes, brown hair, ruddy complexion and was 5'-6½" in height.

DAVERN, EDWARD, Private
    Orderly for Major Marcus Reno. In the valley and hilltop fights. Born in Limerick, Ireland. Enlisted on August 12, 1872, at age 26 in Louisville, Kentucky by Lieut. William Cooke. Lieut. Edward Godfrey wrote, "During the retreat Private Dalvern [sic], troop "F" had a hand-to-hand conflict with an Indian; his horse was killed; he then shot the Indian, caught the Indian's pony, and rode to the command." ("Custer's Last Battle" in *The Century Magazine*, January, 1892, XLIII:3, p. 372). Private Davern was appointed Sergeant on Special Order, Nr. 78, Headquarters, 7th Cavalry, September 25, 1876 to date from September 27, 1876. Discharged on August 12, 1877 at Camp Yellowstone, Montana Territory, upon expiration of service, as a Sergeant of excellent character. He re-enlisted and was on duty at Fort Totten, Dakota. Testified at the Reno Court of Inquiry in Chicago on January 29-30, 1879. Regimental Order Nr. 60, September 15, 1887 continued Corporal Davern, re-enlisted, in the grade of Corporal. He had grey eyes, brown hair, fair complexion and was 5'-6¾" in height.

DOHMAN, ANTON, Private

Killed in battle on June 25. Born in Hanover, Germany. Second enlistment on August 3, 1871, at age 21 in Louisville, Kentucky by Lieut. William Cooke. He had grey eyes, brown hair, fair complexion and was 5'-2½" in height. Listed as Anton Dohman on the battle monument and elsewhere as Anton Dorman.

DONNELLY, TIMOTHY, Private

Killed in battle on June 25. Born in Dallington, England. Enlisted on September 21, 1875, at age 21 5/12 in Boston by Lieut. Henry Lawton. His previous occupation was laborer. He had blue eyes, dark hair, fair complexion and was 5'-6" in height. Listed as Timothy Donnelly on the battle monument and elsewhere as Donnelley.

DOWNING, ALEXANDER, Private

On detached service from May 13, 1876 at Fort Abraham Lincoln, Dakota. Born in New Madison, Ohio. Enlisted on September 18, 1875, at age 24 in Cincinnati, Ohio by Lieut. Patrick Cusack. Previous occupation was farmer. Appointed Blacksmith on Company Order Nr. 5 to date from October 11, 1876. Discharged on September 17, 1880 at Fort Meade, Dakota upon expiration of service, as a Blacksmith of excellent character. He had grey eyes, brown hair, dark complexion and was 5'7½" in height.

EADES, WILLIAM, Private

On Extra Duty in Quartermaster Department as mechanic. Born in Dublin, Ireland. Enlisted on September 9, 1871, at age 27 in Louisville, Kentucky by Lieut. John F. Weston. Previous occupation was clerk. Discharged on August 6, 1876 at camp at the mouth of Rosebud Creek, Montana Territory per General Order Nr. 24, AGO, 1859, as a Private of excellent character. He had grey eyes, black hair, fair complexion and was 5'-7" in height.

FINNEGAN, THOMAS J., Private

Born in Allen County, Ohio. Enlisted on August 19, 1873, at age 23 in Cincinnati by Lieut. Adam Kramer. Previous occupation was farmer. Discharged on August 19, 1878 at Fort Totten, Dakota upon expiration of service, as a Private of excellent character. He had grey eyes, black hair, fair complexion and was 5'-9¾" in height. Listed as Thomas J. Finegan in the Register of Enlistments, U.S. Army.

GARDNER, WILLIAM, Private

Killed in battle on June 25. Born in Hanover, Germany. Second enlistment on August 25, 1875, at age 26 in New York City by Lieut. John Babcock. He had blue eyes, light hair, light complexion and was 5'-7" in height. Listed as Wm. Gardiner on the battle monument and as William Gardner in the Register of Enlistments, U.S. Army.

GREGG, WILLIAM J., Private

Born in Baltimore, Maryland. Re-enlisted on November 11, 1872, at age 25 in Louisville, Kentucky by Lieut. William Cooke. Previous occupation was clerk. Appointed Sergeant from Private per Special Order Nr. 78, Hq. 7th Cavalry, September 25, 1876, to date from September 27. Discharged on

November 11, 1877, at Fort Abraham Lincoln, Dakota upon expiration of service, as a Sergeant of excellent character. He had blue eyes, brown hair, fair complexion and was 5'-7" in height. The Descriptive List and Records File; Custer Battlefield National Monument has Special Order Nr. 484, AGO, November 1, 1867; Item Nr. 7 of the order discharges Corporal William J. Gregg, Company F, 7th Cavalry.

HAMMON, GEORGE W., Private
Killed in battle on June 25. Born in Fulton County, Ohio. Enlisted on September 9, 1873, at age 21 in Cincinnati by Lieut. Adam Kramer. Previous occupation was farmer. He had blue eyes, dark brown hair, florid complexion and was 5'-8" in height. Listed as G. W. Hammon on the battle monument. George was an older brother of Corporal John Hammon of Company G.

HARRIS, LEONARD A., Private
In confinement from May 28, 1875 at Newport, Kentucky. Born in Cincinnati, Ohio. Enlisted on December 21, 1872, at age 21 2/12 in Cincinnati by Lieut. James Wheelan. Previous occupation was laborer. He had blue eyes, light hair, florid complexion and was 5'-7" in height.

HEGNER, FRANCIS, Private
On Extra Duty in Quartermaster Department as laborer. Born in Berlin, Germany. Second enlistment on July 24, 1872, at age 29 in Louisville, Kentucky by Lieut. William Cooke. Discharged on June 7, 1877, at Fort Abercrombie, Dakota per Special Order Nr. 70, Department of Dakota, 1877, as a Private of very good character. He had blue eyes, light hair, fair complexion and was 5'-9" in height.

HOWARD, FRANK, Private
Born in Brooklyn, New York. Enlisted on September 23, 1875 at age 23 in Chicago by Lieut. Edmund Luff. Previous occupation was farmer. Deserted on January 7, 1878; apprehended on January 9, 1878. Dishonorably discharged on March 30, 1878 at Fort Totten, Dakota per General Court Martial Order Nr. 18, Department of Dakota., 1878, as a Private. He had blue eyes, light hair, fair complexion and was 5'-7¾" in height.

HUNTER, FRANK, Private
Born in Ireland. Discharged from his first enlistment in Company F, 7th Cavalry on August 17, 1871. Second enlistment on August 30, 1871 at age 28 in Louisville, Kentucky by Lieut. John Weston. Discharged on August 6, 1876, in camp at the mouth of Rosebud Creek, Montana Territory, per General Order Nr. 24, AGO, 1859, as a Private of excellent character. He had grey eyes, light hair, fair complexion and was 5'-5½" in height. Listed as Frank Hunter in the Register of Enlistments, U.S. Army and elsewhere as Frank Hunt.

KELLY, JOHN P., Private
Killed in battle on June 25. Born in Easton, Pennsylvania. Enlisted on January 3, 1872 at age 23 in Unionville, South Carolina by Lieut. Thomas McDougall. Previous occupation was soldier. He had hazel eyes, light hair, light

complexion and was 5'-6" in height. Listed as Jno. Kelly on the battle monument and elsewhere as John P. Kelley and Kidey.

KLEIN, GUSTAV, Private
Killed in battle on June 25. Born in Wurtemburg, Germany. He was enlisted on March 15, 1871 at age 23 at Fort Leavenworth, Kansas by Lieut. William Cooke. Previous occupation was soldier. Discharged on March 16, 1876, at Fort Abraham Lincoln, Dakota upon expiration of service, as a Private of excellent character and was re-enlisted on the same day at Fort Lincoln by Captain George Yates. He had blue eyes, light hair, fair complexion and was 5'-7½" in height. Listed as Gustav Klein in the Register of Enlistments, U.S. Army and on the battle monument and elsewhere as Gustave Klein.

KLEIN, NIKOLAUS, Private
On detached service from May 13, 1876 at Fort Abraham Lincoln, Dakota. Born in Bavaria, Germany. Enlisted on February 10, 1872 at age 22 in Buffalo, New York by Lieut. Albert Forse. Previous occupation was butcher. Discharged on February 10, 1877, at Fort Abercrombie, Dakota upon expiration of his service, as a Private of good character. Re-enlisted on February 10, 1877, at Fort Abercrombie by Lieut. James M. Bell. He had hazel eyes, light hair, light complexion and was 5'-5¼" in height. Listed as Nikolaus Klein in the Register of Enlistments, U.S. Army and as Nikolaus Kleiner on the 7th Cavalry Returns for June 30, 1876 and elsewhere as Nicholaus Klein.

KNAUTH, HERMAN, Private
Killed in battle on June 25. Born in Dammendorf, Prussia. Enlisted on January 20, 1872 at age 33 in Rochester, New York by Lieut. Albert Forse. Previous occupation was merchant. He had blue eyes, light brown hair, fair complexion and was 5'-8" in height. Listed as Herman Knauth on the battle monument and elsewhere as Krianth.

LEFLER, MEIG, Private
With the pack train detail on June 25? Born in Baden, Germany. Second enlistment on November 25, 1871, at age 24 in Cincinnati, Ohio by Lieut. Myles Moylan. Previous occupation was farmer. Discharged on November 25, 1876, at Fort Abercrombie, Dakota upon expiration of service, as a Private of excellent character. He had grey eyes, brown hair, fair complexion and was 5'-6½" in height.

LEROCK, WILLIAM H., Private
Killed in battle on June 25. Born in Wayne County, New York. Enlisted on February 9, 1872 at age 21 in Buffalo, New York by Lieut. Albert Forse. Previous occupation was laborer. He had hazel eyes, dark hair, fair complexion and was 5'-5¼" in height. Listed as W. H. Lerock on the battle monument, and as Wm. Larock in the Register of Enlistments, U.S. Army.

LIEMANN, WERNER L., Private
Killed in battle on June 25. Born in Bremen, Germany. Enlisted on January 30, 1873 at the age of 30 in New York City by Captain Edwin Sumner. Previous occupation was painter. He had blue eyes, brown hair, light complexion

and was 5'-5" in height. Listed as W. L. Liemann on the battle monument and elsewhere as Luman and Werner L. Lieman.

LOSSEE, WILLIAM A., Private
Killed in battle on June 25. Born in Brewster Station, New York. Enlisted on September 24, 1875, at age 26 in New York City by Lieut. John Babcock. Previous occupation was showman. He had grey eyes, light hair, ruddy complexion and was 5'-5½" in height. Listed as W. A. Lossee on the battle monument and as W. A. Loose in the Register of Enlistments, U.S. Army and as Wm. A. Lossee on his Oath of Enlistment. Listed elsewhere as Losse.

LYNCH, DENNIS, Private
In the pack train detail on June 25? Born in Cumberland, Maryland. Second enlistment on March 3, 1871, at age 24 in Louisville, Kentucky by Lieut. William Cooke. Discharged on August 3, 1876 at the mouth of Rosebud Creek, Montana Territory upon expiration of service, as a Private of excellent character. He had grey eyes, brown hair, dark complexion and was 5'-5¼" in height.

LYONS, BERNARD, Private
In the pack train detail on June 25? Born in Galway, Ireland. Enlisted on September 6, 1875, at age 26 in Boston by Lieut. William Harper, Jr. Previous occupation was clerk. Acquitted on May 2, 1876, of the charge of violation of the 60th Article of War and neglect of duty per General Court Martial Order Nr. 28, Department of Dakota, 1876. Discharged on March 30, 1878, at Fort Totten, Dakota for disability. He had blue eyes, brown hair, fair complexion and was 5'-6 1/8" in height.

MADSON, CHRISTIAN, Private
Killed in battle on June 25. Born in Kjerteminde, Denmark. Enlisted on August 24, 1872, at age 24½ in Cleveland, Ohio by Lieut. James Peale. Previous occupation was tanner. He had blue eyes, light hair, fair complexion and was 5'-11" in height. Listed as Christian Madson on the battle monument and as Christian Madsen in the Register of Enlistments, U.S. Army. Listed elsewhere as Madison.

MEINICKE, ERNST, Private
On detached service from May 13, 1876 at Fort Abraham Lincoln, Dakota. Born in Bamburg, Germany. Enlisted on September 25, 1875, at age 30 in New York City by Lieut. John Babcock. Previous occupation was gardner. Discharged on September 24, 1880, at Fort Totten, Dakota upon expiration of service, as a Private of excellent character. He had blue eyes, brown hair, fair complexion and was 5'-6½" in height.

MILTON, FRANCIS E., Private
Killed in battle on June 25. Born in Hillsdale, Michigan. Second enlistment on August 15, 1871 at age 18 in Louisville, Kentucky by Lieut. William Cooke. Previous occupation was soldier. He had blue eyes, light hair, light complexion and was 5'-7¼" in height. Listed as F. E. Milton on the battle monument and elsewhere as James Milton.

MILTON, JOSEPH, Private
On detached duty in Regimental Band as cook. Born in Glasgow, Scotland. Second enlistment on January 1, 1873, at age 28 in Louisville,. Kentucky by Lieut. Charles Larned. Discharged on January 1, 1878, at Fort Abraham Lincoln, Dakota upon expiration of service, as a Private of excellent character. He had blue eyes, brown hair, fair complexion and was 5'-6½" in height. Listed as Joseph Millton in the Register of Enlistments. U.S. Army.

MONROE, JOSEPH, Private
Killed in battle on June 25. Born in Lorraine, France. Enlisted on September 14, 1875, at age 24 in Cincinnati, Ohio by Lieut. Patrick Cusack. Previous occupation was laborer. Sentenced to four months confinement at hard labor at his post, and a $40 fine per General Court Martial Order Nr. 8, Department of Dakota, January 20, 1876. He had brown eyes, black hair, dark complexion and was 5'-6½" in height. Listed as Joseph Monroe on the battle monument and elsewhere as Joseph Munroe.

MYERS, FRANK, Private
In the pack train detail on June 25? Born in Quebec, Canada. Enlisted on October 8, 1875, at age 21 in Cincinnati, Ohio by Lieut. Patrick Cusack. Previous occupation was farmer. Deserted on December 14, 1876. He had grey eyes, brown hair, dark complexion and was 5'-8¼" in height.

OMLING, SEBASTIAN, Private
Killed in battle on June 25. Born in Windaciler, Bavaria, Germany. Enlisted on December 21, 1871, at age 33 in Louisville, Kentucky by Lieut. William H. Clapp. Previous occupation was blacksmith. He had hazel eyes, light hair, fair complexion and was 5'-5¼" in height. Listed as Sebastian Omling on the battle monument, and elsewhere as Omeling and Smeling.

PICKARD, EDWIN F., Private
Orderly for Captain George Yates on June 25. Assigned to the pack train on the morning of June 25. In the hilltop fight. Went to the river on June 26 with a water party. Born in Boston, Massachusetts. Enlisted on September 6, 1875 at age 23 in Boston by Lieut. William Harper, Jr. Previous occupation was clerk. Discharged January 18, 1878, at Fort Abraham Lincoln, Dakota for disability (stiffened right arm), as a Private of good character. He had blue eyes, light hair, fair complexion and was 5'-8" in height. His story was published in five installments beginning July 31, 1923 in *The Portand* (Oregon) *Journal*; reprinted in *Montana*, Summer, 1954, 4:3, 17-29.

PILCHER, ALBERT, Private
On detached duty at Headquarters Department of Dakota. Born in Parkersburg, West Virginia. Enlisted on September 26, 1871, at age 23 in Wheeling, West Virginia by Lieut. G. W. H. Starck. Assigned to Company D, 13th Infantry. Previous occupation was boilermaker. He deserted and was enlisted in the 7th Cavalry under the name of Henry Barton on September 12, 1873, at a represented age of 23 in Pittsburgh by Lieut. Randolph Norwood. He stated that his birthplace was Wabash County, Illinois and his previous occupation was teamster. His enlistment was cancelled when he surrendered on

December 24, 1873 under General Order Nr. 102, AGO, 1873, as Albert Pilcher, deserter from Company D, 13th Infantry. He had blue eyes, dark brown hair, fair to dark complexion and was 5'-6¼ to 7" in height.

REILEY, MICHAEL, Private

Born in Luzerne County, Pennsylvania. Enlisted on November 6, 1872, at age 21 in Wilkes Barre, Pennsylvania by Captain Eugene Beaumont. Previous occupation was miner. Discharged on November 6, 1877, at Fort Abraham Lincoln, Dakota upon expiration of service, as a Private of good character. He had grey eyes, light brown hair, fair complexion and was 5'-8 7/8" in height. Listed as Michael Reiley in the Register of Enlistments, U.S. Army; and on the Oath of Enlistment.

ROONEY, JAMES M., Private

Born in New York City. Second enlistment on December 3, 1872, at age 24 in Louisville, Kentucky by Lieut. William Cooke. He was appointed a Corporal on Special Order Nr. 81, Headquarters, 7th Cavalry, October 3, 1876 to date from October 1, 1876. Discharged on December 3, 1877, at Fort Buford, Dakota upon expiration of service, as a Sergeant of excellent character. He had blue eyes, brown hair, dark complexion and was 5'-8¼" in height. Listed elsewhere as James H. Rooney.

RUDDEN, PATRICK, Private

Killed in battle on June 25. Born in Newark, New Jersey. Enlisted on September 24, 1875, at age 22 in St. Louis by Lieut. John Thompson. Previous occupation was hatter. He had blue eyes, brown hair, dark complexion and was 5'-5 7/8" in height. Listed as Pat'k Rudden on the battle monument and elsewhere as Ruddew.

SAUNDERS, RICHARD D., Private

Killed in battle on June 25. Born in Yarmouth, Nova Scotia. Enlisted on August 16, 1875 at age 22 in Boston by Lieut. William Harper, Jr. Previous occupation was stonemason. He had blue eyes, brown hair, dark complexion and was 5'-9 5/8" in height. Listed as Rich'd Saunders on the battle monument and elsewhere as Sanders.

SCHLEIFFARTH, PAUL, Private

On Extra Duty in Commissary and Subsistence Department. Born in Berlin, Germany. Enlisted on December 15, 1871, at age 32 in Louisville, Kentucky by Lieut. William Clapp. Previous occupation was soldier. Appointed Corporal on Special Order Nr. 81, Headquarters 7th Cavalry, October 3, 1876 to date from October 1, 1876. Discharged on December 15, 1876, at Fort Abercrombie, Dakota upon expiration of service, as a Private of excellent character. He had grey eyes, brown hair, fair complexion and was 5'-6½" in height. Listed as Paul Schleiffarth in the Register of Enlistments, U.S. Army and on the Company F Muster Roll, October 31, 1876.

SHULTE, FREDERICK, Private

Born in Rohden, Prussia. Enlisted on September 10, 1867, at age 21 in Cincinnati, Ohio by Captain O'Connell. Previous occupation was laborer.

Assigned to Company D, 2nd Cavalry. Deserted on August 2, 1868. His name is listed as Frederick Shulte in the Register of Enlistments, U.S. Army. Enlisted on March 27, 1871 in Company F, 7th Cavalry under the name of Charles Miller. He surrendered on November 20, 1873 under General Order Nr. 102, AGO, 1873 as Frederick Shulte, deserter from the 2nd Cavalry. Discharged on December 28, 1877 upon expiration of service, at Mercer's Ranch Arizona Territory, as a Sergeant with character notation as a "good soldier". He had blue eyes, brown hair and fair complexion and was 5'-5¼" in height. Listed elsewhere as Shutte, Schutte, Schulte and Schuetze.

SICFOUS, FRANCIS W., Private
Killed in battle on June 25. Born in Clarion County, Pennsylvania. Enlisted on October 4, 1875, at age 23 in Pittsburgh by Lieut. Thomas Gregg. Previous occupation was painter. He had grey eyes, light hair, fair complexion and was 5'-5" in height and was illiterate. Listed as F. W. Siclous on the battle monument and as Francis W. Sicfous on his Oath of Enlistment and in the Register of Enlistments, U. S. Army.

SWEENEY, JOHN W., Private
Born in Marion County, Missouri. Second enlistment on January 4, 1872, at age 25 in Louisville, Kentucky by Lieut. John Weston. The Descriptive List and Records File, Custer Battlefield National Monument, includes Company Order Nr. 11, July 10, 1874 promoting Corporal John W. Sweeney to Sergeant, vice Mason reduced. Acquitted of a charge of violation of the 60th Article of War and neglect of duty per General Court Martial Order Nr. 28, Department of Dakota May 2, 1876. Discharged on January 4, 1877 at Fort Abercrombie, Dakota upon expiration of service, as a Private of excellent character. He had grey eyes, light hair, fair complexion and was 5'-8½" in height.

SWEENEY, WILLIAM, Private
In the hands of civil authorities at Bismarck, Dakota from January 23, 1876. Born in Newark, New Jersey. Enlisted on September 7, 1875, at age 21 in St. Louis by Captain Owen Hale. Previous occupation was teamster. Deserted on September 26, 1876. He had grey eyes, brown hair, fair complexion and was 5'-5½" in height.

THORP, MICHAEL, Private
On detached service from May 13, 1876 at Fort Abraham Lincoln, Dakota. Born in Summersett, Ohio. Second enlistment on June 17, 1875, at age 32 4/12 at Fort Lincoln by Lieut. James Calhoun. Assigned to the Band; transferred to Company F. Discharged on April 5, 1877, at Fort Abercrombie, Dakota for disability, as a Private. He had hazel eyes, brown hair, fair complexion and was 5'-10¼" in height.

WALSH, THOMAS, Private
Born in County Rascommon, Ireland. Second enlistment on September 21, 1875, at age 33 at St. Louis by Lieut. John Thompson. Discharged on April 12, 1880 at Fort Totten, Dakota for disability. He had grey eyes, brown hair, dark complexion and was 5'-4½" in height.

WARREN, GEORGE A., Private

Killed in battle on June 25. Born in Gibson County, Indiana. Enlisted on September 7, 1875, at age 35 in St. Louis by Captain Owen Hale. Previous occupation was carpenter. He had hazel eyes, brown hair, fair complexion and was 5'-9½" in height. Listed as Geo. Warren on the battle monument.

COMPANY G IN 1876

The company was stationed at Shreveport, Louisiana, until April 19 when they left by rail with Company B to join the regiment. They were joined by Company K enroute and arrived at St. Paul on April 23. On April 28 they left by rail and arrived at Bismarck, Dakota, on May 1 and went into camp below the post of Fort Abraham Lincoln awaiting the departure of the Sioux expedition The transfer from Shreveport in the Department of the Gulf, to Fort Lincoln in the Department of Dakota involved 2,583 miles of travel.

The regiment, under Lieut. Col. George Custer, departed on May 17 and returned to Fort Lincoln on September 26 and Company G went into camp below the post. Four companies of the regiment, including Company G, departed for Fort Lincoln on October 21 under the command of Major Marcus Reno for Standing Rock Agency to disarm and dismount the Indians at that agency. They returned on November 3 for winter station. During the year the company marched 1,516 miles.

The following officers and men were casualties in the fight on the Little Bighorn River. Killed: First Lieutenant Donald McIntosh, Sergeants Edward Botzer, Martin Considine; Corporals Otto Hagemann and James Martin; Trumpeter Henry Dose; Saddler Crawford Selby; Farrier Benjamin Wells; Privates Andrew Moore, John McGinnis, John Rapp, Benjamin Rogers, Henry Seafferman and Edward Stanley. Wounded: Privates John Morrison, James Boyle, Charles Campbell and John McVay. Private Edward Comtesse committed suicide on January 25 at 8:30 PM in camp near Shreveport by shooting himself through the head with a carbine.

Officers serving with the company in the year were Captain John Tourtellotte, First Lieutenant Donald McIntosh and Second Lieutenants George D. Wallace, Ernest Garlington and John Wilkinson.*

* John William Wilkinson was the replacement in Company G (for Lieut. George Wallace who was promoted.) Lieut. Wilkinson was born in Missouri and appointed to the U.S. Military Academy, July 1, 1868, from Montana Territory. He graduated 30th in the class of 1872 and was appointed Second Lieutenant, 8th Cavalry, to rank from June 14, 1872. He was transferred to the 7th Cavalry effective June 26, 1876, and promoted to First Lieutenant December 9, 1876. Appointed Regimental Adjutant Nov. 30, 1881, to August 14, 1886, and promoted to Captain January 30, 1892. Brevetted Captain on February 27, 1890, for his gallant service in action against the Nez Perce Indians at Canyon Creek, Mont. Sept. 13, 1877. Captain Wilkinson died on March 22, 1892.

COMPANY G AT THE LITTLE BIGHORN

	Absent	Present	Wounded	Died OWRT	Killed	Survived
.Captain	1					1
1st Lieut.		1			1	
2nd Lieut.		1				1
1st Sergt.	1					1
Sergeant	1	5			2	3
Corporal	1	6			2	5
Trumpeter	1	1			1	1
Saddler		1			1	
Farrier		1			1	
Wagoner						
Blacksmith		1				1
Private	18	29	4		6	41
Total	23	46	4	0	14	54

COMPANY G ON JUNE 30, 1876

Enlisted present for duty 28
Enlisted present extra duty 1
Enlisted present sick 2
Officers absent detached service 1
Enlisted absent detached service 20
Enlisted absent with leave 1
Enlisted absent sick 1
Captain 1
First Sergeant 1
Sergeants 4
Corporals 5
Trumpeter 1
Blacksmith 1
Privates 41
Total enlisted 53
Aggregate 54
Aggregate in May 69
Officer transferred to reg. staff 1
Officer killed 1
Enlisted killed 13
Wounded 2
Horses serviceable 25
Horses lost 25

TOURTELLOTTE, JOHN EATON, Captain

On detached service as aide-de-camp to General Sherman. Born in Connecticut. He enlisted from Minnesota in Company H, 4th Minnesota Infantry from September 30 to December 12, 1861. He was commissioned a Captain in the same regiment on December 13, 1861 and was promoted to Lieutenant Colonel of the regiment on September 1, 1862. With his regiment in Mississippi he was engaged in the battles at Iuka and Corinth and the siege at Corinth. He commanded the regiment in the battle of Raymond, the capture of Jackson, the battles of Champion Hill, Missionary Ridge and the assault and siege of Vicksburg. He was commanding a brigade engaged in the defense of Allatoona where he was wounded. He was promoted to Colonel of the 4th Minnesota Volunteers on October 5, 1864. Colonel Tourtellotte was in Sherman's march to the sea and the campaign in the Carolinas and the siege of Atlanta and the battle of Bentonville. On March 2, 1865 he received the brevet of Brigadier General, U.S.V., for his gallant and meritorious services. He was honorably mustered out on June 21, 1865. He was commissioned a Captain in the 28th Infantry on July 28, 1866, the date that the regiment was organized. In March, 1867 he received the brevet of Major, USA, for his gallant and meritorious services at the siege of Vicksburg. On the same date he received the brevet of Lieutenant Colonel, USA, for his gallant and meritorious services in the battle of Allatoona and Colonel, USA for his gallant and meritorious services in the battle of Bentonville. In the reorganization of the army he was unassigned on March 31, 1869. On December 15, 1870, he was assigned to the 7th Cavalry. He was appointed Colonel and aide-de-camp to General W. T. Sherman from January 1, 1871 to February 8, 1884. He received promotion to Major of Cavalry on September 22, 1883; retired on March 20, 1885; died on July 22, 1891.

McINTOSH, DONALD, First Lieutenant

Killed in the valley fight on June 25. Born on September 4, 1838 at Jasper House, near Montreal, Canada, the son of James and Charlotte Robinson McIntosh. He resided at various posts of the Hudson's Bay Company in Canada. From 1846 to 1851 he was at Vancouver and at Oregon City from 1851 to 1853 and at Portland in 1854. From 1854 to 1860 he was at Forts Dalles and Steilacoom and in 1861 he was Chief Clerk for Colonel Daniel Rucker and served with him during the Civil War. He was a resident of Washington, D.C. from June 1, 1864 until he was commissioned. He received appointment as a Second Lieutenant in the 7th Cavalry effective August 17, 1867 and joined the regiment at Fort Harker, Kansas on October 16, 1867. His promotion to First Lieutenant, effective from March 22, 1870, was accepted on July 14, 1870 while in camp near Fort Hays, Kansas. Assigned to Company G and, in the absence of the company commander, McIntosh commanded the company. On May 17, 1876 he departed from Fort Abraham Lincoln to participate with the regiment in the Sioux expedition. His remains were interred on the battlefield on June 27th. In July, 1877; exhumed and re-interred on August 3, 1877, in Fort Leavenworth National Cemetery. On October 28. 1909, his remains were again exhumed and re-interred on October 31, 1909, in Arlington National Cemetery. He was survived by his widow, Molly Garrett McIntosh.

WALLACE, GEORGE DANIEL, Second Lieutenant

In the valley and hilltop fights. Born on June 29, 1849, in York County, South Carolina. He entered the Military Academy September 1, 1868, by appointment from South Carolina and was the 2419th graduate of the Academy, graduating on June 14, 1872. He ranked 9th in his class of 57 graduates. His academy classmates who joined the 7th Cavalry were Charles Varnum and Henry Harrington. He was commissioned a Second Lieutenant, 7th Cavalry on June 14, 1872. After graduation leave he joined his company at Laurens Court House, South Carolina on October 30, 1872. On May 17, 1876, Lieut. Wallace departed from Fort Abraham Lincoln, Dakota with Company G, 7th Cavalry to participate in the Sioux expedition. Engaged in the valley and hilltop fights on the Little Bighorn River on June 25 and 26. Transferred from Company G to the position of regimental adjutant and promoted to First Lieutenant, effective from June 25, 1876; occupying the vacancy created by the death of Lieut. William Cooke. Lieut. Wallace returned to Fort Lincoln on September 26 at the end of that phase of the Sioux campaign. From June 25, 1876, to June 6, 1877, he was the regimental adjutant. Promoted to Captain September 23, 1885, to occupy the vacancy of Captain Andrew Nave who retired. While commanding a company of the 7th Cavalry, Captain Wallace was killed on December 29, 1890, at Wounded Knee Creek, South Dakota, in an engagement with hostile Indians of Big Foot's band of Sioux. His death was due to gunshot wounds in the head and abdomen; interred at Yorkville, South Carolina on January 6, 1891.

GARLICK, EDWARD, First Sergeant
On furlough from April 14, 1876. Born on May 8, 1846, in Chertsey, England. Enlisted on February 3, 1866, in Co. G, 11th Infantry at Richmond, Virginia. Transferred to Co. G, 20th Infantry, on Dec. 6, 1866. Previous occupation was laborer. Honorably discharged on February 3, 1869, upon expiration of service, as a Corporal. Re-enlisted on April 14, 1871, at Jefferson Barracks, Missouri in Co. G, 7th Cavalry by Lieut. Peter Vroom. With his company he participated in the action on August 4, 1873, on the Tongue River and the action on August 11, 1873, at the mouth of the Bighorn River against hostile Sioux, in the Yellowstone Expedition. He was engaged in the Black Hills expedition in July and August, 1874. Discharged on April 14, 1876, at Shreveport, Louisiana as a First Sergeant, upon expiration of service, with a notation of "unexceptionable character." Granted four months furlough with permission to go beyond the sea, to take effect upon his re-enlistment on Special Order Nr. 61, Department of the Gulf, Apr. 1, 1876. His third enlistment was on April 14, 1876, at Shreveport by Lieut. Donald McIntosh. He then went to England on his furlough and returned to detached service. He participated in the 1877 Nez Perce campaign and was engaged in the Canyon Creek fight on September 13, 1877. Discharged on April 13, 1881, at Fort Meade, Dakota, as a First Sergeant of excellent character. His fourth enlistment was on April 14, 1881 at Fort Meade. Discharged April 13, 1886, at Fort Keogh, Montana Terr. as a Sergeant. His fifth enlistment was on April 14, 1886, and he was discharged on November 5, 1887, at Fort Riley, Kansas on a surgeon's certificate of disability. All of his cavalry service was in Troop G, 7th Cavalry. He was pensioned on Nov. 19, 1887, at the rate of $18 per month because of disease of the kidneys and chronic nephritis caused by exposure to cold weather while on duty in troop stables in the winter of 1886-1887 and the spring of 1887. The pension was increased to $50 monthly on June 17, 1927 (for 75 years of age) under the Act of Mar. 3, 1927. Garlick married Elizabeth Hahn, widow of Henry Dose, Co. G, 7th Cavalry Trumpeter, who was killed in the Little Bighorn River fight. The marriage took place on November 22, 1876, at Bismarck, Dakota.

Garlick had blue eyes, sandy hair, light complexion and was 6'-2" in height. He resided in Sturgis, South Dakota, where he served as mail carrier for many years. He died in Sturgis about July, 1931.

AKERS, JAMES, Sergeant
Born in Kings County, Ireland. Enlisted on December 4, 1874, at age 23 in Boston by Lieutenant William Harper, Jr. Previous occupation was plasterer. Assigned to Company G, 7th Cavalry. Honorably discharged on January 12, 1878, at Fort Abraham Lincoln, Dakota for disability, as a Sergeant of good character. He had hazel eyes, auburn hair, fair complexion and was 5'-6" in height. He may have been previously enlisted in the 6th Cavalry.

BOTZER, EDWARD, Sergeant
Killed at the ford in the retreat from the valley fight on June 25. Born in Bremerhaven, Germany. Second enlistment on November 26, 1871, at age 26 in Spartanburg, South Carolina, by Lieutenant Donald McIntosh. In his previous enlistment he had been a Corporal in Company G, 7th Cavalry. He had blue eyes, brown hair, fair complexion and was 5'-6½" in height. Listed as Edw'd Botzer on the battle monument.

BROWN, ALEXANDER, Sergeant
Born in Aberdeen, Scotland on February 19, 1844. Second enlistment on December 13, 1871, at age 26 in Spartanburg, South Carolina by Lieut. Donald McIntosh. Discharged on December 13, 1876, at Fort Abraham Lincoln, Dakota upon expiration of service as a Private of very good character. Re-enlisted. He died April 7, 1884, as a Sergeant in Troop H, 7th Cavalry and was interred in the Fort Meade (South Dakota) Post Cemetery, Grave 1-44. He had hazel eyes, black hair, dark complexion and was 5'-8½" in height. The Descriptive List and Records File, Custer Battlefield National Monument, has a letter from Lieut. Donald McIntosh, Company G, 7th Cavalry, Shreveport, Louisiana, October 14, 1874 requesting a warrant for various non-commissioned officers including First Sergeant Alexander Brown. A partial record of the Sioux campaign is in Charles Reynold's diary. The diary was retained by Sergeant Brown after the Little Bighorn fight and is now in the Minnesota Historical Society Library.

CONSIDINE, MARTIN, Sergeant
Killed in battle on June 25. Born in Clare, Ireland. Second enlistment on January 28, 1875, at age 27 in St. Louis by Lieut. William Volkmar. He had blue eyes, brown hair, fair complexion and was 5'-7½" in height. Listed as Martin Considine on the battle monument.

LLOYD, FRANK, Sergeant
On detached service from May 17, 1876 at Fort Abraham Lincoln, Dakota. Born in London, England. Enlisted on February 12, 1872, at age 23 in Chicago by Captain Samuel Young. Previous occupation was clerk. Discharged on February 12, 1877, at Fort Lincoln upon expiration of service, as a Sergeant of excellent character. He had grey eyes, brown hair, fair complexion and was 5'-6" in height.

NORTHEG, OLANS H., Sergeant
Born in Nannestad, Norway. Second enlistment on March 21, 1872, at age

30 in St. Louis by Lieut. Peter Vroom. Previous occupation was clerk. Discharged on March 21, 1877, at Fort Abraham Lincoln, Dakota upon expiration of service, as a Sergeant of very good character. Re-enlisted. He died November 5, 1882, and was interred in the Fort Meade, Dakota, Post Cemetery, Grave 3-33. He had grey eyes, fair hair, fair complexion and was 5'-9½" in height. Listed as Olans H. Northeg in the Register of Enlistments and as Olans Northeg on his cemetery monument and as Alans Nathey in internment records.

BRINKERHOFF, HENRY M., Corporal
Born in Adam County, Pennsylvania. Enlisted on Dec. 1, 1874, at age 22 in St. Louis by Lieut. William Volkmar. Previous occupation was laborer. Discharged Nov. 30, 1879, at Fort Meade, Dakota upon expiration of service, as a Sergeant of excellent character. He had blue eyes, light hair, fair complexion and was 5'-6" in height. His "Account of the Custer Battle" is in the *Custer Scrapbook*, Billings (Mont.) Public Library. His letter to Albert Johnson, criticizing Lieut. Edward Godfrey for anti-Reno remarks, is in the Dustin Collection, Custer Battlefield National Monument. In 1927 Brinkerhoff resided in Inglewood, California.

FLOOD, PHILLIP, Corporal
In an insane asylum in Washington, D.C. from April 27, 1875. Born in County Meath, Ireland. Enlisted on December 3, 1874, at age 27 in Boston by Lieut. William Harper, Jr. Discharged on September 9, 1878 to date from July 1, 1877, at Washington, D.C. per Special Order Nr. 140, AGO, War Department, with good character, as far as known. He had brown eyes, brown hair, ruddy complexion and was 5'-6¾" in height.

HAGEMANN, OTTO, Corporal
Killed in battle on June 25. Born in Hanover, Germany. Enlisted on October 2, 1873, at age 24 in New York City by Lieut. Edward Hunter. Previous occupation was merchant. He had brown eyes, brown hair, fair complexion and was 5'-9½" in height. Listed as Otto Hagemann on the battle monument and as Otto Hagenann in the Register of Enlistments, U.S. Army and elsewhere as Otto Hageman.

HAMMON, JOHN E., Corporal
In the valley and hilltop fights. Born in Warren County, Ohio. Enlisted on September 1, 1873, at age 18 in Cincinnati, Ohio by Lieut. Adam Kramer. Previous occupation was farmer. Discharged September 1, 1878, at Camp James G. Sturgis, Dakota, upon expiration of service, as a Corporal of very good character. He had blue eyes, dark brown hair, fair complexion and was 5'-7¼" in height. He may have been promoted to the grade of Sergeant in June, 1876. *The Custer Battle*, a statement made to C. E. Deland, February 28, 1898, is in the Dustin Collection, Custer Battlefield National Monument.

LOYD, GEORGE, Corporal
In the valley and hilltop fights. Born in Tyrone, Ireland. Third enlistment on April 13, 1874, at age 31 in St. Louis by Captain Charles Bendire. Discharged on April 12, 1879, at Fort Abraham Lincoln, Dakota, upon expiration of service, as a Sergeant of excellent character. Re-enlisted. As a Sergeant in Company I, 7th Cavalry, he was issued a Medal of Honor on April 16, 1891,

"For bravery especially after having been severely wounded through the lung," in the engagement with Sioux Indians at Wounded Knee Creek, South Dakota on December 29, 1890. He died of the wounds received in the fight and was interred at Fort Robinson, Nebraska. He had grey eyes, light hair, ruddy complexion and was 5'-9" in height.

MARTIN, JAMES, Corporal
Killed in the hilltop fight. Born in County Kildare, Ireland. Enlisted on February 6, 1872, at age 24 in Chicago by Captain Samuel Young. Previous occupation was laborer. He had grey eyes, brown hair, fair complexion and was 5'-5" in height. Listed as James Martin on the battle monument.

WALLACE, JOHN W., Corporal
Born in Salem, Indiana. Enlisted on November 1, 1872, at age 22 10/12 in Kansas City by Lieut. John Morrison. Previous occupation was farmer. Discharged on June 25, 1877, at camp on Sunday Creek, Montana Territory per Special Order Nr. 70, Department of Dakota, 1877, as a Corporal of excellent character. He had blue eyes, auburn hair, florid complexion and was 5'-9" in height.

CARTER, CASSIUS R., Trumpeter
On detached service from April 19, 1876, at Shreveport, Louisiana. Born in Baltimore, Maryland. Enlisted on October 31, 1865, at a stated age of 19 at Carlisle, Pennsylvania, by Lieut. Thomas McGregor. Previous occupation was soldier. Deserted from Carlisle Barracks on November 2, 1865; surrendered August 10, 1866 under the provisions of General Order Nr. 43, AGO, July 3, 1866. Assigned to Company E, 7th Cavalry. Discharged from Company E on August 10, 1869. Re-enlisted in Company F, 7th Cavalry on September 24, 1869 at Fitz-Meadows, Colorado Terr., 25 miles west of Fort Wallace, Kansas by Captain Edw. Myers. Discharged on May 23, 1875. Third enlistment in General Mounted Service on June 22, 1875, at age 26 at St. Louis Barracks, Missouri by Captain James Wheelan. Assigned to Company G, 7th Cavalry. Discharged June 22, 1880, upon expiration of service as a Trumpeter of good character. Fourth enlistment on June 22, 1880, at camp on Box Elder Creek, Montana Terr. by Lieut. William Nicholson. Assigned to Company G. At this time Carter was married with no children. Discharged on June 21, 1885, from Company E. Fifth enlistment on June 22, 1885, at Fort Meade, Dakota by Lieut. John Wilkinson. Assigned to Troop E, 7th Cavalry. Discharged on June 21, 1890. Sixth enlistment on July 1, 1890 in St. Louis by Captain A. B. Kauffman. He had black or grey eyes, black hair, dark complexion and was 5'-5¼" to 6¾" in height and was illiterate. Listed as Cassius R. Caster in the Register of Enlistments, U.S. Army and as Cassius R. Carter on his Oaths of Enlistment.

DOSE, HENRY C., Trumpeter
Killed in battle on June 25. Born in Holstein, Germany. Second enlistment on February 1, 1875, at age 25 in Shreveport, Louisiana by Lieut. Donald McIntosh. Previous occupation was artificer. Dose was previously enlisted in the 3rd Infantry. He had grey eyes, brown hair, fair complexion and was 5'-6" in height. His widow married First Sergeant Edward Garlick.

SELBY, CRAWFORD, Saddler
Killed in battle on June 25. Born in Ashland County, Ohio. Enlisted on

June 21, 1875, at age 30 in Chicago by Lieut. Edmund Luff. Previous occupation was saddler. Listed as Crawford Selby on the battle monument. He had grey eyes, light brown hair, fair complexion and was 5'-5½" in height.

WELLS, BENJAMIN J., Farrier

Killed in the retreat from the valley fight on June 25. His horse bolted into the Indians at the ford and he was killed. His remains were found to the right (south) of the line of retreat. Born in Sangamon, Illinois. Second enlistment on December 5, 1871, at age 28 in Louisville, Kentucky by Lieut. William Cooke. He had blue eyes, fair hair, fair complexion and was 5'-6½" in height. Listed as Benj. Wells on the battle monument.

TAYLOR, WALTER O., Blacksmith

Born in Scituate, Rhode Island. Enlisted on November 22, 1875, at age 21 4/12 in Boston by Lieut. Henry Lawton. Previous occupation was horseshoer. Discharged on November 21, 1880, at Newport, Kentucky, upon expiration of service as a Blacksmith of good character. In 1927 he resided on a rural route at Whitman, Mass. He had grey eyes, light hair, fair complexion and was 5'-6¾" in height.

BARNETT, CHARLES C., Private

On detached service from June 15, 1876, at Yellowstone Depot, Montana Territory. Born in Camden, Ohio. Enlisted on March 21, 1876, at age 19 in Cincinnati, Ohio by Lieut. Patrick Cusack. Previous occupation was carpenter. He was discharged on March 24, 1881, at Fort Meade, Dakota, upon expiration of service, as a Private of excellent character. He had blue eyes, brown hair, fair complexion and was 5'-9" in height. In 1927 he resided at 817 H. Ave. Anacortes, Wash. Listed as Barnet on the Muster Roll of Recruits of the General Mounted Service, St. Louis Barracks, for the period Feb. 29, to April 30, 1876.

BOYLE, JAMES P., Private

Wounded. Returned to duty. Born in County Tyrone, Ireland. Enlisted on December 7, 1874, at age 21 in Boston by Lieut. William Harper, Jr. Previous occupation was laborer. Discharged on December 6, 1879, at Fort Meade, Dakota upon expiration of service, as a Private of good character. He had hazel eyes, auburn hair, ruddy complexion and was 5'-6 3/8" in height. Not listed as wounded on the 7th Cavalry Returns; listed elsewhere as wounded.

CAMPBELL, CHARLES, Private

Wounded in the right shoulder on June 26 in the first water party with Private Michael Madden. Transported to Fort Abraham Lincoln, Dakota, on the steamer *Far West*. Born in Guthrie County, Iowa. Enlisted on April 3, 1876, at age 21 in St. Louis by Lieut. William Thompson. Previous occupation was carpenter. Discharged on April 2, 1881, at Fort Meade, Dakota. Re-enlisted and appointed regimental Quartermaster Sergeant; First Sergeant of Troop I and Post Quartermaster Sergeant. Wounded in an engagement with Sioux Indians at Wounded Knee, South Dakota, on December 29, 1890. He had blue eyes, light hair, ruddy complexion and was 5'-5½" in height. Died of tuberculosis at Fort Bayard, New Mexico. Theodore Goldin, in telling the story of the water party, related that, "We all made the rush in safety, save little Campbell, of G Troop, who went down with a ball in his shoulder, just a few feet from the shelter of the ravine. One or two of the men halted and turned back to his assistance, but he pluckily called out, 'Go on, boys; I can make it back some way.'" In Brininstool *Troopers With Custer*, p. 227.

CORNWALL, MICHAEL, Private
Born in Ireland. Second enlistment on August 19, 1875, at age 32 in Pittsburgh by Lieut. Thomas Gregg. Previous occupation was soldier. Assigned to Company G; transferred to Company K. Discharged on August 18, 1880, at Fort Meade, Dakota, upon expiration of service, as a Private of good character. He had grey eyes, brown hair, ruddy complexion and was 5'-4½" in height.

CRUSSY, MELANCHTON H., Private
On detached service from June 15, 1876, at Yellowstone Depot, Montana Territory. Born in New York City. Enlisted on December 1, 1875, at age 30 in St. Louis by Lieut John Thompson. Previous occupation was clerk. Discharged on November 30, 1880, at Fort Meade, Dakota, upon expiration of service, as a Private. He had blue eyes, brown hair, dark complexion and was 5'-6¼" in height. Listed as Melanchton H. Crussy in the Register of Enlistments, U.S. Army and elsewhere as Corporal Melanchton Cressey and as Melanchlow H. Crussy and as Sgt. Melancthon H. Cressy.

DWYER, EDMOND, Private
In the first water party with Private Michael Madden during the hilltop fight on June 26. Born in Fairfax County, Virginia. Enlisted on April 14, 1876, at age 25 4/12 in St. Louis by Lieut John Thompson. Previous occupation was laborer. Deserted on August 15, 1878; surrendered on November 8, 1880. Dishonorably discharged on January 6, 1881, at Fort Leavenworth, Kansas per General Court Martial Order Nr. 12, Department of Missouri, 1881. He had blue eyes, brown hair, fair complexion and was 5'-5½" in height. His name is listed as Edward Dwyer on the Muster Roll of Recruits of the General Mounted Service, St. Louis Barracks, for the period Feb. 29 to Apr. 30, 1876.

GEIST, FRANK J., Private
On detached service from June 15, 1876 at Yellowstone Depot, Montana Territory. Born in Wurtzburg, Bavaria, Germany. Enlisted on April 14, 1876, at age of 22 2/12 in St. Louis by Lieut. John Thompson. Previous occupation was machinist. Discharged on January 30, 1879, at Fort A. Lincoln, Dakota for disability, as a Private of good character. He had grey eyes, light hair, fair complexion and was 5'-6" in height.

GOLDIN, THEODORE W., (born John Stilwell), Private
In the valley and hilltop fights. Born on July 25, 1858, in Green County, Wisconsin. Enlisted on April 8, 1876 at Chicago by Lieut. Edmund Luff. Previous occupation was brakeman. Cavalry duty was as headquarters clerk. Discharged on November 13, 1877, in the field in Dakota Territory per paragraph 3, Special Order Nr. 174, dated August 16, 1877, AGO, War Department, as a Private of good character, because of a concealed minority enlistment. He had blue eyes, brown hair, fair complexion and was 5'-7¾" in height. On December 21, 1895, upon his own application, he was awarded the Medal of Honor as one of a party of volunteers who, under heavy fire from the

indians, went for and brought water to the wounded in the Little Bighorn River fight. This medal is on display at Prairie du Chien. In 1904 he was chairman of the Republican Central Committee in Wisconsin. He became a prominent attorney and a Colonel in the Wisconsin National Guard. Died on February 15, 1935; interred in King Veteran's Cemetery. Colonel T. W. Goldin, General Staff, Wisconsin National Guard, was the author of "Comment On A United States Army," Vol. XIII, p. 339 and "Meritorious Discharged Soldiers," May, 1891, Vol. XII, Nr. LI, pp. 660-661 in the *Journal of the Military Service Institution*.

GRAHAM, THOMAS, Private

In the hilltop fight. Born in Alton, Ohio. Enlisted on November 4, 1872, at age 18 in Columbus, Ohio by Lieut. James Wheelan. Previous occupation was laborer. Discharged on November 4, 1877, at Fort Abraham Lincoln, Dakota upon expiration of service, as a Private of excellent character. He had grey eyes, light hair, fair complexion and was 5'-6¾" in height.

GRAY, WILLIAM S., Private

On detached servce at Yellowstone Depot, Montana Territory from June 15, 1876. Born in New Bedford, Massachusetts. Enlisted on April 10, 1876, at age 21 in Cincinnati by Lieut. Patrick Cusack. Previous occupation was farmer. Discharged on April 9. 1881, at Fort Meade, Dakota upon expiration of his service, as a Private of excellent character. He had hazel eyes, black hair, brown complexion and was 5'-6¾" in height.

GRAYSON, EDWARD, Private

Born in Providence, Rhode Island. Second enlistment on December 18, 1872, at age 35 in Charlotte, North Carolina by Lieut. Nathaniel Wolfe. Transferred from Company C to Company G to Company B. Discharged on December 18, 1877, at Fort Abraham Lincoln, Dakota upon expiration of service, as a Private of good character. He had blue eyes, brown hair, light complexion and was 5'-5¾" in height.

HACKETT, JOHN, Private

Born in Dublin, Ireland. Enlisted on November 14, 1872, at age 21 in Chicago by Captain Samuel Young. Previous occupation was hostler. Discharged on November 14, 1877 at Fort Abraham Lincoln, Dakota upon expiration of service, as a Private of excellent character. He had grey eyes, brown hair, fair complexion and was 5'-4¼" in height.

HENDERSON, GEORGE W., Private

On detached service from June 15, 1876, at Yellowstone Depot, Montana Territory. Born in Homelsville, New York. Enlisted on March 2, 1876, at age 21 in Baltimore, Maryland by Lieut. William Wallace. Previous occupation was farmer. Deserted on January 2, 1877; apprehended on January 4, 1877 and then escaped on January 20, 1877. He had grey eyes, light hair, ruddy complexion and was 5'-7½" in height.

JOHNSON, BENJAMIN, Private

Born in Lancaster, Pennsylvania. Enlisted on June 22, 1875, at age 29 in Pittsburgh by Lieut. Thomas Gregg. Previous occupation was carpenter. Discharged on June 22, 1880, at Box Elder Creek. Montana Territory upon expiration of service, as a Sergeant of excellent character. He had hazel eyes, dark brown hair, dark complexion and was 5'-5¾" in height.

KATZENMAIER, JACOB, Private
On detached service from June 15, 1876 at Yellowstone Depot, Montana Territory. Born in Germany. Enlisted on March 27, 1876, at age 23 in Pittsburgh, by Lieut. Thomas Gregg. Previous occupation was baker. He died on January 27, 1880 of erysipelas, at Fort Meade, Dakota. He had blue eyes, light brown hair, fair complexion and was 5'-8¼" in height. His remains were interred in the Fort Meade Post Cemetery, Grave 1-2. The name on the gravestone is Jacob Katzemeir. His name is listed as Jacob Katzenmaeir on the 7th Cavalry Returns, June 30, 1876.

KILFOYLE, MARTIN, Private
On detached service from June 15, 1876 at Yellowstone Depot, Montana Territory. Born in County Clare, Ireland. Enlisted on December 4, 1874, at age 21 in St. Louis by Lieut. William Volkmar. Previous occupation was laborer. Discharged on November 30, 1879 at Fort Meade, Dakota upon expiration of service, as a Private. He had blue eyes, light hair, fair complexion and was 5'-6" in height.

LADEN, JOSEPH, Private
On detached service from May 17, 1876, at Fort A. Lincoln, Dakota. Born in Ireland. Enlisted on December 18, 1872, at age 23 in Pittsburgh by Lieut. Calbraith Rodgers. Previous occupation was puddler. Discharged December 18, 1877, at Fort Lincoln upon expiration of service, as a Private of very good character. He had grey eyes, brown hair, fair complexion and was 5'-8½" in height.

LATTMANN, JOHN, Private
Born in Zurich, Switzerland. Enlisted on October 14, 1873, at age 25 in Philadelphia by Lieut. William Volkmar. Previous occupation was laborer. Discharged October 14, 1878, at Fort A. Lincoln, Dakota, upon expiration of service, as a Private of excellent character. He had grey eyes, auburn hair, ruddy complexion and was 5'-6¾" in height. Listed as John Lattmann in the Register of Enlistments, U.S. Army and elsewhere as John Lattman. He homesteaded on 160 acres of land 12 miles northeast of Rapid City, South Dakota, (near Elk Vale Cemetery) where he raised cattle. He remained a bachelor and died about 1915.

LAUPER, FRANK, Private
On detached service from June 15, 1876, at Yellowstone Depot, Montana Terr. Born in Montgomery, Ohio. Enlisted on April 7, 1876, at age 24 in Cincinnati by Lieut. Patrick Cusack. Previous occupation was soldier. Discharged on April 6, 1881, at Fort Meade, Dakota, upon expiration of service, as a Saddler of excellent character. He had blue eyes, light hair, light complexion and was 5'-6½. in height.

LAWLER, JAMES, Private
On detached service from May 17, 1876, at Fort A. Lincoln, Dakota. Born in Kildare, Ireland. Second enlistment on December 21, 1874, at age 36 in Shreveport, Louisiana, by Lieut. Donald McIntosh. Previous occupation was soldier. Died on September 18, 1877, of wounds received in the fight at Canyon Creek, Montana Territory, with Chief Joseph's band of Nez Perce Indians. He was then a Farrier. He had brown eyes, brown hair, dark complexion and was 5'-5¾" in height.

MOORE, ANDREW J., Private
Killed in the hilltop fight on June 26. Born in Camden, New Jersey. Enlisted on January 23, 1872, at age 21 in Philadelphia by Captain Samuel Whitside. Previous occupation was carpenter. He had blue eyes, dark hair, fair complexion and was 5'-8" in height. Listed as A. J. Moore on the battle monument.

MORRISON, JOHN, Private
Wounded. Returned to duty. Born in Zanesville, Ohio. Third enlistment on May 21, 1875, at age 32 in Shreveport, Louisiana by Lieut. Donald McIntosh. Discharged on May 20, 1880 at Fort Meade, Dakota upon expiration of service, as a Private of good character. He had grey eyes, brown hair, ruddy complexion and was 5'-8¾" in height. Listed as wounded in Major Marcus Reno's report in July, 1876; not listed as wounded in the 7th Cavalry Returns, June 30, 1876.

McCORMICK, SAMUEL, Private
In the valley and hilltop fights. He gave his horse to Lieut. Donald McIntosh at the beginning of the withdrawal from the timber in the valley fight. He rejoined the command on the hilltop with George Herendeen, the scout. Born in Tyrone, Ireland. Enlisted on September 29, 1873, at age 25 in Philadelphia by Lieut. William Volkmar. Previous occupation was morocco tanner. Discharged on September 29, 1878, at Fort Lincoln, Dakota upon expiration of service, as a Private of good character. He had grey eyes, brown hair, ruddy complexion and was 5'-6½" in height.

McDONNELL, JOHN, Private
Born in New York City. Enlisted on April 7, 1873, at age 28 in Cairo, Illinois by Lieut. John Walker. Previous occupation was wagoner. Sentenced to 40 days confinement at hard labor and a fine of $10 per General Court Martial Order Nr. 2, Department of the Gulf, January, 1876. Discharged on April 7, 1878, at Fort Lincoln, Dakota upon expiration of service, as a Private of good character. He had blue eyes, auburn hair, fair complexion and was 5'-9" in height.

McEAGEN, JOHN, Private
Born in County Cary, Ireland. Enlisted on February 6, 1872, at age 24 4/12 in Cincinnati, Ohio by Lieut. Myles Moylan. Previous occupation was laborer. Discharged on February 6, 1877, at Fort Lincoln, Dakota upon expiration of service, as a Farrier of excellent character. He had grey eyes, brown hair, ruddy complexion, and was 5'-8¾" in height. Listed as McEgan in Sgt. Alex Brown's roster in Aug. 1876.

McGINNIS, JOHN J., Private
Killed in battle on June 25. Born in Boston. Enlisted on December 2, 1874, at age 25 in Boston by Lieut. William Harper, Jr. Previous occupation was lithographer. Listed as J. J. McGinniss on the battle monument and elsewhere as John J. McGinniss. He had grey eyes, sandy hair, florid complexion and was 5'-7 3/8" in height.

McGONIGLE, HUGH, Private
Born in Philadelphia, Pennsylvania. Third enlistment on July 22, 1872, at age 30 in Philadelphia by Captain Samuel Whitside. Discharged on June 25, 1877, at camp on Sunday Creek, Montana Territory per Special Order Nr. 70, Department of Dakota, 1877, as a Private of excellent character. He had brown eyes, black hair, dark complexion and was 5'-10" in height.

McKAY, EDWARD J., Private
On detached service from June 15, 1876, at Yellowstone Depot, Montana Territory. Born in Galway, Ireland. Enlisted on April 12, 1876, at age 22 in Cincinnati by Lieut. Patrick Cusack. Previous occupation was laborer. He was discharged on April 11, 1881, at Fort Meade, Dakota upon expiration of his service, as a Private of excellent character. He had blue eyes, black hair, ruddy complexion and was 5'-5" in height.

McKEE, JOHN, Private
On detached service from June 15, 1876, at Yellowstone Depot, Montana Territory. Born in Meigs County, Ohio. Enlisted on April 4, 1876, at age 23 in St. Louis by Lieut. John Thompson. Previous occupation was cooper. He was discharged on April 3, 1877, at Fort Meade, Dakota upon expiration of service, as a Private of excellent character. He had hazel eyes, light hair, fair complexion and was 5'-10" in height.

McVAY, JOHN, Private
Wounded in the hips on June 25. Transported to Fort Abraham Lincoln, Dakota on the steamer *Far West*. Born in Ireland. Enlisted on November 21, 1872, at age 24 in Pittsburgh by Lieut. Calbraith Rodgers. Previous occupation was laborer. Discharged on November 21, 1877, at Fort Lincoln upon expiration of service, as a Private of very good character. He had grey eyes, dark hair, dark complexion and was 5'-8¾" in height. Listed elsewhere as James McVey and John Mackey.

O'NEILL, THOMAS, Private
Missing after the valley fight on June 25. Rejoined the Reno battalion on the hilltop. Born in Dublin, Ireland. Second enlistment on January 17, 1872, at age 27 in Chicago by Captain Samuel Young. Deserted on June 18, 1872; surrendered on December 2, 1872. He was cook for Lieut. Donald McIntosh in the 1876 Sioux expedition until June 25. Discharged June 19, 1877, at Fort Lincoln, Dakota, upon expiration of service, as a Private of good character. Re-enlisted on July 15, 1877, at Fort Lincoln, by Lieut. Andrew Nave. Discharged on July 14, 1882, at Fort Snelling, Minnesota, upon expiration of service, as a First Sergeant. He had blue eyes, black hair, fair complexion and was 5'-8½" in height.

PETRING, HENRY, Private

Born in Germany. Enlisted on December 9, 1874, at age 21, in New York City by Lieut. Thomas Gregg. Previous occupation was cabinetmaker. Discharged December 8, 1879, at Fort Meade, Dakota, upon expiration of service, as a Private of good character. He had grey eyes, brown hair, florid complexion and was 5'-6¾" in height.

RAPP, JOHN, Private

Killed in the valley fight on June 25. He was orderly for Lieut. Donald McIntosh and was killed while holding horses. Born in Wurtemburg, Germany. Enlisted on September 29, 1873, at age 25 in Philadelphia by Lieut. William Volkmar. Previous occupation was tanner. He had blue eyes, dark hair, fair complexion and was 5'-5¼" in height. Listed as Jno. Rapp on the battle monument and elsewhere as John Ropp and John Papp.

REED, JOHN A., Private

Born in Chester County, Pennsylvania. Enlisted on April 6, 1871, at age 25¼ in Pittsburgh by Lieut. James M. Bell. Previous occupation was laborer. Discharged on April 6, 1876, at Shreveport, Louisiana, upon expiration of service, as a Private of good character. Re-enlisted on April 18, 1876, at St. Louis by Lieut. Charles Cresson and discharged on April 17, 1881 at Fort Meade, Dakota upon expiration of service, as a Farrier of excellent character. Re-enlisted. Died (as a Sergeant) on July 21, 1897, at Fort Sisseton, South Dakota. Re-interred in the Custer Battlefield National Cemetery, Grave 1A. He had grey eyes, brown hair, fair complexion and was 5'-7" in height.

ROBB, ELDORADO J., Private

Born in Warren County, Kentucky. Enlisted on January 8, 1872, at age 21 in Louisville, Kentucky by Lieut. Edward Ward. Previous occupation was laborer. Acquitted of a charge of "neglect of duty to the prejudice of good order and military discipline" per General Court Martial Order Nr. 2, Department of the Gulf, January, 1876. Discharged on Jan. 8, 1877, at Fort Lincoln, Dakota, upon expiration of service, as a Private of good character. He had hazel eyes, brown hair, ruddy complexion and was 5'-9¾" in height. Listed as Eldorado J. Robb in the Register of Enlistments, U.S. Army.

ROGERS, BENJAMIN F., Private

Killed in battle on June 25. Born in Madison County, Kentucky. Enlisted on January 5, 1872, at age 24 in Louisville, by Lieut. Edward Ward. Previous occupation was farmer. Sentenced to confinement for three months at his post and $30 fine per General Court Martial Order Nr. 8, Department of the Gulf, February 25, 1876. He had blue eyes, light hair, ruddy complexion and was 5'-10" in height. Listed as B. F. Rogers on the battle monument.

ROWLAND, ROBERT, Private

On detached service from June 15, 1876, at Yellowstone Depot, Montana Territory. Born in Warsaw, Poland. Enlisted on April 7, 1876, at age 32 in St. Louis by Lieut. John Thompson. Previous occupation was baker. The *Dakota Pantograph* (Sioux Falls) for Jan. 8, 1879 carries this story: "James Brooks, freighter . . . rode sixty miles before New Year's Eve, in advance of his wagon train coming from Fort Keogh to reach Bismarck to see the old year out with a high time. He attended a dance at Keno hall where a number of fast women and soldiers were waltzing out '78. Brooks record was that no man ever got the drop on him. About eleven o'clock he slapped a woman's face who told him to keep quiet. A regular knockdown followed. After several black eyes were scored Brooks received a ball from a navy revolver passing in at his mouth and out at the back of his head. Corporal John [sic] Rowland, Company G, 7th Cavalry was the last man to clinch with Brooks and he is under arrest. Nobody seemed to see the shot fired. The Pantograph for January 22, 1879 indicates that "Corporal Rowland, 7th Cavalry, charged with killing James Brooks at Bismarck New Years Eve has been discharged on the preliminary examination." Rowland deserted on April 10, 1879. He had brown eyes, brown hair, ruddy complexion and was 5'-8" in height.

SEAFFERMAN, HENRY, Private

Killed in battle on June 25. Born in Strasburg, Germany. Enlisted in Company K, 2nd Cavalry, from August 11, 1860, to July 1, 1864, and in Company K, 5th Cavalry from July 1, 1864 to July 1, 1867. (The 2nd Cavalry was re-designated the 5th Cavalry by Act of Congress August 3, 1861). Enlisted in Company H, 7th Cavalry from July 5, 1867, with detached service to the 7th Cavalry Band. Enlisted on July 11, 1872, at age 32 in Spartanburg, South Carolina, by Lieut. Benjamin Hodgson. He had hazel eyes, brown hair, florid complexion and was 5'-7½" in height. Listed as Henry Seafferman on the battle monument. Listed elsewhere as Staferman. See Descriptive List and Records File, Custer Battlefield National Monument.

SHANAHAN, JOHN, Private

On detached service from June 15, 1876 at Yellowstone Depot, Montana Territory. Born in Ireland. Enlisted on December 9, 1874, at age 21 5/12 in Boston by Lieut. William Harper, Jr. Previous occupation was laborer. Discharged on December 8, 1879 at Fort Meade, Dakota upon expiration of service, as a Private of good character. He had blue eyes, brown hair, fair complexion and was 5'-7" in height.

SMALL, JOHN R., Private

Born in Baltimore, Maryland. Enlisted on March 5, 1873, at age 28 in Philadelphia by Captain G. T. Robinson. Previous occupation was sailor. He had grey eyes, dark hair, fair complexion and was 5'-7½" in height. Small was tried at Shreveport, Louisiana for absence without leave, selling uniform clothing, worthlessness (Small had been sentenced by a garrison court within twelve months for ten different offenses). General Augur, commanding the Department of the Gulf observed, "The trial of enlisted men on the charge of worthlessness, sustained by specifications of offenses which have already been punished by sentence of court- martial, is prohibited by General Order Nr. 11, series of 1873, from the War Department. If officers who prefer charges would keep themselves informed of existing orders concerning offenses of enlisted men, the ends of justice would not have been defeated, as in this case. The sentence is too severe for the offenses of absence without leave and selling clothing, and is of such nature that it cannot well be modified. It is, therefore disapproved, and Private Small will be released from confinement and returned to duty." Private Small was released from confinement at Fort Leavenworth on February 25, 1876 per General Court Martial Order Nr. 8, Department of the Gulf, Feb. 28, 1876.

STANLEY, EDWARD, Private
Killed in battle on June 25. Enlisted on November 22, 1875, at age 25 in Boston by Lieut. Henry Lawton. Previous occupation was clerk. He had blue eyes, brown hair, fair complexion and was 5'-9 3/8" in height. Listed as Edw'd Stanley on the battle monument.

STEPHENS, GEORGE W., Private
On detached service from June 15, 1876, at Yellowstone Depot, Montana Territory. Born in Madison, Indiana. Enlisted on April 4, 1876, at age 23 in St. Louis Barracks, Missouri by Lieut. John Thompson. Previous occupation was cooper. he had brown eyes, black hair, dark complexion and was 5'-8½" in height and was illiterate.

STEVENSON, THOMAS W., Private
Born in Fermaugh, Ireland. Second enlistment on July 19, 1875, at age 27 in Chicago by Lieut. Edmund Luff. Discharged on July 18, 1880 at Fort Totten, Dakota upon expiration of service, as a Private of good character. He had blue eyes, red hair, ruddy complexion and was 5'-5¾" in height.

SULLIVAN, DANIEL, Private
On detached service from June 15, 1876, at Yellowstone Depot, Montana Territory. Born in Cork, Ireland. Enlisted on December 8, 1874, at age 22 in Boston by Lieut. William Harper, Jr. Previous occupation was laborer. Discharged on December 7, 1879, at Fort Meade, Dakota upon expiration of service, as a Private of good character. He had blue eyes, dark hair, medium complexion and was 5'-8" in height. In 1927 he resided at Tragmina, Skibbarson, Ireland.

TULO, JOSEPH, Private
On detached service from June 15, 1876, at Yellowstone Depot, Montana Territory. Born in Rand, France. Enlisted on March 7, 1876, at the age of 23 in St. Louis by Lieut. John Thompson. Previous occupation was laborer. Deserted on September 2, 1877. He had grey eyes, brown hair, fair complexion and was 5'-8½" in height.

WEISS, MARKUS, Private
Born in Caban, Hungary. Second enlistment on February 27, 1876, at age 29½ at Shreveport, Louisiana by Lieut. Donald McIntosh. Died on November 15, 1879, at Fort Meade, Dakota, the result of a fracture of the skull. Interred in the Fort Meade Post Cemetery, Grave 1-6. He had grey eyes, brown hair, fair complexion and was 5'-8" in height. The Descriptive List and Records File, Custer Battlefield National Monument, has Special Order Nr. 135, Depot General Recruiting Service, August 1, 1867 in which the name of Private Marcus Weis, Company G, 7th Cavalry appears on a list of deserters being returned to their units.

WILLIAMSON, PASAVAN, Private
On detached service from June 15, 1876, at Yellowstone Depot, Montana Territory. Born in Petersburg, Ohio. Enlisted on April 18, 1876, at age 28 in Pittsburgh, Pennsylvania by Lieut. Thomas Gregg. Previous occupation was

harness maker. Deserted on July 7, 1876; apprehended on July 13; escaped on December 5, 1876; discharged on February 10, 1877, per General Court Martial Order Nr. 59, Department of Dakota, 1876, at Fort Lincoln, Dak. as a Private. Committed suicide in the federal prison at Fort Leavenworth. He had blue eyes, brown hair, light complexion and was 5'-9¼" in height. See Hugh Scott, *Some Memories of A Soldier*, pp, 44-45.

COMPANY H IN 1876

The company remained a part of the garrison at Fort Rice, Dakota unitl May 5 when they marched to Fort Abraham Lincoln, Dakota and joined the rest of the regiment in camp below the fort to take part in the Sioux expedition. The company arrived at Fort Lincoln on May 6 and the regiment departed on May 17 and returned on September 26.

Company H was one of eight companies under the command of Colonel Samuel Sturgis that went to the Cheyenne Agency via the left bank of the Missouri River to disarm and dismount the Indians at that Agency. The companies left Fort Lincoln on October 17 and left camp opposite the Agency on November 4. Companies H and M left the column as it passed opposite Fort Rice and took winter station at that post. The company marched 1,865 miles during the year.

The following were casualties in the fight on the Little Bighorn River. Those killed were Corporal George Lell; Privates Julien Jones and Thomas Meador. Those wounded were First Sergeant Joseph McCurry, Sergeants Patrick Conelly, Thomas McLaughlin and John Pahl, Corporal Alexander Bishop; Trumpeter William Ramell; Saddler Otto Voit; Privates Henry Bishley, Charles Bishop, Henry Black, John Cooper, William Farley, William George, Thomas Hughes, Jan Moller, John Phillips, David McWilliams, Charles Windolph and William Williams. Private William George died on the steamboat *Far West* on July 3 while enroute to Fort Lincoln, of wounds received in the Little Bighorn River fight.

Officers serving with the company during the year were Captain Frederick Benteen, First Lieutenants Francis Gibson and Charles DeRudio and Second Lieutenant Albert Russell.* Lieut. DeRudio accepted promotion to First Lieutenant on February 25th while in winter station at Fort Rice. Lieut. Russell transferred from the Tenth Regiment of Cavalry to occupy the vacancy created by the promotion of Lieut. Ernest Garlington who was assigned to fill the vacancy of Second Lieutenant in Company H but was transferred to Company G and promoted to First Lieutenant to rank from June 25th.

* *Albert Judson Russell was born in Ohio and appointed to military service from Connecticut as a Cadet at the Military Academy, September 1, 1872. He graduated 41st in his class and was appointed Second Lieut., 10 Cavalry, June 15, 1876. Transferred to the 7th Cavalry effective June 26, 1876. Promoted to First Lieut. Nov. 30, 1881. Retired as Captain April 23, 1896. Died April 15, 1900.*

COMPANY H AT THE LITTLE BIGHORN

	Absent	Present	Wounded	Died OWRT	Killed	Survived
Captain		1	1			1
1st Lieut.		1				1
2nd Lieut.	1					1
1st Sergt.		1	1			1
Sergeants		5	3			5
Corporals		3	2	1		2
Trumpeter		2	1			2
Saddler		1	1			1
Farrier	1					1
Blacksmith		1				1
Private	8	33	13	1	2	38
Totals	10	48	22	2	2	54

COMPANY H ON JUNE 30, 1876

Commissioned present for duty 1
Commissioned present for special duty 1
Enlisted present for duty 34
Enlisted absent detached service 1
Enlisted absent sick 14
Enlisted absent in arrest 3
Captain 1
First Lieutenant 1
First Sergeant 1
Sergeants 5
Corporals 2
Trumpeters 2
Farrier and blacksmith 2
Saddler 1
Privates 39
Total enlisted 52
Agregate 54
Aggregate in May 57
Enlisted killed 3
Enlisted wounded 11
Horses serviceable 44
Horses lost 6

BENTEEN, FREDERICK WILLIAM, Captain

Commanding Company H in the hilltop fight. Born on August 24, 1834, in Petersburg, Virginia. Entered military service from Missouri as First Lieutenant, 10th Missouri Volunteer Cavalry, on September 1, 1861. Promoted to Captain on October 1, 1861; engaged in the action at West Glaze and at Wilson's Creek and the skirmish at Salem. In 1862 he was in the action at Bolivar, the skirmish at Springfield, the skirmish at Sugar Creek, the battle at Pea Ridge, the skirmishes at Batesville, Cotton Plant and Kickapoo Bottom, the defense of Helena, the skirmish at Greenville and the action at Milliken's Bend. Promoted to Major on December 19, 1862. In 1863 he was in the skirmish at Florence, the siege of Vicksburg, the action at Iuka, the capture of Jackson, the action at Brandon Station and the skirmish at Cane Creek. Promoted to Lieut. Colonel on February 27, 1864. In the actions at Bolivar and Pleasant Hill and the action on the Big Blue and the Little Osage and at Charlot, the skirmish at Montevallo, the assault and capture of Selma and the raid on Columbus. Honorably mustered out on June 30, 1865, and appointed Colonel, 138th U.S. Colored Infantry, until July 15, 1865. On June 6, 1865, he was recommended for Brevet Brig. General, Missouri Militia. Appointed Captain, 7th Cavalry, to rank from July 28, 1866. Brevetted Major, USA and Lieut. Colonel, USA, March 2, 1867, for his gallant and meritorious services in the battle of the Osage and the raid on Columbus. Received the brevet of Colonel for his service in an engagement with hostiles on the Saline River on August 13, 1868. Participated in the Washita River fight on November 28, 1868. He fought in the Little Bighorn River fight and was wounded in the right thumb and went to the field hospital with malarious dysentery. Engaged in the Nez Perce Campaign in 1877. In 1878 he commanded a battalion against hostile Indians. In 1879 he was detailed to appear at the Reno Court of Inquiry. Promoted to Major, 9th Cavalry, on December 17, 1882. Court martialed at Fort Du Chesne, Utah on charges of drunkenness and disorderly conduct and suspended from rank for one year at half pay. Retired on July 7, 1888 and resided in Atlanta. Brevetted Brig. General, February 27, 1890, for his service at the Little Bighorn and against the Nez Perce at Canyon Creek. Died in Atlanta on June 22, 1898; interred in the National Cemetery at Arlington, Virginia.

GIBSON, FRANCIS MARION, First Lieutenant

On temporary duty commanding Company G in the hilltop fight. Born on December 14, 1847 in Philadelphia. Appointed to military service from that city and commissioned Second Lieutenant, 7th Cavalry, on October 5, 1867. He joined the regiment on December 7, 1867 and served at Fort Leavenworth until June, 1868. Promoted to First Lieutenant on July 11, 1871. Participated in Colonel David Stanley's Yellowstone expedition, escorting the Northern Pacific Railroad Survey and exploring the valley of the Yellowstone River from May 7 to September 21, 1873. In the expedition to the Black Hills in July and August, 1874. On scouting duty at Fort Randall from May, 1875 to May, 1876. On May 17, 1876 he departed from Fort Abraham Lincoln, Dakota with the 7th Cavalry on the Sioux expedition. Returned to Fort Lincoln on September 26 upon termination of that part of the campaign. His company then proceeded to disarm and dismount agency Indians and then returned to winter station at Fort Rice on November 10. Engaged in the Nez Perce campaign from April 18, 1877 and returned to station on November 8 at Fort Rice. Promoted to Captain to rank from February 5, 1880. On field service until July 25, 1887 and at Fort Riley until June 11, 1889 and on sick leave from then to October 20, 1889 and on recruiting duty until October 1, 1890 and again on sick leave until December 3, 1891, when, after 22 years of service, he was retired for disability. By 1893 he had completely recovered from his illness and requested restoration to active duty. Died in 1919; interred in the National Cemetery, Arlington, Virginia. He was survived by his wife, Katherine Garrett Gibson, and daughter, Katherine.

GARLINGTON, ERNEST ALBERT, Second Lieutenant

On graduation leave of absence. Born on Feburary 20, 1853, at Newberry, South Carolina, the son of Albert Creswell, a planter, lawyer and Brigadier General, CSA and Sally Lark Moon Garlington. On July 1, 1872, he entered the Military Academy by appointment from Georgia. He was the 2622nd graduate, ranking 30th in his class of 48 graduates. Commissioned Second Lieutenant, 7th Cavalry on June 15, 1876 and assigned to Company H. Promoted to First Lieutenant effective June 25, 1876 and transferred to Company G to occupy the vacancy created by the death of Lieut. Donald McIntosh, killed in the Little Bighorn River fight. Lieut. Albert Russell occupied Garlington's vacancy in Company H. Garlington was on graduation leave until August 2, 1876, when he joined the regiment in the field in Montana. He was appointed regimental adjutant from June 6, 1877, to November 30, 1881. Commanded the Arctic Relief Expedition in 1883. Awarded the Medal of Honor on September 26, 1893 for his distinguished gallantry in action against hostile Sioux Indians in the fight on Wounded Knee Creek, South Dakota on December 29, 1890 where he was severely wounded while serving with the 7th Cavalry. He received the Order of the Purple Heart for his wound. Promoted to Captain on December 3, 1891 and served in various expeditions against the Sioux. He served throughout the Spanish-American War in Cuba in 1898. Promoted to Major, Inspector General on January 2, 1895; to Lieutenant Colonel on July 7, 1898 and Colonel on March 1, 1901. He served several tours of duty as Inspector General of the Philippine Division. On October 1, 1906, he was appointed Brigadier General, Inspector General of the Army with station in Washington, D.C. and served in that position until his retirement on February 29, 1917. During World War I he was recalled to active duty in the Office of the Chief of Staff and served from May to September, 1918. Died October 16, 1934, at Coronado, California at the age of 81. He was survived by his wife, Anna B. Garlington and his son, Major Creswell Garlington.

McCURRY, JOSEPH, First Sergeant

Wounded in the hilltop fight. Born in Philadelphia, Pennsylvania. Enlisted on January 22, 1872, at age 21 in Philadelphia by Captain Samuel Whitside. Previous occupation was coachmaker. Discharged on January 22, 1877 at Fort Rice, Dakota upon expiration of service, as a Sergeant of excellent character. He had brown eyes, dark hair, ruddy complexion and was 5'-7" in height. Listed elsewhere as Joseph McCorry and McMurray. Not listed as wounded on the 7th Cavalry Returns.

CONELLY, PATRICK, Sergeant

Wounded in the hilltop fight. Returned to duty. Born in Enniskellen, Tipperary, Ireland. First enlistment on August 12, 1865, at age 21 in Baltimore by Lieut. R. G. Howell. He was an illiterate. Second enlistment on November 1, 1866, in New York City by Captain F. D. Ogilby. He stated in this enlistment that he was born in Lowell, Massachusetts. Assigned to the 14th Infantry. Third enlistment on October 5, 1873, at age 28 at Fort Rice, Dakota, by Captain

156

Frederick Benteen. Deserted on October 2, 1876; surrendered January 26, 1878. The time lost by desertion was made good and he was discharged on January 31, 1880, at Fort Meade, Dakota, upon expiration of service, as a Private of excellent character. He had blue eyes, brown hair, ruddy complexion and was 5'-7" in height. Not listed as wounded in the Little Bighorn fight in the 7th Cavalry returns. Listed elsewhere as being wounded in the fight. Listed as Patrick Conelly in the Register of Enlistments, U.S. Army, and on his Oath of Enlistment.

GEIGER, GEORGE H., Sergeant
In the hilltop fight. The Medal of Honor was awarded to him on October 5, 1878, for his duty as a sharpshooter for the water party in the Little Bighorn River fight. With three comrades he held a position during the entire engagement, that secured water for the command. Born in Cincinnati, Ohio. Second enlistment on December 18, 1872, at the age of 29 in Louisville, Kentucky by Lieut. William Cooke. Promoted from Corporal to Sergeant on May 1, 1876. Discharged on December 18, 1877, at camp near Fort Buford, Dakota upon expiration of service, as a Sergeant of excellent character. He had grey eyes, light hair, fair complexion and was 5'-4½" in height.

MARONEY, MATTHEW, Sergeant
Born in County Clare, Ireland. Second enlistment on January 4, 1872, at age 31 in Huntsville, Alabama by Lieut. Charles DeRudio. Discharged on January 4, 1877, at Fort Rice, Dakota upon expiration of service, as a Sergeant of excellent character. He had blue eyes, brown hair, light complexion and was 5'-7½" in height.

McLAUGHLIN, THOMAS, Sergeant
Wounded in the hilltop fight. Returned to duty. Born in Philadelphia, Pennsylvania. Second enlistment on August 6, 1871, at age 24 in Louisville, Kentucky by Lieut. William Cooke. Discharged on August 6, 1876, at camp on Rosebud Creek, Montana Territory upon expiration of service, as a Sergeant of excellent character. He had blue eyes, light hair, fair complexion and was 5'-4½" in height. Not among those listed as wounded on the Returns of the Seventh Cavalry for June, 1876.

PAHL, JOHN, Sergeant
Wounded in the right shoulder (back) in the hilltop fight on June 25. Transported to Fort Abraham Lincoln, Dakota on the steamboat *Far West*. Born in Bavaria, Germany. Enlisted on November 4, 1872, at age 26 in New York City by Captain Edwin Sumner. Previous occupation was teamster. Discharged on January 4, 1878, at Fort Rice, Dakota, upon expiration of service, as a Sergeant of excellent character. Absent sick at Fort Rice from August 12, 1876 per Muster Roll, Company H, August 31, 1876. Listed elsewhere as John Paul. He had brown eyes, brown hair, fair complexion and was 5'-6¼" in height.

BISHOP, ALEXANDER B., Corporal
Wounded in the right arm in the hilltop fight on June 25; transported to Fort Abraham Lincoln, Dakota on the steamboat *Far West*. Born in Brooklyn,

New York. Enlisted on April 15, 1875, at age 22 in New Orleans, Louisiana by Captain Frederick Benteen. Previous occupation was sailor. Appointed Corporal on May 1, 1876. Discharged on October 29, 1876, at Fort Rice, Dakota per Special Order Nr. 21, AGO, 1876, as a Sergeant. Absent sick at Fort Rice from August 12, 1876 per Muster Roll, Company H, August 31, 1876. He had hazel eyes, light hair, fair complexion and was 5'-6" in height. In 1927 he resided at 310 Clermont Ave., Brooklyn, N.Y.

LELL, GEORGE, Corporal

Died on the afternoon of June 26 in the hilltop hospital of wounds in the abdomen received on June 26 in the hilltop fight. Born in Hamilton County, Ohio. Enlisted on September 18, 1873, at age 26 in Cincinnati by Lieut. Adam Kramer. Previous occupation was gasfitter. He had blue eyes, dark hair, dark complexion and was 5'-9" in height. In the Returns of the 7th Cavalry he is listed as having died on June 27. His name is mentioned in the Windolph letters in the Dustin Collection, Custer Battlefield National Monument. "I will never forget Sgt. Lell. He was fatally wounded and dragged to the hospital. He was dying and knew it. 'Lift me up, boys,' he said to some of the men. 'I want to see the boys again before I go.' So they held him up to a sitting position where he could see his comrades in action. A smile came to his face as he saw the beautiful fight the Seventh was making. Then they laid him down and he died soon after." From "The Battle of the Big Horn" by Charles Windolph, *The Sunshine Magazine*, September 30, 1930.

NEALON, DANIEL, Corporal

Born in Newport, Rhode Island. Enlisted on February 9, 1872, at age 22 in Buffalo, New York by Lieut. Albert Forse. Previous occupation was clerk. Discharged on February 9, 1877, at Fort Rice, Dakota upon expiration of service, as a Sergeant of good character. He had grey eyes, brown hair, fair complexion and was 5'-7" in height.

MARTIN, JOHN (Giovanni Martini), Trumpeter

In the hilltop fight. He carried the last message from Lieut. Col. George Custer to Captain Frederick Benteen. Born in Sola Conzalina, Italy. He was a drummer boy in the Italian Army at the age of 14. It has been said that he fought against the Austrians at Custoza in 1866. He arrived in the United States from Italy in 1873 and was enlisted on June 1, 1874, at age 22 in New York City by Lieut. Edward Hunter. Previous occupation was musician. Discharged May 3, 1879, at Fort A. Lincoln, Dakota upon expiration of service, as a Trumpeter of excellent character. Re-enlisted. Testified at the Reno Court of Inquiry in Chicago January 31, 1879. Retired as a Sergeant in 1904 after 30 years of service. He had hazel eyes, dark hair, dark complexion and was 5'-6" in height. Employed as a ticket agent on a subway in New York City after his retirement. Died on December 24, 1922, at age 69 in Brooklyn, New York; interred in Cypress Hills Cemetery, New York City.

RAMELL, WILLIAM, Trumpeter

Wounded in the hilltop fight. Returned to duty. Born at Staten Island, New York. He was enlisted on June 1, 1874, at age 21 in Philadelphia by Lieut. William Volkmar. Previous occupation was trumpeter. Deserted on February 1.

1877. Not listed among the wounded on the Returns of the Seventh Cavalry for June, 1876. He had brown eyes, dark hair, dark complexion and was 5'-3¼" in height. Listed elsewhere as Ramel.

VOIT, OTTO, Saddler
Wounded in the hilltop fight. Returned to duty. Born in Baden, Germany. Second enlistment on October 9, 1875, at age 30 in St. Louis by Lieut. John Thompson. Awarded the Medal of Honor on October 5, 1878, for bravery in action, as a sharpshooter for the water party in the Little Bighorn River fight. Discharged October 8, 1880, at Fort Meade, Dakota, upon expiration of service, as a Saddler of excellent character. He had hazel eyes, dark hair, dark complexion and was 5'-3¾" in height. Listed elsewhere as Voik. Not listed among the wounded on the *Returns of the Seventh Cavalry* in June, 1876. Listed elsewhere as wounded.

MARSHALL, JOHN M., Farrier
Sick in the hospital from May 5, 1876 at Fort Rice, Dakota. Born in Scarbrough, England. Enlisted on February 6, 1872, at age 32 9/12 in Cincinnati by Lieut. Myles Moylan. Previous occupation was laborer. Discharged on February 6, 1877 at Fort Rice, Dakota upon expiration of service, as a Farrier of good character. He had blue eyes, light hair, fair complexion and was 5'-6" in height.

MECKLIN, HENRY W. B., Blacksmith
In the hilltop fight. Awarded the Medal of Honor for participation as a sharpshooter for the water party in the Little Bighorn River fight. With three comrades, during the entire engagement, he courageously held a position that secured water for the command. Born in Westmoreland County, Pennsylvania. Enlisted on August 5, 1875, at age 23 in Pittsburgh by Lieut. Thomas Gregg. Previous occupation was blacksmith. Discharged on August 4, 1880, at Fort Meade, Dakota, upon expiration of service, as a Blacksmith. He had grey eyes, dark hair, fair complexion and was 5'-9¾" in height. Listed elsewhere as Henry Meckling and Henry W. B. Mechlin.

ADAMS, JACOB, Private
With the pack train on June 25. In the hilltop fight. In the water party with Michael Madden. Born in Stark County, Ohio, June 25, 1852. Enlisted on April 13, 1873, at age 21 in Yankton, Dakota by Captain Frederick Benteen. Previous occupation was farmer. Adams was in Captain George Yates' detachment when Rain-In-The-Face was arrested at Standing Rock Agency, Dakota in 1875. The unexecuted portion of a sentence of military convict, J. Adams, formerly Private, Company H, Seventh Cavalry, was remitted on June 21, 1876 per Special Order Nr. 116, Department of the Gulf. Discharged on April 13, 1878 at Fort Rice, Dakota upon expiration of service, as a Private of excellent character. He had brown eyes, brown hair, fair complexion and was 5'-8" in height. After discharge from the service he resided for a time in Vincennes, Indiana. "A Survivor's Story of the Custer Massacre On The American Frontier" is Adams' story told in *The Journal of American History*. Another story told by Adams is in *The National Republic Magazine*. His story was also published in a pamphlet in 1930. In 1927 he resided on Rural Route 12, Kalamazoo, Michigan.

159

AVERY, CHARLES E., Private
In confinement from May 17, 1876 at Fort Abraham Lincoln, Dakota. Born in Peterboro, New Hampshire. Enlisted on September 30, 1872, at age 21 in Lowell, Massachusetts by Captain Moses Harris. Previous occupation was laborer. Discharged on June 24, 1877, at camp near Sunday Creek, Montana Territory per Special Order Nr. 70, Department of Dakota, 1877, as a Private of very good character. He had blue eyes, dark hair, dark complexion and was 5'-8" in height. Listed as Charles Avrey on the Muster Roll of Company H, August 31, 1876.

BISHLEY, P. HENRY, Private
Wounded in the hilltop fight. Returned to duty. Born in Chicago. Enlisted on October 6, 1875, at age 34 in St. Louis by Lieut. John Thompson. Previous occupation was soldier. Discharged on June 9, 1879 at Fort Abraham Lincoln, Dakota for disability, as a Private. Not listed among the wounded on the Returns of the Seventh Cavalry for June, 1876. He had hazel eyes, brown hair, fair complexion and was 5'-7" in height.

BISHOP, CHARLES H., Private
Wounded in the right arm in the hilltop fight on June 25th and transported to Fort A. Lincoln, Dakota, on the supply steamer *Far West*. Born in Washington, D.C. Enlisted on April 15, 1875, at age 22 in New Orleans by Captain Frederick Benteen. Previous occupation was watchmaker. Discharged on April 14, 1880 at Fort Meade, Dakota upon expiration of service, as a Sergeant of excellent character. He had hazel eyes, light hair, fair complexion and was 5'-8" in height. In 1927 he resided at 1503 North 66th Street, East St. Louis, Illinois.

BLACK, HENRY, Private
Wounded in the right arm in the hilltop fight on June 25th and transported to Fort A. Lincoln, Dakota on the supply steamer *Far West*. Born in Donegal, Ireland. Enlisted on November 13, 1872, at age 22 in St. Louis, Mo. by Lieut. Oscar Elting. Previous occupation was laborer. Discharged on November 23, 1877 at Camp Buford, Dakota upon expiration of service, as a Private. He had blue eyes, light brown hair, fair complexion and was 6'-0½" in height. Listed elsewhere as William Black.

CHANNELL, WILLIAM, Private
Born in Dorchester, Massachusetts. Enlisted on September 27, 1875, at age 26 in Boston by Lieut. Henry Lawton. Previous occupation was shoemaker. Deserted on July 26, 1876; apprehended on the same day. Dishonorably discharged on October 30, 1876 at Fort Rice, Dakota, per General Court Martial Order Nr. 48, Department of Dakota, 1876, as a Private. He had brown eyes, dark hair, dark complexion and was 5'-6 7/8" in height.

COOPER, JOHN, Private
Wounded in the right elbow on June 25. Transported to Fort Abraham Lincoln, Dakota, on the steamboat *Far West*. Born in Cork, Ireland. Enlisted on September 27, 1873, at age 27 in New York City by Lieut. Edward Hunter. Previous occupation was laborer. Discharged on September 27, 1878 at Fort

Lincoln upon expiration of service, as a Private of excellent character. Listed as absent sick at Fort Rice, Dakota from August 12, 1876 on the Company H Muster Roll, August 31, 1876. He had blue eyes, brown hair, dark complexion and was 5'-5" in height.

DAY, JOHN, Private

Born in Warren County, Indiana. Enlisted on September 23, 1873, at age 22 1/12 at Chicago, Illinois by Captain Henry Carroll. Previous occupation was shoemaker. Discharged on September 23, 1878, at Fort Abraham Lincoln, Dakota, upon expiration of service, as a Private. He had hazel eyes, auburn hair, fair complexion and was 5'-7" in height.

DEWEY, GEORGE W., Private

Born in Middlebury, Vermont. Enlisted on April 13, 1873, at age 22 at Yankton, Dakota by Captain Frederick Benteen. Previous occupation was carpenter. Discharged on April 13, 1878 at Fort Rice, Dakota upon expiration of service, as a Private. He had grey eyes, dark hair, ruddy complexion and was 5'-6" in height.

DIAMOND, EDWARD, Private

Born in Stoughton, Massachusetts. Enlisted on September 18, 1875, at age 22 in Boston by Lieut. Henry Lawton. Previous occupation was crimper. Discharged on September 17, 1880 at Fort Meade, Dakota upon expiration of service, as a Private of fair character. He had grey eyes, dark hair, ruddy complexion and was 5'-5¾" in height.

FARLEY, WILLIAM, Private

Wounded in the hilltop fight on June 25. Returned to duty. Born in Ireland. Enlisted on June 1, 1875, at age 25 in New Orleans by Captain Frederick Benteen. Previous occupation was blacksmith. Discharged on April 30, 1880 at Fort Meade, Dakota, as a Private of good character. He had blue eyes, dark hair, florid complexion and was 5'-7" in height.

GEORGE, WILLIAM, Private

Wounded in the left side on June 25. Died of wounds on the steamer *Far West* at 4 AM, July 3, 1876. Interred on the river bank at Yellowstone Depot, Montana Territory, by Major Orlando Moore's company. Not listed on the battle monument at Custer Battlefield. Born in Lexington, Kentucky. Second enlistment on May 1, 1875, at age 28 in New Orleans by Captain Frederick Benteen. Previous occupation was laborer. He had blue eyes, sandy hair, fair complexion and was 5'-9" in height.

"The wounded were given every care but one of them, a man named George from H Company died right beside me. He was badly shot and suffered terribly and begged for an opiate to stop the pain. The doctor gave it to him but it did no good." Daniel Newell in *The Sunshine Magazine*, Sept. 30, 1930.

"The heroic Doctor Porter, working without interruption, lost one of his patients in the early morning hours of the 4th, Private William George, of H Troop, shot through the left side on Reno's Hill. At

161

Powder River the boat stopped long enough to have his body interred . . ." Joseph Hanson, *Conquest of the Missouri*, p. 305.

"The steamboat stopped long enough to remove the body of William George, private of company "H" who died on July 3, for burial at Powder River . . ." *Jacob Horner and the Indian Campaigns of 1876 and 1877* by U. L. Burdick and E. D. Hart, 1942, Baltimore, Wirth Press, p. 16.

GLEASE, GEORGE W., Private

Born in Boston, Massachusetts. Third enlistment on September 3, 1875, at age 30 in Cincinnati, Ohio by Lieut. Patrick Cusack. Deserted on October 15, 1877; apprehended on April 26, 1880. Dishonorably discharged on July 31, 1880 at Fort Meade, Dakota by General Court Martial Order Nr. 69, Department of Dakota, 1880. He had blue eyes, brown hair, ruddy complexion and was 5'-5½" in height.

HAACK, HENRY, Private

Born in York County, Pennsylvania. Enlisted on October 4, 1872, at age 34 in Nashville, Tennessee by Captain Frederick Benteen. Previous occupation was shoemaker. Discharged on June 24, 1877 at camp on Sunday Creek, Montana Territory per Special Order Nr. 70, Department of Dakota, 1877, as a Corporal of excellent character. He had black eyes, black hair, dark complexion and was 5'-7½" in height.

HALEY, TIMOTHY, Private

Born in Cork, Ireland. Third enlistment on January 15, 1875, at age 30 in New Orleans, Louisiana by Captain Frederick Benteen. Previous occupation was soldier. Discharged on April 16, 1879, at Fort Abraham Lincoln, Dakota for disability, as a Private of good character. He had blue eyes, brown hair, fair complexion and was 5'-6½" in height.

HOOD, CHARLES N., Private

Sick in the hospital from May 17, 1876 at Fort Abraham Lincoln, Dakota. Born in Seneca County, New York. Enlisted on August 25, 1873, at age 24 1/3 in Cincinnati by Lieut. Adam Kramer. Previous occupation was painter. Sentenced by Garrison Court Martial to forfeit to the United States, $5.00 of his monthly pay for one month on General Order Nr. 40, Headquarters, Fort Lincoln, July 24, 1876. Discharged on August 25, 1878, at Camp James G. Sturgis, Dakota upon expiration of service, as a Sergeant of good character. He had light brown eyes, light brown hair, fair complexion and was 5'-6" in height.

HUGHES, THOMAS, Private

Wounded. Returned to duty. Born in County Mayo, Ireland. Discharged from enlistment in Company H, Seventh Cavalry, on December 30, 1877. His third enlistment was on May 25, 1878, at age 29 at 100 Walker St. New York City (Mounted Recruiting Service Office) by Captain R. S. Morris, 18th Infantry. He had grey eyes, dark hair, fair complexion and was 5'-8" in height. Not among those listed as wounded in the Returns of the Seventh Cavalry for June, 1876.

HUNT, JOHN, Private

Born in Boston, Massachusetts. Second enlistment on September 1, 1871, at age 36 in Nashville, Tennessee, by Captain Frederick Benteen. Previous occupation was clerk. Discharged on August 6, 1876, at the mouth of Rosebud Creek, Montana Territory per General Order Nr. 24, AGO, War Department, 1859, as a Private of excellent character. He had blue eyes, auburn hair, ruddy complexion and was 5'-5¼" in height.

JONES, JULIEN D., Private

Killed beside Charles Windolph in the hilltop fight on June 25. Born in Boston, Massachusetts. Enlisted on August 7, 1871, at age 22 in Nashville, Tennessee by Captain Frederick Benteen. Previous occupation was painter. Listed as J. D. Jones on the battle monument. Listed elsewhere as Corporal Julian D. Jones. He had grey eyes, dark brown hair, dark complexion and was 5'-6½" in height.

"My buddy, a young fellow named Jones, who hailed from Milwaukee [sic], was lying alongside of me [on Reno Hill]. Together we had scooped out a wide shallow trench and piled up the dirt to make a little breastwork in front of us. It was plumb light now and sharpshooters on the knob of a hill south of us and maybe a thousand yards away, were taking pot shots at us."

Jones said something about taking off his overcoat, and he started to roll on his side so that he could get his arms and shoulders out, without exposing himself to fire. Suddenly I heard him cry out. He had been shot straight through the heart . . ." Charles Windolph in Frazier Hunt, *I Fought With Custer*, p. 103.

KELLY, GEORGE, Private

Born in New York City. Second enlistment on April 16, 1875, at age 27 in New Orleans, Louisiana by Captain Frederick Benteen. Discharged on April 15, 1880 at Fort Meade, Dakota upon expiration of service, as a Private of excellent character. He had hazel eyes, brown hair, dark complexion and was 5'-5" in height.

KELLY, JAMES, Private

Born in Boston, Massachusetts. Enlisted on August 28, 1866 at age 26 in Chicago by Major Arthur McArthur. Previous occupation was soldier. He was enlisted under the name James Kelley and assigned to Company H, 7th Cavalry. Deserted on February 9, 1868; surrendered on November 25, 1873 under General Order Nr. 102, AGO, 1873. Discharged on July 3, 1877, at Fort Abraham Lincoln, Dakota, as a Private, upon expiration of his service, the time lost by desertion having been made good. He had blue eyes, light hair, florid complexion and was 5'-4¼" in height.

LAMPERTIN, FRANK, Private

Sick in the hospital at Fort Abraham Lincoln, Dakota from May 17, 1876. Born in Cologne, Germany. Second enlistment in Company H, 7th Cavalry on August 27, 1875, at age 23 in St. Louis by Captian Owen Hale. His previous occupation was musician. Discharged on August 26, 1880, at Fort Meade, Dakota upon expiration of service, as a Private of fair character. Third enlistment, in the 11th Infantry Band, on September 25, 1880 at Fort Sully, Dakota, by Leiut. George G. Lott, Adjutant, 11th Infantry. Discharged on September 24, 1885 upon expiration of service. Fourth enlistment on September 25, 1885 at Fort Sully in the 11th Infantry Band by Lieut. Lott. By 1885 he was married and had two children. Discharged on September 24, 1890 upon expiration of service. Fifth enlistment on September 29, 1890, at age 38 at Madison Barracks, New York by Lieut. P.B.M. Travis, Adjutant, 11th Infantry. He had brown eyes, dark brown hair, ruddy to dark complexion and was 5'-7½" to 7¾" in height.

LAWHORN, THOMAS, Private
Born in Caldwell County, Kentucky. Second enlistment on May 12, 1875, at age 24 at Yankton, Dakota, by Captain Frederick W. Benteen. Deserted on February 7, 1877. He had hazel eyes, dark hair, fair complexion and was 5'-9" in height.

MOLLER, JAN, Private
Wounded in the right thigh in the hilltop fight on June 25. Transported to Fort Abraham Lincoln, Dakota on the steamboat *Far West*. Born in Orsle, Denmark. Enlisted on January 15, 1872, at age 22 in Chicago, Illinois by Captain Samuel Young. Previous occupation was laborer. Discharged on January 15, 1877 upon expiration of service, as a Corporal of excellent character. He had grey eyes, light hair, sandy complexion and was 5'-8" in height. Listed as absent sick at Fort Rice, Dakota from August 12, 1876 on the Company H Muster Roll, August 31, 1876. Listed as Jan Moller on pension records and elsewhere as John Muller or James Mullen or James Muller. In 1927 he resided at 63 Stewart St., Deadwood, South Dakota.

MEADOR, THOMAS E., Private
Killed beside Charles Windolph in the hilltop fight on June 26. Born in Bedford County, Virginia. Enlisted on January 19, 1872, at age 23 in Lexington, Kentucky by Lieut. Robert Smither. Previous occupation was farmer. He had brown eyes, brown hair, ruddy complexion and was 5'-5¼" in height. Listed as T. E. Meador on the battle monument and elsewhere as Meader.

McDERMOTT, THOMAS, Private
In the hilltop fight. Born in New York City. Second enlistment on May 18, 1872, at age 27 in Pittsburgh, Pennsylvania, by Lieut. James M. Bell. Previous occupation was teamster. Discharged on May 28, 1877 at camp near Fort Buford, Dakota upon expiration of service, as a Sergeant of excellent character. He had grey eyes, black hair, fair complexion and was 5'-6¾" in height.

McNAMARA, JAMES, Private
Born in Rascommon, Ireland. Enlisted on November 12, 1872, at age 24 4/12 in Troy, New York by Captain Theodore Wint. Previous occupation was laborer. Discharged on November 12, 1877 at Fort Buford, Dakota upon expiration of service, as a Private of excellent character. He had blue eyes, light hair, light complexion and was 5'-5" in height. In 1927 he resided at Pittsfield, Massachusetts.

McWILLIAMS, DAVID, Private
Wounded in the right knee. Transported to Fort Abraham Lincoln, Dakota

on the steamboat *Far West*. Born in Edinburgh, Scotland. Second enlistment on August 29, 1871, at age 22 in Louisville, Kentucky, by Lieut. William Cooke. In *The Diary and Letters of Dr. James M. DeWolf* the entry for June 6, 1876 relates. "Man accidently shot through calf of leg coming out on back of right foot pistol accidently went off while mounting." In Mark Kellogg's diary for June 6 is this entry, "Priv. McWilliams . . . accidently shot himself with a revolver today; ball took effect calf leg ran down tendon and lodged just under skin top of foot, flesh wound lay him up a month." This happened on the west fork of O'Fallon's Creek, Montana Territory. Discharged on August 29, 1876, at Fort Rice, Dakota upon expiration of service, as a Private of good character. Re-enlisted; transferred to Company A. Died on December 28, 1881, as a Private. Interred in the Fort Meade (Dakota) Post Cemetery, Grave 2-14. He had blue eyes, brown hair, fair complexion and was 5'-5½" in height. Listed elsewhere as Daniel McWilliams.

MULLER, JOHN, Private
In confinement from December 22, 1875 at Columbus Barracks, Ohio. for desertion with $30 paid for his apprehension. Born in Hamburg, Germany. Enlisted on March 13, 1870, at age 28 at Fort Hays, Kansas, by Captain Frederick Benteen. Previous occupation was teamster. Assigned to Company H, 7th Cavalry. He had blue eyes, brown hair, fair complexion and was 5'-5" in height.

NEES, ELDER, Private
Born in Ornirhessen, Germany. Enlisted on September 7, 1875, at age 22 in New York City by Lieut. John Babcock. Previous occupation was clerk. Deserted on July 26, 1876; apprehended on July 28, 1876. Discharged on November 30, 1876 at Fort Abraham Lincoln, Dakota per General Court Martial Order Nr. 48, Department of Dakota, October 30, 1876. He had blue eyes, brown hair, ruddy complexion and was 5'-7½" in height.

NICHOLAS, JOSHUA S., Private
Born in London, England. Enlisted on February 2, 1872, at age 21 in Chicago, Illinois by Captin Samuel Young. Previous occupation was carpenter. Discharged on February 2, 1877 at Fort Rice, Dakota upon expiration of service, as a Sergeant of excellent character. He had blue eyes, light hair, light complexion and was 5'-6" in height. Listed elsewhere as Joshua S. Nichols.

O'RYAN, WILLIAM, Private
Born in Limerick, Ireland. Enlisted on October 2, 1875, at age 21 in New York City by Lieut. John Babcock. Previous occupation was clerk. Deserted on February 1, 1877. He had blue eyes, sandy hair, ruddy complexion and was 5'-7¾" in height.

PHILLIPS, JOHN J., Private
Wounded in the face and both hands in the hilltop fight on June 25. Transported to Fort Abraham Lincoln, Dakota on the steamboat *Far West*. Born in Alleghany County, Pennsylvania. Enlisted on September 12, 1873, at age 21 in Pittsburgh by Lieut. Randolph Norwood. Previous occupation was packer. Discharged on November 1, 1876, at Fort Lincoln for disability, as a Private of good character. Listed absent sick from July 5, 1876, on the Muster Roll for

Company H, August 31, 1876. He had blue eyes, light hair, fair complexion and was 5'-5" in height.

PINKSTON, JOHN S., Private
Born in St. Clair County, Michigan. Enlisted on March 1, 1872, at age 21 9/12 in Nashville, Tennessee by Captain Frederick Benteen. Previous occupation was laborer. Deserted on September 26, 1872; apprehended on January 27, 1873. He again deserted on April 24, 1873 and surrendered on November 5, 1874 and then deserted on May 22, 1877. He had grey eyes, dark hair, fair complexion and was 5'-7" in height.

PITTET, FRANCIS, Private
Sick in the hospital from May 5, 1876, at Fort Rice, Dakota. Born in Tribourg, Switzerland. Enlisted on January 20, 1873, at age 34 in Nashville, Tennessee by Captain Frederick Benteen. Previous occupation was carpenter. Discharged on January 20, 1878, at Fort Rice upon expiration of service, as a Private of excellent character. He had grey eyes, black hair, dark complexion and was 5'-7" in height.

SEVERS, SAMUEL, Private
Wounded in both thighs in the hilltop fight on June 25. Transported to Fort Abraham Lincoln, Dakota on the steamboat *Far West.* Born in St. Louis, Missouri. Enlisted on February 16, 1875, at age 21 in New Orleans, Louisiana by Captain Frederick Benteen. Previous occupation was laborer. Discharged on September 22, 1876 at Fort Rice, Dakota for disability. Listed as absent sick from August 12, 1876 on the Muster Roll of Company H, August 31, 1876. He had black eyes, black hair, dark complexion and was 5'-6" in height. Listed elsewhere as Samuel Severes and Severn.

TAPLY, DANIEL, Private
Sick in the hospital from May 17, 1876 at Fort Rice, Dakota. Born in Halifax, England. Enlisted on May 1, 1875, at age 34 in New Orleans by Captain Frederick Benteen. Previous occupation was tailor. Discharged on November 25, 1878 at Fort Abraham Lincoln, Dakota per Special Order Nr. 250, AGO, 1878, as a Private with character reference of "None". Listed as Daniel Taply in the Register of Enlistments, U.S. Army and elsewhere as David Taply. He had blue eyes, brown hair, fair complexion and was 5'-10" in height.

WALSH, MICHAEL J., Private
In confinement from May 10, 1876, at Jackson Barracks, New Orleans, Louisiana. Born in Ireland. Enlisted on June 15, 1873, at age 34 at Fort Rice, Dakota, by Capt. Frederick Benteen. Previous occupation was barber. Deserted at New Orleans on April 6, 1875; surrendered at Jackson Barracks May 10, 1876. Sentenced to confinement in prison for two years from August, 1876, and dishonorably discharged with the loss of all pay per General Court Martial Order Nr. 23, Department of the Gulf, 1876, on July 29, 1876, as a Private. He had blue eyes, brown hair, florid complexion and was 5'-5¼" in height.

WALTER, ALOYSE L., Private
On detached service from June 16, 1876 at Yellowstone Depot, Montana

Territory. Born in Willen, France. Sixth enlistment on March 1, 1875, at age 40 in New Orleans by Captain Frederick Benteen. Discharged on March 5, 1877 at Fort Rice, Dakota for disability, as a Private of excellent character. He had hazel eyes, brown hair, fair complexion and was 5'-7" in height. Absent on detached service at Fort Rice from August 14, 1876 per Company H Muster Roll, August 31, 1876.

WILLIAMS, WILLIAM C., Private

Wounded. Returned to duty. Born in Wheeling, Virginia. Enlisted on September 27, 1873, at age 21 in Cincinnati, Ohio by Lieut. Adam Kramer. Previous occupation was farmer. Discharged on September 27, 1878, at Fort Abraham Lincoln, Dakota upon expiration of service, as a Sergeant of excellent character. He had grey eyes, light hair, fair complexion and was 5'-10" in height. Not listed among the wounded on the Returns of the Seventh Cavalry for June, 1876 but he is listed as wounded by both Finerty and Forrest. He inscribed his name as W. C. Williams Co. H, 7 Cav. on May 28, 1876, on a rock near camp while on the Sioux expedition.

WINDOLPH, CHARLES (Charles Wrangel), Private

Wounded in the buttock in the hilltop fight on June 25. Returned to duty. Born on December 9, 1851 in Bergen, Germany. Departed from Germany in 1871. He was enlisted in the 7th Cavalry on July 23, 1872 under the name of Charles Wrangel at age 21½ in Nashville, Tennessee by Captain Frederick Benteen. Previous occupation was shoemaker. He arrived at Yankton, Dakota in April, 1873 with the 7th Cavalry. His enlistment was cancelled when he surrendered on November 19, 1873 under General Order Nr. 102, AGO, 1873 as Charles Windolph, a deserter from Company A, 2nd Infantry. He was in the expedition exploring the Black Hills in July and August, 1874 and in the Sioux campaign from May 17 to September 26, 1876. In the campaign against the Nez Perce Indians under Chief Joseph in 1877. His last re-enlistment was on March 22, 1878. Awarded the Medal of Honor on October 5, 1878 as a member of the sharpshooters protecting the water party in the Little Bighorn River fight. The Medal of Honor citation read, "With three comrades, during the entire engagement, courageously held a position that secured water for the command." Awarded the Order of the Purple Heart for the wound sustained in the Little Bighorn River fight. Discharged on March 21, 1883, at Fort Meade, Dakota as First Sergeant of Troop H. He had brown eyes, brown hair, dark complexion and was 5'-6" in height. After discharge he was employed by the Homestake Mining Company in Deadwood, South Dakota for 49 years. In 1927 he resided at 6 Old Abe Street, Lead, South Dakota. In 1880, he married Mathilda L. Windolph who died on March 23, 1924 and was interred in the Black Hills National Cemetery, Grave A225. Windolph died on March 11, 1950 and was interred in the Black Hills National Cemetery on March 14, 1950 in Grave A239.

The company remained part of the garrison at Fort A. Lincoln, Dakota, until May 5 when they joined the rest of the regiment in camp below the post to take part in the Sioux expedition. The company left Fort Lincoln on May 17 and returned on September 26.

On October 17 Co. I, with seven other companies under the command of Colonel Samuel Sturgis, departed for the Cheyenne Agency via the left bank of the Missouri to disarm and dismount the Indians at that agency. Return to Fort Lincoln was made on November 11. The company marched 2,206 miles in the year.

The following members were casualties in the Little Bighorn River fight. Killed: Captain Myles Keogh, Lieut. James Porter, First Sergeant Frank Varden, Sergeant James Bustard, Corporals George Morris, Samuel Staples, John Wild; Trumpeters John McGucker and John Patton, Blacksmith Henry Bailey, Privates John Barry, Joseph Broadhurst, Thomas Connors, Thomas Downing, Edward Driscoll, David Gillette, George Gross, Adam Hetesimer, Edward Holcomb, Marion Horn, Patrick Kelley, Friederick Lehman, Henry Lehmann, Edward Lloyd, John Mitchell, Archibald McIlhargey, Jacob Noshang, John O'Bryan, John Parker, Felix Pitter, George Post, James Quinn, William Reed, John Rossbury, Darwin Symms, James Troy, Charles Van Bramer, and William Whaley. Private David Cooney was wounded with Major Marcus Reno's command and died in the hospital at Fort Lincoln on July 20 of wounds received in the fight. Private Andrew McAllister died in the hospital at Fort Lincoln on October 4 of typhoid fever.

Officers serving with the company in the year were: Captain Myles Keogh and Henry Nowlan; First Lieutenants James Porter and Luther Hare; Second Lieutenants Andrew Nave, George Chase and Hugh Scott. Lieut. George Chase was a replacement for Lieut. Nave who was transferred to Company A. Lieut. Chase was transferred from the 3rd Cavalry. On his own application Lieut. Hugh Scott was transferred from Co. E to Co. I as a replacement, per Special Order, War Department, Dec. 8, 1876.*

* *Hugh Lenox Scott was born in Kentucky, September 22, 1853. He was appointed at large from New Jersey July 1, 1871, to be a Cadet at the Military Academy. He graduated June 14, 1876, ranking 36th in his class and was appointed 2nd Lieut. 9th Cavalry. Transferred to the 7th Cavelry June 26, 1876. On the Sioux expedition in October, 1876; on the Nez Perce expedition in 1877; on a scout from Fort Lincoln towards the Black Hills in Dec. 1877; on the Black Hills and Cheyenne Indian expedition in 1878. Promoted to 1st Lieut. June 28, 1876. On garrison duty at Fort Totten, Dak. from Dec. 1878 to Oct. 1882; on frontier and garrison duty at Fort Meade, Dak. from November, 1882. Promoted to Captain June 24, 1895. Married the daughter of Major Lewis Merrill. Promoted to Major, AAG Vols. May 12, 1898; Lieut. Col. AAG, Vols. Aug. 17, 1899. Honorably discharged from volunteers June 30, 1901. Promoted to Major, 3rd Cavalry Feb. 25, 1903. Transferred to 14th Cavalry March 16, 1903.*

COMPANY I AT THE LITTLE BIGHORN

	Absent	Present	Wounded	Died OWRT	Killed	Survived
Captain		1			1	
1st Lieut.		1			1	
2nd Lieut.	1					1
1st Sergt.		1			1	
Sergeant	1	4			1	4
Corporal	1	3			3	1
Trumpeter		2			2	
Saddler	1					1
Farrier	1					1
Blacksmith		1			1	
Private	12	38	1	1	28	21
Totals	17	51	1	1	38	29

COMPANY I ON JUNE 30, 1876

Enlisted present for duty 12
Enlisted absent detached service 10
Enlisted absent sick 6
Enlisted absent in arrest 1
Commissioned absent sick 1
Second Lieutenant 1
Sergeants 4
Corporal 1
Farrier 1
Saddler 1
Privates 22
Aggregate 30
Total enlisted 29
Aggregate in May 68
Commissioned officers killed 2
Enlisted killed 36
Wounded 1
Horses serviceable 15
Horses lost 44

KEOGH, MYLES WALTER, Captain

Killed with the Custer battalion on June 25. Born on March 25, 1842 at Orchard House in County Carlow, Ireland, the son of John and Margaret Blanchfield Keogh. He served with distinction in the Pope's army and was a Second Lieutenant on August 7, 1860 in the Battalion of St. Patrick of the Papal Army. On November 9, 1860 he was commissioned a Lieutenant in the Papal Guards. He arrived in New York on April 9, 1862. Appointed Captain, U.S. Volunteers, effective April 9, 1862 and additional aide-de-camp to General Patterson, commanding in the valley of the Shenendoah. Later he was on the staff of General Shields and then General Buford's staff. He was engaged at South Mountain, Antietam, Mine Run and other actions in 1863. After General Buford's death he was on the staff of General Stoneman and was captured with Stoneman at Sunshine Church, Georgia on July 31, 1864 and was held until September 30, 1864. Engaged in the raid on Galesville with Stoneman and in the operations in West Virginia. In 1865 he accompanied Stoneman into North Carolina. On March 13, 1865 he was brevetted Lieut. Colonel, U.S.V. for his uniform gallantry and good conduct during the war. Honorably mustered out of volunteer service on September 1, 1865 after having participated in over thirty general engagements. Commissioned Second Lieutenant, 4th Cavalry, on May 4, 1866 and transferred to the 7th Cavalry; commissioned Captain of Cavalry to rank from July 28, 1866, the date that the regiment was organized. On March 2, 1867 he received the brevets of Major and Lieutenant Colonel, USA, for his services in the battles of Gettysburg and Dallas. On May 17, 1876 Captain Keogh departed from Fort Abraham Lincoln, Dakota in command of Company I, 7th Cavalry to participate in the Sioux expedition. His remains were interred on the battlefield. In July of the following year his remains were exhumed and re-interred in Throop Martin Lot, Fort Hill Cemetery, Auburn, New York on October 25, 1877. Captain Keogh was the owner of Comanche, the only surviving horse found on the battlefield. Fort Keogh, Montana, was established in June, 1877, at the confluence of the Tongue and Yellowstone Rivers and named in his honor. Captain Keogh was unmarried and survived by his brother, Thomas Keogh of Park, County Carlow, Ireland and sisters, Margaret and Mrs. Ellen Donahue, both of County Clifden, Ireland.

PORTER, JAMES EZEKIEL, First Lieutenant

Missing with the Custer battalion on June 25 and presumed killed. Born February 2, 1847 in Strong, Franklin County, Maine. He entered the Military Academy in September, 1864, by appointment from Maine. He was the 2288th graduate, ranking 16th in his class of 39 graduates in 1869. Commissioned Second Lieutenant in the 7th Cavalry June 15, 1869; accepted on July 6, 1869. After graduation leave he joined the regiment at Fort Leavenworth, Kansas in October, 1869. His academy classmates who joined the 7th Cavalry were William Craycroft and Charles Braden. On frontier duty in Kansas in 1870; stationed in various cities in the south in 1871-73. Promoted to First Lieutenant effective March 1, 1872, and transferred to Company I. In June, 1873, he left Fort Snelling, Minnesota, escorting the Northern Boundary Survey Commission until October, 1873, and again the following summer from May to September. On May 17, 1876, he departed from Fort Abraham Lincoln, Dakota with Company I to participate in the Sioux expedition. He was with Company I in the Little Bighorn River fight and was presumed killed, though his remains were not identified. He was survived by his wife.

171

NAVE, ANDREW HUMES, Second Lieutenant

Absent on sick leave. Born in Tennessee. Entered the Military Academy on July 1, 1867, by appointment from Tennessee. He was the 2388th graduate, ranking 19th in his class of 41 graduates. Commissioned Second Lieutenant, 7th Cavalry, June 12, 1871; accepted on August 5, 1871, while he was on graduation leave in Knoxville, Tennessee. After graduation leave he joined his company in garrison at Shelbyville, Kentucky on October 10, 1871, and remained there until September 30, 1872, when he went on detached service with Company D at Opelika, Alabama, to November 8, 1872, when he returned to his company. From April 10 to July 19 he was at Fort Snelling. On May 31, 1873, he was sick in quarters at Fort Snelling and did not rejoin his company until August 17. On that date he departed on frontier duty escorting the Northern Boundary Survey Commission (NBSC) until September 2, 1873, when he went on detached service to Fort Stevenson, Dakota, until October 20 and then into winter station at Fort Totten, Dakota, until May 30, 1874. From April 6 to May 18, 1874, he was conducting prisoners to Stillwater, Minnesota. About May, 1874, he injured his arm or shoulder and, on a surgeon's certificate of disability, he went on leave of absence from August 15, 1874, for two years and one month. While on leave he taught at East Tennessee University (now the University of Tennessee) at Knoxville and was Commandant of Cadets there. He was ordered to appear before a Retiring Board on August 11, 1876, in Washington. The Board found him not permanently incapacitated but partially and temporarily disqualified for active duty. He was escort for the NBSC from May 30 to July 14, 1876, and was then placed on sick leave of absence until August 31, 1876. He was directed to report at Fort Abraham Lincoln for light duty. When he arrived he found that he had been transferred from Company I to Company A and promoted to First Lieutenant, the promotion antedated to June 25, 1876, to occupy the vacancy created by the death of Lieut. Algernon Smith. He was on detached service in St. Paul buying horses from August 17 to September 26 when he rejoined his company which had just returned from the Sioux expedition. On October 17 his company took to the field on an expedition to disarm and dismount agency Indians. Nave was left behind in command of dismounted men until his company returned to Fort Lincoln on November 3. Early 1877 he was on duty at Fort Rice and returned to Fort Lincoln in April as Acting Ordnance Officer, Post Adjutant and Band commander until early 1878, when he rejoined his company. Beginning in 1879 he went on leave of absence until his retirement. He was promoted to Captain on January 16, 1884, and retired on September 23, 1885, for disability in line of duty. From October 6, 1899 to August 31, 1907 he taught at the University of Tennessee. He passed away on December 7, 1924 at the age of 78.

VARDEN, FRANK E. First Sergeant

Killed with the Custer battalion on June 25. Born in Yarmouth, Maine. Second enlistment on May 26, 1872, at age 26 in Shelbyville, Kentucky by Captain Myles Keogh. He had blue eyes, brown hair, light complexion and was 5'-10" in height. Listed as F. E. Varden on the battle monument.

BUSTARD, JAMES, Sergeant

Killed in battle on June 25. Born in Donegal, Ireland. Second enlistment on July 21, 1875, at age 29 at Fort A. Lincoln, Dakota, by Captain Myles

Keogh. Previous occupation was soldier. He had hazel eyes, light hair, fair complexion and was 5'-6½" in height. Listed as James Bustard on the battle monument and elsewhere as Burtard.

CADDLE, MICHAEL C., Sergeant
On detached service from June 15, 1876, at Yellowstone Depot, Montana Territory. Born in New York City. Enlisted on September 29, 1873, at age 22 in New York City by Lieut. Edward Hunter. Previous occupation was conductor. Discharged on September 29, 1878 at Fort A. Lincoln, Dakota, upon expiration of service, as a Sergeant of excellent character. He had blue eyes, light hair, fair complexion and was 5'-5½" in height. Caddle and Private Archibald McIlhargey of Co. I were close friends and McIlhargey asked Caddle to take care of his family should he be killed. Caddle married McIlhargey's widow in 1877 or 1878. The widow had two children, Rosalie and Archibald, who, after her re-marriage, took the name of Caddle. Thomas and Julia were two of the children born after her re-marriage. In all, ten children were born to Mrs. Caddle. She died in 1902. After his discharge Caddle moved to Oliver County, Dakota, and, in 1883, he squatted on land two miles north of Fort Rice on the west side of the Missouri River. He was a mail carrier from the Gwyther farm to Livonia on the Bismarck-Winona stage line. Michael Caddle died May 1, 1919. See Annie R. Gwyther "Pioneer Days on the Ft. Rice Military Reserve," *North Dakota History*, 26:3, 127-131, Summer, 1959. His name is listed elsewhere as Caddell.

DE LACY, MILTON J., Sergeant
Born in Ulster County, New York. Second enlistment on May 13, 1875, at age 28 at Fort Abraham Lincoln, Dakota by Captain Myles Keogh. Deserted on May 9, 1877. He had blue eyes, red hair, light complexion and was 5'-5¾" in height.

GAFFNEY, GEORGE, Sergeant
On detached duty in Quartermaster Department. Born in Cavan, Ireland. Discharged on November 19, 1876, at Fort Abraham Lincoln, Dakota on expiration of service, as a Sergeant. Third enlistment on November 21, 1876, at age 32 at Fort Lincoln by Lieut. George Wallace. Discharged on November 20, 1881 at Fort Totten, Dakota upon expiration of service, as a Sergeant of good character. He had grey eyes, dark hair, dark complexion and was 5'-2" in height.

MURPHY, ROBERT, Sergeant
On detached service at Headquarters, Department of Dakota, in the field. Born in Stanford, New York. Enlisted on January 24, 1872, at age 21 in New Jersey by Captain Edwin Sumner. Previous occupation was fireman. Discharged January 24, 1877, at Fort A. Lincoln, Dakota, upon expiration of service, as a Sergeant of very good character. He had brown eyes, brown hair, fair complexion and was 5'-8¾" in height.

McCALL, JOSEPH, Corporal
On detached service from May 17, 1876 at Fort Abraham Lincoln, Dakota. Born in Chester County, Pennsylvania. Enlisted on September 23, 1873, at age 21 in Philadelphia by Lieut. William Volkmar. Previous occupation was painter. Deserted on February 10, 1878. He had blue eyes, brown hair, fair complexion and was 5'-6½" in height.

MORRIS, GEORGE C., Corporal

Killed in battle on June 25. Born in Georgetown, Delaware. Enlisted on October 26, 1872, at age 21 in Philadelphia by Captain Samuel Whitside. Previous occupation was carriagemaker. He had brown eyes, brown hair, fair complexion and was 5'-5¾" in height. Listed as G. C. Morris on the battle monument.

STAPLES, SAMUEL F., Corporal

Killed in battle on June 25. Born in Worcester, Massachusetts. Enlisted on January 9, 1872, at age 22 in New York City by Captain Edwin Sumner. Previous occupation was painter. He had brown eyes, dark hair, dark complexion and was 5'-6½" in height Listed on the battle monument as S. F. Staples and elsewhere as S. T. Staples.

WILD, JOHN, Corporal

Killed with the Custer battalion on June 25 (near where Captain Myles Keogh fell). Born in Buffalo, New York. Enlisted on May 21, 1873, at age 23 5/12 in Chicago by Captain Henry Carroll. Previous occupation was printer. Listed as Jno. Wild on the battle monument. He had hazel eyes, brown hair, fair complexion and was 5'-9¾" in height.

McGUCKER, JOHN, Trumpeter

Killed in battle on June 25. Born in Albany, New York. Discharged from Co. B, 4th Artillery on November 22, 1871. Enlisted on November 27, 1871, at age 35 in St. Louis by Lieut. Peter Vroom. Assigned to the 7th Cavalry. He had hazel eyes, black hair, ruddy complexion and was 5'-5" in height. Listed on the battle monument and elsewhere as J. M. Gucker.

"Trumpeter McGucker—Whereas, The Cavalry Detachment Library Association has learned with profound sorrow of the death of the esteemed ex-member, John McGucker, trumpeter of Co. I, 7th U.S. Cavalry, killed in the battle of the Little Big Horn, Montana, June 25.

Resolved, That in the death of John McGucker, the C.D.L.A. has lost a true friend and a man whom all admired for his activity, and loved his hearty kindness.

Resolved that these proceedings be published in the Army and Navy Journal."
James Greer, Secretary   James Guinane, President

PATTON, JOHN W., Trumpeter

Killed in battle on June 25. Born in Philadelphia, Pennsylvania. Enlisted on October 21, 1872, at age 21 by Captain Samuel Whitside. Previous occupation was clerk. He had brown eyes, brown hair, ruddy complexion and was 5'-3½" in height. Listed as J. W. Patton on the battle monument and elsewhere as Patten.

HAYWARD, GEORGE, Saddler

Sick in the hospital from May 17, 1876, at Fort Abraham Lincoln,

Dakota. Born in Walton County, Canada. Enlisted on May 14, 1873, at age 22 in St. Louis by Lieut. Lewis Warrington. Previous occupation was harness maker. Discharged on May 14, 1878, at Fort Lincoln, upon expiration of service, as a Saddler of excellent character. He had brown eyes, light hair, fair complexion and was 5'-7" in height. Listed elsewhere as Haywood.

RIVERS, JOHN, Farrier
On detached service from June 15, 1876 at Yellowstone Depot, Montana Territory. Born in Westchester, New York. Enlisted on September 11, 1871, at age 37 in Bagdad, Kentucky by Lieut. Francis Gibson. Previous occupation was Farrier. He was discharged on August 7, 1876 on Rosebud Creek, Montana Territory, *prior to expiration of service,* as a Private of good character. He had grey eyes, dark hair, dark complexion and was 5'-9" in height.

BAILEY, HENRY A., Blacksmith
Killed in battle on June 25. Born on March 25, 1852, at Foster, Rhode Island, the son of Hannah Boswell Bailey and Henry F. Bailey, a carriagemaker. Enlisted on October 24, 1872, at a represented age of 22 in Springfield, Massachusetts by Captain Theodore Wint. Previous occupation was blacksmith. Transferred to St. Louis, thence to Fort Totten, Dakota, and then to Fort Abraham Lincoln, Dakota. He had grey eyes, brown hair, fair complexion and was 5'-7¼" in height. Listed as H. A. Bailey on the battle monument and elsewhere as Henry Baily.

BARRY, JOHN, Private
Killed in battle on June 25. Born in Waterford, Ireland. Enlisted on September 21, 1875, at age 26 in Boston by Lieut. Henry Lawton. Previous occupation was laborer. He had grey eyes, dark hair, ruddy complexion and was 5'-7¾" in height. Listed as Jno. Barry on the battle monument.

BRAUN, FRANZ C., Private
Born in Aix-la-Chapelle, Germany. Enlisted on May 13, 1873, at age 28 in Chicago by Captain Henry Carroll. Previous occupation was turner. Discharged on May 13, 1878, at Fort Abraham Lincoln, Dakota, upon expiration of service, as a Private of excellent character. He had blue eyes, light hair, fair complexion and was 5'-8½" in height. Listed as Franz C. Braun in the Register of Enlistments, U.S. Army and on his Oath of Enlistment.

BROADHURST, JOSEPH F., Private
Killed in battle on June 25. Born in Philadelphia, Pennsylvania. Enlisted on September 22, 1873, at age 21 in Philadelphia by Lieut. William Volkmar. Previous occupation was weaver. He had brown eyes, dark hair, ruddy complexion and was 5'-5" in height. Listed as J. F. Broadhurst on the battle monument and elsewhere as Jos. E. Broadhurst.

CONNORS, THOMAS, Private
Killed in battle on June 25. Born in Harlem, New York. Second enlistment on August 20, 1875, at age 29 in St. Louis by Lieut. John Thompson. He had blue eyes, dark hair, fair complexion and was 5'-7½" in height. Listed as Thos. Connors on the battle monument and elsewhere as Thomas Conners and J. Conners.

COONEY, DAVID, Private

Wounded in the right hip in the hilltop fight on June 26. Promoted to Sergeant on June 28. Transported to Fort Abraham Lincoln, Dakota, on the steamboat *Far West*. Died of wounds on July 20, 1876, at Fort Lincoln. Re-interred in the Custer Battlefield National Cemetery, Grave 529A. Born in Cork, Ireland. Enlisted on December 16, 1872, at age 24 in Boston by Captain Moses Harris. Previous occupation was laborer. He had grey eyes, dark hair, fair complexion and was 5'-5¾" in height. Not listed on the battle monument. Listed elsewhere as Dore Cooney, David Corey and Davis Corey.

DOWNING, THOMAS P., Private

Killed in battle on June 25. Born in Limerick, Ireland. Enlisted on February 12, 1873, at age 21 in Lebanon, Kentucky, by Lieut. Andrew Nave. Previous occupation was laborer. He had blue eyes, sandy hair, florid complexion and was 5'-8¼" in height. Listed as T. P. Downing on the battle monument.

DRISCOLL, EDWARD C., Private

Killed in battle on June 25. Born in Waterford, Ireland. Enlisted on May 19, 1873, at age 22 in Chicago by Captain Henry Carroll. Previous occupation was laborer. He had hazel eyes, light hair, light complexion and was 5'-6" in height. Listed as Edw'd Driscoll on the battle monument.

FARBER, CONRAD, Private

On detached service at Headquarters, Department of Dakota in St. Paul from June 1, 1876. Born in Hungary. Enlisted on July 10, 1871, at age 34 in Louisville, Kentucky by Lieut. William Cooke. Previous occupation was soldier. Discharged on July 10, 1876, at St. Paul upon expiration of his service, as a Private. He had brown eyes, brown hair, light complexion and was 5'-7½" in height.

FOX, FREDERICK, Private

On detached service from May 17, 1876, at Fort A. Lincoln, Dakota. Born in Wurtemburg, Germany. Enlisted on October 22, 1872, at age 22 in Philadelphia by Captain Samuel Whitside. Previous occupation was machinist. Discharged on July 14, 1877, at camp on the Tongue River per Special Order Nr. 70, Department of Dakota, 1877, as a Private of good character. He had brown eyes, brown hair, dark complexion and was 5'-7¾" in height.

GEESBACHER, GABRIEL, Private

On detached service from June 15, 1876 at Yellowstone Depot, Montana Territory. Born in Bavaria, Germany. Enlisted on October 6, 1873, at age 27 in Philadelphia by Lieut. William Volkmar. Previous occupation was miller. Discharged by Lieut. Luther Hare on October 6, 1878, at Camp Ruhlen, Dakota, upon expiration of service, as a Private of excellent character. Second enlistment on October 7, 1878, at Camp Ruhlen by Lieut. Luther Hare. Discharged from Company I on October 6, 1883, upon expiration of service. Third enlistment, in Company M, on October 14, 1883, at Fort Snelling, Minnesota by Lieut. E. F. Glenn. At this time he was 37 years old and unmarried. He had light brown eyes, brown hair, ruddy complexion and was 5'-5¼" in height. Listed as Gabriel Geesbacher in the Register of Enlistments, U.S. Army.

GILLETTE, DAVID C., Private
Killed in battle on June 25. Born in Onandoga County, New York. Enlisted on October 1, 1873, at age 22 in Detroit, Michigan by Lieut. Johnathan Stevenson. Previous occupation was schoolteacher. He had blue eyes, light hair, fair complexion and was 5'-5" in height. Listed as D. C. Gillette on the battle monument and elsewhere as Gillett.

GRIMES, ANDREW, Private
On detached service from May 17, 1876, at Fort Abraham Lincoln, Dakota. Born in Alleghany, Pennsylvania. Enlisted on September 24, 1875, at age 28 in St. Louis by Lieut. John Thompson. Previous occupation was laborer. Discharged on June 3, 1880, at Fort Lincoln for disability, as a Private of excellent character. He had blue eyes, light hair, fair complexion and was 5'-9¼" in height.

GROSS, GEORGE H., Private
Killed in battle on June 25. Born in Germany. Enlisted on October 18, 1872, at age 27 in Pittsburgh, Pennsylvania by Lieut. Calbraith Rodgers. Previous occupation was farmer. Deserted on April 20, 1873; surrendered on November 15, 1873. He had blue eyes, light hair, fair complexion and was 5'-6½" in height. Listed as G. H. Gross on the battle monument and elsewhere as C. H. Gross and G. H. Cross.

HAACK, CHARLES L., Private
Sick in the hospital at Fort Abraham Lincoln, Dakota from May 17, 1876. Born in Leipsig, Saxony. Enlisted on April 29, 1856, to February 28, 1861, and from March 1, 1861, to December 4, 1864, in the Mounted Rifles. Enlisted from January 4, 1865, to January 4, 1869, in the Post Band, Fort Leavenworth, Kansas. Enlisted in the 7th Cavalry Band in April 1869. Fifth enlistment on April 25, 1874, at the age of 48 at Fort Lincoln by Lieut. James Calhoun. Assigned to the 7th Cavalry Band; transferred to Company I. Discharged on August 1, 1876, to be effective from July 25, 1876, at Fort Lincoln to enable him to enter The Soldier's Home, Washington, D.C., per Special Order Nr. 147, AGO, War Department, July, 1876, as a Private of excellent character. He had grey eyes, grey hair, fair complexion and was 5'-6½" in height. Listed as Chas. L. Hauck in the Register of Enlistments, U.S. Army.

HETESIMER, ADAM, Private
Killed in battle on June 25. Born in Cincinnati, Ohio. Enlisted on October 6, 1875, at age 28 by Lieut. Patrick Cusack. Previous occupation was barber. He had blue eyes, black hair, dark complexion and was 5'-7½" in height. Sentenced to two months confinement at hard labor at his post and a fine of $20 per General Court Martial Order Nr. 8, Department of Dakota, January 20, 1876. Listed as Adam Hetesimer on the battle monument and in the Register of Enlistments, U.S. Army and elsewhere as Hitismer and Hetismer.

HOLCOMB, EDWARD P., Private
Killed in battle on June 25. Born in Granby, Connecticut. Enlisted on October 28, 1872, at age 27 in Cleveland, Ohio by Lieut. James Peale. Previous occupation was clerk. He had black eyes, black hair, dark complexion and was

5'-6½" in height. Listed as E. P. Holcomb on the battle monument and elsewhere as F. P. Holcomb and Halcomb.

HORN, MARION E., Private
Killed in battle on June 25. Born on August 26, 1853 in Richmond, Wayne County, Indiana, the son of John and Sarah Ellen Anderson Horn. Enlisted on November 15, 1872, at age 21 at Cincinnati, Ohio by Lieut. James Wheelan. Previous occupation was laborer. He had hazel eyes, brown hair, florid complexion and was 5'-6½" in height. Listed as M. E. Horn on the battle monument.

JONES, HENRY P., Private
Born in Lancaster, Pennsylvania. Enlisted on October 8, 1873, at age 29 in Philadelphia by Lieut. William Volkmar. Previous occupation was plumber. This enlistment was in violation of the 50th Article of War in that he deserted from Company B, 4th Cavalry on August 10, 1873 under the name of John Bush. Discharged on October 8, 1878 at Fort Clark upon expiration of service, as a Private of excellent character. He had dark eyes, brown hair, dark complexion and was 5'-8¼" in height.

KELLEY, PATRICK, Private
Killed in battle on June 25, Born in Mayo, Ireland. Second enlistment on September 13, 1871, at age 30 in Bagdad, Kentucky by Lieut. Francis Gibson. Deserted on June 10, 1873; apprehended on June 14, 1873. He had grey eyes, sandy hair, fair complexion and was 5'-5" in height. Listed as Pat'k Kelley on the battle monument and elsewhere as Kelly.

KENNEDY, FRANCIS JOHNSON (Francis Johnson), Private
With the pack train column. In the hilltop fight. Born in Franklin County, Missouri. Enlisted on September 27, 1875, at a represented age of 21 at St. Louis by Lieut. John Thompson, under the name of Francis Johnson. Previous occupation was laborer. Discharged on September 26, 1880, at Camp Houston, Dakota upon expiration of service, as a Private of excellent character. He had blue eyes, brown hair, dark complexion and was 5'-7¼" in height. In 1900 he was a resident of St. Paul, Minnesota.

KORN, GUSTAVE, Private,
In the valley and hilltop fights. His horse bolted and was killed near the river. Korn rejoined the command of Major Marcus Reno on the night of June 25. Born in Sprollow, Silesia. Enlisted on May 17, 1873, at age 21 in St. Louis by Lieut. Lewis Warrington. Previous occupation was clerk. Discharged on May 17, 1878, at Fort Abraham Lincoln, Dakota upon expiration of service, as a Blacksmith of excellent character. He re-enlisted and was promoted to Sergeant. Killed on December 29, 1890, at Wounded Knee Creek, South Dakota, in an engagement with Sioux Indians of Big Foot's band. Interred at Fort Robinson, Nebraska.

LEE, MARK E., Private
On detached service from June 26, 1876, on the Yellowstone River as attendant for the wounded. He may have been with the pack train detail on June

25 (?). Born in Castine, Maine. Enlisted on September 27, 1875, at age 26 in Boston by Lieut. Henry Lawton. Previous occupation was barber. Discharged on August 19, 1878, at Fort Abraham Lincoln, Dakota for disability, as a Sergeant of good character. He had grey eyes, light brown hair, ruddy complexion and was 5'-8¼" in height.

LEHMAN, FRIEDERICK, Private
Killed in battle on June 25. Born in Berne, Switzerland. Enlisted on October 17, 1871, at age 23 in Louisville, Kentucky by Lieut. William Cooke. Previous occupation was upholsterer. He had blue eyes, light hair, fair complexion and was 5'-7½" in height. Listed as Fred'k Lehman on the battle monument and as Friederick Lehman in the Register of Enlistments, U.S. Army and elsewhere as Fred Lehman.

LEHMANN, HENRY, Private
Killed in battle on June 25. Born in Berlin, Germany. Enlisted on November 11, 1872, at age 33 in New York City by Captain Edwin Sumner. Previous occupation was confectioner. He had brown eyes, dark hair, fair complexion and was 5'-4" in height. Listed as Henry Lehmann on the battle monument and in the Register of Enlistments, U.S. Army and elsewhere as Henry Lehman.

LLOYD, EDWARD W., Private
Killed in battle on June 25. Born in Gloucester, England. Enlisted on September 30, 1873, at age 21 in Pittsburgh, Pennsylvania by Lieut. Randolph Norwood. Previous occupation was engineer. He had grey eyes, light brown hair, fair complexion and was 5'-6" in height. Listed as E. W. Lloyd on the battle monument and elsewhere as E. P. Lloyd.

LYNCH, PATRICK, Private
On detached service at Headquarters, Department of Dakota, in the field. Born in Caragaholt, County Clare, Ireland. Enlisted on October 16, 1872, at age 21 in Toledo, Ohio by Captain Samuel Young. Previous occupation was laborer. Discharged July 14, 1877, at camp on the Tongue River, Montana Territory, per Special Order Nr. 70, Department of Dakota, 1877, as a Sergeant of excellent character. He had blue eyes, auburn hair, sandy complexion and was 5'-6½" in height.

MILLER, WILLIAM E., Private
Sick in the hospital from May 17, 1876 at Fort Abraham Lincoln, Dakota. Born in Exeter, New Hampshire. Enlisted on October 19, 1871, at age 26 in Boston by Lieut. Nesmith. Previous occupation was saddler. Discharged on October 19, 1876, at Fort Lincoln upon expiration of service, as a Private. He had brown eyes, brown hair, dark complexion and was 5'-6½" in height.

MITCHELL, JOHN, Private
Killed with the Custer battalion on June 25. He carried the second message from Major Marcus Reno to Lieut. Colonel George Custer. Born in Galway, Ireland. Enlisted on September 14, 1871, at age 29 in Bagdad, Kentucky, by Lieut. Francis Gibson. He had blue eyes, brown hair, ruddy complexion and was 5'-6¼" in height. Listed as Jno. Mitchell on the battle monument.

McGINNESS, JOHN, Private
Sick in the hospital from May 17, 1876 at Fort Abraham Lincoln, Dakota. Born in Lanford, Ireland. Enlisted on August 5, 1873, at age 40 at Camp Terry, Dakota by Captain Myles Keogh. Previous occupation was soldier. Discharged on August 5, 1878 at Camp James G. Sturgis, Dakota, upon expiration of service, as a Private of good character. He had blue eyes, brown hair, ruddy complexion and was 5'-8½" in height.

McILHARGEY, ARCHIBALD, Private
Killed with the Custer battalion on June 25. He carried the first message from Major Marcus Reno to Lt. Col. George Custer, which reported that the Indians were in front of Major Reno's command in strong force. Born in Antrim, Ireland. Discharged from his first enlistment on November 19, 1872; re-enlisted on the same day at age 27 in Shelbyville, Kentucky by Lieut. James Porter. He had brown eyes, black hair, dark complexion and was 5'-5" in height. Listed as Arch'd McIlhargey on the battle monument. He was survived by his widow and daughter (Rosalie McIlhargey Caddle Watson of Huff, North Dakota) and son (Archibald F. Caddell, Minneapolis, Minnesota) who was born five months after his father's death. His widow married Michael Caddle of Co. I, 7th Cavalry.

McNALLY, JAMES P., Private
In the pack train detail on June 25? Born in Kildare, Ireland. Enlisted on November 12, 1872, at age 25 in Troy, New York by Captain Theodore Wint. Previous occupation was laborer. Discharged on November 12, 1877, at Fort Abraham Lincoln, Dakota upon expiration of service, as a Private of excellent character. He had grey eyes, dark hair, ruddy complexion and was 6'-0½" in height.

McSHANE, JOHN, Private
In the pack train detail on June 15? Born in Montreal, Canada. Enlisted on September 20, 1875, at age 26 in Boston by Lieut. Henry Lawton. Previous occupation was cooper. Discharged on April 13, 1877, at Fort Abraham Lincoln, Dakota for disability resulting from a gunshot wound. He had grey eyes, black hair, dark complexion and was 5'-6" in height.

MYERS, FRED, Private
On detached service from June 15, 1876 at Yellowstone Depot, Montana Territory. Born in Brunswick, Germany. Enlisted on May 14, 1873, at age 25 in St. Louis by Lieut. Lewis Warrington. Previous occupation was laborer. Discharged on May 17, 1878, at Fort Abraham Lincoln, Dakota upon expiration of service, as a Private of very good character. He had hazel eyes, dark hair, dark complexion and was 5'-9¼" in height.

NOSHANG, JACOB, Private
Killed in battle on June 25. Born in Hamilton County, Ohio. Enlisted on January 23, 1872, at age 21 in Louisville, Kentucky by Lieut. Edward Ward. Previous occupation was laborer. Listed as Jacob Noshang on the battle monument and elsewhere as Noshaug. He had hazel eyes, brown hair, dark complexion and was 5'-5¾" in height.

O'BRYAN, JOHN, Private
 Killed in battle on June 25. Born in Pennsylvania. Enlisted on June 8, 1873, at age 22 in Breckenridge, Minnesota by Captain Myles Keogh. Previous occupation was laborer. He had blue eyes, dark brown hair, light complexion and was 5'-6½" in height. Listed as Jno. O'Bryan on the battle monument.

OWENS, EUGENE, Private
 In the pack train detail on June 25? Born in Kildare, Ireland. Enlisted on March 15, 1875, at age 26 in Boston by Lieut. William Harper, Jr. Previous occupation was carpenter. Discharged on March 14, 1880, at Fort A. Lincoln upon expiration of service as a Private of very good character. He had blue eyes, brown hair, fair complexion and was 5'-7¾" in height.

PARKER, JOHN, Private
 Killed in battle on June 25. Born in Birmingham, England. Enlisted on February 3, 1872, at age 22 in Chicago by Captain Samuel Young. Previous occupation was gunsmith. He had grey eyes, light hair, light complexion and was 5'-7" in height. Listed as Jno. Parker on the battle monument.

PITTER, FELIX JAMES, Private
 Killed in battle on June 25. Born in Alesford, England. Enlisted on September 4, 1873, at age 23½ in St. Louis by Captain Charles Bendire. Previous occupation was grocer. He had hazel eyes, dark brown hair, fair complexion and was 5'-6¼" in height. Listed as F. J. Pitter on the battle monument.

PORTER, JOHN, Private
 In confinement from June 1, 1876 at Columbus Barracks, Ohio. Born in London, England. Enlisted on July 24, 1866, at age 21 in Chicago by Brevet Captain Edwin Conway (1st Lt. 4th Cav.) in the 7th Cavalry. Previous occupation was sailor. He had blue eyes, brown hair, florid complexion and was 5'-5" in height.

POST, GEORGE, Private
 Killed in battle on June 25. Born in Adrian, Michigan. Enlisted on June 28, 1875, at age 27 in Chicago by Lieut. Edmund Luff. Previous occupation was saddler. He had blue eyes, light hair, ruddy complexion and was 5'-7¼" in height. Listed as Geo. Post on the battle monument.

QUINN, JAMES, Private
 Killed in battle on June 25. Born in Watkins, New Jersey. Enlisted on February 13, 1872, at age 21 in Buffalo, New York by Lieut. Albert Forse. Previous occupation was boatman. He had blue eyes, red hair, light complexion and was 5'-6" in height. Listed as James Quinn on the battle monument.

RAMSEY, CHARLES, Private
 In the hilltop fight. Born in Macon, Michigan. Enlisted on January 26, 1872, at age 21 in Chicago by Captain Samuel Young. Previous occupation was laborer. Deserted on July 1, 1873; surrendered on November 17, 1873. Discharged on June 11, 1877, at Fort Abraham Lincoln, Dakota, upon expiration of service, as a Private of good character. He had grey eyes, light hair, dark complexion and was 5'-7" in height. Listed as Charley Ramsey in the Register of Enlistments, U.S. Army.

REED, WILLIAM, Private

Killed in battle on June 25. Born in Baltimore, Maryland. Second enlistment on January 2, 1872, at age 28 in Shelbyville, Kentucky, by Lieut. Andrew Nave. He had grey eyes, light hair, light complexion and was 5'-9¾" in height. Listed as Wm. Reed on the battle monument.

kOSSBURY, JOHN W., Private

Killed in battle on June 25. Born in Rochester, New York. Enlisted on January 26, 1872, at age 22 in Rochester by Lieut. Albert Forse. Previous occupation was salesman. He had hazel eyes, dark hair, fair complexion and was 5'-6½" in height. Listed as J. W. Rossbury on the battle monument and elsewhere as J. W. Rossberg and James Rossbury.

SAAS, WILLIAM, Private

On detached service from May 17, 1876 at Fort Abraham Lincoln, Dakota. Born in Strasburg, Germany. Enlisted on January 2, 1872, at age 23 in Cincinnati by Lieut. Myles Moylan. Previous occupation was cigarmaker. Discharged on January 2, 1877 at Fort Lincoln upon expiration of service, as a Private of good character. Re-enlisted on January 2, 1877. He had blue eyes, light hair, fair complexion and was 5'-7" in height.

SYMMS, DARWIN L., Private

Killed in battle on June 25. Born in Montreal, Canada. Enlisted on August 25, 1875, at age 23 in Chicago by Lieut. Edmund Luff. Previous occupation was clerk. He had blue eyes, light hair, fair complexion and was 5'-9" in height. Listed as D. L. Symms on the battle monument, and elsewhere as D. L. Lymons and D. E. Symmes.

THOMAS, HERBERT P., Private

On detached service from May 17, 1876 at Fort Abraham Lincoln, Dakota. Born in South Wales, England. Enlisted on May 5, 1873, at age 22 in Pittsburgh, Pennsylvania by Lieut. Randolph Norwood. Previous occupation was miner. Discharged from Company 1, 7th Cavalry on May 5, 1878, at Fort Lincoln upon expiration of service, as a Private of excellent character. He had blue eyes, light hair, fair complexion and was 5'-6¼" in height. Re-enlisted on September 25, 1884, at Fort Omaha, Nebraska, by Lieut. B. D. Price.

TROY, JAMES E., Private

Killed in battle on June 25. Born in Richmond, Massachusetts. Enlisted on December 30, 1871, at age 22 in Boston by Lieut. Moses Harris. Previous occupation was shoemaker. He had grey eyes, brown hair, dark complexion and was 5'-5¼" in height. Listed as J. E. Troy on the battle monument.

VAN BRAMER, CHARLES, Private

Killed in battle on June 25. Born in Canterbury, New Jersey. Enlisted on January 3, 1872, at age 21 4/12 in Chicago by Captain Samuel Young. Previous occupation was laborer. He had grey eyes, dark hair, dark complexion and was 5'-9½" in height. Listed as Chas. Van Bramer on the battle monument, and elsewhere as Chas. Van Bramar and Chas. Von Bramer.

WHALEY, WILLIAM B., Private
Killed in battle on June 25. Born in Harrison County, Kentucky. Enlisted on September 24, 1873, at age 24 in Cincinnati, Ohio by Lieut. Adam Kramer. Previous occupation was farmer. He had brown eyes, dark hair, florid complexion and was 5'-6" in height. Listed on the battle monument as W. B. Whaley and elsewhere as W. P. Whaley. Whaley may have been raised in Clinton County, Missouri, south of Cameron, Missouri. He was alleged to have attended the Military Academy at West Point but there appears to be no record of such attendance.

COMPANY K IN 1876

By Special Order, Department of the Gulf, Jan. 5, 1876, Co. K was ordered from the discontinued post at Colfax, Louisiana, to New Orleans taking with it all stores, supplies and means of transportation. The company remained until January 12 at Colfax and then proceeded via the boat *Bart Able* to New Orleans, arriving there Jan. 14. Departing the next day by rail the company arrived in McComb City, Mississippi for new station. Lieut. Hare and seven men stayed at Colfax in charge of public property and rejoined the company on Jan. 23. Lieut. Godfrey and five men escorted the U.S. Internal Revenue Collector from Feb. 3 to Feb. 8 and traveled 87 miles. On Mar. 6 Lieut. Hare and 15 men left for temporary station at Bayou Sara, La. and arrived there at 9:00 AM after traveling 79 miles. A detachment escorted the Department Internal Revenue Collector from Mar. 17, traveling 110 miles and later in March traveling 50 miles.

The company left McComb City by rail April 18 and joined Companies B and G enroute and proceeded to St. Paul, Minn. arriving there April 28 and arriving at Fort A. Lincoln, Dak. on May 1. The company went into camp below the post awaiting departure of the Sioux expedition. The transfer from McComb City in the Department of the Gulf to Fort Lincoln in the Department of Dakota covered a distance of 2,894 miles.

The regiment left Fort Lincoln on May 17 and returned on September 26 and went into camp. After obtaining recruits, Co. K was one of six cavalry companies and two infantry companies (accompanied by two pieces of artillery) that left Fort Lincoln on October 17 and went to Cheyenne Agency via the left bank of the Missouri to disarm and dismount the Indians. The company returned in November for winter station at Fort Lincoln. Distance marched in the year was 1,848 miles. Distance journeyed by detachments was 326 miles.

The following members were casualties in the Little Bighorn River fight June 25-26. Killed: First Sergeant Dewitt Winney, Sergeant Robert Hughes, Corporal John Callahan, Privates Elihu Clear and Julius Helmer. Wounded: Sergeant Michael Madden, Privates Patrick Corcoran and Max Mielke. Private Wm. Crawford died in the Fort Lincoln hospital on August 28 of typhoid fever. Private John Steintker died in company quarters at Fort Lincoln on Nov. 28 of suicide by poison.

Officers serving with the company were Captain Owen Hale, First Lieuts. Charles Braden and Edward Godfrey, Second Lieuts. Luther Hare and Jonathan Biddle. Lieut. Edwin Proctor Andrus was a replacement for Lieut. Hare who was promoted but Lieut. Andrus declined transfer from the 5th Cavalry. Lieut. Biddle was replacement for Lieut. Andrus.*

Jonathan Williams Biddle was born in Pennsylvania and entered military service from there. Appointed Second Lieut. 7th Cavalry Aug. 31, 1876. Killed on September 30, 1877 in action against Nez Perce Indians at Snake River, Montana Territory.

COMPANY K AT THE LITTLE BIGHORN

	Absent	Present	Wounded	Died OWRT	Killed	Survived
Captain	1					1
1st Lieut.		1				1
2nd Lieut.		1				1
1st Sergt.		1			1	
Sergeants		6			1	5
Corporals	2	1			1	2
Trumpeter		2			1	1
Saddler		1	1			1
Farrier		1				1
Wagoner	1					1
Blacksmith		1				1
Private	24	28	2		1	51
Totals	28	43	3	0	5	66

COMPANY K ON JUNE 30, 1876

Officers present for duty 2
Enlisted present for duty 25
Enlisted present extra duty 8
Officers absent detached service 1
Enlisted absent detached service 24
Enlisted absent sick 6
Captain 1
First Lieutenant 1
Second Lieutenant 1
Sergeants 5
Corporals 2
Trumpeter 1
Farrier and blacksmith 2
Saddler 1
Wagoner 1
Privates 51
Total enlisted 63
Aggregate 66
Aggregate in May 71
Enlisted killed 5
Wounded 3
Horse serviceable 26
Horses unserviceable 7
Horses lost 11

HALE, OWEN, Captain

On detached service at St. Louis, Missouri. Born on July 23, 1843, in Troy, New York. On October 18, 1861 he enrolled in the 1st New York Mounted Rifles at Troy. Honorably mustered out on April 9, 1862 as Sergeant Major. He again enrolled on August 13, 1862, and was mustered in on July 23, 1862, as a Private, Company B, 1st New York Mounted Rifles and was promoted to Sergeant Major on April 20, 1863. He served in that rank until May 8, 1863, when he accepted appointment as Second Lieutenant, Company F, in the same regiment. He participated in actions against the 42nd Battalion, Virginia Cavalry and in the skirmish at Bottom's Bridge and the operations around Drewry's Bluff; the siege of Suffolk and in the advance of General Butler's army on the Peninsula. Promoted to First Lieutenant on October 19, 1864, and was transferred to Company E, 4th Provisional Cavalry, New York Volunteers. Brevetted Captain, U.S.V., to date from March 13, 1865 for his gallant and meritorious services during the Civil War. Honorably mustered out of volunteer service on November 29, 1865. He received appointment as First Lieutenant, 7th Cavalry to rank from July 28, 1866, the date that the regiment was organized. He received the brevets of Captain and Major, U.S.A. on January 17, 1869. Promoted to Captain of Cavalry on March 1, 1869. From May 7 to September 21, 1873 he was with Colonel David Stanley's expedition, escorting the Northern Pacific Railroad Survey and exploring the valley of the Yellowstone River. In 1876, during the Sioux expedition, Captain Hale was on detached service in St. Louis—he did not participate in the Little Bighorn River fight. Engaged with the regiment in 1877 in the Nez Perce campaign. He was in the action against Chief Joseph's band at Snake Creek near the Bear Paw Mountains on September 30. Captain Hale was killed in the first charge, by a shot in the neck. He was survived by his brother, Henry H. Hale of Troy.

GODFREY, EDWARD SETTLE, First Lieutenant

In the hilltop fight commanding Company K. Born on October 9, 1843 in Kalida, Putnam County, Ohio, the son of Charles Moore and Mary Chambers Godfrey. Enlisted on April 26, 1861, in Company D, 21st Ohio Volunteer Infantry; in the action at Scarey Creek, West Virginia on July 17, 1861. Honorably discharged on August 12, 1861. He entered the Military Academy July 1, 1863, and graduated, as the 2208th graduate, on June 17, 1867, ranking 53rd in his class of 63 graduates. Appointed Second Lieutenant, Company G, 7th Cavalry on June 17, 1867. Promoted to First Lieutenant on February 1, 1868 and served with the regiment in Kansas. On November 27, 1868, he engaged in the fight against Black Kettle's Cheyenne village on the Washita River and was in General Sheridan's expedition in Indian Territory until February, 1869. In 1871 he served in South Carolina and in 1873 he was in Colonel David Stanley's expediton escorting the Northern Pacific Railroad Survey and exploring the valley of the Yellowstone River. Engaged in the action against Sioux Indians on August 11, 1873, at the mouth of the Bighorn River, Montana. Assistant Engineering Officer in the expedition exploring the Black Hills in 1874. From 1874 to 1876 he was commanding the post at Colfax, Louisiana and later at McComb City, Mississippi. He departed on May 17, 1876 in the Sioux expedition under Brig. General Terry and was engaged in the Little Bighorn River fight on June 25-26 while commanding Company K. From October 15 to November 16 he was on an expedition to disarm and dismount agency Indians.

Promoted to Captain of Company D to rank from December 9, 1876. In 1877 he participated in the expedition against Chief Joseph and was severely wounded near the Bear Paw Mountains. In 1879 he testified in the Reno Court of Inquiry. Brevetted Major, U.S.A., February 27, 1890 for his services at the Bear Paw Mountains. On December 29, 1890, he was engaged in the fight at Wounded Knee Creek, South Dakota. Promoted to Major, 1st Cavalry December 8, 1896; Lieut. Colonel, 12th Cavalry, February 2, 1901 following service in Cuba; Colonel, 9th Cavalry on June 26, 1901 and to Brigadier General on January 17, 1907. Retired at Fort Riley on October 9, 1907 after over 40 years service. Died on April 1, 1932 at the age of 88 at Cookstown, New Jersey, the last surviving officer (except Colonel Charles Varnum) of the Little Bighorn River fight. Interred in the National Cemetery, Arlington, Virginia. He was survived by his children and wife, Ida.

HARE, LUTHER RECTOR, Second Lieutenant

On duty with the Detachment of Indian Scouts under Lieut. Varnum in the Reno battalion. Born on August 24, 1851, at Greencastle, Indiana, the son of Silas and Elizabeth Rector Hare. He entered the Military Academy on September 1, 1870, and graduated on June 17, 1874, as the 2533rd graduate, ranking 25th in his class of 41 graduates. Appointed a Second Lieutenant, 7th Cavalry on June 17, 1874, and served in the garrison at Colfax, Louisiana until 1876. Engaged in the Sioux expedition from May 17 to September 26, 1876 and participated in the Little Bighorn River fight on June 25-26. After the valley fight on June 25, he joined Company K and engaged in the hilltop fight. Promoted to First Lieutenant to date from June 25, 1876, and transferred to Company I to occupy the vacancy created by the death of Lieut. James Porter. Engaged in the campaign against Chief Joseph in 1877. He continued to serve on frontier duty and was promoted to Captain on December 29, 1890 as a result of a vacancy created after the fight against Big Foot's band of Sioux at Wounded Knee Creek, South Dakota. On May 14, 1898 he was promoted to Lieutenant Colonel, 1st Texas Volunteer Cavalry and on June 14 of the same year received promotion to Colonel of the regiment. Honorably mustered out of volunteer service in November, 1898. On July 5, 1899 he received appointment as Colonel, 33rd U.S. Volunteer Infantry and took the regiment to the Philippines. He fought in the battles at San Fabian, Mangatani Bridge, San Jacinto and San Quentin. Appointed Brigadier General, U.S.V, on June 1, 1900; discharged from volunteer service on June 20, 1901. On February 2, 1901, he was promoted to Major, 12th Cavalry and on July 16, 1903 he was retired for disability. From October 10, 1903 to June 30, 1905 he was on active duty as Inspection Instructor of Militia. From May 29, 1908 to January 15, 1911 he was Professor of Military Science and Tactics at the University of Texas when he again retired. He was promoted to Lieut. Colonel, Retired, on July 9, 1916 and was appointed Commander of the Student Army Training Corps at Simmons College from January 23, 1918 to February 15, 1919 when he was relieved from active service for the last time. Died at the age of 78 at Walter Reed Hospital on December 22, 1929; interred in the National Cemetery at Arlington, Virginia. Besides his brother, Judge Silas Hare, of Sherman, Texas, he was survived by his three daughters, Mrs. Camilla Lippincott, Mrs. Charles Field Mason, and the Vicomtesse de Beughem of Brussels, Belgium.

WINNEY, DEWITT, First Sergeant
Killed in the hilltop fight on June 25. Born in Saratoga, New York. Enlisted on November 6, 1872, at age 27 in New York City by Captain Edwin Sumner. Previous occupation was laborer. He had grey eyes, brown hair, dark complexion and was 5'-4½" in height. Listed as De Witt Winney on the battle monument. An account of his death is in Lieut. Edward Godfrey's diary for June 25, 1876, manuscript p. 4-2, book, p. 17.

CAMPBELL, JEREMIAH, Sergeant
Born in Sangamon County, Illinois. Second enlistment on January 16, 1872, at age 27 in Cincinnati, Ohio by Lieut. Myles Moylan. Previous occupation was laborer. Discharged on January 16, 1877, at Fort Abraham Lincoln, Dakota upon expiration of service, as a Private of good character. He had grey eyes, dark hair, fair complexion and was 5'-7¾" in height.

FREDERICK, ANDREW, Sergeant
Born in Bedford County, Pennsylvania. Second enlistment on April 23, 1872, at age 28 in Yorkville, South Carolina by Captain Owen Hale. Discharged on April 23, 1877, at Fort Abraham Lincoln, Dakota, upon expiration of service, as a Private of excellent character. He had hazel eyes, dark hair, light complexion and was 5'-3½" in height.

HOSE, GEORGE, Sergeant
Born in Hesse Cassel, Germany. Second enlistment on January 1, 1875, at age 26 in Colfax, Louisiana by Lieut. Edward Godfrey. Previous occupation was soldier. Discharged on April 5, 1878 at Fort Rice, Dakota for disability, as a Corporal of excellent character. He had grey eyes, brown hair, dark complexion and was 5'-7½" in height.

HUGHES, ROBERT H., Sergeant
Killed with the Custer battalion on June 25. Sergeant Hughes carried Lieut. Colonel George Custer's battle flag and was killed on Custer Hill. Born in Dublin, Ireland. Second enlistment on October 1, 1873, at age 33 at Fort Rice, Dakota by Captain Owen Hale. He had blue eyes, brown hair, fair complexion and was 5'-9" in height. Listed as R. H. Hughes on the battle monument and elsewhere as B. H. Hughes.

RAFTER, JOHN, Sergeant
Born in Lansingburgh, New York. Enlisted on January 20, 1872, at age 21 in Troy, New York by Lieut. Oscar Elting. Previous occupation was brushmaker. Discharged on January 20, 1877, at Fort Abraham Lincoln, Dakota upon expiration of service, as a Sergeant of good character. Re-enlisted on January 26, 1877, at Fort Lincoln by Lieut. Hugh Scott and discharged on January 25, 1882, at Fort Lincoln upon expiration of service, as a Private of fair character. He had blue eyes, brown hair, ruddy complexion and was 5'-9¼" in height.

ROTT, LOUIS, Sergeant
Born in Germany. Second enlistment on January 17, 1875, at age 26 in Colfax, Louisiana by Lieut. Edward Godfrey. Discharged on May 26, 1878 at Fort Rice, Dakota for disability, as a Sergeant of excellent character. He had brown eyes, black hair, dark complexion and was 5'-9" in height.

CALLAHAN, JOHN J., Corporal
Killed in battle on June 25. Born in Salem, Massachusetts. Enlisted on November 5, 1872, at age 21 in Boston by Captain Moses Harris. Previous occupation was currier. He had grey eyes, dark hair, fair complexion and was 5'-7" in height. Listed as J. J. Callahan on the battle monument.

MURRAY, HENRY, Corporal
On detached service from June 15, 1876 at Yellowstone Depot, Montana Territory. Born in Boston, Massachusetts. Enlisted on October 14, 1875, at age 27 in St. Louis by Lieut. John Thompson. Previous occupation was soldier. Promoted to Sergeant about September 5, 1876 by Lieut. Edward Godfrey. By 1876 Murray had been on NCO for 11 years according to Lieut. Godfrey (Godfrey **Diary**, p. 47). Appointed Commissary Sergeant on June 12, 1879. Discharged on October 12, 1880, at Fort Benton, Montana Territory, upon expiration of service, as a Commissary Sergeant of excellent character. He had hazel eyes, dark hair, dark complexion and was 5'-11" in height.

NOLAN, JOHN, Corporal
On detached service from June 15, 1876 at Yellowstone Depot, Montana Territory. Born in Tipperary, Ireland. Enlisted on December 4, 1874, at age 26 in New York City by Lieut. Thomas Gregg. Previous occupation was groom. Wounded on September 30, 1877, in the Snake Creek fight near the Bear Paw Mountains, Montana Territory in an engagement with Chief Joseph's band of Nez Perce Indians. Discharged on February 1, 1878, at Fort Rice, Dakota for disability, as a Sergeant of excellent character. He had blue eyes, brown hair, fair complexion and was 5'-7¼" in height.

HELMER, JULIUS, Trumpeter
Killed in battle on June 25. Born in Hanover, Germany. Third enlistment on July 10, 1875, at age 29 in Cincinnati, Ohio by Lieut. Patrick Cusack. He had grey eyes, brown hair, light complexion and was 5'-9¾" in height. Listed as Julius Helmer on the battle monument.

PENWELL, GEORGE B., Trumpeter
In the hilltop fight. Born in Philadelphia. Pennsylvania. Enlisted on June 22, 1869 in Philadelphia by Lieut Humbert. Previous occupation was painter. Assigned to Company L, 5th Cavalry. Deserted on July 28, 1870, at Lodge Pole Station, Union Pacific, Railroad, Nebraska. Enlisted on January 16, 1871, at age 22 at Fort Leavenworth, Kansas by Lieut. William Cooke. Assigned to Company K, 7th Cavalry. His enlistment was cancelled on November 14, 1873 when he surrendered at Fort Rice, Dakota under General Order Nr. 102, AGO, 1873 as a deserter from Company L, 5th Cavalry. Restored to duty without trial. He had grey eyes, brown hair, fair complexion and was 5'-5" in height.

MADDEN, MICHAEL P., Saddler
Wounded in the right leg (double fracture below the knee) in the first water party in the hilltop fight on June 26. Dr. Porter amputated his leg on the battlefield. Promoted to Sergeant on June 26 for his gallantry on the field. Transported to Fort Abraham Lincoln, Dakota on the steamboat *Far West*. "In our venture to the stream, we found Trooper Mike Madden lying in the coulee, shot through the ankle. Mike was a big husky fellow and had accompanied the

first detachment. He lost his leg in the hospital, where it was amputated. An amusing incident happened in connection with it. Before amputating the member, the surgeon gave Mike a stiff horn of brandy to brace him up. Mike went through the ordeal without a whimper, and was then given another drink. Smacking his lips in appreciation, he whispered to the surgeon, 'Doctor, cut off me other leg!'" William Slaper in Brininstool **Troopers With Custer**, p. 59. Born in Galcony, Ireland. Second enlistment on August 28, 1871, in Louisville, Kentucky by Lieut. William Cooke. Discharged on August 28, 1876, at Fort Lincoln upon expiration of service, as a Sergeant of excellent character. Later employed in the harness depot at the Department of Dakota in St. Paul. He may have been interred in the old Fort Snelling Cemetery, Minnesota.

STEINTKER, JOHN R., Farrier
Born in Hanover, Germany. Second enlistment on November 30, 1872, at age 37 in Louisville, Kentucky by Lieut. William Cooke. Died in company quarters on November 28, 1876 at Fort Abraham Lincoln, Dakota. Death was suicide by poison. Reinterred in the Custer Battlefield National Cemetery, Grave 574A. He had brown eyes, dark hair, ruddy complexion and was 5'-11½" in height.

WHYTEFIELD, ALBERT, Wagoner
On detached service from June 15, 1876 at Yellowstone Depot, Montana Territory. Born in Sandusky, Ohio. Enlisted on September 10, 1866 at age 20 in Detroit, Michigan by Brevet Major C. B. McLellan (Lieut. 6th Cav.). Previous occupation was painter. Assigned to the 7th Cavalry. He had blue eyes, light hair, fair complexion and was 5'-4½" in height and was illiterate. Also listed as Albert Whyterfield and Albert Whytenfield.

BURKE, EDMUND H., Blacksmith
In the valley and hilltop fights. Born in Manchester, England. Third enlistment on December 14, 1871, at age 30 in Yorkville, South Carolina by Lieut. Henry Nowlan. Previous occupation was horseshoer. Discharged on December 14, 1876, upon expiration of service, as a Corporal of good character. He had hazel eyes, black hair, dark complexion and was 5'-8½" in height.

ACKERMAN, CHARLES, Private
On detached service from June 15, 1876 at Yellowstone Depot, Montana. He was cook for Lieut. Edward Godfrey after August 5, 1876, replacing Private Charles Burkhardt. Born in Baden, Germany. Enlisted on September 9, 1875, at age 27 in St. Louis by Captain Owen Hale. Previous occupation was cook. Discharged on September 8, 1880 at Fort Totten, Dakota upon expiration of service, as a Private of excellent character. He had hazel eyes, brown hair, fair complexion and was 5'-7¾" in height. In 1927 he resided at 1032 Grand Ave. St. Paul, Minnesota. Listed as Charles Ackerman in the Register of Enlistments, U.S. Army.

ANDERSON, GEORGE, Private
On detached service at Fort Abraham Lincoln, Dakota from May 17, 1876. Born in St. Catharine, Canada. Enlisted on August 16, 1871, at age 29 in Louisville, Kentucky by Lieut. John Weston. Previous occupation was soldier.

Discharged on September 16, 1876 at Fort Lincoln upon expiration of service, as a Private of excellent character. He had blue eyes, light hair, light complexion and was 5'-5½" in height.

BAUER, JACOB, Private
Sick in hospital from May 17, 1876 at Fort A. Lincoln, Dakota. Born in Baden, Germany. Enlisted on March 4, 1876, at age 33 in McComb City, Miss. by Lieut. Edward Godfrey. Previous occupation was soldier. Discharged on March 3, 1881 at Fort Totten, Dakota upon expiration of service, as a Private of very good character. He had brown eyes, black hair, sallow complexion and was 5'-5" in height.

BLAIR, JAMES C., Private
On detached service at Fort Abraham Lincoln, Dakota from May 17, 1876. Born in Camden, New Jersey. Enlisted on December 29, 1874, at age 24 in Pittsburgh, Pennsylvania by Lieut. Thomas Gregg. Previous occupation was carpenter. Discharged on December 28, 1879 at Fort Totten, Dakota upon expiration of service, as a Private of good character. He had blue eyes, light brown hair, fair complexion and was 5'-8¼" in height. Listed elsewhere as James E. Blair.

BLUNT, GEORGE, Private
Born in Baltimore, Maryland. Second enlistment on September 11, 1871, at age 26 in Yorkville, South Carolina, by Captain Owen Hale. Previous occupation was carpenter. Discharged on August 6, 1876 at camp at the mouth of Rosebud Creek, Montana per General Order Nr. 24, AGO, War Department, 1859, as a Private of excellent character. He had blue eyes, dark hair, sallow complexion and was 5'6¾" in height.

BOISSEN, CHRISTIAN, Private
Born in Denmark. Enlisted on March 25, 1873, at age 31 in Memphis, Tennessee by Captain Owen Hale. Previous occupation was bootmaker. Discharged on March 25, 1878, upon expiration of service, as a Private of excellent character. He had blue eyes, brown hair, fair complexion and was 5'-6" in height. Boissen may have been promoted to Saddler to replace Michael Madden who was promoted to Sergeant.

BRESNAHAN, CORNELIUS, Private
Born in Mount Auburn, Massachusetts. Enlisted on October 3, 1873, at age 21¼ in Boston by Lieut. James Ropes. Previous occupation was laborer. Dishonorably discharged on May 31, 1878 at Fort Rice, Dakota as a Private, per General Court Martial Order Nr. 36, Department of Dakota, May 8, 1878. He had hazel eyes, red hair, medium complexion and was 5'-9" in height.

BROWN, JOSEPH, Private
Born in Berlin, Germany. Second enlistment on January 27, 1875, at age 30 in St. Louis by Lieut. William Volkmar. Previous occupation was carpenter. Discharged on January 26, 1880, at Fort Abraham Lincoln, Dakota, upon expiration of service, as a Private of very good character. He had blue eyes, light hair, fair complexion and was 5'-11" in height.

BURGDORF, CHARLES J., Private
On detached service at Yellowstone Depot, Montana Territory from June 15, 1876. Born in Hanover, Germany. Second enlistment on February 28, 1876, at age 30 in Chicago by Lieut. Edmund Luff. Previous occupation was soldier. Discharged on February 27, 1881, at Fort Totten, Dakota upon expiration of service, as a Private of very good character. He had blue eyes, fair hair, ruddy complexion and was 5'-5¾" in height.

BURKHARDT, CHARLES, Private
In the hilltop fight. He was cook for Lieut. Edward Godfrey during the march from Fort Abraham Lincoln, Dakota. Born in Summerville, Ohio. Third enlistment on September 1, 1871, at age 25 in Louisville, Kentucky by Lieut. John Weston. Previous occupation was soldier. Discharged on August 6, 1876, at camp on Rosebud Creek, Montana Territory per General Order Nr. 24, AGO, War Department, 1859, as a Private of excellent character. Not listed on the 7th Cavalry Muster Roll for June 30, 1876. Listed as Burckhardt by Lieut. Godfrey in his diary, p. 14, 31. He had hazel eyes, brown hair, dark complexion and was 5'-3" in height.

CLEAR, ELIHU F., Private
Killed while climbing the bluff during the retreat from the valley fight on June 25. He was an orderly for Dr. James DeWolf who was killed nearby. Born in Randolph County, Indiana. Second enlistment on January 4, 1872, at age 28 in Yorkville, South Carolina by Captain Owen Hale. He had light blue eyes, brown hair, dark complexion and was 5'-6½" in height. Listed as E. F. Clear on the battle monument and elsewhere as Eli U. T. Clair and Elihue M. T. Clair and Elihue F. Clear.

COAKLEY, PATRICK, Private
Born in Kings County, Ireland. Second enlistment on December 26, 1871, at age 29 in Yorkville, South Carolina by Captain Owen Hale. Deserted on March 12, 1872; surrendered on April 18, 1872. Discharged on February 8, 1877 at Fort Abraham Lincoln, Dakota upon expiration of service, as a Private of excellent character. He had hazel eyes, brown hair, fair complexion and was 5'-7½" in height.

CORCORAN, PATRICK, Private
Wounded in the right shoulder in the hilltop fight on June 25. Transported to Fort Abraham Lincoln, Dakota on the steamboat *Far West*. Born in Cattaraugus County, New York. Second enlistment on August 23, 1872, at age 27 in Kansas City, Missouri by Lieut. John Morrison. Discharged on January 29, 1877 at Fort Lincoln for disability, as a Private. He had hazel eyes, brown hair, fair complexion and was 5'-9½" in height. Listed as wounded on June 26 by Lieut. Edward Godfrey in his diary, p. 17. Listed as Patrick Cocoran in the Register of Enlistments, U.S. Army.

CRAWFORD, WILLIAM L., Private
On detached service from June 15, 1876 at Yellowstone Depot, Montana Territory. Born in Newfield, New York. Enlisted on February 13, 1875, at age 25 in St. Louis by Lieut. William Volkmar. Previous occupation was boat

builder. Died of typhoid fever on August 20, 1876 at Fort Abraham Lincoln, Dakota. Re-interred in the Custer Battlefield National Cemetery, Grave 569A. He had grey eyes, light hair, fair complexion and was 5'-9½" in height.

CREIGHTON, JOHN C. (Charles Chesterwood), Private
In the hilltop fight. Born on March 4, 1850, in Massilon, Ohio, the son of Hugh and Jean McPherson Creighton. In the Register of Enlistments, U.S. Army, his birthplace is listed as Memphis, Tennessee. Enlisted on January 6, 1872, at age 22 in Chicago by Captain Samuel Young. Previous occupation was machinist. He participated in an engagement against Sioux Indians on June 13, 1873, at Camp Hancock, Dakota, and in a skirmish at the mouth of the Little Bighorn River, Montana Territory, on August 11, 1873 and in the Little Bighorn River fight on June 25-26, 1876. Discharged on January 6, 1877, at Fort A. Lincoln, Dakota upon expiration of service, as a Private of good character. Re-enlisted and mustered out in 1882. Married Mrs. Susan Andrews in 1882 at Fort Lincoln. In 1927 he resided at 107 Seventh Ave. N.W., Mandan, North Dakota. Died in the winter of 1934-35.

DELANEY, MICHAEL, Private
On detached service from June 15, 1876 at Yellowstone Depot, Montana Territory. Born in Broom County, New York. Enlisted on May 20, 1875, at age 21 in Cincinnati by Lieut. Patrick Cusack. Previous occupation was clerk. Engaged in the Nez Perce campaign and wounded on September 30, 1877, in the Snake Creek fight near the Bear Paw Mountains in Montana Territory in an engagement with Chief Joseph's band of Nez Perce. He was a Corporal at this time. Discharged on May 1, 1878, at Fort Rice, Dakota for disability, as a Sergeant of excellent character. He had blue eyes, brown hair, dark complexion and was 5'-8¼" in height.

DONAHUE, JOHN F., Private
Born in Tipperary, Ireland. Enlisted on December 14, 1872, at age 22 in Boston by Lieut. William Harper, Jr. Previous occupation was laborer. Discharged on December 13, 1879 at Fort Totten, Dakota upon expiration of service, as a Private of very good character. He had hazel eyes, dark hair, medium complexion and was 5'-9" in height. Listed as John F. Donahue in the Register of Enlistments, U.S. Army.

DOOLEY, PATRICK, Private
Sick in the hospital from May 17, 1876 at Fort Abraham Lincoln, Dakota. Born in County Queens, Ireland. Second enlistment on September 13, 1871, at age 40 in Yorkville, South Carolina by Captain Owen Hale. Previous occupation was soldier. Discharged on September 11, 1876, at Fort Lincoln, Dakota upon expiration of service, as a Private of excellent character. He had blue eyes, dark hair, ruddy complexion. His height is not listed in the Register of Enlistments, U.S. Army.

FISHER, CHARLES, Private
On detached service from June 15, 1876 at Yellowstone Depot, Montana Territory. Born in Bavaria, Germany. Enlisted on March 7, 1876, at age 27 in Chicago by Lieut. Edmund Luff. Previous occupation was soldier. Transferred to

Company H, 7th Cavalry. Discharged on March 19, 1881, at Fort Meade, Dakota upon expiration of his service, as a Farrier. He had grey eyes, dark hair, dark complexion and was 5'-6½" in height.

FOLEY, JOHN, Private
Born in Dublin, Ireland. Second enlistment on August 22, 1871, at age 32 in Louisville, Kentucky, by Lieut. William Cooke. Previous occupation was farmer. Discharged on August 6, 1876, at the camp at the mouth of Rosebud Creek, Montana Territory per General Order Nr. 24, AGO, War Department, 1859, as a Private of excellent character. He had grey eyes, black hair, dark complexion and was 5'-9" in height.

GIBBS, WILLIAM, Private
Born in Manchester, England. Enlisted on December 15, 1874, at age 22 in New York City by Lieut. Thomas Gregg. Previous occupation was butcher. Discharged on April 5, 1878, at Fort Rice, Dakota for disability, as a Private of excellent character. He had blue eyes, brown hair, fair complexion and was 5'-7¼" in height. In 1927 he resided at the Veteran's Home, Sawtelle, California.

GORDON, THOMAS A., Private
Born in Boston, Massachusetts. Enlisted on September 26, 1873, at age 22 9/12 in Boston by Lieut. James Ropes. Previous occupation was laborer. Discharged on September 26, 1878, at Camp R. Williams, Nebraska upon expiration of service, as a Private of very good character. He had grey eyes, black hair, dark complexion and was 5'-6½ in height. In 1927 he resided on George St., Mendon, Massachusetts.

GREEN, THOMAS, Private
On detached service from June 15, 1876 at Yellowstone Depot, Montana Territory. Born in Aurora, Illinois. Enlisted on December 10, 1875, at age 21 11/12 in Boston by Lieut. Henry Lawton. Previous occupation was laborer. Discharged on January 29, 1879 at Fort Abraham Lincoln, Dakota for disability, as a Private of good character. He had blue eyes, dark hair, dark complexion and was 5'-6¾" in height. Listed as Thomas Green in the Register of Enlistments, U.S. Army.

GUNTHER, JULIUS, Private
Sick in the hospital at Fort Abraham Lincoln, Dakota from May 17, 1876. Born in Wurtemburg, Germany. Second enlistment on August 24, 1872, at age 28 in Kansas City, Missouri, by Lieut. John Morrison. Previous occupation was farrier. His enlistment was cancelled when he surrendered on December 7, 1873 under General Order Nr. 102, AGO, Oct. 10, 1873, as Julius Gunther, a deserter from Company D, 5th Cavalry. He was restored to duty without trial and transferred from Company D, 5th Cavalry to Company K, 7th Cavalry effective November 10, 1874. He had grey eyes, brown hair, fair complexion and was 5'-5¼" in height.

HOLAHAN, ANDREW, Private
On detached service from June 15, 1876 at Yellowstone Depot, Montana Territory. Born in Kilkenny, Ireland. Enlisted on December 22, 1874, at age 25

in St. Louis by Lieut. William Volkmar. Previous occupation was miner. Discharged on December 21, 1879 at Fort Totten, Dakota upon expiration of service, as a Sergeant of very good character. He had blue eyes, brown hair, ruddy complexion and was 5'-7¼" in height. Listed as Holohan on the Muster Roll of Recruits of the General Mounted Service, St. Louis Barracks, for the period Feb. 29 to April 30, 1876.

HORNER, JACOB, Private

On detached service at Yellowstone Depot, Montana Territory from June 15, 1876. Born October 6, 1854 in New York City, the son of Jacob and Anna Mary Richard Horner. His parents came to the United States from Alsace-Lorraine in 1848 and engaged in the bakery business in New York City until 1857 when they returned to the old country with their son. Jacob, the son, returned to the United States at the age of 15 and then returned on September 20, 1874 to visit his parents. He arrived in New Orleans in January, 1875 and worked as a meat cutter in the French market there. In 1875 he embarked on a Mississippi River steamer and arrived in St. Louis in April where he became employed in the meat business. He was enlisted April 8, 1876, at Jefferson Barracks by Captain Owen Hale and assigned to Company K which he joined at Fort Snelling on April 18. He traveled by special train to Fort A. Lincoln, stopping at Brainerd, Minnesota, and Fargo and Bismarck, Dakota. He participated in the Sioux expedition, marching afoot from May 17 until July when he was mounted. He departed on May 17, 1877 from Fort Lincoln on the Nez Perce campaign, arriving at Fort Keogh on June 28 and proceeding up the Yellowstone. Engaged in the Canyon Creek fight on September 13 against Chief Joseph's band of Nez Perce. Accompanied a band of Cheyenne Indians (brought in by Co. K in December, 1877) to Bismarck. Horner arrived at Fort Rice in January, 1878 and then went to the Black Hills to aid in the capture of Brule Sioux in that vicinity. He returned to Fort Lincoln in November, 1878 and thence to Fort Totten on November 15. He married Kathryn Stewart (or Catherine Stuart) daughter of an enlisted man, on April 18, 1880, at Fort Totten (Kathryn died September 3, 1933). Discharged April 7, 1881 at Fort Totten upon expiration of service, as a Sergeant of fine character. He had black eyes, black hair, dark complexion and was 5'-6" in height. He lived in Bismarck, employed by the Northern Pacific railroad, for a year and then entered trade as a butcher. In his declining years he spent his winters in Los Angeles. Died on September 21, 1951, of respiratory infection at the Bismarck Hospital. Survived by three of his five children: Mrs. Emily Morrison and Leo A. Horner, St. Paul, Minn. and John C. Horner, Savage, Minn. His story is in U. L. Burdick and E. D. Hart *Jacob Horner And The Indian Campaigns of 1876 and 1877.* He was the last surviving member of the 7th Cavalry who participated, from May 17, in the Sioux campaign.

HAYT, WALTER, Private

On detached service from June 15, 1876 at Yellowstone Depot, Montana Territory. Born in Steuben County, New York. Second enlistment on May 19, 1875, at age 27 in St. Louis by Captain James Wheelan. Previous occupation was soldier. Discharged on May 18, 1880 at Fort Totten, Dakota upon expiration of service, as a Private of excellent character. He had blue eyes, brown hair, florid complexion and was 5'-6¾" in height. Listed as Walter Hayt in the Register of Enlistments, U.S. Army and elsewhere as Walter Hoyt. Listed as Walker Hoyt on the Muster Roll of Recruits of the General Mounted Service, St. Louis Barracks, for the period Feb. 29 to April 30, 1876.

JENNYS, ALONZO, Private
Born in New York City. Second enlistment on March 14, 1876, at age 27 in McComb City, Mississippi by Lieut. Edward Godfrey. He deserted on April 18, 1877. He had grey eyes, brown hair and florid complexion and was 5'-7" in height.

LASLEY, WILLIAM W., Private
Born in St. Louis County, Missouri. Enlisted on October 17, 1872, at age 29 in Kansas City, Missouri, by Lieut. John Morrison. Previous occupation was farmer. He was discharged on June 23, 1877 at camp on Sunday Creek, Montana Territory per Special Order Nr. 70, Department of Dakota, 1877, as a Private of excellent character. He had blue eyes, brown hair, fair complexion and was 5'-7½" in height.

LIEBERMANN, ANDREW, Private
On detached service from May 17, 1876 at Fort Abraham Lincoln, Dakota. Born in Wurtemburg, Germany. Enlisted on November 3, 1875, at age 28 in Cincinnati by Lieut. Patrick Cusack. Previous occupation was tailor. Deserted on *May 25, 1876*. He had brown eyes, black hair, dark complexion and was 5'-5¾" in height. Listed elsewhere as Andrew Liberman.

LYONS, DANIEL, Private
On detached service from June 15, 1876, at Yellowstone Depot, Montana Territory. Born in Brooklyn, New York. Enlisted on April 4, 1876, at age 23 in St. Louis by Lieut. John Thompson. Previous occupation was blacksmith. Discharged April 9, 1878, at Fort Rice, Dakota, for disability, as a Blacksmith of excellent character. He had blue or hazel eyes, brown or black hair, fair complexion and was 5'-6 1/8 or 9¼" in height.

MIELKE, MAX, Private
Wounded in the left foot in the hilltop fight on June 26. Transported to Fort Abraham Lincoln, Dakota on the steamboat *Far West*. Born in Frankfort, Germany. Third enlistment on March 24, 1876, at age 30 in McComb City, Mississippi by Lieut. Edward Godfrey. Killed in the Snake Creek fight on September 30, 1877, near the Bear Paw Mountains, Montana Territory in the engagement with Chief Joseph's band of Nez Perce Indians. (He was then a Sergeant.) Re-interred in the Custer Battlefield National Cemetery, Grave 1412 (2) B. He had blue eyes, dark hair, fair complexion and was 5'-10" in height. Listed elsewhere as M. Wilke and Max Wilke.

MURPHY, MICHAEL, Private
Born in Cork, Ireland. Second enlistment on September 11, 1871, at age 33 in York, South Carolina by Captain Owen Hale. Discharged on August 6, 1876, at camp at the mouth of Rosebud Creek, Montana Territory, per General Order Nr. 24, AGO, War Department, 1859, as a Private of excellent character. He re-enlisted and was wounded on September 30, 1877, in the Snake Creek fight near the Bear Paw Mountains, Montana in the engagement with Chief

Joseph's band of Nez Perce Indians. He had blue eyes, black hair, fair complexion and was 5'-3½" in height.

MURPHY, THOMAS, Private
Born in Cork, Ireland, Enlisted on December 18, 1874, at age 21 in Boston by Lieut. William Harper, Jr. Previous occupation was shoemaker. Deserted on March 20, 1875; apprehended on March 22, 1875. Discharged on June 29, 1878 at Fort Rice, Dakota for disability, as a Private of good character. He had grey eyes, dark hair, fair complexion and was 5'-9¾" in height.

McCONNELL, WILSON, Private
Born in Lawrence County, Pennsylvania. Second enlistment on January 3, 1872, at Yorkville, South Carolina, at age 32 by Captain Owen Hale. Discharged on January 3, 1877, at Fort Abraham Lincoln, Dakota upon expiration of service, as a Private of good character. He had grey eyes, light hair, ruddy complexion and was 5'-9" in height.

McCUE, MARTIN, Private
Born at sea. Enlisted on October 28, 1872, at age 21 in Philadelphia by Captain Samuel Whitside. Previous occupation was stripper. Discharged on June 23, 1877, at camp on Sunday Creek, Montana Territory, per Special Order Nr. 70, Department of Dakota, 1877, as a Private of excellent character. He had grey eyes, brown hair, ruddy complexion and was 5'-6½" in height.

RAGAN, MICHAEL, Private
On detached service from June 15, 1876 at Yellowstone Depot, Montana Territory. "When Custer started his last march up the Rosebud, on the morning of June 22, 1876, many of the recruits had obtained horses and accompanied him. Horner's buddy, Charles Schmidt, private in "L" company, secured the horse of Michael Ragan of "K" company, a Civil War veteran, and went in Ragan's place." Burdick and Hart, *Jacob Horner and the Indian Campaign of 1876 and 1877*, p. 14, Baltimore, 1942. Ragan was born in Queenstown, Ireland. Enlisted on November 8, 1873, at age 27 in Boston by Captain Moses Harris. Previous occupation was shoemaker. Discharged November 8, 1877, at Fort A. Lincoln, Dakota, upon expiration of service, as a Private of good character. He had grey eyes, dark hair, fair complexion and was 5'-7" in height. Re-enlisted on December 26, 1877, at Fort Rice, Dakota by Captain Edward Mathey. Listed as Michael Ragan in the Register of Enlistments, U.S. Army and on his Oath of Enlistment and on the Muster Roll for June 30, 1876. Listed elsewhere as Michael Reagan.

RAICHEL, HENRY W., Private
Born in Hamilton County, Ohio. Second enlistment on May 8, 1875, in Cincinnati, Ohio by Lieut. Patrick Cusack. Previous occupation was baker. Promoted to Sergeant. Killed in the Snake Creek fight with Chief Joseph's band of Nez Perce Indians on September 30, 1877, near the Bear Paw Mountains, Montana Territory. Re-interred in the Custer Battlefield National Cemetery, Grave 1412 (2) B. He had blue eyes, brown hair, florid complexion and was 5'-9" in height.

REILLY, MICHAEL, Private
   On detached service from June 15, 1876 at Yellowstone Depot, Montana Territory. Born in Langford, Ireland. Second enlistment on June 8, 1875, at age 23 in St. Louis by Lieut. James Wheelan. Previous occupation was soldier. Discharged on June 5, 1879, at Fort Totten, Dakota per Special Order Nr. 124, AGO, 1879, as a Sergeant of excellent character. He had hazel eyes, dark hair, dark complexion and was 5'-6¼" in height. Listed as Michael Reilly in the Register of Enlistments, U. S. Army.

ROBERS, JOHNATHAN, Private
   Born in Surrey County, North Carolina. Enlisted on December 4, 1872, at age 21 in Yorkville, South Carolina by Lieut. John Aspinwall. Previous occupation was farmer. Appointed Farrier on December 1, 1876. Discharged on December 4, 1877, at Fort Buford, Dakota, upon expiration of service, as a Private of excellent character. Re-enlisted in Company E, 7th Cavalry on December 17, 1877 at Fort Rice, Dakota by Lieut. Edward Mathey. Discharged on December 16, 1882 at Fort Meade, Dakota upon expiration of service, as a Private of excellent character. Listed as Johnathan Robers in the Register of Enlistments, U.S. Army and is so signed on his Oath of Enlistment. He had blue eyes, brown hair, fair complexion and was 5'-8" in height.

ROTH, FRANCIS, Private
   On detached service from June 15, 1876 at Yellowstone Depot, Montana Territory. Born in Frankfort, Germany. Second enlistment on March 30, 1876, at age 29 in St. Louis by Lieut. John Thompson. Killed in the Snake Creek fight on September 30, 1877, near the Bear Paw Mountains, Montana Territory in an engagement with Chief Joseph's band of Nez Perce Indians Re-interred in the Custer Battlefield National Cemetery, Grave 1412 (2) B. He had grey eyes, brown hair, fair complexion and was 5'-7" in height.

SCHAUER, JOHN, Private
   Born in Bavaria. Enlisted on November 21, 1872, at age 21 in Pittsburgh, Pennsylvania by Lieut. Calbraith Rodgers. Previous occupation was laborer. Wounded in the Snake Creek fight near the Bear Paw Mountains, Montana Territory in the engagement with Chief Joseph's band of Nez Perce Indians on September 30, 1877. Discharged on November 21, 1877, at Fort Abraham Lincoln, Dakota upon expiration of service, as a Private of good character. Re-enlisted on December 17, 1877, at Fort Rice, Dakota by Captain Edward Mathey. Discharged on December 16, 1882 at Fort Meade, Dakota upon expiration of service, as a Private of very good character. He had grey eyes, dark hair, sallow complexion and was 5'-8" in height. Listed as John Shauer in the Register of Enlistments, U.S. Army.

SCHLAFER, CHRISTIAN, Private
   Born in Cincinnati, Ohio. Enlisted on March 24, 1875, at age 29 in Cincinnati by Lieut. Patrick Cusack. Previous occupation was soldier. Discharged on March 23, 1880, at Fort Totten, Dakota upon expiration of service, as a Trumpeter of good character. He had grey eyes, light hair, fair complexion and was 5'-5¾" in height.

SCHWERER, JOHN, Private
Born in Germany. Enlisted on November 12, 1872, at age 31 in New York City by Captain Edwin Sumner. Previous occupation was hatmaker. Wounded on September 30, 1877, in the engagement on Snake Creek, Montana Territory with Chief Joseph's band of Nez Perce Indians. Discharged on November 2, 1877, at Fort Abraham Lincoln, Dakota, upon expiration of service, as a Private of good character. He had brown eyes, dark hair, fair complexion and was 5'-5¾" in height. Listed as John Schwerer in the Register of Enlistments, U.S. Army and as John Schmerer in the *Army and Navy Journal*, October 13, 1877.

SEIFERT, AUGUST, Private
Born in Hesse, Darmstadt, Germany. Second enlistment on January 16, 1875, at age 27½ in Colfax, Louisiana by Lieut. Edward Godfrey. Previous occupation was baker. Discharged on January 15, 1880, at Fort Totten, Dakota upon expiration of service, as a Private of excellent character. He had grey eyes, brown hair, light complexion and was 5'-5" in height. Listed as August Siefort in the Register of Enlistments, U.S. Army.

SMITH, FREDERICK, Private
On detached service from June 15, 1876, at Yellowstone Depot, Montana Territory. Born in Muhlhausen, Germany. Discharged from Troop K, 7th Cavalry on March 6, 1886, and enlisted for the 5th time in Troop K, on March 7, 1886, at Fort Meade, Dakota, at the age of 39 by Lieut. John Wilkinson. He had blue eyes, dark brown hair, florid complexion, was 5'-10½" in height and was unmarried.

TAUBE, EMIL, Private
On detached service from June 15, 1876, at Yellowstone Depot, Montana Territory. Born in Damuan, Germany. Enlisted on March 21, 1876, at age 28 in St. Louis by Lieut. John Thompson. Previous occupation was laborer. Wounded on September 30, 1877, in the Snake Creek fight near the Bear Paw Mountains, Montana Territory in an engagement with Chief Joseph's band of Nez Perce Indians. Discharged on January 20, 1879, at Fort Abraham Lincoln, Dakota for disability, as a Private of excellent character. He had hazel eyes, black hair, dark complexion and was 5'-5½" in height.

VAN PELT, WILLIAM E., Private
On detached service from June 15, 1876, at Yellowstone Depot, Montana Territory. Born in New York City. Enlisted on January 13, 1876, at age 27 in St. Louis by Lieut. John Thompson. Previous occupation was clerk. Discharged on January 26, 1880, at Fort Meade, Dakota per Special Order Nr. 12, AGO, 1880, as a Quartermaster Sergeant of excellent character. He had blue eyes, brown hair, fair complexion and was 5'-7" in height. Listed elsewhere as Wm. A. Van Pelt.

WASMUS, ERNEST, Private
Born in Brunswick, Germany. Enlisted on December 17, 1874, at age 27 in New York City by Lieut. Thomas Gregg. Previous occupation was bookkeeper. Discharged on December 16, 1879, at Fort Totten, Dakota upon expiration of service, as a Sergeant of excellent character. He had brown eyes, brown hair, fair

complexion and was 5'-8¾" in height. Listed as Earnest Wasmus on the Muster Roll of the General Mounted Service, St. Louis Barracks for the period Feb. 29, to April 30, 1876.

WHITLOW, WILLIAM, Private

Born in Cavandish, Vermont. Enlisted on December 10, 1872, at age 27 in Troy, New York by Captain Owen Hale. Previous occupation was barber. Killed on September 30, 1877 in the Snake Creek fight with Chief Joseph's band of Nez Perce Indians, near the Bear Paw Mountains, Montana Territory. Re-interred in the Custer Battlefield National Cemetery, Grave 1412 (2) B. He had black eyes, black hair, dark complexion and was 5'-5" in height. Listed as Wm. Whitelaw in *The Army and Navy Journal*, October 13, 1877.

WILSON, GEORGE A., Private

On detached service from June 15, 1876, at Yellowstone Depot, Montana Territory. Born in Madison County, Ohio. Second enlistment on October 2, 1871, at age 32 in Louisville, Kentucky by Lieut. William Cooke. Previous occupation was blacksmith. Discharged on October 2, 1876, at Fort Abraham Lincoln, Dakota upon expiration of service, as a Private of excellent character. He had black eyes, dark hair, dark complexion and was 5'-7¾" in height.

WITT, HENRY, Private

On detached service from June 15, 1876, at Yellowstone Depot, Montana Territory. Born in Cincinnati, Ohio. Enlisted on December 9, 1875, at age 23 in Cincinnati by Lieut. Patrick Cusack. Previous occupation was piano maker. Discharged on December 8, 1880, at Fort Totten, Dakota upon expiration of service, as a Sergeant of excellent character. He had blue eyes, brown hair, fair complexion and was 5'-9" in height. In 1927 he resided at Ellison Apartments, Venice, California.

COMPANY L IN 1876

The company was a part of the garrison at Fort Totten, Dakota, until March 10 and then left with Co. E and arrived at Jamestown, Dakota, on March 13, traveling 83 miles. Lieut. Craycroft was relieved of temporary command on March 22 and left to join his company. Lieut. James Calhoun arrived from Fort Abraham Lincoln and assumed temporary command. The company arrived at Fort Lincoln on April 17 and joined the regiment in camp below the post, to take part in the Sioux expedition. The regiment left Fort Lincoln on May 17 and returned on September 26 and Company L occupied quarters.

Company L was one of eight companies that marched to the Cheyenne Agency via the left bank of the Missouri under the command of Colonel Samuel Sturgis, to disarm and dismount the Indians there. The company left Fort Lincoln on October 17 and returned on November 11 for winter station. Distance marched by the company during the year was 2,210 miles.

The following members were casualties in the Little Bighorn River fight: Killed: Second Lieut. John Crittenden, First Sergeant James Butler, Sergeants William Cashan and Amos Warren, Corporals William Gilbert, William Harrison, and John Seiler, Trumpeter Frederick Walsh, Saddler Charles Perkins, Farrier William Heath, Blacksmith Charles Siemon, Privates George Adams, William Andrews, Anthony Assadaly, Elmer Babcock, John Burke, Ami Chreer, James Galvan, Charles Graham, Henry Hamilton, Weston Harrington, Louis Hauggi, Francis Hughes, Thomas Kavanagh, Louis Lobering, Bartholomew Mahoney, Thomas Maxwell, John Miller, Charles McCarthy, Peter McGue, David O'Connell, Christian Reibold, Henry Roberts, Walter Rogers, Charles Scott, Bent Siemonson, Andrew Snow, Byron Tarbox, Edward Tessier, Thomas Tweed and Michael Vetter. Private Jasper Marshall was wounded with Major Marcus Reno's command.

Officers serving with the company in the year were: Captain Michael Sheridan, First Lieuts. Charles Braden and Edward Godfrey, Second Lieuts. John Crittenden, Edwin Eckerson and Loyd McCormick.*

* *Loyd Stone McCormick was born in Beverly, Ohio on Nov. 18, 1854. He entered the Military Academy from Ohio on July 1, 1872, and graduated 38th in his class. He was appointed Second Lieut. 10th Cavalry June 15, 1876. Transferred to the 7th Cavalry effective June 26, 1876, as a replacement for Lieut. Edwin Eckerson who was promoted. Promoted to First Lieut. June 30, 1878. Appointed regimental adjutant Sept. 14, 1887, to Sept. 13, 1891. Promoted to Captain July 17, 1895. Assigned to Subsistence Dept. Aug. 22, 1902. Promoted to Major, 7th Cavalry Apr. 15, 1903. Died at Fort Leavenworth, October 14, 1928.*

COMPANY L AT THE LITTLE BIGHORN

	Absent	Present	Wounded	Died OWRT	Killed	Survived
Captain	1					1
1st Lieut.	1					1
2nd Lieut.	1	1			1	1
1st Sergt.		1			1	
Sergeant	2	3			2	3
Corporal	1	3			3	1
Trumpeter		1			1	
Saddler		1			1	
Farrier		1			1	
Wagoner						
Blacksmith		1			1	
Private	7	46	1		34	19
Totals	13	58	1	0	45	26

RETURNS OF COMPANY L ON JUNE 30, 1876

Enlisted present for duty 11
Enlisted present for extra duty 1
Officers absent detached service 1
Officers absent sick 1
Enlisted absent detached service 8
Enlisted absent sick 3
Captain 1
First Lieutenant 1
Sergeants.. 3
Corporal 1
Privates 19
Total enlisted 23
Aggregate 25
Aggregate in May 69
Enlisted killed 44
Wounded 1
Horses serviceable 13
Horses lost 49

SHERIDAN, MICHAEL VINCENT, Captain

On detached service as aide-de-camp to the Lieutenant General of the Army. Born in Ohio, entered military service from there as a volunteer aide-de-camp to Brig. General Philip Sheridan from July 1, 1862, to September 7, 1863. Appointed Second Lieutenant, 2nd Missouri Volunteers, from September 7, 1863, to June 28, 1864. On June 29, 1864, he accepted appointment as Captain, aide-de-camp of Volunteers to date from May 18, 1864, and served on Maj. General Sheridan's staff until August 1, 1866. He participated in numerous engagements during the Civil War. After the surrender of Lee's Army of Northern Virginia at Appomattox Court House on April 9, 1865, he was transferred to the Department of the Gulf where he served until August 1, 1866, when he was mustered out of volunteer service. He received appointment as a Second Lieutenant, Fifth Regiment of Cavalry from February 23, 1866 until he received a commission as Captain, Seventh Regiment of Cavalry to rank from July 28, 1866. He served with the regiment until July 1, 1867, when he was appointed aide-de-camp to Maj. General Sheridan and served in that position for many years. Appointed aide-de-camp, with the rank of Lieutenant Colonel, on August 1, 1870, and Military Secretary to General Sheridan on April 9, 1878, to June 1, 1888. He was Colonel, aide-de-camp to General Sheridan from June 1 to August 5, 1888; Lieutenant Colonel, AAG, to July 9, 1892 and Colonel, AAG to January 25, 1897. Appointed Brigadier General, Volunteers on May 27, 1898, and honorably discharged from volunteer service on May 12, 1899. Promoted to Brigadier General, USA on April 15, 1902, and retired on April 16, 1902.

BRADEN, CHARLES, First Lieutenant

On sick leave from March 13, 1874. Born in Michigan; entered the Military Academy on October 17, 1865, by appointment from Michigan. He was the 2291st graduate, ranking 19th in his class of 39 which graduated on June 15, 1869. He was commissioned that day in the Seventh Regiment of Cavalry. He served with the regiment at Fort Leavenworth, Kansas and was in the expedition under Colonel Richard Dodge locating a road from Fort Lyon to Fort Union in 1870. His winter station was Fort Wallace, Kansas. In garrison in Columbia, Winnsborough and Yorkville, South Carolina until 1872 engaged in operations against the Ku Klux Klan. In April 1873 the regiment assembled at Yankton, Dakota and journeyed up the Missouri River to Fort Rice, Dakota from whence they departed on the Yellowstone expedition under Colonel David Stanley until September, 1873. Lieut. Braden was engaged in a chase after hostile Indians on August 4, 1873 and he was in a fight with Sioux Indians near the mouth of the Bighorn River on August 11 where, in command of the advance guard of 17 men, he was wounded in the left thigh, the bone being shattered. He was carried 400 miles on a litter and then sent to Fort Abraham Lincoln for treatment where he remained until October 31, 1873. From there he went to St. Paul until March, 1874, when he went on sick leave. He remained on leave until his retirement except for a brief period, from August to September, 1876 when he was on duty with the Mounted Recruiting Service. He received promotion to First Lieutenant on December 9, 1875, and on June 28, 1878, he was retired for disability for wounds received in action. He taught in private schools and was engaged in a manufacturing enterprise until 1882 when he returned to West Point. He received the brevet of First Lieutenant on February 27, 1890 for his gallant and meritorious services in action against the Indians on the Yellowstone expedition.

CRITTENDEN, JOHN JORDAN, Attached Second Lieutenant

Killed with Custer battalion on June 25 while attached for duty with Company L. Born on June 7, 1854, in Frankfort, Kentucky, the son of Colonel Thomas L. Crittenden. Appointed Second Lieutenant, 20th Infantry, to rank from October 15, 1875. On October 25 of the same year he suffered a gunshot wound in his eye due to an explosion of a cartridge at Fort Abercrombie, Dakota. He received operative treatment in Cincinnati and removal of one eye on November 25. John Crittenden departed with the Dakota column on May 17, 1876, to participate in the Sioux expedition. He was attached to Company L for duty in the absence of Lieut. Edwin Eckerson. On June 25 he was killed with the Custer battalion, and his remains were interred on the battlefield on June 28. On September 11, 1931, his remains were exhumed and re-interred on September 15, 1931, in the Custer Battlefield National Cemetery.

ECKERSON, EDWIN PHILIP, Second Lieutenant

On delay enroute to join Company L until June 19 and on change of station until June 27. Joined regiment on July 30th. Born in Washington Territory. A Presidential appointee from Fort Monroe, Virginia, to the Second Lieutenancy in Company L, 5th Cavalry on December 12, 1872. At Camp Grant, Arizona Territory he was placed in arrest, tried by general court for conduct to the prejudice of good order and military discipline and other offenses. He was found guilty and dismissed from the service. The promotion of Lieut. Charles Braden created a vacancy for a Second Lieutenant in Company L and, by direction of the President, Eckerson received the appointment on May 2, 1876. He accepted on May 19 and was granted a delay until June 19. He joined the regiment on July 30 and served in Montana and Dakota. Transferred to Company D and promoted to First Lieutenant to rank from June 25, 1876, to occupy the vacancy created by the promotion of Lieut. James M. Bell of Company D. He was tried by a general court and was dismissed from the service effective June 30, 1878. He died at Hays City, Kansas August 17, 1885.

BUTLER, JAMES, First Sergeant

Killed near the Custer battalion on June 25. Born in Albany, New York. Second enlistment on May 31, 1875, at age 33 at Fort A. Lincoln, Dakota by Lieut. Thomas Custer. The appointment of Butler as Commissionary Sergeant, U.S. Army, (from First Sergeant, Co. L, 7th Cavalry) was revoked on October 21, 1875 and he was re-assigned to the 7th Cavalry. His remains were probably re-interred in the Custer Battlefield National Cemetery. Listed as James Butler on the battle monument. He had grey eyes, black hair, fair complexion and was 5'-5½" in height.

> "Many corpses were found scattered over the field between Custer's line of defense, the river, and in the direction of Reno's Hill. These, doubtless, were of men who had attempted to escape; some of them may have been sent as couriers, by Custer. One of the first bodies I recognized and one of the nearest to the ford was that of Sergeant Butler of Tom Custer's troop. Sergeant Butler was a soldier of many years' experience and of known courage. The indications were that he had sold his life dearly, for near and under him were found many empty cartridge-shells." Edward Godfrey "Custer's Last Battle" *The Century Magazine,* January, 1892, XLIII:3, p. 381.

BENDER, HENRY, Sergeant
On detached service from June 15, 1876 at Yellowstone Depot, Montana Territory. Born in Berlin, Germany. Enlisted on January 28, 1873, at age 29 in New Orleans by Lieut. John Weston. Previous occupation was clerk. Discharged on January 24, 1878, at Fort Abraham Lincoln, Dakota, upon expiration of service, as a Sergeant of excellent character. He had hazel eyes, black hair, dark complexion and was 5'-9" in height.

CASHAN, WILLIAM, Sergeant
Killed in battle on June 25. Born in County Queens, Ireland. Third enlistment on December 17, 1872, at age 27 in Boston, by Captain Moses Harris. He had blue eyes, brown hair, fair complexion and was 5'-9" in height. Listed as Wm. Cashan on the battle monument. Listed as a Private in the *Bismarck Tribune Extra* July 6, 1876.

FINDEISEN, HUGO, Sergeant
On detached service from May 17, 1876, at Fort Abraham Lincoln, Dakota. Born in Altenburg, Germany. Enlisted on January 14, 1872, at age 36 in Yorkville, South Carolina by Lieut. Charles Braden. Previous occupation was clerk. Discharged on January 14, 1877, at Fort Lincoln upon expiration of service, as a Sergeant of excellent character. He had grey eyes, light hair, fair complexion and was 5'-11" in height. Listed as Hugo Findeisen on the Register of Enlistments, U.S. Army and the 7th Cavalry Returns, June 30, 1876 and elsewhere as Finderson.

MULLEN, JOHN, (JAMES HUGHES), Sergeant
Born in Baltimore, Maryland. Second enlistment on April 24, 1872, at age 22 at Fort Wallace, Kansas, by Lieut. Henry Nowlan. Previous occupation was laborer. His enlistment was cancelled when he surrendered on November 27, 1873, under General Order Nr. 102, AGO, War Department, 1873 as John Mullen, a deserter from Company K, 1st Artillery. He had grey eyes, light hair, fair complexion and was 5'-6" in height. Manuscript letter to Mrs. E. B. Custer from J. J. Mullin, Newburg, New York regarding his service with G. A. Custer, dated January 14, 1908, is in the E. B. Custer Collection, Custer Battlefield National Monument.

WARREN, AMOS B., Sergeant
Killed in battle on June 25. Born in Brooklyn, New York. Enlisted on September 13, 1873, at age 24¼ at Brooklyn by Captain Henry Carroll. Previous occupation was cooper. He had hazel eyes, brown hair, dark complexion and was 5'-10" in height. Listed as A. B. Warren on the battle monument.

GILBERT, WILLIAM H., Corporal
Killed in battle on June 25. Born in Philadelphia, Pennsylvania. Enlisted on October 2, 1873, at age 22 in New York City by Lieut. Edward Hunter. Previous occupation was butcher. He had blue eyes, brown hair, dark complexion and was 5'-7¼" in height. Listed as W. H. Gilbert on the battle monument.

HARRISON, WILLIAM H., Corporal
Killed in battle on June 25. Born in Gloucester, Massachusetts. Third

enlistment on October 9, 1875, at age 30 at Fort Totten, Dakota by Lieut. John Weston. He had hazel eyes, auburn hair, dark complexion and was 5'-7¾" in height. Listed as W. H. Harrison on the battle monument.

NUNAN, JOHN, Corporal
On detached service from June 15, 1876, at Yellowstone Depot, Montana Territory. Born in Fort Wayne, Indiana. Enlisted January 14, 1872, at age 25 in Yorkville, South Carolina, by Lieut. Charles Braden. Previous occupation was soldier. Discharged January 14, 1877, at Fort A. Lincoln, Dakota, upon expiration of service, as a Sergeant of excellent character. He had blue eyes, dark hair, fair complexion and was 5'-7" in height. Re-enlisted. A dispatch from Bismarck, Dakota dated October 31, 1878: "A singular development transpired at Fort Lincoln today. Mrs. Sergeant Noonan, who died last night, turns out to be a man. Mrs. Noonan was a laundress at the post and a most popular midwife. She was married three times and was one of the widows of the Custer massacre. Her husband is a member of the 7th Cavalry, now in the field. There is no explanation of the unnatural union except that the supposed Mexican woman was worth $10,000 and was able to buy her husband's silence. She had been with the 7th Cavalry nine years." *The Army and Navy Journal*, XVI:18, p. 284, December 7, 1878. In G. D. Wagner *Old Neutriment,* pp. 114-115, John Burkman related that Nonan (Nunan) was married to "Mrs. Nash" (after "Mrs. Nash" had been married to Clifton, a quartermaster clerk who deserted). "Corporal Noonan shot and killed himself at Fort Lincoln . . . He was the third husband of the supposed woman who recently died at Fort Lincoln, but who proved to be a perfectly formed man." *Dakota* (Sioux Falls) *Pantograph*, Dec. 11, 1878. Nunan died on November 3, 1878, and was interred at Fort Lincoln and re-interred in the Custer Battlefield National Cemetery, Grave 573A.

SEILER, JOHN, Corporal
Killed in battle on June 25. Born in Bavaria, Germany. Enlisted on February 12, 1872, at age 21 in Buffalo, New York by Lieut. Albert Forse. Previous occupation was laborer. He had grey eyes, light hair, fair complexion and was 5'-8" in height. Listed as Jno. Seiler on the battle monument and elsewhere as Seiller.

WALSH, FREDERICK, Trumpeter
Killed with the Custer battalion on June 25. Born in Carlisle, Pennsylvania. Enlisted on December 1, 1872, at age 21 in Louisville, Kentucky by Lieut. William Cooke. Previous occupation was laborer. He had hazel eyes, brown hair, dark complexion and was 5'-7" in height. Listed as Fred'k Walsh on the battle monument.

PERKINS, CHARLES, Saddler
Killed in battle on June 25. Born in York County, Maine. Enlisted on August 18, 1875, at age 27 in St. Louis, Missouri by Lieut. John Thompson. Previous occupation was shoemaker. He had black eyes, dark hair, dark complexion and was 5'-10" in height. Listed as Chas. Perkins on the battle monument.

HEATH, WILLIAM H., Farrier
Killed in battle on June 25. Born in Staffordshire, England. Enlisted on

October 9, 1875, at age 27 in Cincinnati, Ohio by Lieut. Patrick Cusack. Previous occupation was coachman. He had blue eyes, brown hair, dark complexion and was 5'-7¼" in height. Listed as W. H. Heath on the battle monument and elsewhere as Kiefer.

SIEMON, CHARLES, Blacksmith
Killed in battle on June 25. Born in Copenhagen, Denmark. Second enlistment on July 19, 1872, at age 28 in Yorkville, South Carolina by Lieut. John Aspinwall. He had grey eyes, brown hair, dark complexion and was 5'-7½" in height. Listed as Chas. Siemon on the battle monument and elsewhere as Chas. Seimon, Charles Swan, Charles Simon and Pvt. Lunon.

ABRAMS, WILLIAM G., Private
Born in Baltimore, Maryland. Enlisted on September 1, 1871, at age 33 in Winnsboro, South Carolina, by Lieut. Charles Braden. Previous occupation was soldier. Discharged on August 5, 1876, at camp at the mouth of Rosebud Creek, Montana Territory per General Order Nr. 24, War Department, AGO, 1859, as a Private. He had black eyes, dark hair, dark complexion and was 5'-10" in height.

ADAMS, GEORGE E., Private
Killed in battle on June 25. Born in Minorsville, Pennsylvania. Second enlistment on January 27, 1874, at age 27½ at Fort Abraham Lincoln, Dakota by Lieut. John Weston. Previous occupation was soldier. He had blue eyes, light hair, fair complexion and was 5'-8½" in height. Listed as G. E. Adams on the battle monument.

ANDREWS, WILLIAM, Private
Killed in battle on June 25. Born in Prussia. Enlisted on May 21, 1875, at age 30 at Fort Abraham Lincoln, Dakota by Lieut. John Walker. Previous occupation was soldier. He had blue eyes, dark hair, fair complexion and was 5'-6½" in height. Listed as Wm. Andrews on the battle monument.

ASSADALY, ANTHONY, Private
Killed in battle on June 25. Born in Prussia. First enlistment on June 23, 1865, at age 23 in Philadelphia by Lieut. J. Mix. Discharged on June 22, 1868, from Company I, 3rd New York Volunteer Cavalry. Second enlistment on July 21, 1868, at Fort Leavenworth, Kansas by Lieut. Myles Moylan. Assigned to Company F, 7th Cavalry. Discharged on July 27, 1873. Third enlistment on July 21, 1873, at age 31 in St. Paul, Minnesota by Colonel Samuel Sturgis. He had blue eyes, dark hair, fair complexion and was 5'-3" in height and was illiterate. Listed as Anthony Assadalig on his first Oath of Enlistment; as Anthony Assadaly on the second Oath and as Antony Assadily on the third Oath. Listed as Anthony Assadily on the battle monument, Custer Battlefield. Listed elsewhere as Arodelsky and as Assdely.

BABCOCK, ELMER, Private
Killed in battle on June 25. Born in Pharsalia, New York. Enlisted on September 21, 1875, at age 21¼ by Lieut. Henry Lawton. Previous occupation was farmer. He had brown eyes, dark hair, dark complexion and was 5'-6½" in height. Listed as Elmer Babcock on the battle monument.

BANKS, CHARLES, Private
Born in Dublin, Ireland. Second enlistment on September 29, 1873, at age 28 in St. Paul, Minnesota by Lieut. Henry Nowlan. Discharged on September 29, 1878, at Camp James G. Sturgis, near Bear Butte, Dakota, upon expiration of service, as a Private of good character. He had brown eyes, brown hair, fair complexion and was 5'-6½" in height.

BROWN, NATHAN T., Private
Born in Marion County, Indiana. Second enlistment on November 25, 1874, at age 31 at Fort A. Lincoln, Dakota by Lieut. William Cooke. Killed on Sept. 13, 1877, at Canyon Creek, Montana Territory, in an engagement with Nez Perce Indians. Interred on the battlefield; later re-interred at the Custer Battlefield National Cemetery, Grave 1415 (5) B. He had grey eyes, black hair, dark complexion and was 5'-7" in height. Listed as Nathan T. Brown in the Register of Enlistments, U.S. Army and on the internment records at the Custer Battlefield National Cemetery and elsewhere as Nathan J. Brown.

BURKE, JOHN, Private
Killed in battle on June 25. Born in Oneida, New York. Enlisted on September 29, 1873, at age 21 in New York City by Lieut. Edward Hunter. Previous occupation was blacksmith. He had brown eyes, brown hair, dark complexion and was 5'-8¾" in height. Listed as Jno. Burke on the battle monument.

BURKMAN, JOHN, Private
On duty with the pack train. In the hilltop fight. Born January 10, 1839, in Alleghany County, Pennsylvania. At the time of enlistment he gave his birthplace as Pennsylvania but in G. D. Wagner *Old Neutriment*, p. 33, he stated that he was actually born in Germany. Burkman was a teamster for William Bent prior to the Civil War. He enlisted in the Fifth Missouri Volunteers and was engaged in the battle of Wilson's Creek on August 10, 1861. In Gen. Sibley's expedition of 1863 and Colonel David Stanley's expedition to the Yellowstone River in 1873 and in the Black Hills expedition under Lieut. Col. George Custer in July and August, 1874. First enlistment in the 7th Cavalry was in the fall of 1870 at age 28 in Company A. He was re-enlisted on September 1, 1875, at age 35 at Fort A. Lincoln, Dakota by Lieut. James Calhoun. In the Sioux expedition of 1876 and the Nez Perce campaign of 1877 with Colonel Samuel Sturgis. Discharged May 17, 1879, at Fort A. Lincoln for disability, as a Private of good character. Died on November 6, 1925, at Billings, Montana of gunshot wounds by his own hand. Interred on Nov. 10, 1925, in the Custer Battlefield National Cemetery, Grave 1463 (941) A. He had hazel eyes, dark hair, ruddy complexion and was 5'-7" in height.

CHREER, AMI, Private
Killed in battle on June 25. Born in Pittsburgh, Pennsylvania. Enlisted on September 21, 1872, at age 21 in Harrisburg, Pennsylvania by Lieut. John Mahnken. Previous occupation was farmer. He had grey eyes, dark hair, light complexion, was 5'-11¾" in height and was illiterate. Listed as Ami Chreer in the Register of Enlistments, U.S. Army and on his Oath of Enlistment and elsewhere as Ami Cheever and Andrew Hester.

COLWELL, JOHN R., Private

Sick in the hospital at Fort Abraham Lincoln, Dakota from May 17, 1876. Born in Champaign County, Illinois. Enlisted on September 16, 1875, at age 30 in Chicago by Lieut. Edmund Luff. Previous occupation was clerk. Discharged on September 15, 1880, at Fort Lincoln upon expiration of service, as Sergeant of good character. He had brown eyes, brown hair, fair complexion and was 5'-4" in height.

CONLON, MICHAEL, Private

On detached service from May 17, 1876 at Yellowstone Depot, Montana Territory. Born in Rondout, New York. Second enlistment on April 13, 1872, at age 27 at Yorkville, South Carolina by Lieut. Charles Braden. Discharged on April 13, 1877, at Fort A. Lincoln, Dakota upon expiration of service, as a Private of very good character. He had hazel eyes, brown hair, dark complexion and was 5'-7" in height.

CRISFIELD, WILLIAM B., Private

Killed in battle on June 25. Born in Kent, England. Second enlistment on February 1, 1875, at age 39 at Fort Abraham Lincoln, Dakota by Lieut. Thomas Custer. He had grey eyes, black hair, ruddy complexion and was 5'-7" in height. Listed as W. B. Crisfield on the battle monument.

DUGGAN, JOHN, Private

Killed in battle on June 25. Born in Worcester, Massachusetts. Enlisted on September 24, 1873, at age 24 in Boston by Lieut. James Ropes. Previous occupation was carpenter. He had grey eyes, dark hair, fair complexion and was 5'-9½" in height. Listed as Jno. Duggan on the battle monument.

DYE, WILLIAM, Private

Killed in battle on June 25. Born in Marietta, Ohio. Enlisted on September 23, 1875, at age 25 in Cincinnati by Lieut. Patrick Cusack. Previous occupation was butcher. He had brown eyes, black hair, fair complexion and was 5'-9½" in height. Listed as Wm. Dye on the battle monument.

ETZLER, WILLIAM, Private

Born in Wheeling, West Virginia. Enlisted on September 9, 1873, at age 21 in Cincinnati, Ohio by Lieut. Adam Kramer. Previous occupation was cigar maker. Discharged on September 9, 1878, at Fort Abraham Lincoln, Dakota, upon expiration of service, as a Private of good character. He had blue eyes, dark hair, fair complexion and was 5'-6½" in height.

GALVAN, JAMES J., Private

Killed in battle on June 25. Born in Liverpool, England. Enlisted on September 28, 1875, at age 26 in Boston, Massachusetts by Lieut. Henry Lawton. Previous occupation was laborer. He had grey eyes, dark hair, dark complexion and was 5'-6¾" in height. Listed as J. J. Galvan on the battle monument and elsewhere as Galvin and Calran.

GRAHAM, CHARLES, Private

Killed in battle on June 25. Born in Tyrone County, Ireland. Second enlistment on July 1, 1872, at age 35 in Yorkville, South Carolina by Lieut. John Weston. He had blue eyes, brown hair, florid complexion and was 5'-6¾" in height. Listed as Chas. Graham on the battle monument.

HAMILTON, HENRY, Private

Killed in battle on June 25. Born in Dexter, New York. Served in the Civil War. Second enlistment in the 7th Cavalry on January 20, 1872, at age 29 in New Orleans, Louisiana by Lieut. John Weston. Previous occupation was cook. He had blue eyes, brown hair, fair complexion and was 5'-6¼" in height. Listed as Henry Hamilton on the battle monument. His niece, Mrs. Susan Kirschermann of Yakima, Washington, stated that Henry Hamilton ran away from home when he was very young and became a drummer boy in the Civil War.

HARRINGTON, WESTON, Private

Killed in battle on June 25. Born in Alton, Ohio on February 9, 1855, the son of Peter and Mary A. Harrington. Peter Harrington was born July 14, 1820, and died February 17, 1904. Mary Harrington was born May 10, 1828, and died July 14, 1875. Ella, a sister of Weston, was born January 29, 1859, and died August 27, 1860. Weston Harrington was enlisted on November 4, 1872, at a stated age of 21 in Columbus, Ohio by Lieut. James Wheelan. Previous occupation was laborer. He had brown eyes, brown hair, fair complexion and was 5'-8" in height. Listed as Weston Harrington on the battle monument and on a gravestone in Alton Cemetery, Prairie Township, Franklin County, Ohio. Listed elsewhere as Harnington.

HAUGGI, LOUIS, Private

Killed in battle on June 25. Born in Alsace, Germany. Enlisted on October 6, 1873, at age 21½ in Cincinnati, Ohio by Lieut. Adam Kramer. Previous occupation was farmer. He had brown eyes, light hair, fair complexion and was 5'-7" in height. Listed as Louis Hauggi on the battle monument and as a Louis Hanggi in the Register of Enlistments, U.S. Army and elsewhere as Louis Hange.

HOEHN, MAX, Private

On detached service from June 15, 1876 at Yellowstone Depot, Montana Territory. Born in Berlin, Germany. Enlisted on October 4, 1873, at age 21½ at St. Louis Barracks by Captain Charles Bendire. Previous occupation was clerk. Discharged on October 4, 1878, at Fort Abraham Lincoln, Dakota upon expiration of service, as a Private of excellent character. He had grey eyes, light hair, fair complexion and was 5'-6¾" in height.

HUGHES, FRANCIS F., Private

Killed in battle on June 25. Born in Leavenworth, Kansas. Enlisted on May 22, 1875, at age 21 at Fort Abraham Lincoln, Dakota by Lieut. Thomas Custer. Previous occupation was laborer. He had blue eyes, brown hair, light complexion and was 5'-7¾" in height. Listed as F. F. Hughes on the battle monument and in the Register of Enlistments, U.S. Army and elsewhere as F. L. Hughes and Francis T. Hughes.

KAVANAGH, THOMAS G., Private

Killed in battle on June 25. Born in Dublin, Ireland. Second enlistment on January 16, 1873, at age 28 in New Orleans, Louisiana by Lieut. John Weston.

Previous occupation was farmer. He had grey eyes, red hair, ruddy complexion and was 5'-11¼" in height. Listed as T. G. Kavanagh on the battle monument and elsewhere as Kavaugh.

KEEGAN, MICHAEL, Private
On detached service from June 15, 1876, at Yellowstone Depot, Montana Territory. Born in Wexford, Ireland. Fifth enlistment on August 6, 1872, at age 40 in Yorkville, South Carolina, by Lieut. John Weston. Previous occupation was soldier. Discharged on December 15, 1876, at Fort Abraham Lincoln, Dakota for disability, as a Private of good character. He had blue eyes, light hair, ruddy complexion and was 5'-6" in height.

LEPPER, FREDERICK, Private
On detached service (sick?) from June 15, 1876, at Yellowstone Depot, Montana Territory. Born in Hamilton County Ohio. Enlisted on November 12, 1872, at age 23 in Cincinnati by Lieut. James Wheelan. Previous occupation was carriage painter. Discharged on November 12, 1877, at Fort Abraham Lincoln, Dakota upon expiration of service, as a Private of excellent character. He had hazel eyes, brown hair, fair complexion and was 5'-7¾" in height.

LOBERING, LOUIS, Private
Killed in battle on June 25. Born in Hanover, Germany. Third enlistment on May 20, 1875, at age 40 at Fort Abraham Lincoln, Dakota by Lieut. Thomas Custer. He had blue eyes, brown hair, ruddy complexion and was 5'-6¾" in height. Listed as Louis Lobering on the battle monument and elsewhere as Lewis Lovering.

LOGUE, WILLIAM J., Private
With the pack train detail on June 25? Born in New York City. Enlisted on April 7, 1873, at age 27 in Cairo, Illinois, by Lieut. Charles Braden. Previous occupation was carpenter. Discharged on April 7, 1878, at Fort Abraham Lincoln, Dakota upon expiration of service, as a Private of good character. He had grey eyes, light hair, fair complexion and was 5'-8½" in height. Listed as William J. Logue in the Register of Enlistments, U.S. Army.

MAHONEY, BARTHOLOMEW, Private
Killed in battle on June 25. Born in Cork, Ireland. Enlisted on October 29, 1872, at age 26 in Boston by Captain Moses Harris. Previous occupation was teamster. He had hazel eyes, dark hair, sallow complexion and was 5'-10" in height. Listed as Bartholomew Mahoney on the battle monument and elsewhere as Berthol Mahoney.

MARSHALL, JASPER, Private
With the pack train detail on June 25 (?). Wounded in the left foot in the hilltop fight on June 26. Transported to Fort Abraham Lincoln, Dakota, on the steamer *Far West*. Born in Warren County, Ohio. Enlisted on September 22, 1875, at age 22 in Cincinnati, Ohio, by Lieut. Patrick Cusack. Previous occupation was farmer. Discharged on February 9, 1877, at Fort Lincoln for disability, as a Private. He had grey eyes, black hair, dark complexion and was 5'-5½" in height. Listed as Jasper Marshall in the Register of Enlistments, U.S. Army, and elsewhere as Thomas Marshall.

MAXWELL, THOMAS E., Private

Killed in battle on June 25. Born in Alleghany, Pennsylvania. Enlisted on December, 27, 1872, at age 22 in St. Louis, Missouri by Lieut. Oscar Elting. Previous occupation was laborer. He had blue eyes, brown hair, ruddy complexion and was 5'-5½" in height. Listed as T. E. Maxwell on the battle monument.

MILLER, JOHN, Private

Killed in battle on June 25. Born in Philadelphia, Pennsylvania. Second enlistment on September 4, 1875, at age 26 in St. Louis, Missouri by Lieut. John Thompson. He had hazel eyes, brown hair, dark complexion and was 5'-8" in height. Listed as Jno. Miller on the battle monument.

MOORE, LANSING, Private

In the pack train detail on June 25. Born September 27, 1846, at Hoboken, New Jersey. He left home at about the age of 14 and was enlisted on September 27, 1875, at a represented age of 21 in New York City by Lieut. John Babcock. Previous occupation was carpenter. In the Sioux expedition of 1876, during the march up Rosebud Creek, he was detailed to the pack train and was subsequently in the hilltop fight on the Little Bighorn. Discharged on September 26, 1880, at Fort A. Lincoln, Dakota upon expiration of service, as a Private of excellent character. He had blue eyes, brown hair, ruddy complexion and was 5'-8" in height. He married Sarah, daughter of John Belcher, on July 4, 1881, at the Belcher ranch, Custer County, Montana Territory, and settled in Sheridan County, near Sheridan, Wyoming in 1882. Leaving his squatter claim in 1885 he was employed on ranches near Lily Park, Colorado until 1890 when he went to Rawlins, Wyoming, where he freighted for five or six years, hauling from Rawlins to Lander and Fort Washakie. He attended the 50th Anniversary celebration of the Little Bighorn River fight on June 25, 1926 at the Custer Battlefield National Monument. For two or three years prior to his death he was employed as a guard at the Wyoming State Penitentiary, later receiving a pension. He died July 28, 1931, at Rawlins and was interred there. His wife, Sarah, died on January 19, 1951, and was interred beside Lansing.

McCARTHY, CHARLES, Private

Killed in battle on June 25. Born in Philadelphia, Pennsylvania. Second enlistment on September 30, 1873, at age 28 in St. Paul, Minnesota by Lieut. Henry Nowlan. He had blue eyes, brown hair, dark complexion and was 5'-7¼" in height. Listed as Chas. McCarthy on the battle monument.

McGUE, PETER, Private

Killed in battle on June 25. Born in Port Henry, New York. Enlisted on December 23, 1872, at age 25 5/12 in Troy, New York by Captain Theodore Wint. Previous occupation was laborer. He had brown eyes, black hair, dark complexion and was 5'-4" in height. Listed as Peter McGue on the battle monument.

McHUGH, PHILIP, Private

Born in Donigal, Ireland. Second enlistment on June 4, 1874, at age of 35 in St. Paul, Minnesota by Lieut. William Cooke. Discharged on June 4, 1879, at

Fort Abraham Lincoln, Dakota upon expiration of service, as a Private of good character. He had hazel eyes, black hair, ruddy complexion and was 5'-6½" in height.

McPEAKE, ALEXANDER, Private

On detached service from June 15, 1876, at Yellowstone Depot, Montana Territory. Born in Canonsburg, Washington County, Pennsylvania, the son of Harmon and Jane Rankin McPeake and the youngest of seven brothers and two sisters. Resided at McConnell's Mills, Pennsylvania. Enlisted on March 15, 1871, at age 21 7/12 in Pittsburgh by Lieut. James M. Bell. Previous occupation was teamster. He had grey eyes, light hair, fair complexion and was 5'-7¾" in height. Discharged on June 24, 1877, at camp on Sunday Creek, Montana Territory, as a Private in Company L. Re-enlisted on April 19, 1878, and discharged on April 18, 1883 at Fort Yates, Dakota, as a Private in Company D, 17th Infantry. Enlisted on May 7, 1883 in Pittsburgh and assigned to Company C, 6th Infantry. Deserted on April 13, 1885 at Fort Douglas, Utah, as a Private. No record of apprehension. An account of this soldier in *The Morning Observer*, Washington, Pennsylvania, October 3-19, 1932.

O'CONNELL, DAVID J., Private

Killed in battle on June 25. Born in Cork, Ireland. Third enlistment on May 20, 1874, at age 30 at Fort Abraham Lincoln, Dakota, by Lieut. Goerge Wallace. He had dark eyes, brown hair, ruddy complexion and was 5'-7½" in height. Listed as D. J. O'Connell on the battle monument and elsewhere as Daniel J. O'Connell.

REIBOLD, CHRISTIAN, Private

Killed in battle on June 25. Born in Buffalo, New York. Enlisted on August 1, 1871, at age 21 in Chicago by Captain Samuel Young. Previous occupation was shoemaker. Deserted on April 30, 1872; apprehended on April 29, 1874. He had grey eyes, light hair, light complexion and was 5'-6" in height. Listed as Christian Reibold on the battle monument and elsewhere as Riebold and Reinbold.

ROBERTS, HENRY, Private

Killed in battle on June 25. Born in London, England. Enlisted on November 11, 1872, at age 22¾ in Toledo, Ohio by Captain Samuel Young. Previous occupation was laborer. He had blue eyes, light hair, light complexion and was 5'-9" in height. Listed as Henry Roberts on the battle monument. Not listed among the casualties in the *Bismarck Tribune Extra*, July 6, 1876.

ROGERS, WALTER B., Private

Killed in battle on June 25. Born in Washington, Pennsylvania. Enlisted on June 6, 1873, at age 26 in Baltimore, Maryland by Lieut. Rafris. Previous occupation was clerk. Deserted on September 8, 1873; apprehended on September 12, 1873. He had brown eyes, dark hair, medium complexion and was 5'-8¼" in height. Listed as W. B. Rogers on the battle monument and elsewhere as Rodgers and W. B. Roberts and Walter D. Rogers.

ROSE, PETER E., Private

Born in Rockford, Illinois, Enlisted on September 28, 1875, at age 23 in

Chicago by Lieut. Edmund Luff. Previous occupation was cooper. Deserted on March 19, 1878. He had brown eyes, black hair, dark complexion and was 5'-9" in height.

SCHMIDT, CHARLES, Private
Killed in battle on June 25. Born in Wurtemburg, Germany. Enlisted on November 14, 1872, at age 23 in New York City by Captain Edwin Sumner. Previous occupation was laborer. He had brown eyes, brown hair, fair complexion and was 5'-8½" in height. Listed as Chas. Schmidt on the battle monument and as Henry Schmidt elsewhere.

"When Custer started his last march up the Rosebud on the morning of June 22, 1876, many of the recruits had obtained horses and accompanied him. Horner's buddy, Charles Schmidt, private in "L" company, secured the horse of Michael Ragan of "K" company, a Civil War veteran, and went in Ragan's place. *Jacob Horner and the Indian Campaigns of 1876 and 1877* by U. L. Burdick and E. D. Hart, 1942, Baltimore, p. 14.

SCOTT, CHARLES, Private
Killed in battle on June 25. Born in Scotland. Enlisted on November 20, 1873, at age 22 at Fort Abraham Lincoln, Dakota by Lieut. Francis Gibson. Previous occupation was cook. He had blue eyes, brown hair, fair complexion and was 5'-9" in height. Listed as Chas. Scott on the battle monument.

SIEMONSON, BENT, Private
Killed in battle on June 25. Born in Milwaukee, Wisconsin. Enlisted on February 6, 1872, at age 21¼ at Chicago by Captain Samuel Young. Previous occupation was laborer. He had blue eyes, light hair, light complexion and was 5'-5½" in height. Listed as Bent Siemonson on the battle monument and as Bernt Siemonson in the Register of Enlistments, U.S. Army and elsewhere as Semonson and Bent Seimonson and Burt Semenson.

SNOW, ANDREW, Private
Killed in battle on June 25. Born in Surrell, Canada. Enlisted on September 24, 1875, at age 22 in Boston by Lieut. Henry Lawton. Previous occupation was hostler. He had hazel eyes, black hair, ruddy complexion and was 5'-5 1/8" in height. Listed as And'w Snow on the battle monument.

SPRAGUE, OTTO, Private
On detached service from May 17, 1876, at Fort Abraham Lincoln, Dakota. Born in Mineral Point, Wisconsin. Enlisted on August 27, 1875, at age 21 in Chicago by Lieut. Edmund Luff. Previous occupation was machinist. Discharged on August 26, 1880, at Fort Lincoln, upon expiration of service, as a Private of good character. He had grey eyes, light brown hair, dark complexion and was 5'-7¾" in height.

STOFFEL, HENRY, Private
Born in Philadelphia, Pennsylvania. Enlisted on January 22, 1872, at age 21 in Philadelphia by Captain Samuel Whitside. Previous occupation was farmer.

Deserted on July 6, 1873; surrendered on November 2, 1874. Discharged on May 18, 1878, at Fort Abraham Lincoln, Dakota upon expiration of service, as a Private of excellent character. He had blue eyes, light hair, fair complexion and was 5'-9" in height.

SULLIVAN, TIMOTHY, Private
   Born in Chelsea, Massachusetts. Second enlistment on September 17, 1875, at age 31 in Chicago by Lieut. Edmund Luff. Discharged on September 16, 1880, at Fort Abraham Lincoln, Dakota upon expiration of service, as a Private of good character. He had hazel eyes, brown hair, dark complexion and was 5'-4½" in height.

TARBOX, BYRON L., Private
   Killed in battle on June 25. Born in Brookville, Maine. Enlisted on September 22, 1875, at age 23 in Boston by Lieut. Henry Lawton. Previous occupation was shoemaker. He had grey eyes, dark hair, fair complexion and was 5'-6¼" in height. Tarbox was a half-brother of Private William Morris, Company M, 7th Cavalry. Listed on the battle monument as Byron Tarbox.

TESSIER, EDMOND D., Private
   Killed in battle on June 25. Born in Montreal, Canada. Second enlistment on November 26, 1871, at age 24 in Yorkville, South Carolina by Lieut. Henry Nowlan. Previous occupation was clerk. He had hazel eyes, dark hair, dark complexion and was 5'-7½" in height. Listed as E. D. Tessier on the battle monument, and as Edmond D. Tessier in the Register of Enlistments, U.S. Army, and elsewhere as Tessler.

TWEED, THOMAS S., Private
   Killed in battle on June 25. Born in North Liberty, Ohio. Enlisted on September 1, 1875, at age 22 in Cincinnati, Ohio by Lieut. Patrick Cusack. Previous occupation was printer. He had grey eyes, brown hair, fair complexion and was 5'-5¼" in height. Listed as T. S. Tweed on the battle monument and elsewhere as T. W. Tweed and Thomas L. Tweed.

VETTER, MICHAEL, Private
   Killed in battle on June 25. Born in Hessen, Germany. Enlisted on October 4, 1875, at age 23 in Pittsburgh, Pennsylvania by Lieut. Thomas Gregg. Previous occupation was carpenter. He had blue eyes, light hair, fair complexion and was 5'-9¼" in height. Listed as Mich'l Vetter on the battle monument and elsewhere as Veller.

COMPANY M IN 1876

The company was a part of the garrison at Fort Rice, Dakota, until May 5 when they marched to Fort A. Lincoln and joined the regiment in camp below the post to take part in the Sioux expedition. The regiment left Fort Lincoln on May 17 and Company M was part of a scouting party that Lieut. Col. George Custer took up the Little Missouri for 22 miles and returned on May 30. The regiment returned to Fort Lincoln on September 26 and the company went into camp.

Company M was one of eight companies that went to the Cheyenne Agency via the left bank of the Missouri under the command of Colonel Samuel Sturgis to disarm and dismount the Indians there. The company left Fort Lincoln on October 17 and left the camp across the river from the Cheyenne Agency on November 4. As the command passed opposite Fort Rice, Companies M and H left the column and took winter station there. The company marched 1,777 miles in the year.

The following members were casualties in the Little Bighorn River fight. Killed: Sec. Lieut. James Sturgis; Sergeant Miles O'Hara, Corporals Frederick Streing and Henry Cody (Henry Scollin), Privates Henry Gordon, Henry Klotzbucher, George Lorentz, William Meyer, George Smith, David Summers, Henry Turley, Henry Voight. Wounded: Sergeants Patrick Carey, and Charles White; Privates, Frank Braun, John H. Meier, William Morris, Daniel Newell, Edward Pigford, James Tanner, Roman Rutten, Thomas Varner, Charles Wiedman and James Wilbur. Private John Ryan died in the hospital at Fort Rice on February 16 of consumption. Private Frank Braun died on October 4 in the hospital at Fort Lincoln of wounds received in the Little Bighorn River fight.

Officers serving with the company in the year were: Captain Thomas French, First Lieutenant Edward Mathey, Second Lieutenants James Sturgis and John Gresham.* Lieut. Gresham was replacement for Lieut. Sturgis.

* John Chowning Gresham was born in Virginia and was appointed to the Military Academy from that state. He graduated from the Academy in 1876, and was appointed a Second Lieut. 3rd Cavalry on June 15 that year. Transferred to the 7th Cavalry on June 26, 1876. Promoted to First Lieut. June 28, 1878, and Captain April 8, 1892, and Major, 6th Cavalry September 17, 1901. Awarded the Medal of Honor May 26, 1895, for distinguished gallantry in voluntarily leading a party to dislodge Indians concealed in a ravine at Wounded Knee Creek, South Dakota December 29, 1890, while serving as a First Lieut. 7th Cavalry.

COMPANY M AT THE LITTLE BIGHORN

	Absent	Present	Wounded	Died OWRT	Killed	Survived
Captain		1				1
1st Lieut.		1				1
2nd Lieut.		1			1	
1st Sergt.		1				1
Sergeant	1	4	2		1	4
Corporal		3			2	1
Trumpeter		2				2
Saddler		1				1
Farrier	1					1
Wagoner	1					1
Blacksmith						
Private	6	44	11	3	7	40
Totals	9	58	13	3	11	53

COMPANY M ON JUNE 30, 1876

Officers present for duty 2
Enlisted present for duty 27
Enlisted present extra duty 6
Enlisted present sick 10
Enlisted absent detached service 7
Enlisted absent sick 1
Enlisted absent in arrest 1
Captain 1
First Lieutenant 1
First Sergeant 1
Sergeants 4
Corporal 1
Trumpeters 2
Farrier 1
Saddler 1
Wagoner 1
Privates 41
Total enlisted 52
Aggregate 54
Aggregate in May 67
Officer killed 1
Enlisted killed 12
Wounded 10
Horses serviceable 37
Horses unserviceable 8
Horses lost 19

FRENCH, THOMAS HENRY, Captain

In command of Company M in the valley and hilltop fights. Born on March 4, 1843, near Baltimore, Maryland. He enlisted in the Tenth Regiment of Infantry from January 13 to June 9, 1864, and was commissioned a Second Lieutenant in that regiment to rank from May 18, 1864. Promoted to First Lieutenant on June 23, 1864. He served in the field in the war and was brevetted Captain August 18, 1864, for his gallant services in operations on the Weldon Railroad. Promoted to Captain on March 26, 1868; unassigned during the organization on May 19, 1869; assigned to the 7th Cavalry on January 1, 1871. While with the 7th Cavalry he was in several engagements with Indians. In the Sioux expedition from May 17, 1876. On September 13, 1877, he was in the encounter with Chief Joseph and the Nez Perce Indians at Canyon Creek. In October, 1878, Captain French was escorting a wagon train and a detachment of the 7th Cavalry from Fort Abraham Lincoln to Camp Ruhlen, Dakota. Court martialed on January 13, 1879, and sentenced to be dismissed from the service. President Hayes, upon the recommendation of the department commander, commuted the sentence to suspension from rank on half pay for one year. Retired on February 5, 1880; the unexecuted portion of the court martial was remitted. At the age of 39, Captain French died at Planter's House, Leavenworth, Kansas on March 27, 1882. Interred in the National Cemetery, Fort Leavenworth.

MATHEY, EDWARD GUSTAVE, First Lieutenant

In command of the pack train. In the hilltop fight. Born on October 27, 1837, in France. He enlisted from Indiana as a Private, 17th Indiana Volunteer Infantry in June, 1861, and was promoted to Sergeant, Company C, to rank from May 31, 1861. Appointed Second Lieutenant in the same regiment effective May 1, 1862. On August 10, 1862, he resigned and was appointed a Second Lieutenant in the 81st Indiana Volunteer Infantry to rank from September 1, 1862. He fought with his regiment during the rest of the Civil War and was engaged in the battle at Stone River, the skirmish at Liberty Gap and the battle of Chickamauga. Promoted to First Lieutenant effective March 21, 1863, and Captain on November 8, 1863. He participated in the demonstration before Rocky Faced Ridge, the battle of Resaca, the action near Kingston, the battle of Kenesaw Mountain, the action at Marietta and the siege of Atlanta. Engaged in the battle of Jonesborough, the action at Lovejoy Station, the battle at Franklin and the battle of Nashville. Promoted to Major effective September 12, 1864; mustered out of volunteer service on June 13, 1865. Appointed a Second Lieutenant, Seventh Regiment of Cavalry, to rank from September 24, 1867, and promoted to First Lieutenant on May 10, 1870. On May 17, 1876, Lieut. Mathey departed with the 7th Cavalry to participate in the Sioux expedition. From June 22 he commanded the pack train accompanying the 7th Cavalry and on June 25-26 he was in the hilltop fight on the Little Bighorn River. He returned to Fort Lincoln on September 26. Engaged in the 1877 campaign against Chief Joseph's band of Nez Perce. Promoted to Captain to rank from September 30, 1877, after the Snake Creek fight near the Bear Paw Mountains. On December 11, 1896, Mathey retired with the rank of Major for disability incurred in line of duty and was promoted to Lieut. Colonel, USA, retired, on April 23, 1904. Died July 17, 1915, at Mercy Hospital, Denver, Colorado in his 78th year. Interred in the National Cemetery, Arlington, Virginia. Survived by his invalid wife and his daughter, Julia P. Mathey.

STURGIS, JAMES GARLAND, Second Lieutenant

Killed with the Custer battalion on June 25. Born on January 24, 1854, in Albuquerque, New Mexico, the son of Colonel (Brevet Major General) Samuel Davis Sturgis, commanding officer of the Seventh Regiment of Cavalry, and Mamie T. Sturgis. He entered the Military Academy on July 1, 1871, by an appointment at large. He was the 2578th graduate, ranking 29th in his class of 43 graduates. He graduated on June 16, 1875, and was commissioned Second Lieutenant in the 7th Cavalry on the same day. He accepted the commission on July 3rd. After graduation he was on leave until August 16th. At the request of his father he was placed on temporary court martial duty at St. Louis Depot until October 15. He departed from St. Louis in October to join his company at Fort Rice, Dakota, where he arrived on October 29, remaining in winter station there. Lieut. Sturgis departed on May 17, 1876, from Fort Abraham Lincoln, Dakota with the 7th Cavalry to participate in the Sioux expedition. He was assigned to Company M but was on duty with Company E (Lieut. Algernon Smith, commanding) on June 25 when he was missing with the Custer battalion and presumed killed at the age of 22. Camp James G. Sturgis, on the northwest slope of Bear Butte, Dakota, was established on July 1, 1878, and named in his honor. Colonel Sam Sturgis joined the command there on July 18, 1878. The camp was abandoned on August 28 by the move to Camp Ruhlen (now Fort Meade), a few miles to the east. Lieut. J. C. Gresham was transferred from the 3rd Cavalry to Company M, 7th Cavalry to occupy the vacancy created by the death of Jack Sturgis.

RYAN, JOHN M., First Sergeant

In the valley and hilltop fights. Born on August 25, 1845, at West Newton, Massachusetts. Enlisted in Company C, 28th Massachusetts Regiment in 1861. Discharged on December 19, 1864. Enlisted in Company K, 61st Massachusetts Regiment in 1865. Wounded four times during the Civil War. First enlistment in the 7th Cavalry in 1866. Second enlistment on December 21, 1871, at the age of 26 at Union, South Carolina by Captain Thomas H. French. Previous occupation was carpenter. Discharged on December 21, 1876, at Fort Rice, Dakota upon expiration of service, as a Sergeant. He had grey eyes, auburn hair, ruddy complexion and was 5'-6½" in height. He was Chief of Police in West Newton, Massachusetts, for nine years and retired in 1912. Died October 14, 1926 in West Newton. A steel knife with Sergeant John Ryan's name on the handle was found on Sibley Island below Bismarck and is in the North Dakota Historical Society Museum, Bismarck.

CAPES, WILLIAM, Sergeant

On detached service from June 15, 1876, at Yellowstone Depot, Montana Territory. Joined company from detached service at Yellowstone Depot on July 30, 1876. Born in Portland, Maine. Enlisted on December 30, 1872, at age 25 in New York City by Captain Edwin Sumner. Previous occupation was laborer. Discharged on December 30, 1877, at Fort A. Lincoln, Dakota upon expiration of service, as a Sergeant, with character good in every respect. He had grey eyes, black hair, ruddy complexion and was 5'-9½" in height.

CAREY, PATRICK, Sergeant

Wounded in the right hip in the hilltop fight on June 26. Transported to Fort A. Lincoln, Dakota on the steamer *Far West*.

"... some 10 or 12 men became separated from the command and hid themselves in the brush or in the woods, or under the river embankment, and some of those men told me afterwards that they stood in water up to their necks, under the embankment, to keep out of sight of the Indians. Two of these men were sergeants in my company, Charles White and Patrick Carney. They joined the command in the intrenchments on the bluff, after dark." John Ryan in the *Hardin* (Montana) *Tribune*, June 22, 1923.

Born in Tipperary, Ireland. Second enlistment on March 22, 1875, at age 39 at Fort Rice, Dakota, by Captain Thomas French. Discharged March 21, 1880, at Fort Meade, Dakota, upon expiration of service, as a Private of good character. He had grey eyes, grey hair, light complexion and was 5'-7½" in height. Listed elsewhere as Patrick Carney.

McGLONE, JOHN, Sergeant

Born in Sligo, Ireland. Enlisted on December 18, 1872, at age 28 in Philadelphia by Captain Samuel Whitside. Previous occupation was laborer. Discharged on December 18, 1877 at Fort Abraham Lincoln, Dakota upon expiration of service, as a Sergeant of excellent character. He had brown eyes, dark hair, ruddy complexion and was 5'-9½" in height.

O'HARA, MILES F., Sergeant

Killed by a shot through the breast, on the skirmish line in the valley fight.

"It was on this line that I saw the first one of my own company comrades fall. This was Sergeant O'Hara." Wm. Slaper in Brininstool *Troopers With Custer*, p. 48.

Born in Alton, Ohio. Enlisted on October 30, 1872, at age 21 1/12 in New York City by Captain Charles Wikoff. Also recorded as having enlisted at Columbus, Ohio. Previous occupation was laborer. Promoted to Sergeant in June, 1876. He had grey eyes, light hair, ruddy complexion and was 5'-8¼" in height. Listed as M. F. O'Hara on the battle monument and as Miles F. O'Harra in the Register of Enlistments, U.S. Army and elsewhere as Myles O'Hara.

"This (the skirmish line) was where the first man was killed, Sergt. Miles F. O'Hara of my troop M. He was a corporal going out on the expedition and was promoted to sergeant a few days before his death to replace Sergt. John Dolan, who was discharged, as his term of service had expired, and was back with the wagon train at Powder River. Sergt. O'Hara was considered a very fine soldier in M troop, and we missed him very much." John Ryan in the *Hardin* (Montana) *Tribune*, June 22, 1923.

WHITE, CHARLES, Sergeant

Wounded in the right arm in the valley fight on June 25. His horse was killed when the retreat from the valley fight began. He was left in the timber and later rejoined the command on the hilltop. Transported to Fort Abraham Lincoln, Dakota on the steamer *Far West*. Born in Saxony, Germany. Enlisted on March 8, 1871, at age 24 in Philadelphia by Captain Eugene Beaumont. Previous occupation was farmer. Discharged on March 8, 1876, at Fort Rice, Dakota upon expiration of service, as a Sergeant of excellent character. Second enlistment on March 8, 1876, at the age of 29 at Fort Rice by Captain Thomas French. Discharged on October 5, 1879, at Fort Meade, Dakota, per General Court Martial Order No. 100, Department of Dakota, 1879, as a Private, for threatening to "gunsling" a man out of the Army (while at Fort Lincoln). He had grey eyes, brown hair, fair complexion and was 5'-3¾" in height. "Sergeant White though badly wounded in the elbow stayed on his feet and did everything he could to relieve the sufferers. He had a glassful of jelly in his bags and each wounded man got a small spoonful of that." Daniel Newell, "The Story of the Big Horn Campaign of 1876" in *The Sunshine Magazine*, September 30, 1930.

CODY, HENRY, (HENRY M. SCOLLIN), Corporal

Killed in the valley fight, during the retreat on June 25. Born in Nashua, New Hampshire. Enlisted on September 24, 1873, at age 22 at Boston, Massachusetts by Lieut. James Ropes. Previous occupation was painter. He had blue eyes, dark hair, medium complexion and was 5'-7" in height. Listed elsewhere as Henry Scollen and also as Scollier. Daniel Newell related that on June 24th, "While I was swimming, my bunkie, Scollen, had been sleeping but when I got back he was writing in his diary and he read to me what he had written. I said to him, "What in hell are you thinking about, you don't count on dying do you?" He said to me, 'Dan, if anything happens to me notify my sister Mary who lives in Gardiner, Mass. My name is Henry Cody and the name Henry Scollen is assumed.' He had told me this before when we were in camp on the Tongue [River]. I think he had a premonition of what was in store for him, and in less than 24 hours he was lying dead on the bottom of the Little Big Horn, his body riddled with bullets . . . Soon after we started with Sergeant Ryan on retreat, I saw my bunkie, Scollen, fall. He was on ahead and when I got up there I saw his horse had fallen in a sort of a wallow and thrown him out of the saddle. He had been shot but was still alive when I got to him. I couldn't help him and he was beyond help anyway. All he could say was, 'Goodbye boys.' . . . The body of my bunkie, Henry Scollen or Henry Cody, was all hacked up. Later I sent his sister his prayer book which was found in his trunk at Fort Rice when his effects were sold. She wrote wanting to know whether his body had been mutilated. I answered and told her it had not, but it had. I wanted to spare her feelings all I could. I suppose she is dead now and there is no harm in telling it. I would have given most anything if I could have recovered his diary but I suppose the squaws got that when they stripped his body. Poor boy. His life's biggest adventure never got into that diary." "Story of the Big Horn Campaign of 1876" in *The Sunshine Magazine* Sept. 30, 1930, II:1, pp. 2-7. "Corporal Henry Scollen of M Troop was found badly mutilated, with his right leg severed from his body." William Slaper in Brininstool *Troopers With Custer*. p. 65.

LALOR, WILLIAM, Corporal

Born in New York City. Enlisted on September 29, 1875, at age 30 in St. Louis by Lieut. William Hall. Previous occupation was laborer. Promoted to Sergeant effective August 1, 1876. Discharged on September 28, 1880, at Fort Meade, Dakota, upon expiration of service, as a Corporal of good character. He had blue eyes, brown hair, fair complexion and was 5'-8" in height.

STREING, FREDERICK, Corporal
Killed in battle on June 25. Born in Ripley County, Indiana. Enlisted on October 19, 1872, at age 21 in Louisville, Kentucky by Lieut. Peter Vroom. Previous occupation was laborer. He had grey eyes, light hair, fair complexion and was 5'-5¼" in height. Listed as Fred'k Streing on the battle monument and elsewhere as Fred Stringer.

WEAVER, HENRY C., Trumpeter
Born in Philadelphia, Pennsylvania. Second enlistment on May 1, 1875, at age 32 in Pittsburgh by Lieut. Thomas Gregg. Discharged on February 4, 1879, at Fort Meade, Dakota as a Private per General Court Martial Order Nr. 3, Department of Dakota, 1879. He had grey eyes, dark hair, ruddy complexion and was 5'-4¾" in height.

FISCHER, CHARLES, Trumpeter
Born in Breslau, Germany. Third enlistment on September 14, 1875, at age 31 in St. Louis by Lieut. John Thompson. Previous occupation was soldier. Discharged June 16, 1878, at Fort A. Lincoln, Dakota, for disability, as a Trumpeter. He had grey eyes, dark brown hair, fair complexion and was 5'-4½" in height. Listed as Charles Fischer in the Register of Enlistments, U. S. Army.

> ". . . Lieutenant Hodgson asked one of the men to carry him across [the river], he being wounded and his horse being shot. It was reported that a trumpeter from my company named Fisher, better known as 'Bounce', told him to hold on to his stirrup, and the horse drew the lieutenant as well as the rider across the river. He was shot a second time and killed. Now I know of three men who claim to have aided Hodgson." John Ryan in the *Hardin* (Montana) *Tribune*, June 22, 1923.

> "As I glanced about me, the first thing that engaged my attention was Trumpeter Henry Fisher of M Troop riding in the river some distance up, with Lieut. Benny Hodgson hanging to one stirrup." Wm. Slaper in Brininstool *Troopers With Custer*, p. 52.

DONAHUE, JOHN, Saddler
Born in Galway, Ireland. Second enlistment on Oct. 20, 1871, at age 23 in Chicago by Captain Samuel Young. Discharged October 20, 1876, at camp near Fort A. Lincoln, Dakota, upon expiration of service, as a Saddler of excellent character. He had hazel eyes, brown hair, light complexion and was 5'-3" in height. Listed as John Donahue in the Register of Enlistments, U.S. Army and elsewhere as Donohue.

WOOD, WILLIAM M., Farrier
On detached service from May 5, 1876, at Fort Rice, Dakota in charge of company property. Born in Grafton, New York. Enlisted on January 11, 1872, at age 23 2/12 in Troy, New York by Lieut. Oscar Elting. Previous occupation was farmer. Discharged on January 11, 1877, at Fort Rice upon expiration of service, as a Farrier of excellent character. He had blue eyes, red hair, fair complexion and was 5'-10¼" in height.

RICKETS, JOSEPH, Wagoner

On detached service from June 15, 1876, at Yellowstone Depot, Montana Territory. Born in Warren County, Ohio. Enlisted on January 16, 1873, at age 23 11/12 in Cincinnati by Lieut. Adam Kramer. Previous occupation was farmer. He was discharged on January 16, 1878, at Fort Abraham Lincoln, Dakota upon expiration of service, as a Private of good character. He had blue eyes, dark hair, ruddy complexion and was 5'-9" in height. Listed as Joseph Rickets in the Register of Enlistments, U.S. Army and elsewhere as Ricketts. In relating the march from Fort Lincoln to Power River, Daniel Newell remarked, "I had given an Indian a dollar for the hind quarters of an antelope and so had a feast in sight but no way to cook it. But we had a man with us called 'Buckeye' – Ricketts was his name – and he contracted to cook if we would take him into our mess. The bargain was struck and pretty soon he came along with some pieces of an oak wagon tongue and a reach. We had pork and bacon and a bunch of us got the antelope cooked and had a feast. . ." as told to John P. Everett in "The Story of the Big Horn Campaign of 1876" in *The Sunshine Magazine*, September, 1930.

BATES, JOSEPH, Private

Born in Providence, Rhode Island. Enlisted on July 18, 1870, at age 31 in Carlisle, Penna. by Lieut. Cain. Previous occupation was soldier. Deserted on May 11, 1872; apprehended on Dec. 20, 1873. Joined Company M by transfer from Company F, 7th Cavalry on January 7, 1874 per Special Order Nr. 274, Headquarters, Department of Dakota, December 12, 1874. Discharged on February 27, 1877, at Fort Rice, Dakota upon expiration of service, as a Private. He had blue eyes, brown hair, fair complexion and was 5'-0" in height.

BOWERS, FRANK, Private

In confinement from Feb. 14, 1876, at Fort Wayne, Michigan. Born in Detroit, Michigan. Enlisted on January 4, 1870, at age 25 in Fort Leavenworth, Kansas by Lieut. Myles Moylan, Adjutant, 7th Cavalry. Previous occupation was shoemaker. Discharged on May 29, 1876 without character per Special Order Nr. 104, AGO, May 27, 1876 as F. Volkenstein, alias Frank Bowers. He had brown eyes, brown hair, ruddy complexion and was 5'-11" in height.

BRAUN, FRANK, Private

Wounded in the face and left thigh on June 25. Transported to Fort Abraham Lincoln, Dakota on the steamer *Far West*. Died of gunshot wounds on October 4, 1876, at Fort Lincoln. Born in Berne, Switzerland. Enlisted on September 23, 1875, at age 27 in Louisville, Kentucky by Lieut. William Beck. Previous occupation was laborer. Re-interred in the Custer Battlefield National Cemetery, Grave 571A. He had hazel eyes, fair hair, fair complexion and was 5'-6¼" in height. Listed elsewhere as Baum and Brunn.

CAIN, MORRIS, Private

Born in Barkersville, Massachusetts. Enlisted on September 16, 1875, at age 22 in Boston by Lieut. Henry Lawton. Previous occupation was farmer. Discharged on July 4, 1877, at camp on Sunday Creek, Montana Territory per Special Order Nr. 124, AGO, War Department, 1877, as a Private of excellent character. He had brown eyes, black hair, dark complexion and was 5'-7" in height.

DAVIS, HARRISON, Private

Born in Westmoreland County, Pennsylvania. Second enlistment on December 21, 1871, at age 26 in Union, South Carolina by Captain Thomas French. Previous occupation was miner. Promoted to Corporal on August 1, 1876. Discharged on December 21, 1876, at Fort Rice, Dakota upon expiration of service, as a Private of excellent character. He had brown eyes, sandy hair, ruddy complexion and was 5'-6½" in height.

DOLAN, JOHN, Private

On detached service from June 15, 1876, at Yellowstone Depot, Montana Territory. Born in Dublin, Ireland. Enlisted in Company H, 1st Cavalry on February 16, 1866, at age 22 in Philadelphia by Captain J. Mix, 2nd Cavalry. Previous occupation was laborer. Honorably discharged on February 15, 1869, from Company H, 1st Cavalry at Camp Harney, Oregon, upon expiration of service, as a Corporal. Re-enlisted on March 13, 1869, at Portland, Oregon, by Lieut. Duncan Sherman, 1st Cavalry. Deserted. Re-enlisted as Thomas Brown on October 1, 1873, at age 29 in New York City by Lieut. Edward Hunter. He stated that his birthplace was New York City and that his previous occupation was machinist. Assigned to Company M, 7th Cavalry. His enlistment was cancelled and he surrendered on November 17, 1873, under the President's proclamation published in General Order Nr. 102, AGO, 1873, as John Dolan, deserter from Company I, 1st Cavalry. Discharged from Company M, 7th Cavalry on July 3, 1876, at camp on the Bighorn River, Montana Territory, upon expiration of service as a Private. His character on discharge was excellent and no objection was known to his being re-enlisted. Third enlistment was on August 2, 1876, at age 32 in the General Mounted Service at St. Louis Barracks, Missouri by Lieut. John Thompson, 3rd Cavalry. Discharged on August 1, 1881, at Fort Yates, Dakota, upon expiration of service, as a Sergeant in Troop B, 7th Cavalry. At this time he was married and had two children. Fourth enlistment on January 1, 1882, at the age of 37 at Fort Abraham Lincoln, Dakota by Lieut. Ernest Garlington. Assigned to Troop L, 7th Cavalry. Discharged on December 31, 1886, at Fort Buford, Dakota, as a Sergeant in Troop L, 7th Cavalry. At this time Dolan was a single man. He had gunshot wound scars on the back of his head and on the left leg below the knee, in front and below the left ankle. Fifth enlistment on January 1, 1887, at Fort Buford by Lieut. Ernest Garlington. Discharged on December 31, 1891, at Fort Riley, Kansas from Troop C, 7th Cavalry, as a Sergeant of good character. Sixth enlistment on January 26, 1892, in Troop B, 7th Cavalry, at Fort Riley by Lieut. James F. Bell. Discharged on April 10, 1896, at Camp Grant, Arizona Territory for disability, as a Sergeant in Troop I, 7th Cavalry, of very good character. He had hazel grey, or brown eyes, brown or dark hair, ruddy or dark complexion and was 5'-9½" to 10" in height. His account of the Little Bighorn River fight was published in *The New York Herald*, July 23, 1876, p. 4.

GALLENNE, JEAN B. D., Private

Born in Lorient, France. Enlisted on September 30, 1873, at age 24 in New York City by Lieut. Edward Hunter. Previous occupation was student. Discharged on April 27, 1878, at Fort Rice, Dakota, for disability, as a Private of good character. He had blue eyes, black hair, dark complexion and was 5'-5¼" in height. The Descriptive List and Records File, Custer Battlefield National

227

Monument, includes an order for stoppage of pay against Captain Thos. French for tobacco issued and not charged to Private Gallenne. Details of the indorsement of this record indicate that Gallenne was detailed to the Medical Department as a 2nd Class Hospital Steward. The Muster Roll for Company M, 7th Cavalry, June 30, 1876, lists Gallenne in the hospital at Fort Abraham Lincoln, Dakota.

GOLDEN, BERNARD, Private
Born in Cavan, Ireland. Second enlistment on October 5, 1875, at age 33 in St. Louis by Lieut. John Thompson. He deserted on December 8, 1877. He had grey eyes, brown hair, ruddy complexion and was 5'-7" in height.

GORDON, HENRY, Private
Killed by a shot in the neck while climbing the bluffs during the retreat on June 25. Born in Chatham, England. Enlisted on December 5, 1872, at age 21 in Boston by Captain Moses Harris. Previous occupation was laborer. He had brown eyes, brown hair, fair complexion and was 5'-6" in height. Listed as Henry Gordon on the battle monument.

HEID, GEORGE, Private
Born in Bavaria, Germany. Second enlistment on June 17, 1870, at age 28 in Cincinnati by Captain J. S. Tomkins. Previous occupation was farmer. Assigned to Company M, 7th Cavalry. Discharged on March 15, 1877. Re-enlisted in Company G, 7th Cavalry on March 19, 1877, at Fort Abraham Lincoln, Dakota, by Lieut. Ernest Garlington. Transferred to Company I, 7th Cavalry. Discharged on March 18, 1882. Re-enlisted on March 24, 1882 at Fort Totten, Dakota, in Troop I at age 39, by Lieut. J. D. Nickerson. Died at Fort Totten, re-interred in the Custer Battlefield National Cemetery, Grave 97A. He had grey eyes, dark hair, ruddy complexion and was 5'-6¼" in height.

KAVANAUGH, CHARLES, Private
Born in Pittsburgh, Pennsylvania. Enlisted on August 7, 1867, at age 26 in St. Louis by Captain P. Dwyer. Discharged on August 7, 1872, from Company G, 7th Cavalry, upon expiration of service. Second enlistment on September 13, 1875, at age 34 in New York City by Lieut. John Babcock. Discharged from Company E, 7th Cavalry, on September 12, 1880, at Fort Meade, Dakota, upon expiration of service, as a Private of excellent character. Third enlistment on June 7, 1881 at age 40 at Fort Schuyler, New York by Captain G. Parslow. Enlisted in Battery G, 3rd Artillery. Sick in hospital from September 23, 1885. Discharged on August 10, 1886 at Fort McHenry, Baltimore, for total disability (consumption-right lung). He had grey eyes, fair hair, dark complexion and was 5'-8¾" in height. His name is written as Charles Kavanaugh on his first Oath of Enlistment and as Charles Kavanagh on his third Oath of Enlistment and as Charles Kavanuagh on the Company M Muster Roll, June 30, 1876, and as Charles Kavanaugh in the Register of Enlistments, U.S. Army.

KLOTZBUCHER, HENRY, Private
Killed in the valley fight on June 25. Born in Baden, Germany. Enlisted on October 4, 1873, at age 25 in Philadelphia, Pennsylvania, by Lieut. William Volkmar. Previous occupation was cooper. He had brown eyes, ruddy complexion, brown hair and was 5'-6½" in height. Listed as Henry Klotzbucher

on the battle monument.

> "When I got my horse there were not many of us left in the timber that I could see. Soon after Private Henry Koltzbucher [sic] who was "striker" for Capt. French was shot through the stomach, just as he was in the act of mounting his horse. He fell to the ground, and I saw Private Francis Neely dismount to help him. I thereupon got off my horse and helped Neely drag the wounded trooper into a clump of heavy underbrush, where we thought he might not be found by Indians. Wm. E. Morris, another comrade, came up at this juncture and helped us care for Koltzbucher. We saw that he was probably mortally wounded, so we left him a canteen of water and hurriedly mounted again, dashing toward the river in the wake of our flying trooper comrades. After the battle we found the body of Koltzbucher where we had dragged him. He was not mutilated, and consequently had not been discovered by the Indians or their squaws in their fiendish work of killing and mutilating . . ." William Slaper in Brininstool *Troopers With Custer*, p. 51.

LORENTZ, GEORGE, Private

Killed in the valley fight on June 25. Born in Holstein, Germany. Enlisted on November 13, 1872, at age 21 in St. Louis by Lieut. Oscar Elting. Previous occupation was painter. He had grey eyes, dark brown hair, fair complexion and was 5'-6¾" in height. Listed as Geo. Lorentz on the battle monument and elsewhere as Lawrence and Lawerence. See also Wm. Morris letter in Brady *Indian Fights and Fighters*.

> "As we mounted (in the timber in the valley fight) I looked to the rear in the direction of the river and saw Indians completing the circle, riding through the brush and lying flat on their ponies . . . Just at that moment one of these Indians fired and Private George Lorentz of my company, who was number one of the first set of fours, was shot, the bullet striking him in the back of his neck and coming out of his mouth. He fell forward on his saddle and dropped to the ground." John Ryan in the *Hardin* (Montana) *Tribune*, June 22, 1923.

MAHONEY, DANIEL, Private

Born in Cork, Ireland. Enlisted on September 28, 1875, at age 23 in Boston by Lieut. Henry Lawton. Previous occupation was laborer. Discharged on April 14, 1878, at Fort Abraham Lincoln, Dakota for disability, as a Private of good character. He had grey eyes, brown hair, fair complexion and was 5'-9¼" in height. Listed as Daniel Mahony in the Register of Enlistments, U.S. Army.

McCORMICK, JAMES, Private

On detached service from June 15, 1876, at Yellowstone Depot, Montana Territory. Born in New York City. Second enlistment on April 2, 1873, at age 27 in Memphis, Tennessee by Captain Thomas French. Previous occupation was soldier. Listed as detached service with the regimental band on the Company M Muster Roll, June 30, 1876. Discharged on April 2, 1878, at Fort Abraham

Lincoln, Dakota upon expiration of service, as a Private of excellent character. He had dark eyes, dark hair, sallow complexion and was 5'-6½" in height.

MEIER, JOHN H., Private

Wounded in the back of the neck in the valley fight on June 25. Transported to Fort A. Lincoln, Dakota, on the steamer *Far West*. Born in Hanover. Germany. Enlisted on September 3, 1873, at age 26 in Boston by Lieut. James Ropes. Previous occupation was varnisher. He recuperated from his wound at the Fort Rice hospital. Lieut. Edward Godfrey wrote that Meier lost control of his horse at the beginning of the valley fight. Discharged on September 3, 1878, at Camp Ruhlen, Dakota upon expiration of service, as a Private of excellent character. He had blue eyes, red hair, light complexion and was 5'-5" in height. He is listed as John H. Meyer in various publications and as J. R. Meyer in Edgar Stewart *Custer's Luck*, p. 353.

> " 'Snopsy' Meyer's horse got away from him and bolted through the Indian's line on our right, but he got back to us, shooting his way out with his six gun. How he ever did it is a mystery . . . As 'Snopsy' got to the river his horse was shot from under him and he started for the river afoot. I saw him and Benny Hodgson — we called him the Jack of Clubs — starting for the same horse. 'Snopsy' got on the horse and Hodgson hung on to the stirrup and was dragged to the other side of the river and was hit by a bullet and killed just as he got across." Daniel Newell as related to John Everett "The Story Of The Big Horn Campaign," *The Sunshine Magazine*, Sept. 1930.

MEYER, WILLIAM D., Private

Killed by a shot in the eye while climbing the bluffs after the valley fight on June 25.

> "In scaling the bluff, Dr. DeWolf, a contract surgeon on the expedition, was killed; also Sergeant Clair of Company K, William D. Meyer, a farrier of Company M, and Henry Gordon of the same company. Their bodies, with a number of others, lay under our guns, so that the Indians did not get a chance to scalp them." John Ryan in the *Hardin* (Montana) *Tribune*, June 22, 1923.

Born in Pittsburgh, Pennsylvania. Enlisted on December 16, 1875, at age 22 7/12 in Pittsburgh by Lieut. Calbraith Rodgers. Previous occupation was laborer. He had blue eyes, light hair, fair complexion and was 5'-9½" in height. Listed as W. D. Meyer on the battle monument.

MOORE, HUGH N., Private

Born in Dorchester County, Maryland. Enlisted on August 24, 1872, in Louisville. Kentucky by Lieut. Charles Larned. Previous occupation was sailmaker. Promoted to Corporal on August 1, 1876. Discharged on August 24, 1877, at camp on the Yellowstone River, Montana Territory upon expiration of service, as a Sergeant. He had grey eyes, brown hair, fair complexion and was 5'-7½" in height.

MORRIS, WILLIAM E., Private

Wounded in the left breast while climbing the bluffs after the valley fight on June 25. Transported to Fort Abraham Lincoln, Dakota, on the steamer *Far West*. Born in Boston, Massachusetts. Enlisted on September 22, 1875, at age 21 1/3 in Boston by Lieut. Henry Lawton. Previous occupation was salesman. Discharged on December 11, 1877, at Fort Lincoln, for disability as a Private of worthless character. He had brown eyes, auburn hair, fair complexion and was 5'-7½" in height. He was a half-brother of Private Byron L. Tarbox, Company L, 7th Cavalry. His name is listed in various publications as W. E. Harris. Morris was later a judge in New York City and a Captain, 69th Infantry Regiment, New York National Guard. In 1927 he resided at 2780 Pond Place, New York City.

NEELY, FRANK, Private

In the valley and hilltop fights.   Born in Collinsville, Ohio.   Enlisted on April 8, 1871 at age 21-1/12 in Cincinnati by Lieut. Myles Moylan. Previous occupation was painter. Deserted on June 20, 1873; surrendered on November 21, 1873. Promoted to Corporal on August 1, 1876. Discharged on September 9, 1876, at camp on the Yellowstone River, Montana Territory upon expiration of service, as a Corporal of excellent character. Re-enlisted on September 9, 1876, at camp on Yellowstone River at age of 26 5/12 by Lieut. Edward Mathey. Discharged on September 8, 1881, at Fort Meade, Dakota, upon expiration of service, as a Private of good character. He had grey eyes, light hair, light complexion and was 5'-10" in height. Listed as Frank Neely on the Muster Roll of Company M, June 30, 1876. He inscribed "F. Neely, Co. M. 7th Cav." on May 28, 1876, on a rock near camp while on the Sioux expedition.

NEWELL, DANIEL, Private

Wounded in the left thigh (leg) at the beginning of the retreat in the valley fight on June 25. Transported to Fort Abraham Lincoln, Dakota, on the steamer *Far West*. Born on March 17, 1847, in Ballinlough, Rascommon County, Ireland, one of a family of 13 children. Worked in London from the age of 15 learning the blacksmithing trade. Enlisted on October 8, 1873, at age 25 in Philadelphia by Lieut. William Volkmar. Previous occupation was listed as blacksmith. In the expedition exploring the Black Hills in 1874. Appointed Blacksmith on July 1, 1876. Discharged on October 8, 1878, at Camp Ruhlen, Dakota upon expiration of service, as a Private of good character. Resided in North Dakota in 1878, and was post blacksmith at Fort Meade, Dakota from 1879 to 1884. He married Mary Harlow on July 9, 1882, at the Fort Meade Chapel and resided in Sturgis, South Dakota, from 1882. Interred in the Post Cemetery at Fort Meade. He had grey eyes, brown hair, dark complexion and was 5'7½" in height. His story of the fight was published in *The Sunshine Magazine*, September 30, 1930, as "The Story of the Big Horn Campaign of 1876."

PIGFORD, EDWARD A., Private

Wounded in the right hip in the retreat from the valley fight on June 25. Slightly wounded in the right forearm by a small caliber bullet on June 26. (This statement is made by Earle Forrest but is not borne out by the Returns of the 7th Cavalry). Born near West Elizabeth in Alleghany County, Pennsylvania. Enlisted on September 13, 1875, at age 21 in Pittsburgh by Lieut. Thomas Gregg. Sent to Jefferson Barracks, near St. Louis, and then to Fort A. Lincoln, Dakota. Discharged on October 15, 1876, at Fort A. Lincoln per Special Order Nr. 180, AGO, War Department, 1876, as a Private of excellent character. He had grey eyes, auburn hair, light complexion and was 5'6¾" in height. In 1927, he resided at Lock Three, Pennsylvania. Died on December 6, 1932, at Lock Three and was interred at Richland Cemetery, Dravosberg, Pennsylvania.

ROBINSON, WILLIAM, Private
Born in Down, Ireland. Enlisted on September 30, 1873, at age 31 in Philadelphia by Lieut. William Volkmar. Previous occupation was cloth finisher. On daily duty at regimental headquarters per Muster Roll of Company M, June 30, 1876. Discharged on September 30, 1878 at Camp Ruhlen, Dakota, upon expiration of service, as a Private of excellent character. He had blue eyes, dark brown hair, fair complexion and was 5'-9" in height. In 1927 he resided in Seattle, Washington.

RUTTEN, ROMAN, Private
Wounded in the right shoulder in the hilltop fight on June 26. Transported to Fort Abraham Lincoln, Dakota on the steamer *Far West*. Born in Baden, Germany. Enlisted on July 17, 1872, at age 26 in Philadelphia by Captain Samuel Whitside. Previous occupation was tailor. Discharged on July 17, 1877, at Fort Rice, Dakota upon expiration of service, as a Private of very good character. Re-enlisted on July 17, 1877 at Fort Rice by Lieut. Ogle. Discharged on July 16, 1882, at Fort Meade, Dakota upon expiration of service, as a Private of excellent character. He recuperated from his wound in the hospital at Fort Rice. He had brown eyes, light brown hair, ruddy complexion and was 5'-6¼" in height. Listed elsewhere as Rutler and as Roman Bolten and as Roman Rullin.

RYDER, HOBART, Private
In the valley and hilltop fights. Born in New York City. Enlisted on September 15, 1873, at age 27 in Chicago by Captain Henry Carroll. Previous occupation was broker. Sentenced to three months confinement at hard labor at his post and $30 fine per General Court Martial Order Nr. 8, January 20, 1876, Department of Dakota. His name was listed as Hobart Rider in this order. On detached service with the field hospital with the wagon train, an extra duty according to the Company M Muster Roll, June 30, 1876. Discharged on September 15, 1878, at Camp Ruhlen, Dakota upon expiration of service, as a Corporal of excellent character. He had grey eyes, dark brown hair, fair complexion and was 5'7¼" in height. Daniel Newell related that during the valley fight, ". . . a man named St. Rider [sic], a corporal in my company came out from under some cover and asked me if I was wounded. I said, "Yes, and I can't walk." "Crawl around here under cover" he said, and I did so and we stayed there [on the hillside during the retreat from the valley fight] until the fire slackened . . . As soon as we could we crawled up the hill." *The Sunshine Magazine*, Sept. 1930.

RYE, WILLIAM W., Private
In the valley and hilltop fights. Born in Pike County, Georgia. Enlisted on October 9, 1875, at the age of 26 in St. Louis by Lieut. John Thompson. Previous occupation was farmer. Deserted on October 20, 1876, surrendered on June 8, 1877. Escaped on September 14, 1877. He had grey eyes, brown hair, fair complexion and was 5'-8½" in height.

SEAMANS, JOHN, Private
Born in New London, New Hampshire. Enlisted on September 21, 1875,

at age 21 2/3 in Boston by Lieut. Henry Lawton. Previous occupation was clerk. Deserted on May 12, 1877. He had blue eyes, brown hair, fair complexion and was 5'-9" in height.

SENN, ROBERT, Private

Born in Zurich, Switzerland. Enlisted on September 23, 1875, at age 27 in Louisville, Kentucky by Lieut. Rick. Previous occupation was farmer. Discharged on September 22, 1880, at Fort Meade, Dakota upon expiration of service, as a Private of fair character. He had blue eyes, brown hair, fair complexion and was 5'-7¼" in height.

SEVERS, JAMES, Private

In the valley and hilltop fights. Born in Wayne County, New York. Enlisted on November 12, 1872, at age 21 1/12 in Chicago by Captain Samuel Young. Previous occupation was teamster. Discharged on November 12, 1877, at Fort Rice, Dakota upon expiration of service, as a Private of excellent character. Re-enlisted on November 12, 1877, at Fort Rice by Lieut. Frank Gibson and discharged on November 11, 1882, at Fort Meade, Dakota upon expiration of service. He had blue eyes, light brown hair, fair complexion and was 5'-5¾" in height. He was illiterate and unmarried. Listed as James Severs in the Register of Enlistments, U.S. Army. Mulford, on p. 109 of *Fighting Indians in the Seventh Cavalry*, related that "Crazy Jim" Severs was from Indiana and had saved a pack mule and its load of ammunition under heavy fire in the Little Bighorn River fight. "While the fighting was the thickest [in the advance from the hilltop toward Custer's position] one of the pack mules with the load on its back started to leave. He had gone maybe a hundred yards when he was overtaken by a man we called "Crazy Jim" Seivers [sic] who brought him back. He was exposed to fire of the Sioux from the minute he started until he got back. I saw this and it was a mighty brave deed but Seivers never got any medal of honor for it that I know of." Daniel Newell in *The Sunshine Magazine*, September 30, 1930.

SIVERTSEN, JOHN, Private

Missing after the valley fight (with Lieut. Charles DeRudio in the timber). Rejoined the command later and participated in the hilltop fight. Born in Norway. Enlisted on June 19, 1873, at age 31 at Fort Rice, Dakota, by Captain Thomas French. Previous occupation was blacksmith. Discharged on June 19, 1878 at Fort Abraham Lincoln, Dakota, upon expiration of service, as a Private of excellent character. He had blue eyes, sandy hair, light complexion and was 5'-10" in height. He was later retired to The National Soldier's Home, Washington, D. C.

SLAPER, WILLIAM C., Private

In the valley and hilltop fights. Born on November 23, 1855, in Cincinnati, Ohio. Enlisted on September 10, 1875, in Cincinnati by Lieut. Patrick Cusack. Previous occupation was safemaker. Discharged September 9, 1880 at Fort Meade, Dakota, upon expiration of service, as a Private of good character. He had blue eyes, brown hair, fair complexion and was 5'-8½" in height. In 1927 he resided at the Soldier's Home, Sawtelle, Calif. He died November 13, 1931, at the Soldier's Home. His story was told by Brininstool in *Troopers With Custer*.

SMITH, GEORGE E., Private
Missing and presumed killed in the valley fight on June 25. Before the skirmish line formed at the beginning of the valley fight he lost control of his horse which stampeded into the hostile Indians.

"His horse ran away with him and took him right in the direction of the village. We never even found his body." Daniel Newell in *The Sunshine Magazine*, Sept. 30, 1930.

"Our horses were scenting danger before we dismounted, and several at this point became unmanageable and started straight for the opening among the Indians, carrying their helpless riders with them. One of the boys, a young fellow named Smith of Boston, we never saw again, either dead or alive." **Wm. Slaper in Brininstool** *Trooper's With Custer*, p. 48.

Smith was born in Kennebunk, Maine. Enlisted on September 6, 1875, at age 25 in Boston by Lieut. William Harper, Jr. Previous occupation was shoemaker. He had grey eyes, brown hair, fair complexion and was 5'-6½" in height. A man named Smith in Company M is referred to in Mulford *Fighting Indians in the 7th Cavalry*, as a "New York City bum" who was given a "bobtail" discharge (character reference torn off). This reference to Smith seems undoubtedly to be in error.

SNIFFIN, FRANK, Private
Carried the company colors in the valley fight. Born in New York City. Enlisted on September 1, 1875, at age 22 in St. Louis by Captain Owen Hale. Previous occupation was laborer. Discharged on August 31, 1880, at Fort Meade, Dakota, upon expiration of service, as a Private of good character. He had blue eyes, light hair, fair complexion and was 5'-7" in height.

STERLAND, WALTER S., Private
On detached service from June 15, 1876 at Yellowstone Depot, Montana Territory with the wagon train as a butcher. Born in England. Enlisted on November 18, 1872, at age 21½ in Pittsburgh, Pennsylvania by Lieut. Calbraith Rodgers. Previous occupation was teamster. Discharged on November 18, 1877, at Fort Rice, Dakota upon expiration of service, as a Corporal of good character. He had blue eyes, light hair, fair complexion and was 5'-5½" in height.

STRATTON, FRANK, Private
Born in Nottingham, England. Enlisted on September 18, 1875, at age 27 in St. Louis by Lieut. John Thompson. Previous occupation was printer. He deserted on July 28, 1877. He had hazel eyes, brown hair, fair complexion and was 5'-5½" in height.

SUMMERS, DAVID, Private
Killed in the valley fight as the retreat began, on June 25. Born in Pettis County, Missouri. Discharged on April 24, 1876, from Company I, 6th Infantry. Enlisted on May 13, 1876, at age 27 in camp near Fort Abraham Lincoln, Dakota by Captain Thomas French. Assigned to Company M, 7th Cavalry. He had blue eyes, sandy hair, ruddy complexion and was 5'-8½" in height. Listed as

David Summers on the battle monument and in the Register of Enlistments, U.S. Army, and elsewhere as Somers and Sommers.

TANNER, JAMES J., Private
Killed in battle on June 26. Born in Altoona, Pennsylvania. Enlisted on September 18, 1875, at age 26 in Chicago by Lieut. Edmund Luff. He had brown eyes, black hair, dark complexion and was 5'-7¾" in height. Listed as J. J. Tauner on the battle monument and as James J. Tanner in the Register of Enlistments, U. S. Army.

> "Private James Tanner of Company M, was badly wounded in this charge, and his body lay on the side of the bluffs in an exposed position. There was a call for volunteers to bring him down, and I grabbed a blanket with three other men, rushed to his assistance, rolled him into the blanket, and made quick tracks in getting him from the side of the bluffs to where our wounded lay. Fortunately none of the rescue party received anything more than a few balls through their clothing. After placing Tanner with the rest of the wounded, he died in a few minutes." John Ryan in the *Hardin* (Montana) *Tribune*, June 22, 1923.

> "Early in the morning of the 26th the Sioux got to pressing pretty close to Benteen's company which was guarding the south side of the hill. Benteen decided to charge and M Company came over from the north to reinforce him. They charged and drove the enemy back but Tanner of my company was badly wounded in the charge. He was carried back to the hospital and I said to him, "Poor old Tanner they got you." "No" he gasped, "but they will in a few minutes." To this day I choke every time I try to tell of his death." Daniel Newell, as told to John Everett in "The Story of The Big Horn Campaign Of 1876," in *The Sunshine Magazine*, September, 1930.

THORNBERRY, LEVI, Private
Born in Marietta, Ohio. Enlisted on September 20, 1875, at age 22 in Cincinnati, Ohio by Lieut. Patrick Cusack. Previous occupation was teamster. He deserted on June 7, 1878. He had blue eyes, brown hair, dark complexion and was 5'-6¼" in height.

THORPE, ROLLINS L., Private
Born in New York City. Enlisted on September 7, 1875, at age 21 in Chicago by Lieut. Edmund Luff. Previous occupation was hostler. Discharged on July 7, 1876, at camp on the Bighorn River, Montana Territory per Special Order Nr. 101, AGO, War Department, May 17, 1876, as a Private of good character. He had grey eyes, dark brown hair, dark complexion and was 5'-7½" in height.

TURLEY, HENRY, Private
Killed in the valley fight on June 25. Born in Troy, New York. Enlisted on October 29, 1872, at age 21 7/12 in Troy by Captain Theodore Wint. Previous occupation was laborer. He had brown eyes, black hair, dark complexion and was 5'-4 1/8" in height. Listed as Henry Turley on the battle monument and

elsewhere as Henry Farley and Tenley and James Turley.

> "Private James Turley of my troop when we arrived at the timber
> and had orders to halt, could not control his horse which carried him
> towards the Indian camp. That was the last I saw of him. He was a
> very nice young man. A little incident happened a day or two before
> we left Fort Rice to go on the expedition. Turley asked me if I
> would allow him to put some of his property in my clothes chest. I
> told him that I would with the understanding that if he was killed
> the contents of the chest would belong to me and if I was killed it
> would belong to him. After coming back from the expedition the
> property belonging to those men that were killed was sold at public
> auction and the proceeds turned over to the paymaster." John Ryan
> in the *Hardin* (Montana) *Tribune*, June 22, 1923.

> "Jim Turley's body was found (in the valley woods) with his hunting
> knife driven to the hilt in one (his right) eye." Wm. Slaper in
> Bininstool *Troopers With Custer*, p. 65.

VARNER, THOMAS B., Private
Wounded in the right ear in the hilltop fight on June 26. Transported to
Fort Abraham Lincoln, Dakota on the steamer *Far West*. Born in Franklin
County, Missouri. Enlisted on August 24, 1875, at age 22 in Louisville,
Kentucky, by Lieut. William Beck. Previous occupation was farmer. Deserted on
June 7, 1878. He had blue eyes, brown hair, fair complexion and was 5'-8¼" in
height. Listed elsewhere as T. P. Norman and as Thos. P. Varner. He recuperated
from his wound in the hospital at Fort Rice.

VOIGHT, HENRY C., Private
Born in Hanover, Germany. Enlisted on October 1, 1873, at age 18 in
Philadelphia by Lieut. William Volkmar. Previous occupation was baker. He
had blue eyes, brown hair, fair complexion and was 5'-5½" in height. Listed
as H. C. Voigt on the battle monument and elsewhere as Voygt.

> "There was a gray horse belonging in my company, that was ridden
> by Captain French, and he was the best buffalo horse in the
> command. He was among the other horses near the wounded, and an
> Indian shot him through the head. He was staggering about among
> the other horses, and Private Henry C. Voyt, of my company took
> hold of him to lead him out of the way of the other horses, and
> Voyt, at the same instant had his brains blown out. We buried
> Private Tanner . . . and Voyt in the same grave the next morning.
> Then we made a head board out of a piece of hardtack box, and
> marked their names with a lead pencil on the board, and drove it
> into the ground." John Ryan in the *Hardin* (Montana) *Tribune*, June
> 22, 1923.

WEAVER, GEORGE, Private
Born in Lancaster, Pennsylvania. Second enlistment on March 15. 1876. at

age 33 at Fort Rice, Dakota, by Captain Thomas French. Discharged on March 14, 1881, at Fort Meade, Dakota upon expiration of service, as a Farrier of excellent character. He died on October 14, 1886 and was interred in the Post Cemetery at Fort Meade, Grave 1-65. He had blue eyes, brown hair, florid complexion and was 5'-7" in height.

WEEKS, JAMES, Private
In the hilltop fight. Born in Halifax, Nova Scotia. Enlisted on August 23, 1875, at age 21 2/12 in Boston by Lieut. William Harper, Jr. Previous occupation was laborer. Deserted on February 3, 1877; apprehended on February 16, 1877. Died on August 26, 1877, at Crow Agency, Montana Territory, of pistol shot wound. He had blue eyes, brown hair, fair complexion and was 5'-9 7/8" in height. William Slaper related, concerning the hilltop fight, "I had made the trip for water with a young comrade named Jim Weeks. On our way back, Jim was hailed by Capt. Moylan, requesting a drink. I was surprised to hear Jim blurt out, 'You go to hell and get your own water; this is for the wounded.' Nothing more was said but I know that must have been a hard pill for Moylan to swallow." In Brininstool *Troopers With Custer*, p. 59.

WHISTEN, JOHN, Private
Born in New York City. Enlisted on September 22, 1873, at age 21 in New York City by Lieut. Edward Hunter. Previous occupation was laborer. Discharged on September 22, 1878, at Camp Ruhlen, Dakota upon expiration of service, as a Private of excellent character. He had blue eyes, light hair, fair complexion and was 5'-5½" in height.

WIDMAYER, FERDINAND, Private
On detached service from June 15, 1876, at Yellowstone Depot, Montana Territory. Born in Wurtemburg, Germany. Enlisted on September 26, 1873, at age 24 in Philadelphia by Lieut. William Volkmar. Previous occupation was dyer. He joined his company from detached service at Yellowstone Depot, July 30, 1876. Discharged on September 26, 1878, at Camp Ruhlen, Dakota upon expiration of service, as a Private of excellent character. He had blue eyes, brown hair, fair complexion and was 5'-5" in height.

WIEDMAN, CHARLES T., Private
Wounded in the hilltop fight on June 26. Born in Boston, Massachusetts. Enlisted on September 23, 1875, at age 21 1/3 in Boston by Lieut. Henry Lawton. Previous occupation was machinist. Discharged on March 20, 1878, at Fort Abraham Lincoln, Dakota for disability, as a Private of excellent character. He had grey eyes, brown hair, dark complexion and was 5'-9¼" in height. Listed elsewhere as Charles G. Wiedman and Charles W. Wiedman.

WILBER, JAMES, Private
Wounded in the left leg in the hilltop fight on June 26. Transported to Fort Abraham Lincoln, Dakota on the steamer *Far West*. Born in Baltimore, Maryland. Enlisted on September 8, 1875, in Chicago by Lieut. Edmund Luff. Previous occupation was laborer. Discharged on November 1, 1876, at Fort Lincoln for disability, as a Private of good character. Retired to The National Soldier's Home, Washington, D.C. He had hazel eyes, light hair, fair complexion

and was 5'-8¾" in height. Listed as James Wilber on the Muster Roll of Company M, June 30, 1876, and in *The Teepee Book*, 1916.

WILLIAMS, CHARLES, Private
Born in Delaware County, Pennsylvania. Second enlistment on August 3, 1875, at age 26 in Baltimore by Lieut. Charles Cresson. Discharged on August 3, 1880, at Fort Meade, Dakota, upon expiration of service, as a Private of good character. He had blue eyes, brown hair, fair complexion and was 5'-5" in height.

ZAMETZER, JOHN, Private
Sick in the hospital from May 14, 1876, at Fort Rice, Dakota. Born in Bavaria, Germany. Second enlistment on December 23, 1874, at age 34 in Boston by Lieut. William Harper, Jr. Previous occupation was soldier. Assigned to Company A. Transferred to Company M. Discharged on August 19, 1877, for disability at Fort Rice, as a Corporal of excellent character. He had grey eyes, brown hair, medium complexion and was 5'-9¼" in height.